125 Problems in Text Algorithms

String matching is one of the oldest algorithmic techniques, yet still one of the most pervasive in computer science. The past 20 years have seen technological leaps in applications as diverse as information retrieval and compression. This copiously illustrated collection of puzzles and exercises in key areas of text algorithms and combinatorics on words offers graduate students and researchers a pleasant and direct way to learn and practice with advanced concepts.

The problems are drawn from a large range of scientific publications, both classic and new. Building up from the basics, the book goes on to showcase problems in combinatorics on words (including Fibonacci or Thue–Morse words), pattern matching (including Knuth–Morris–Pratt and Boyer–Moore–like algorithms), efficient text data structures (including suffix trees and suffix arrays), regularities in words (including periods and runs) and text compression (including Huffman, Lempel–Ziv and Burrows–Wheeler–based methods).

MAXIME CROCHEMORE is Emeritus Professor at Université Gustave Eiffel and of King's College London. He holds an honorary doctorate from the University of Helsinki. He is the author of more than 200 articles on algorithms on strings and their applications, and co-author of several books on the subject.

THIERRY LECROQ is a professor in the Department of Computer Science at the University of Rouen Normandy (France). He is currently head of the research team Information Processing in Biology and Health of the Laboratory of Computer Science, Information Processing and System. He has been one of the coordinators of the working group in stringology of the French National Centre for Scientific Research for more than 10 years.

WOJCIECH RYTTER is a professor at the Faculty of Mathematics, Informatics and Mechanics, University of Warsaw. He is the author of a large number of publications on automata, formal languages, parallel algorithms and algorithms on texts. He is a co-author of several books on these subjects, including *Efficient Parallel Algorithms*, *Text Algorithms* and *Analysis of Algorithms and Data Structures*. He is a member of Academia Europaea.

125 Problems in Text Algorithms

With Solutions

MAXIME CROCHEMORE
Gustave Eiffel University

THIERRY LECROQ
University of Rouen Normandy

WOJCIECH RYTTER
University of Warsaw

CAMBRIDGE
UNIVERSITY PRESS

University Printing House, Cambridge CB2 8BS, United Kingdom

One Liberty Plaza, 20th Floor, New York, NY 10006, USA

477 Williamstown Road, Port Melbourne, VIC 3207, Australia

314–321, 3rd Floor, Plot 3, Splendor Forum, Jasola District Centre, New Delhi – 110025, India

103 Penang Road, #05–06/07, Visioncrest Commercial, Singapore 238467

Cambridge University Press is part of the University of Cambridge.

It furthers the University's mission by disseminating knowledge in the pursuit of education, learning, and research at the highest international levels of excellence.

www.cambridge.org
Information on this title: www.cambridge.org/9781108835831
DOI: 10.1017/9781108869317

© Maxime Crochemore, Thierry Lecroq, Wojciech Rytter 2021

Illustrations designed by Hélène Crochemore

First published 2021

Printed in the United Kingdom by TJ Books Ltd, Padstow Cornwall

A catalogue record for this publication is available from the British Library.

Library of Congress Cataloging-in-Publication Data
Names: Crochemore, Maxime, 1947– author. | Lecroq, Thierry, author. | Rytter, Wojciech, author.
Title: One twenty five problems in text algorithms / Maxime Crochemore, Thierry Lecroq, Wojciech Rytter.
Other titles: 125 problems in text algorithms
Description: New York : Cambridge University Press, 2021. | The numerals 125 are superimposed over "One twenty five" on the title page. | Includes bibliographical references and index.
Identifiers: LCCN 2021002037 (print) | LCCN 2021002038 (ebook) | ISBN 9781108835831 (hardback) | ISBN 9781108798853 (paperback) | ISBN 9781108869317 (epub)
Subjects: LCSH: Text processing (Computer science)–Problems, exercises, etc. | Computer algorithms–Problems, exercises, etc.
Classification: LCC QA76.9.T48 C758 2021 (print) | LCC QA76.9.T48 (ebook) | DDC 005.13–dc23
LC record available at https://lccn.loc.gov/2021002037
LC ebook record available at https://lccn.loc.gov/2021002038

ISBN 978-1-108-83583-1 Hardback
ISBN 978-1-108-79885-3 Paperback

Contents

Preface

This book is about algorithms on texts, also called algorithmic stringology. Text (word, string, sequence) is one of the main unstructured data types and the subject is of vital importance in computer science.

The subject is versatile because it is a basic requirement in many sciences, especially in computer science and engineering. The treatment of unstructured data is a very lively area and demands efficient methods owing both to their presence in highly repetitive instructions of operating systems and to the vast amount of data that needs to be analysed on digital networks and equipments. The latter is clear for information technology companies that manage massive data in their data centres but also holds for most scientific areas beyond Computer science.

The book presents a collection of the most interesting representative problems in stringology. They are introduced in a short and pleasant way and open doors to more advanced topics. They were extracted from hundreds of serious scientific publications, some of which are more than a hundred years old and some are very fresh and up to date. Most of the problems are related to applications while others are more abstract. The core part of most of them is an ingenious short algorithmic solution except for a few introductory combinatorial problems.

This is not just yet another monograph on the subject but a series of problems (puzzles and exercises). It is a complement to books dedicated to the subject in which topics are introduced in a more academic and comprehensive way. Nevertheless, most concepts in the field are included in the book, which fills a missing gap and is very expected and needed, especially for students and teachers, as the first problem-solving textbook of the domain.

The book is organised into seven chapters:

'The Very Basics of Stringology' is a preliminary chapter introducing the terminology, basic concepts and tools for the next chapters and that reflects six main streams in the area.

'Combinatorial Puzzles' is about combinatorics on words, an important topic because many algorithms are based on combinatorial properties of their input.

'Pattern Matching' deals with the most classical subject, text searching and string matching.

'Efficient Data Structures' is about data structures for text indexing. They are used as fundamental tools in a large number of algorithms, such as special arrays and trees associated with texts.

'Regularities in Words' concerns regularities that occur in texts, in particular repetitions and symmetries, that have a strong influence on the efficiency of algorithms.

'Text Compression' is devoted to several methods of the practically important area of conservative text compression.

'Miscellaneous' contains various problems that do not fit in earlier chapters but certainly deserve presentation.

Problems listed in the book have been accumulated and developed over several years of teaching on string algorithms in our own different institutions in France, Poland, UK and USA. They have been taught mostly to master's students and are given with solutions as well as with references for further readings. The content also profits from the experience authors gained in writing previous textbooks.

Anyone teaching graduate courses on data structures and algorithms can select whatever they like from our book for their students. However, the overall book is not elementary and is intended as a reference for researchers, PhD and master's students, as well as for academics teaching courses on algorithms even if they are not directly related to text algorithms. It should be viewed as a companion to standard textbooks on the domain. The self-contained presentation of problems provides a rapid access to their understanding and to their solutions without requiring a deep background on the subject.

The book is useful for specialised courses on text algorithms, as well as for more general courses on algorithms and data structures. It introduces all required concepts and notions to solve problems but some prerequisites in bachelor- or sophomore-level academic courses on algorithms, data structures and discrete mathematics certainly help in grasping the material more easily.

1 The Very Basics of Stringology

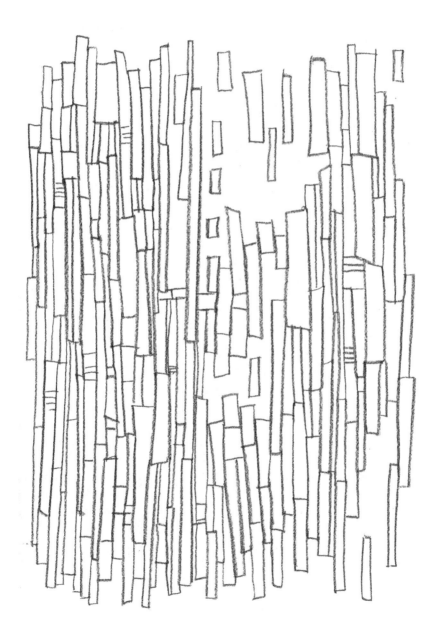

In this chapter we introduce basic notation and definitions of words and sketch several constructions used in text algorithms.

Texts are central in 'word processing' systems, which provide facilities for the manipulation of texts. Such systems usually process objects that are quite large. Text algorithms occur in many areas of science and information processing. Many text editors and programming languages have facilities for processing texts. In molecular biology, for example, text algorithms arise in the analysis of biological molecular sequences.

Words

An **alphabet** is a non-empty set whose elements are called **letters** or symbols. We typically use alphabets $\mathbf{A} = \{a, b, c, \ldots\}$, $\mathbf{B} = \{0, 1\}$ and natural numbers. A **word** (*mot*, in French) or **string** on an alphabet A is a sequence of elements of A.

The zero letter sequence is called the **empty word** and is denoted by ε. The set of all finite words on an alphabet A is denoted by A^*, and $A^+ = A^* \setminus \{\varepsilon\}$.

The **length** of a word x, length of the sequence, is denoted by $|x|$. We denote by $x[i]$, for $i = 0, 1, \ldots, |x| - 1$, the letter at **position** or **index** i on a non-empty word x. Then $x = x[0]x[1]\cdots x[|x| - 1]$ is also denoted by $x[0 \ldots |x| - 1]$. The set of letters that occur in the word x is denoted by $alph(x)$. For the example $x = \text{abaaab}$ we have $|x| = 6$ and $alph(x) = \{a, b\}$.

The **product** or **concatenation** of two words x and y is the word composed of the letters of x followed by the letters of y. It is denoted by xy or by $x \cdot y$ to emphasise the decomposition of the resulting word. The neutral element for the product is ε and we denote respectively by zy^{-1} and $x^{-1}z$ the words x and y when $z = xy$.

A **conjugate**, **rotation** or **cyclic shift** of a word x is any word y that factorises into vu, where $uv = x$. This makes sense because the product of words is obviously non-commutative. For example, the set of conjugates of abba, its conjugacy class because conjugacy is an equivalence relation, is $\{\text{aabb}, \text{abba}, \text{baab}, \text{bbaa}\}$ and that of abab is $\{\text{abab}, \text{baba}\}$.

A word x is a **factor** (sometimes called **substring**) of a word y if $y = uxv$ for two words u and v. When $u = \varepsilon$, x is a **prefix** of y, and when $v = \varepsilon$, x is a **suffix** of y. Sets $Fact(x)$, $Pref(x)$ and $Suff(x)$ denote the sets of factors, prefixes and suffixes of x respectively.

When x is a non-empty factor of $y = y[0..n-1]$ it is of the form $y[i..i + |x| - 1]$ for some i. An **occurrence** of x in y is an interval $[i..i + |x| - 1]$ for which $x = y[i..i + |x| - 1]$. We say that i is the **starting position** (or left position) on y of this occurrence, and that $i + |x| - 1$ is its **ending position** (or right position). An occurrence of x in y can also be defined as a triple (u, x, v) such that $y = uxv$. Then the starting position of the occurrence is $|u|$. For example, the starting and ending positions of $x = $ aba on $y = $ babaababa are

i	0	1	2	3	4	5	6	7	8
$y[i]$	b	a	b	a	a	b	a	b	a
starting positions		1			4		6		
ending positions				3			6		8

For words x and y, $|y|_x$ denotes the number of occurrences of x in y. Then, for instance, $|y| = \Sigma\{|y|_a : a \in alph(y)\}$.

The word x is a **subsequence** or **subword** of y if the latter decomposes into $w_0 x[0] w_1 x[1] \ldots x[|x| - 1] w_{|x|}$ for words $w_0, w_1, \ldots, w_{|x|}$.

A factor or a subsequence x of a word y is said to be **proper** if $x \neq y$.

Periodicity

Let x be a non-empty word. An integer p, $0 < p \leq |x|$, is called a **period** of x if $x[i] = x[i + p]$ for $i = 0, 1, \ldots, |x| - p - 1$. Note that the length of a word is a period of this word, so every non-empty word has at least one period. **The period** of x, denoted by $per(x)$, is its smallest period. For example, 3, 6, 7 and 8 are periods of the word aabaabaa, and $per(\text{aabaabaa}) = 3$. Note that if p is a period of x, its multiples not larger than $|x|$ are also periods of x.

Here is a series of properties equivalent to the definition of a period p of x. First, x can be factorised uniquely as $(uv)^k u$, where u and v are words, v is non-empty, k is a positive integer and $p = |uv|$. Second, x is a prefix of ux for a word u of length p. Third, x is a factor of u^k, where u is a word of length p and k a positive integer. Fourth, x can be factorised as $uw = wv$ for three words u, v and w, verifying $p = |u| = |v|$.

The last point leads to the notion of border. A **border** of x is a proper factor of x that is both a prefix and a suffix of x. **The border** of x, denoted by $Border(x)$, is its longest border. Thus, ε, a, aa, and aabaa are the borders of aabaabaa and $Border(\text{aabaabaa}) = $ aabaa.

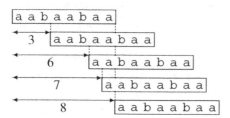

Borders and periods of x are in one-to-one correspondence because of the fourth point above: a period p of x is associated with the border $x[p \mathinner{\ldotp\ldotp} |x| - 1]$.

Note that, when defined, the border of a border of x is also a border of x. Then $\langle Border(x), Border^2(x), \ldots, Border^k(x) = \varepsilon \rangle$ is the list of all borders of x. The (non-empty) word x is said to be ***border free*** if its only border is the empty word or equivalently if its only period is $|x|$.

Lemma 1 (Periodicity lemma) *If p and q are periods of a word x and satisfy $p + q - \gcd(p,q) \le |x|$ then $\gcd(p,q)$ is also a period of x.*

The proof of the lemma may be found in textbooks (see Notes). The Weak Periodicity lemma refers to a variant of the lemma in which the condition is strengthened to $p + q \le |x|$. Its proof comes readily as follows.

$$\begin{array}{c}
\quad 0 \qquad\qquad i \qquad\qquad\quad i+p-q \quad\ i+p \\
x \;\boxed{\;\;\boxed{a}\;\;\;\;\;\;\;\;\;\;\boxed{a}\;\;\;\boxed{a}\;\;} \\
\qquad\qquad\quad p \qquad\qquad\quad q
\end{array}$$

The conclusion obviously holds when $p = q$. Else, w.l.o.g. assume $p > q$ and let us show first that $p - q$ is a period of x. Indeed, let i be a position on x for which $i + p < |x|$. Then $x[i] = x[i + p] = x[i + p - q]$ because p and q are periods. And if $i + p \ge |x|$, the condition implies $i - q \ge 0$. Then $x[i] = x[i - q] = x[i + p - q]$ as before. Thus $p - q$ is a period of x. Iterating the reasoning or using a recurrence as for Euclid's algorithm, we conclude that $\gcd(p,q)$ is a period of x.

To illustrate the Periodicity lemma, let us consider a word x that admits 5 and 8 as periods. Then, if we assume moreover that x is composed of at least two distinct letters, $\gcd(5,8) = 1$ is not a period of x. Thus, the condition of the lemma cannot hold, that is, $|x| < 5 + 8 - \gcd(5,8) = 12$.

$$\begin{array}{l}
\texttt{a b a b a a b a b a a b a b a} \\
\texttt{a b a a b a b a a b a} \\
\texttt{b a b a a b a a b a b a a b a a}
\end{array}$$

The extreme situation is displayed in the picture and shows (when generalised) that the condition required on periods in the statement of the Periodicity lemma cannot be weakened.

Regularities

The powers of a word x are defined by $x^0 = \varepsilon$ and $x^i = x^{i-1}x$ for a positive integer i. The kth **power** of x is x^k. It is a **square** if k is a positive even integer and a **cube** if k is a positive multiple of 3.

The next lemma states a first consequence of the Periodicity lemma.

Lemma 2 *For words x and y, $xy = yx$ if and only if x and y are (integer) powers of the same word. The same conclusion holds when there exist two positive integers k and ℓ for which $x^k = y^\ell$.*

The proofs of the two parts of the lemma are essentially the same (in fact the conclusion derives from a more general statement on codes). For example, if $xy = yx$, both x and y are borders of the word, then both $|x|$ and $|y|$ are periods of it and $\gcd(|x|, |y|)$ as well by the Periodicity lemma. Since $\gcd(|x|, |y|)$ divides also $|xy|$, the conclusion follows. The converse implication is straightforward.

The non-empty word x is said to be **primitive** if it is not the power of any other word. That is to say, x is primitive if $x = u^k$, for a word u and a positive integer k, implies $k = 1$ and then $u = x$. For example, abaab is primitive, while ε and $\text{bababa} = (\text{ba})^3$ are not.

It follows from Lemma 2 that a non-empty word has exactly one primitive word it is a power of. When $x = u^k$ and u is primitive, u is called the **primitive root** of x and k is its **exponent**, denoted by $\exp(x)$. More generally, the exponent of x is the quantity $\exp(x) = |x|/per(x)$, which is not necessarily an integer, and the word is said to be **periodic** if its exponent is at least 2.

Note the number of conjugates of a word, the size of its **conjugacy class**, is the length of its (primitive) root.

Another consequence of the Periodicity lemma follows.

Lemma 3 (Primitivity Lemma, Synchronisation lemma) *A non-empty word x is primitive if and only if it is a factor of its square only as a prefix and as a suffix, or equivalently if and only if $per(x^2) = |x|$.*

The picture illustrates the result of the lemma. The word abbaba is primitive and there are only two occurrences of it in its square, while ababab is not primitive and has four occurrences in its square.

The notion of **run** or **maximal periodicity** encompasses several types of regularities occurring in words. A run in the word x is a maximal occurrence of a periodic factor. To say it more formally, it is an interval $[i \mathbin{..} j]$ of positions on x for which $\exp(x[i \mathbin{..} j]) \geq 2$ and both $x[i-1 \mathbin{..} j]$ and $x[i \mathbin{..} j+1]$ have periods larger than that of $x[i \mathbin{..} j]$ when they exist. In this situation, since the occurrence is identified by i and j, we also say abusively that $x[i \mathbin{..} j]$ is a run.

Another type of regularity consists in the appearance of reverse factors or of palindromes in words. The **reverse** or **mirror image** of the word x is the word $x^R = x[|x| - 1]x[|x| - 2] \cdots x[0]$. Associated with this operation is the notion of **palindrome**: a word x for which $x^R = x$.

For example, noon and testset are English palindromes. The first is an even palindrome of the form uu^R while the second is an odd palindrome of the form uau^R with a letter a. The letter a can be replaced by a short word, leading to the notion of gapped palindromes as useful when related to folding operations like those occurring in sequences of biological molecules. As another example, integers whose decimal expansion is an even palindrome are multiples of 11, such as $1661 = 11 \times 151$ or $175571 = 11 \times 15961$.

Ordering

Some algorithms benefit from the existence of an ordering on the alphabet, denoted by $\leq$. The ordering induces the **lexicographic ordering** or **alphabetic ordering** on words as follows. Like the alphabet ordering, it is denoted by $\leq$. For $x, y \in A^*$, $x \leq y$ if and only if either x is a prefix of y or x and y can be decomposed as $x = uav$ and $y = ubw$ for words u, v and w, letters a and b, with $a < b$. Thus, ababb < abba < abbaab when considering a < b and more generally the natural ordering on the alphabet **A**.

We say that x is **strongly less** than y, denoted by $x \ll y$, when $x \leq y$ but x is not a prefix of y. Note that $x \ll y$ implies $xu \ll yv$ for any words u and v.

Concepts of **Lyndon words** and of **necklaces** are built from the lexicographic ordering.

A Lyndon word x is a primitive word that is the smallest among its conjugates. Equivalently but not entirely obvious, x is smaller than all its proper non-empty suffixes, and as such is also called a **self-minimal word**. As a consequence, x is border-free. It is known that any non-empty word w factorises uniquely into $x_0 x_1 \cdots x_k$, where x_is are Lyndon words and

$x_0 \geq x_1 \geq \cdots \geq x_k$. For example, the word aababaabaaba factorises as aabab · aab · aab · a, where aabab, aab and a are Lyndon words.

A necklace or **minimal word** is a word that is the smallest in its conjugacy class. It is a (integer) power of a Lyndon word. A Lyndon word is a necklace but, for example, the word aabaab $=$ aab^2 is a necklace without being a Lyndon word.

Remarkable Words

Besides Lyndon words, three sets of words have remarkable properties and are often used in examples. They are Thue–Morse words, Fibonacci words and de Bruijn words. The first two are prefixes of (one-way) infinite words. Formally an **infinite word** on the alphabet A is a mapping from natural numbers to A. Their set is denoted by A^∞.

The notion of (monoid) **morphism** is central to defining some infinite sets of words or an associate infinite word. A morphism from A^* to itself (or another free monoid) is a mapping $h : A^* \mapsto A^*$ satisfying $h(uv) = h(u)h(v)$ for all words u and v. Consequently, a morphism is entirely defined by the images $h(a)$ of letters $a \in A$.

The **Thue–Morse word** is produced by iterating the **Thue–Morse morphism** μ from $\{a,b\}^*$ to itself, defined by

$$\begin{cases} \mu(a) = ab, \\ \mu(b) = ba. \end{cases}$$

Iterating the morphism from letter a gives the list of Thue–Morse words $\mu^k(a)$, $k \geq 0$, that starts with

$$\begin{aligned}
\tau_0 = \mu^0(a) &= \text{a} \\
\tau_1 = \mu^1(a) &= \text{ab} \\
\tau_2 = \mu^2(a) &= \text{abba} \\
\tau_3 = \mu^3(a) &= \text{abbabaab} \\
\tau_4 = \mu^4(a) &= \text{abbabaabbaababba} \\
\tau_5 = \mu^5(a) &= \text{abbabaabbaababbabaababbaabbabaab}
\end{aligned}$$

and eventually produces its infinite associate:

$$\mathbf{t} = \lim_{k \to \infty} \mu^k(a) = \text{abbabaabbaababbabaababbaabbabaab} \cdots .$$

An equivalent definition of Thue–Morse words is provided by the following recurrence:

$$\begin{cases} \tau_0 = \mathtt{a}, \\ \tau_{k+1} = \tau_k \overline{\tau_k}, \quad \text{for } k \geq 0, \end{cases}$$

where the bar morphism is defined by $\overline{\mathtt{a}} = \mathtt{b}$ and $\overline{\mathtt{b}} = \mathtt{a}$. Note the length of the kth Thue–Morse word is $|\tau_k| = 2^k$.

A direct definition of **t** is as follows: the letter $\mathbf{t}[n]$ is b if the number of occurrences of digit 1 in the binary representation of n is odd, and is a otherwise.

The infinite Thue–Morse word is known to contain no overlap (factor of the form $auaua$ for a letter a and a word u), that is, no factor of exponent larger than 2. It is said to be ***overlap-free***.

The ***Fibonacci word*** is similarly produced by iterating a morphism, the ***Fibonacci morphism*** ϕ, from $\{\mathtt{a}, \mathtt{b}\}^*$ to itself, defined by

$$\begin{cases} \phi(\mathtt{a}) = \mathtt{ab}, \\ \phi(\mathtt{b}) = \mathtt{a}. \end{cases}$$

Iterating the morphism from letter a gives the list of Fibonacci words $\phi^k(\mathtt{a})$, $k \geq 0$, that starts with

$$\begin{aligned} fib_0 &= \phi^0(\mathtt{a}) &=& \quad \mathtt{a} \\ fib_1 &= \phi^1(\mathtt{a}) &=& \quad \mathtt{ab} \\ fib_2 &= \phi^2(\mathtt{a}) &=& \quad \mathtt{aba} \\ fib_3 &= \phi^3(\mathtt{a}) &=& \quad \mathtt{abaab} \\ fib_4 &= \phi^4(\mathtt{a}) &=& \quad \mathtt{abaababa} \\ fib_5 &= \phi^5(\mathtt{a}) &=& \quad \mathtt{abaababaabaab} \\ fib_6 &= \phi^6(\mathtt{a}) &=& \quad \mathtt{abaababaabaababaababa} \end{aligned}$$

and eventually its infinite associate:

$$\mathbf{f} = \lim_{k \to \infty} \phi^k(\mathtt{a}) = \mathtt{abaababaabaababaababaabaababaabaab} \cdots .$$

An equivalent definition of Fibonacci words comes from the recurrence relation:

$$\begin{cases} fib_0 = \mathtt{a}, \\ fib_1 = \mathtt{ab}, \\ fib_{k+1} = fib_k fib_{k-1}, \quad \text{for } k \geq 1. \end{cases}$$

The sequence of lengths of these words is the sequence of Fibonacci numbers, that is, $|fib_k| = F_{k+2}$. Recall that **Fibonacci numbers** are defined by the recurrence

$$\begin{cases} F_0 = 0, \\ F_1 = 1, \\ F_{k+1} = F_k + F_{k-1}, \quad \text{for } k \geq 1. \end{cases}$$

Among many properties they satisfy are

- $\gcd(F_n, F_{n-1}) = 1$, for $n \geq 2$,
- F_n is the nearest integer of $\Phi^n/\sqrt{5}$, where $\Phi = \frac{1}{2}(1 + \sqrt{5}) = 1.61803\cdots$ is the **golden ratio**.

The interest in Fibonacci words comes from the combinatorial properties they satisfy and the large number of repeats they contain. However, the infinite Fibonacci word contains no factor of exponent larger than $\Phi^2 + 1 = 3.61803\cdots$.

De Bruijn words are defined here on the alphabet $A = \{a, b\}$ and are parameterised by a positive integer k. A word $x \in A^+$ is a de Bruijn word of order k if each word of A^k occurs exactly once in x. As a first example, ab and ba are the only two de Bruijn words of order 1. As a second example, the word aaababbbaa is a de Bruijn word of order 3, since its eight factors of length 3 are the eight words of A^3, that is, aaa, aab, aba, abb, baa, bab, bba and bbb.

The existence of a de Bruijn word of order $k \geq 2$ can be verified with the help of the **de Bruijn automaton** defined by

- States are the words of A^{k-1}.
- Arcs are of the form (av, b, vb) with $a, b \in A$ and $v \in A^{k-2}$.

The picture displays the automaton for de Bruijn words of order 3. Note that exactly two arcs exit each of the states, one labelled by a, the other by b; and that exactly two arcs enter each of the states, both labelled by the same letter. The graph associated with the automaton thus satisfies the Euler condition: every vertex has an even degree. It follows that there exists an Eulerian circuit in the graph. Its label is a **circular de Bruijn word**. Appending to it its prefix of length $k - 1$ gives an ordinary de Bruijn word.

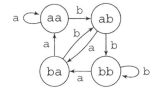

It can also be verified that the number of de Bruijn words of order k is exponential in k.

De Bruijn words can be defined on larger alphabets and are often used as examples of limit cases because they contain all the factors of a given length.

Automata

A finite **automaton** M on the finite alphabet A is composed of a finite set Q of **states**, of an **initial** state q_0, of a set $T \subseteq Q$ of **terminal** states and of a set $F \subseteq Q \times A \times Q$ of **labelled edges** or **arcs** corresponding to state **transitions**. We denote the automaton M by the quadruplet (Q, q_0, T, F) or sometimes by just (Q, F) when, for example, q_0 is implicit and $T = Q$. We say of an arc (p, a, q) that it leaves state p and enters state q; state p is the **source** of the arc, letter a its **label** and state q its **target**. A graphic representation of an automaton is displayed below.

The number of arcs exiting a given state is called the **outgoing degree** of the state. The **incoming degree** of a state is defined in a dual way. By analogy with graphs, the state q is a **successor** by the letter a of the state p when $(p, a, q) \in F$; in the same case, we say that the pair (a, q) is a **labelled successor** of state p.

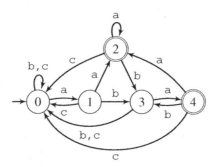

A **path** of length n in the automaton $M = (Q, q_0, T, F)$ is a sequence of n consecutive arcs $\langle (p_0, a_0, p_0'), (p_1, a_1, p_1'), \ldots, (p_{n-1}, a_{n-1}, p_{n-1}') \rangle$ that satisfies $p_k' = p_{k+1}$ for $k = 0, 1, \ldots, n - 2$. The **label** of the path is the word $a_0 a_1 \ldots a_{n-1}$, its **origin** the state p_0 and its **end** the state p_{n-1}'. A path in the automaton M is **successful** if its origin is the initial state q_0 and if its end is in T. A word is **recognised** or **accepted** by the automaton if it is the label of a successful path. The language composed of the words recognised by the automaton M is denoted by $Lang(M)$.

An automaton $M = (Q, q_0, T, F)$ is **deterministic** if for every pair $(p, a) \in Q \times A$ there exists at most one state $q \in Q$ for which $(p, a, q) \in F$. In such a case, it is natural to consider the **transition function** $\delta \colon Q \times A \to Q$ of the automaton defined for every arc $(p, a, q) \in F$ by $\delta(p, a) = q$ and undefined elsewhere. The function δ merely extends to words.

It is known that any language accepted by an automaton is also accepted by a deterministic automaton and that there is a unique (up to state naming) minimal deterministic automaton accepting it.

Trie

A **trie** $\mathcal{T}$ on the alphabet A, a kind of digital tree, is an automaton whose paths from the initial state, the root, do not converge. A trie is used mostly to represent finite sets of words. If no word of the set is a prefix of another word of the set, words are associated with the leaves of the trie.

Below is the trie $\mathcal{T}(\{aa, aba, abaaa, abab\})$. States correspond to prefixes of words in the set. For example, state 3 corresponds to the prefix of length 2 of both abaaa and abab. Terminal states (doubly circled) 2, 4, 6 and 7 correspond to the words in the set.

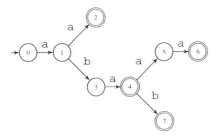

Suffix Structures

Suffix structures that store the suffixes of a word are important data structures used to produce efficient indexes. Tries can be used as such but their size can be quadratic. One solution to cope with that is to compact the trie, resulting in the Suffix tree of the word. It consists in eliminating non-terminal nodes with only one outgoing edge and in labelling arcs by factors of the word accordingly. Eliminated nodes are sometimes called implicit nodes of the Suffix tree and remaining nodes are called explicit nodes.

Below are the trie $\mathcal{T}(Suff(aabab))$ of suffixes of aabab (on the left) and its **Suffix tree** $\mathcal{ST}(aabab)$ (on the right). To get a complete linear-size structure, each factor of the word that labels an arc needs to be represented by a pair of integers such as (position, length).

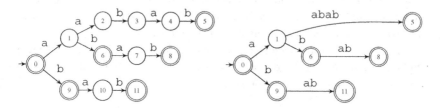

A second solution to reduce the size of the Suffix trie is to minimise it, which means considering the minimal deterministic automaton accepting the suffixes of the word, its **Suffix automaton**. Below (left) is $\mathcal{S}$(aabab), the Suffix automaton of aabab.

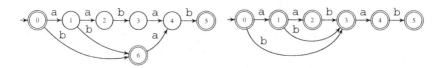

It is known that $\mathcal{S}(x)$ possesses fewer than $2|x|$ states and fewer than $3|x|$ arcs, for a total size $O(|x|)$, that is, linear in $|x|$. The Factor automaton $\mathcal{F}(x)$ of the word, minimal deterministic automaton accepting its factors, can even be smaller because all its states are terminal. In the above picture, the right part is the Factor automaton of aabab in which state 6 of $\mathcal{S}$(aabab) is merged with state 3.

Suffix Array

The **Suffix array** of a word is also used to produce indexes but proceeds differently than with trees or automata. It consists primarily in sorting the non-empty suffixes of the word to allow binary search for its factors. To get actually efficient searches another feature is considered: the longest common prefixes of successive suffixes in the sorted list.

The information is stored in two arrays, SA and LCP. The array SA is the inverse of the array Rank that gives the rank of each suffix attached at its starting position.

Below are the tables associated with the example word aababa. Its sorted list of suffixes is a, aababa, aba, ababa, ba and baba whose starting positions are 5, 0, 3, 1, 4 and 2. This latter list is stored in SA indexed by suffix ranks.

i	0	1	2	3	4	5							
$x[i]$	a	a	b	a	b	a							
Rank$[i]$	1	3	5	2	4	0							
r	0	1	2	3	4	5	6	7	8	9	10	11	12
SA$[r]$	5	0	3	1	4	2							
LCP$[r]$	0	1	1	3	0	2	0	0	1	0	0	0	0

The table LCP essentially contains **longest common prefixes** stored as maximal lengths of common prefixes between successive suffixes:

$$\text{LCP}[r] = |lcp(x[\text{SA}[r-1]\mathbin{..}|x|-1], x[\text{SA}[r]\mathbin{..}|x|-1])|,$$

where lcp denotes the longest common prefix between two words. This gives LCP$[0\mathbin{..}6]$ for the example. The next values in LCP$[7\mathbin{..}12]$ correspond to the same information for suffixes starting at positions d and f when the pair (d, f) appears in the binary search. Formally, for such a pair, the value is stored at position $|x| + 1 + \lfloor (d+f)/2 \rfloor$. For example, in the above LCP array the value 1 corresponding to the pair $(0, 2)$, maximal length of prefixes between $x[5\mathbin{..}5]$ and $x[3\mathbin{..}5]$, is stored at position 8.

The table Rank is used in applications of the Suffix array that are mainly other than searching.

Compression

The most powerful **compression** methods for general texts are based either on the Ziv–Lempel factorisation of words or on easier techniques on top of the Burrows–Wheeler transform of words. We give a glimpse of both.

When processing a word online, the goal of **Ziv–Lempel compression scheme** is to capture information that has been met before. The associated factorisation of a word x is $u_0 u_1 \cdots u_k$, where u_i is the longest prefix of $u_i \cdots u_k$ that appears before this occurrence in x. When it is empty, the first letter of $u_i \cdots u_k$, which does not occur in $u_0 \cdots u_{i-1}$, is chosen. The factor u_i is sometimes called abusively the **longest previous factor** at position $|u_0 \cdots u_{i-1}|$ on x.

For example, the factorisation of the word abaabababaaababb is a · b · a · aba · baba · aabab · b.

There are several variations to define the factors of the decomposition; here are a few of them. The factor u_i may include the letter immediately following the occurrence of the longest previous factor at position $|u_0 \cdots u_{i-1}|$, which amounts to extending a factor occurring before. Previous occurrences of factors may be chosen among the factors $u_0, \ldots, u_{i-1}$ or among all the factors of $u_0 \cdots u_{i-1}$ (to avoid an overlap between occurrences) or among all factors occurring before. This results in a large variety of text compression software based on the method.

When designing word algorithms the factorisation is also used to reduce some online processing by storing what has already been done on previous occurrences of factors.

The **Burrows–Wheeler transform** of a word x is a reversible mapping that transforms $x \in A^k$ into $\mathrm{BW}(x) \in A^k$. The effect is mostly to group together letters having the same context in x. The encoding proceeds as follows. Let us consider the sorted list of rotations (conjugates) of x. Then $\mathrm{BW}(x)$ is the word composed of the last letters of sorted rotations, referred to as the last column of the corresponding table.

For the example word banana, rotations are listed below on the left and their sorted list on the right. Then $\mathrm{BW}(\mathrm{banana}) = \mathrm{nnbaaa}$.

0	b	a	n	a	n	a		5	a	b	a	n	a	n
1	a	n	a	n	a	b		3	a	n	a	b	a	n
2	n	a	n	a	b	a		1	a	n	a	n	a	b
3	a	n	a	b	a	n		0	b	a	n	a	n	a
4	n	a	b	a	n	a		4	n	a	b	a	n	a
5	a	b	a	n	a	n		2	n	a	n	a	b	a

Two conjugate words have the same image by the mapping. Choosing the Lyndon word as a representative of the class of a primitive word, the mapping becomes bijective. To recover the original word x other than a Lyndon word, it is sufficient to keep the position on $\mathrm{BW}(x)$ of the first letter of x.

The main property of the transformation is that occurrences of a given letter are in the same relative order in $\mathrm{BW}(x)$ and in the sorted list of all letters. This is used to decode $\mathrm{BW}(x)$.

To do it on nnbaaa from the above example, we first sort the letters getting the word aaabnn. Knowing that the first letter of the initial word appears at position 2 on nnbaaa, we can start the decoding: the first letter is b followed by letter a at the same position 2 on aaabnn. This is the third occurrence of a in aaabnn corresponding to its third occurrence in nnbaaa, which is followed by n, and so on.

The decoding process is similar to following the cycle in the graph below from the correct letter. Starting from a different letter produces a conjugate of the initial word.

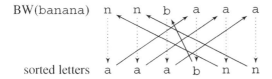

Writing Conventions of Algorithms

The style of the algorithmic language used here is relatively close to real programming languages but at a higher abstraction level. We adopt the following conventions:

- Indentation means the structure of blocks inherent to compound instructions.
- Lines of code are numbered in order to be referred to in the text.
- The symbol ▷ introduces a comment.
- The access to a specific attribute of an object is signified by the name of the attribute followed by the identifier associated with the object between brackets.
- A variable that represents a given object (table, queue, tree, word, automaton) is a pointer to this object.
- The arguments given to procedures or to functions are managed by the 'call by value' rule.
- Variables of procedures and functions are local to them unless otherwise mentioned.
- The evaluation of boolean expressions is performed from left to right in a lazy way.
- Instructions of the form $(m_1, m_2, \ldots) \leftarrow (exp_1, exp_2, \ldots)$ abbreviate the sequence of assignments $m_1 \leftarrow exp_1, m_2 \leftarrow exp_2, \ldots$.

Algorithm TRIE below is an example of how algorithms are written. It produces the trie of a dictionary X, finite set of words X. It successively considers each word of X during the **for** loop of lines 2–10 and inserts them into the structure letter by letter during execution of the **for** loop of lines 4–9. When the latter loop is over, the last considered state t, ending the path from the initial state and labelled by the current word, is set as terminal at line 10.

TRIE(X finite set of words)

1    $M \leftarrow$ NEW-AUTOMATON()
2   **for** each string $x \in X$ **do**
3          $t \leftarrow initial(M)$
4   **for** each letter a of x, sequentially **do**
5                $p \leftarrow$ TARGET(t, a)
6   **if** $p =$ NIL **then**
7                      $p \leftarrow$ NEW-STATE()
8                      $Succ[t] \leftarrow Succ[t] \cup \{(a, p)\}$
9                $t \leftarrow p$
10         $terminal[t] \leftarrow$ TRUE
11   **return** M

Notes

Basic elements on words introduced in this section follow their presentation in [74]. They can be found in other textbooks on text algorithms, like those by Crochemore and Rytter [96], Gusfield [134], Crochemore and Rytter [98] and Smyth [228]. The notions are also introduced in some textbooks dealing with the wider topics of combinatorics on words, such as those by Lothaire [175–177], or in the tutorial by Berstel and Karhumäki [34].

1   Stringologic Proof of Fermat's Little Theorem

In 1640 the great French number theorist Pierre de Fermat proved the following property:

If p is a prime number and k is any natural number
then p divides $k^p - k$.

The statement is known as *Fermat's little theorem*. For example:

7 divides $2^7 - 2$ and 101 divides $10^{101} - 10$.

Question. Prove Fermat's little theorem using only stringologic arguments.

[**Hint:** Count conjugacy classes of words of length p.]

Solution

To prove the property we consider conjugacy classes of words of the same length. For example, the conjugacy class containing aaaba is the set $C(\texttt{aaaba}) = \{\texttt{aaaab}, \texttt{aaaba}, \texttt{aabaa}, \texttt{abaaa}, \texttt{baaaa}\}$. The next fact is a consequence of the Primitivity Lemma.

Observation. The conjugacy class of a primitive word w contains exactly $|w|$ distinct words.

Let us consider the set of words of length p, a prime number, over the alphabet $\{1, 2, \ldots, k\}$ and let $S_k(p)$ be its subset of primitive words. Among the k^p words only k of them are not primitive, namely words of the form a^p for a letter a. Thus we arrive at the following observation.

Observation. The number $|S_k(p)|$ of primitive words of length p, a prime number, on a k-letter alphabet is $k^p - k$.

Since words in $S_k(p)$ are primitive, the conjugacy class of each of them is of size p. Conjugacy classes partition $S_k(p)$ into sets of size p, which implies that p divides $k^p - k$ and that there are $(k^p - k)/p$ classes. This proves the theorem.

Notes

When a word $w = u^q$ of length n on a k-letter alphabet has a primitive root u of length d, we have $n = qd$ and the conjugacy class of w contains d elements. Running d over the divisors of n we get the equality $k^n = \Sigma\{d\psi_k(d) : d \text{ divisor of } n\}$, where $\psi_k(m)$ denotes the number of classes of primitive words of length m. It proves the theorem when n is prime. Further details are in the book by Lothaire [175, chapter 1].

2   Simple Case of Codicity Testing

A set $\{w_1, w_2, \ldots, w_n\}$ of words drawn from an alphabet A is a (uniquely decipherable) code if for every two sequences (noted as words) $i_1 i_2 \cdots i_k$ and $j_1 j_2 \cdots j_\ell$ of indices from $\{1, 2, \ldots, n\}$ we have

$$i_1 i_2 \cdots i_k \neq j_1 j_2 \cdots j_\ell \;\Rightarrow\; w_{i_1} w_{i_2} \cdots w_{i_k} \neq w_{j_1} w_{j_2} \cdots w_{j_\ell}.$$

In other words, if we define the morphism h from $\{1, 2, \ldots, n\}^*$ to A^* by $h(i) = w_i$, for $i \in \{1, 2, \ldots, n\}$, the condition means that the morphism is injective.

For an arbitrary integer n there is no known linear-time algorithm for testing the codicity property. However, the situation is extremely simple for $n = 2$: it is enough to check if the two codewords commute, that is, if $w_1 w_2 = w_2 w_1$.

Question. Show that $\{x, y\}$ is a code if and only if $xy \neq yx$.

Solution

A proof idea is given on page 5 as a consequence of the Periodicity Lemma. Below is a self-contained inductive proof.

If $\{x, y\}$ is a code, the conclusion follows by definition. Conversely, let us assume $\{x, y\}$ is not a code and prove the equality $xy = yx$. The equality holds if one of the words is empty, so we are left to consider the two words are not empty.

The proof is by induction on the length of $|xy|$. The induction base is the simple case $x = y$, for which the equality obviously holds.

Assume that $x \neq y$. Then one of the words is a proper prefix of the other and assume w.l.o.g. that x is a proper prefix of y: $y = xz$ for a non-empty word z. Then $\{x, z\}$ is not a code because the two distinct concatenations of x's and y's producing the same word translate into two distinct concatenations of x's and z's producing the word.

The inductive hypothesis applies because $|xz| < |xy|$ and yields $xz = zx$. Consequently $xy = xxz = xzx = yx$, which shows that the equality holds for x and y, and achieves the proof.

Notes

The same type of proof shows that $\{x, y\}$ is not a code if $x^k = y^\ell$ for two positive integers k and ℓ.

We do not know if there is a special codicity test for three words in terms of a fixed set of inequalities. For a finite number of words, an efficient polynomial-time algorithm using a graph-theoretical approach is given in Problem 52.

3   Magic Squares and the Thue–Morse Word

The goal of the problem is to build magic squares with the help of the infinite Thue–Morse word $\mathbf{t}$ on the binary alphabet $\{0, 1\}$ (instead of $\{a, b\}$). The word $\mathbf{t}$ is $\mu^{\infty}(0)$ obtained by iterating the morphism μ defined by $\mu(0) = 01$ and $\mu(1) = 10$:

$$\mathbf{t} = 0110100110010110 1001 \cdots .$$

The $n \times n$ array S_n, where $n = 2^m$ for a positive natural number m is defined, for $0 \le i, j < n$, by

$$S_n[i, j] = \mathbf{t}[k](k + 1) + (1 - \mathbf{t}[k])(n^2 - k),$$

where $k = i.n + j$. The generated array S_4 is

16	2	3	13
5	11	10	8
9	7	6	12
4	14	15	1

The array is a magic square because it contains all the integers from 1 to 16 and the sum of elements on each row is 34, as well as the sums on each column and on each diagonal.

> **Question.** Show the $n \times n$ array S_n is a magic square for any natural number n power of 2.

Solution

To understand the structure of the array S_n let T_n be the Thue–Morse 2-dimensional word of shape $n \times n$, where $n = 2^m$, defined, for $0 \le i, j < n$, by $T_n[i, j] = \mathbf{t}[i.n + j]$. The picture displays T_4 and T_8, where $*$ substitutes for 0 and space substitutes for 1.

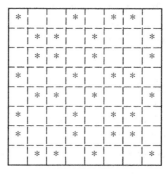

Notice that the table T_n satisfies two simple properties:

(i) Every row and every column is made up of blocks `0110` and `1001`.

(ii) Each of the two main diagonals is homogeneous, consisting only of 0's or only of 1's (respectively stars and spaces on the picture).

It is clear from the definition that the $n \times n$ matrix S_n is filled with all the integers from 1 to n^2. To prove it is a magic square we have to show that the sum of all entries in any row, in any column or in any of the two diagonals is the same, that is, $\frac{n}{2}(n^2 + 1)$.

Correctness for rows. According to property (i) each block in a row is of type `0110` or type `1001`. Consider a block `0110` whose first element is the kth element in the array. Then

$$S[k, k+1, k+2, k+3] = [n^2 - k, k+2, k+3, n^2 - k - 3],$$

which sums to $2n^2 + 2$. For a block whose type is different from `0110` we get $[k+1, n^2 - k - 1, n^2 - k - 2, k+4]$, whose sum is the same value. Since we have $n/4$ such blocks in a row, the sum of all their contributions is

$$\frac{n}{4} \cdot (2n^2 + 2) = \frac{n}{2}(n^2 + 1),$$

as required.

The correctness for columns can be shown similarly.

Correctness for diagonals. Let us consider only the diagonal from $(0,0)$ to $(n-1, n-1)$ since the other diagonal can be treated similarly. Entries on the diagonal are $1, 1+(n+1), 1+2(n+1), \ldots, 1+(n-1)(n+1)$, listed bottom-up. Their sum is

$$n + (n+1)\sum_{i=0}^{n-1} i = n + (n+1)\frac{n}{2}(n-1) = \frac{n}{2}(n^2 + 1),$$

as required.

This achieves the proof that S_n is a magic square.

Notes

More on magic squares and their long history may be found on Wikipedia: `https://en.wikipedia.org/wiki/Magic_square`.

---

4   Oldenburger–Kolakoski Sequence

The Oldenburger–Kolakoski sequence is an autodescriptive and self-generating infinite sequence of symbols $\{1, 2\}$. More technically, it is its own run-length encoding. The sequence, denoted here by $\mathbf{K}$, is one of the strangest sequences. Despite the simplicity of its generation it appears to have a random behaviour.

By a block of letters in a word we mean a run of letters, that is, a maximal factor consisting of occurrences of the same letter. The operation $blocks(S)$ replaces each block of a word S by its length. For example,

$$blocks(2\,1\,1\,1\,2\,2\,1\,2\,2\,2) = 1\,3\,2\,1\,3.$$

The sequence $\mathbf{K}$ is the unique infinite sequence over the alphabet $\{1, 2\}$ that starts with 2 and satisfies $blocks(\mathbf{K}) = \mathbf{K}$.

Remark. Usually the sequence is defined to start with 1, but it is more convenient here that it starts with 2. In fact, these are the same sequences after removing the first occurrence of 1.

> **Question.** Show that we can generate online the first n symbols of the sequence $\mathbf{K}$ in $O(n)$ time and $O(\log n)$ space.

[**Hint:** Produce $\mathbf{K}$ by iterating $h = blocks^{-1}$ from 2.]

The very small space used for the generation of $\mathbf{K}$ is the most interesting element of the question.

Solution

As h is defined, $h(x) = y$ if and only if y starts with 2 and $blocks(y) = x$.

How to generate $h^{k+1}(2)$ from $h^k(2)$. Let $x = h^k(2)$. Then $y = h^{k+1}(2) = h(x)$ results by replacing the letter $x[i]$ of x either by $x[i]$ occurrences of letter 2 if i is even or by $x[i]$ occurrences of letter 1 if i is odd. The word $\mathbf{K}$ is the limit of $\mathbf{K}_k = h^k(2)$ when k goes to infinity. The first iterations of h give

$$\begin{cases} h(2) & = 2\,2 \\ h^2(2) & = 2\,2\,1\,1 \\ h^3(2) & = 2\,2\,1\,1\,2\,1 \\ h^4(2) & = 2\,2\,1\,1\,2\,1\,2\,2\,1 \end{cases}$$

We leave for the reader the following technical fact.

Observation. $n = O(\log |\mathbf{K}_n|)$ and $\sum_{k=0}^{n} |\mathbf{K}_k| = O(|\mathbf{K}_n|)$.

Let T be the parsing tree associated with $\mathbf{K}_n$. Its leaves correspond to positions on $\mathbf{K}_n$. For a position i, $0 \leq i < |\mathbf{K}_n|$, $RightBranch(i)$ denotes the path from the ith leaf upwards to the first node on the leftmost branch of the tree (see picture).

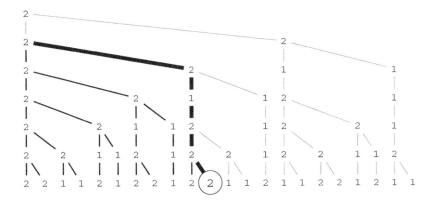

The figure illustrates the parsing tree of $\mathbf{K}_6 = h^6(2)$. Each level represents $h^k(2)$ for $k = 0, 1, \ldots, 6$. The RightBranch of position 10 (circled leaf) consists of the thick edges and their endpoints. It starts from the leaf and goes up to finish at the first node on the leftmost branch.

To every node on the RightBranch is attached one bit of information: the parity of the numbers of nodes to the left on its level.

If for each node we know its label and whether it is a left child, then from *RightBranch*(i) the symbol at position ($i + 1$) as well as the whole *RightBranch*($i + 1$) are computed in logarithmic space and amortised constant time due to the observation (since lengths of paths are logarithmic and the size of the whole tree is linear). The process works as follows on a suffix of the RightBranch. It goes up the tree to find the first left child, then goes down to the right from its parent and continues until it reaches the next leaf. Basically it goes up to the lowest common ancestor of leaves i and $i + 1$ and in a certain sense each iteration can be seen as an in-order traversal of the parsing tree using small memory.

The RightBranch may grow upwards, as happens when changing *RightBranch*(13) to *RightBranch*(14) in the example. This is a top-level description of the algorithm and technical details are omitted.

Notes

The Oldenburger–Kolakoski sequence, often referred to as just the Kolakoski sequence, was designed by Oldenburger [197] and later popularised by Kolakoski [166]. The sequence is an example of a smooth word, see [46]. Our sketch of the algorithm is a version of the algorithm by Nilsson [195]; see also https://en.wikipedia.org/wiki/Kolakoski_sequence.

5   Square-Free Game

A non-trivial square is a word over an alphabet A of the form uu, where $|u| > 1$, and it is an odd-square if in addition $|u|$ is an odd number.

The *square-free game* of length n over A is played between two players, Ann and Ben. The players extend an initially empty word w by alternately appending letters to the word. The game ends when the length of the emerging word is n or a non-trivial square has been created earlier. We assume that Ben makes the first move and that n is even. Ann wins if there are no non-trivial squares in the final word. Otherwise, Ben is the winner.

Odd square-free game. In this limited game Ann wins if no odd-square occurs. On the alphabet $A = \{0, 1, 2\}$ we describe Ann's winning strategy as follows. Ann never makes the same move as Ben's last move, and if Ben repeats Ann's last move then she does not repeat his previous move.

To do so, Ann remembers the pair (b, a), where a is the letter appended during her previous move and b is that from Ben's previous move. In other terms, the word w is of even length and after the first move is of the form $w = vba$. Then Ben adds c and Ann responds by adding d to get $w = vbacd$, where

$$ d = \begin{cases} a & \text{if } c \neq a, \\ 3 - b - a & \text{otherwise.} \end{cases} $$

Ann behaves like a finite deterministic automaton whose output has six states. A possible sequence of moves starting with 1 2, potentially winning for Ann, is

$$ 1\,2\,1\,2\,2\,0\,1\,0\,0\,2\,1\,2\,2\,0. $$

> **Question. (A)** Show that Ann always wins against Ben in the odd square-free game of any even length n.
>
> **(B)** Describe a winning strategy for Ann in the square-free game over an alphabet of size 9.

[**Hint:** To prove (A) show w contains no odd-square. For point (B) mix a simple even-square strategy with the former strategy.]

Solution

Point (A). We show point (A) by contradiction that Ann's strategy is winning and assume the word w (history of the game) contains an odd-square uu ($|u| > 1$).

Case 1. The first letter of uu is from a move by Ben.

The square is of the form

$$uu = b_0 a_1 b_1 a_2 b_2 \cdots a_k b_k \; a_0' b_1' a_1' b_2' a_2' \cdots b_k' a_k',$$

where the letters b_i and b_j' correspond to Ben's moves and the others to Ann's moves.

Since uu is a square we get $b_0 = a_0'$, $a_1 = b_1'$, ..., $b_k = a_k'$. Due to Ann's strategy we have $a_1 \neq b_0$, $a_2 \neq b_1$, etc.; that is, each two adjacent letters in uu are distinct. In particular, this implies that Ben never repeats the last move of Ann in uu.

Consequently all moves of Ann are the same; that is, all letters a_i, a_j' are the same. Hence $a_k = a_k'$ but at the same time $a_k' = b_k$ since uu is a square. This implies $b_k = a_k$ and that Ben repeats the last move of Ann, a contradiction. This completes the proof for this case.

Case 2. The first letter of uu is from a move by Ann.

The square is of the form

$$uu = a_0 b_1 a_1 b_2 a_2 \cdots b_k a_k \; b_0' a_1' b_1' a_2' b_2' \cdots a_k' b_k',$$

where as before the letters b_i, b_j' correspond to Ben's moves and the others to Ann's moves.

Similarly to the previous case we can prove that Ben always makes a move different from the last move of Ann, except that it can happen that $a_k = b_0'$. If so, $a_1' \neq b_k$, since $a_1' = 3 - a_k - b_k$, and later $a_1' = a_2' = \cdots = a_k'$. Consequently $a_k' \neq b_k$ but at the same time $a_k' = b_k$, since uu is a square, a contradiction.

If $a_k \neq b_0'$ all moves of Ben are different from those of Ann, who consequently always does the same move in uu. This leads to a contradiction in the same way as in case 1.

This completes the proof of this case and shows that Ann's strategy is winning.

Point (B). If the game concerns non-trivial even squares on the alphabet $\{0, 1, 2\}$ a winning strategy for Ann is extremely simple: in her kth move she adds the kth letter of any (initially fixed) square-free word over the same alphabet.

Combining in a simple way strategies (using them simultaneously) for non-trivial odd and even square-free games, Ann gets a winning strategy avoiding general non-trivial squares on a 9-letter alphabet. The alphabet now consists of pairs (e, e') of letters in $\{0, 1, 2\}$. The history of the game is a word of the form

$w = (e_1, e_1')(e_2, e_2') \cdots (e_k, e_k')$ for which $e_1 e_2 \cdots e_k$ contains no odd-square and $e_1' e_2' \cdots e_k'$ contains no non-trivial even square.

Notes

The solution of the game presented in the problem is described in [132], where the number of letters was additionally decreased to 7 using more complicated arguments. However, a flaw was discovered by Kosinski et al.; see [169], where the number of letters is reduced just to 8.

6   Fibonacci Words and Fibonacci Numeration System

Let $r(m)$ denote the Fibonacci representation of a non-negative integer m. It is a word x of length ℓ on the alphabet $\{0,1\}$ ending with 1 except for $m = 0$, containing no two consecutive occurrences of 1 and that satisfies $m = \sum_{i=0}^{\ell-1} x[i] \cdot F_{i+2}$, where F_{i+2} is the $(i + 2)$th Fibonacci number (recall that $F_0 = 0$, $F_1 = 1$, $F_2 = 1$, $F_3 = 2$, etc.).

For example: $r(0) = 0, r(1) = 1, r(2) = 01, r(3) = 001, r(4) = 101, r(5) = 0001, r(6) = 1001, r(7) = 0101$.

Note that the usual positional Fibonacci representation of an integer m is $r(m)^R$, the reverse of $r(m)$. Also note that Fibonacci coding used to encode an integer m in a data stream is $r(m)1$, terminating with 11 to allow its decoding.

> **Question.** Show that the sequence of first digits of Fibonacci representations of natural numbers in increasing order is the infinite Fibonacci word when letters are identified to digits: a to 0, b to 1.

Let $pos(k, c), k > 0$, denote the position of the kth occurrence of letter c in the infinite Fibonacci word $\mathbf{f}$.

> **Question.** Show how to compute the position of the kth occurrence of letter a in the Fibonacci word $\mathbf{f}$ in time $O(\log k)$. The same applies for the letter b.

[**Hint:** Show the following formulas: $r(pos(k, \text{a})) = 0 \cdot r(k - 1)$ and $r(pos(k, \text{b})) = 10 \cdot r(k - 1)$.]

Solution

To understand the structure of Fibonacci representations, let us consider the rectangle R_n whose rows are representations of the first $|fib_n| = F_{n+2}$ natural numbers. Representations are possibly right padded with 0's to get n digits. The rectangles are given by the recurrence shown in the picture below.

$$R_1 = \begin{bmatrix} 0 \\ 1 \end{bmatrix} \qquad R_2 = \begin{bmatrix} 0 & 0 \\ 1 & 0 \\ 0 & 1 \end{bmatrix} \qquad R_3 = \begin{bmatrix} 0 & 0 & 0 \\ 1 & 0 & 0 \\ 0 & 1 & 0 \\ 0 & 0 & 1 \\ 1 & 0 & 1 \end{bmatrix} \qquad R_{n+2} = \begin{bmatrix} R_{n+1} & & 0 \\ & & \cdot \\ & & \cdot \\ & & \\ \hline & & 0 & 1 \\ R_n & & \cdot & \cdot \end{bmatrix}$$

Answer to the first question. Rows of rectangles R_1 and R_2 are representations of first $|fib_1|$ and $|fib_2|$ integers in increasing order respectively. Let us show by recurrence it holds for R_{n+2}, $n > 0$. Indeed, the first $|fib_{n+1}|$ rows of R_{n+2} are representations padded with 0 of the first $|fib_{n+1}|$ integers by the recurrence hypothesis. The next $|fib_n|$ rows are representations of the form $x \cdot 01$ (they cannot end with 11). Since x is a row of R_n and using again the recurrence hypothesis, the next rows represent the next $|fib_n|$ integers, which shows that R_{n+2} satisfies the property and ends the recurrence.

It is clear from the recurrence that the sequence of first digits (the first column at the limit) corresponds to the infinite Fibonacci word. This answers the first question.

Answer to the second question. The limit of tables R_n is the infinite table R_∞ of Fibonacci representations of all consecutive natural numbers in increasing order. In each row, letters to the right of the rightmost occurrence of 1 are non-significant digits equal to zero.

Zeros in the first column of R_∞ correspond to a's in the Fibonacci word. Rows starting with 0's are of the form

$$0 \cdot x_0, \ 0 \cdot x_1, \ 0 \cdot x_2, \ \dots,$$

where

$$x_0, \ x_1, \ x_2, \ \dots$$

is the sequence of representations of consecutive natural numbers.

Hence the kth zero corresponds to x_{k-1} and occurs at position $0 \cdot x_{k-1}$, which gives $r(pos(k, \mathtt{a})) = 0 \cdot r(k-1)$.

Similarly we get $r(pos(k, \mathtt{b})) = 10 \cdot r(k-1)$, since all rows containing 1 in the first column of R_∞ start in fact with 10.

Therefore, computing the kth occurrence of a letter in the Fibonacci word amounts to computing the Fibonacci representation of an integer and doing the inverse operation, both taking $O(\log k)$ time as expected.

0	a	0	0	0	0	0	·
1	b	1	0	0	0	0	·
2	a	0	1	0	0	0	·
3	a	0	0	1	0	0	·
4	b	1	0	1	0	0	·
5	a	0	0	0	1	0	·
6	b	1	0	0	1	0	·
7	a	0	1	0	1	0	·
8	a	0	0	0	0	1	·
9	b	1	0	0	0	1	·
10	a	0	1	0	0	1	·
11	a	0	0	1	0	1	·
12	b	1	0	1	0	1	·
·	·	·	·	·	·	·	·

positions of the

5th occurrence of a:
$(0 \cdot 101)_F = 7$

4th occurrence of b:
$(10 \cdot 001)_F = 9$

Notes
The problem material is by Rytter [216].

---

7 Wythoff's Game and Fibonacci Word

Wythoff's game, a variant of the game of Nim, is a two-player game of strategy. It is played with two piles of tokens, one being initially non-empty. Players take turns removing either a positive number of tokens from one pile or the same number of tokens from both piles. When there are no tokens left, the game ends and the last player is the winner.

A configuration of the game is described by a pair of natural numbers (m, n), $m \leq n$, where m and n are the number of tokens on the two piles. Note that $(0, n)$ as well as (n, n), $n > 0$ are winning configurations. The smallest losing configuration is $(1, 2)$ and all configurations of the form $(m + 1, m + 2)$, $(1, m)$ and $(2, m)$ for $m > 0$ are winning configurations.

It is known that losing configurations follow a regular pattern determined by the golden ratio. Thus we pose the following question.

Question. Is there any close relation between Wythoff's game and the infinite Fibonacci word?

Solution

Losing configurations in Wythoff's game are closely related to the Fibonacci word. Let *WytLost* denote the set of losing configurations. It contains pairs of the form (m,n), $0 < m < n$:

$$WytLost = \{(1,2),(3,5),(4,7),(6,10),(8,13),\ldots\}.$$

Denoting by (m_k,n_k) the kth lexicographically smallest pair of the set we get

$$WytLost = \{(m_1,n_1),(m_2,n_2),(m_3,n_3),\ldots\},$$

with $m_1 < m_2 < m_3 < \cdots$ and $n_1 < n_2 < n_3 < \cdots$

Let $pos(k,c)$, $k > 0$, denote the position of the kth occurrence of the letter c in the infinite Fibonacci word $\mathbf{f}$. The following property relating $\mathbf{f}$ to Wythoff's game is stated as follows.

Fact 1. $m_k = pos(k,\mathsf{a}) + 1$ and $n_k = pos(k,\mathsf{b}) + 1$.

Let $M = \{m_1,m_2,m_3,\ldots\}$ and $N = \{n_1,n_2,n_3,\ldots\}$. The following fact is well known and not proved here.

Fact 2.

(i) $M \cap N = \emptyset$ and $M \cup N = \{1,2,3,\ldots\}$.

(ii) $n_k = m_k + k$ for every $k > 0$.

Fact 2 is used to derive Fact 1. It is enough to prove that both properties (i) and (ii) hold for the sets $M' = \{pos(k,\mathsf{a}) + 1 : k > 0\}$ and $N' = \{pos(k,\mathsf{b}) + 1 : k > 0\}$.

Property (i) obviously holds and property (ii) follows from the hint presented and proved in Problem 6:

$$r(pos(k,\mathsf{a})) = 0 \cdot r(k-1) \text{ and } r(pos(k,\mathsf{b})) = 10 \cdot r(k-1),$$

where $r(i)$ stands for the Fibonacci representation of the natural number i. To show that $pos(k,\mathsf{b}) + 1 - pos(k,\mathsf{a}) + 1 = k$ it is sufficient to prove that for any Fibonacci representation x of a positive integer we have $(10x)_F - (0x)_F = (x)_F + 1$, where $(y)_F$ denotes the number i for which $r(i) = y$. But this follows directly from the definition of the Fibonacci representation and achieves the proof.

Notes

The game was introduced by Wythoff [240] as a modification of the game of Nim. He discovered the relation between losing configurations and the golden ratio; see `https://en.wikipedia.org/wiki/Wythoff's_game`. Specifically, the kth losing configuration (m_k, n_k), $k > 0$, is given by $m_k = \lfloor k\Phi \rfloor$ and $n_k = \lfloor k\Phi^2 \rfloor \doteq m_k + k$. He also showed that sequences of m_k's and of n_k's are complementary; that is, each positive integer appears exactly once in either sequence.

Another consequence of the above properties is a surprising algorithm that generates the infinite Fibonacci word (or prefixes of it as long as required). To do so, assume we start with the infinite word $Fib = \sqcup^\infty$ and apply the following instruction.

```
1   for k ← 1 to ∞ do
2       i ← smallest position on Fib of ⊔
3       Fib[i] ← a
4       Fib[i + k] ← b
```

Then properties (i) and (ii) imply Fib becomes the Fibonacci word.

8   Distinct Periodic Words

In this problem we examine how much different two periodic words of the same length can be. The difference is measured with the Hamming distance. The Hamming distance between x and y of the same length is $\mathrm{HAM}(x, y) = |\{j : x[j] \neq y[j]\}|$.

We consider a word x whose period is p, a word y of length $|x|$ whose period q satisfies $q \leq p$ and we assume there is at least a mismatch between them. Let i be the position on x and on y of a mismatch, say, $x[i] = $ a and $y[i] = $ b. On the picture $x = u^2$, $|u| = p$, and $|v| = q$.

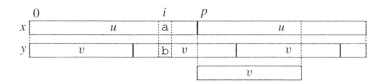

Example. Let $x = $ (abaababa)^2 of period 8 and $y = $ (abaaa)^{3}a of period 5. The words are distinct and have more than one mismatch. They are at positions 4, 9, 11, 12 and 14.

0	1	2	3	**4**	5	6	7	8	**9**	10	**11**	**12**	13	**14**	15
x	a	b	a	a	b	a	b	a	a	b	a	a	b	a	b	a
y	a	b	a	a	a	a	b	a	a	a	a	b	a	a	a	a

Question. What is the minimal Hamming distance between two distinct periodic words of the same length?

[**Hint:** Consider different cases of position i according to periods p and q.]

Solution

Since x is periodic its length is at least $2p$. W.l.o.g. it can be assumed that $x = x[0..2p - 1] = u^2$. By symmetry we can also consider the mismatch position i satisfies $0 \le i < p$. Let $v = y[0..q - 1]$ be the prefix period of y. Note that u and v are primitive words.

For example, aa and bb of period 1 have exactly two mismatches, as well as bbcabcbbcabc and abcabcabcabc of respective periods 6 and 3. In fact, if p is a multiple of q, that is, $p = hq$ for a positive integer h, it is clear that there is another mismatch at position $i + p$. Then $\mathrm{HAM}(x, y) \ge 2$.

If p is not a multiple of q, we prove the same inequality by contradiction, then assume the two words x and y match except at position i on them. Let us consider three cases illustrated by the three pictures that follow.

Case $i \ge q$. The word v as a prefix of u occurs at position p on both x and y. It is then an internal factor of v^2, which contradicts its primitivity by the Primitivity Lemma.

Case $i < q$ **and** $i + q < p$**.** Since $y[i] = y[i + q] = x[i + q]$, we get $x[i] \neq x[i + q]$. Then q is not a period of u though its occurrence at position p has period q, a contradiction.

Case $i < q$ **and** $i + q \geq p$**.** Let us first show that $w = y[i + 1 .. i + p - 1]$ has period $p - q$. Indeed, for a position j, if $i < j < p$ we have

$$y[j] = x[j] = x[j + p] = y[j + p] = y[j + p - q]$$

and if $p \leq j < i + q$, we get

$$y[j] = y[j - q] = x[j - q] = x[j + p - q].$$

Then, w of length $p - 1$ has period $p - q$ in addition to period q as a factor of y longer than v. The Periodicity Lemma implies that $\gcd(q, p - q)$ is also a period, which contradicts the primitivity of v because $p - q < q$.

To conclude, when p is not a multiple of q, we have $\mathrm{HAM}(x, y) \geq 2$ as before, which achieves the whole proof.

Notes
A different proof of the result is by Amir et al. [12], and more developments can be found in [9].

9   A Relative of the Thue–Morse Word

Let $\mathbf{c} = (c_0, c_1, c_2, \dots)$ be the least increasing sequence of positive integers starting with 1 and satisfying the condition

$$(*) \qquad n \in \mathbf{C} \Leftrightarrow n/2 \notin \mathbf{C},$$

where $\mathbf{C}$ is the set of elements in the sequence $\mathbf{c}$. The first elements of the sequence $\mathbf{c}$ are

$$1, 3, 4, 5, 7, 9, 11, 12, 13, 15, 16, 17, 19, 20, 21, 23, 25, 27, 28, 29, \dots$$

Observe both that all odd integers are in the sequence and that gaps between two consecutive elements are either 1 or 2.

> **Question.** What is the relation between the sequence $\mathbf{c}$ and the infinite Thue–Morse word $\mathbf{t}$?

Solution

Recall the Thue–Morse word $\mathbf{t}$ is $\mu^\infty(\mathsf{a})$, where the morphism μ is defined from $\{\mathsf{a}, \mathsf{b}\}$ to itself by $\mu(\mathsf{a}) = \mathsf{ab}$ and $\mu(\mathsf{b}) = \mathsf{ba}$. Let $end\text{-}pos(x, y)$ denote the set of ending positions of occurrences of a word x inside a word y.

Key property. For a positive integer n,

$$(**) \qquad n \notin \mathbf{C} \Leftrightarrow n \in end\text{-}pos(\mathsf{aa}, \tau) \cup end\text{-}pos(\mathsf{bb}, \tau).$$

The table below shows a prefix of $\mathbf{t}$ and a few first elements of $\mathbf{C}$ associated with it (even values in bold) to illustrate the property.

0	1	2	3	4	5	6	7	8	9	10	11	12	13	14	15	16	17
t	a	b	b	a	b	a	a	b	b	a	a	b	a	b	b	a	b	a
c		1		3	4	5		7		9		11	**12**	13		15	**16**	17

From its definition, the word $\mathbf{t}$ satisfies, for $k > 0$:

(i) $\mathbf{t}[n] = \overline{\mathbf{t}[k]}$ and $\mathbf{t}[n-1] = \mathbf{t}[k]$ if $n = 2k + 1$.

(ii) $\mathbf{t}[n] = \mathbf{t}[k]$ and $\mathbf{t}[n-1] = \overline{\mathbf{t}[k-1]}$ if $n = 2k$.

Then property (i) rules out equivalence $(**)$ for odd integers and property (ii) does it by induction for even integers, which shows the relation between $\mathbf{c}$ and $\mathbf{t}$.

Notes

Referring to the equivalent definition of the Thue–Morse word using the parity of the number of 1's in the binary representation of integers (see page 8) the property '$n \in \mathbf{C} \Leftrightarrow v(n)$ is even,' where $v(n)$ denotes the length of the end-block of 0's in the binary representation of n and also characterises the sequence **c**. (Note $v(n) = 0$ if and only if n is odd.)

10   Thue–Morse Words and Sums of Powers

For a finite set of natural numbers I let $Sum_k(I) = \sum_{i \in I} i^k$. Given two finite sets I and J of natural numbers we consider the property $\mathbf{P}(n, I, J)$:

$$\text{for any } k, 0 < k < n, \ Sum_k(I) = Sum_k(J),$$

which we examine with regards to sets of positions on the nth Thue–Morse word τ_n of length 2^n. Namely, the sets are

$$T_a(n) = \{i : \tau_n[i] = a\} \text{ and } T_b(n) = \{j : \tau_n[j] = b\}.$$

For example, the Thue–Morse word $\tau_3 = abbabaab$ provides

$$T_a(3) = \{0, 3, 5, 6\} \text{ and } T_b(3) = \{1, 2, 4, 7\}.$$

The property $\mathbf{P}(3, T_a(3), T_b(3))$ holds due to the equalities:
$0 + 3 + 5 + 6 = 1 + 2 + 4 + 7 = 14,$
$0^2 + 3^2 + 5^2 + 6^2 = 1^2 + 2^2 + 4^2 + 7^2 = 70.$

> **Question.** Show that the property $\mathbf{P}(n, T_a(n), T_b(n))$ holds for any integer $n > 1$.

Solution
For a natural number d let $I + \{d\} = \{a + d : a \in I\}$. Note the following fact, whose proof is a matter of simple calculation, for any number d and sets I, J.

Observation. Assume $\mathbf{P}(n, I, J)$ holds. Then the two other properties hold as well:

$$\mathbf{P}(n, I + \{d\}, J + \{d\}) \text{ and } \mathbf{P}(n + 1, I \cup (J + \{d\}), J \cup (I + \{d\})).$$

The solution of the problem, that is, the proof of the statement in the question, reduces then to a simple induction on n, using the observation above and the following recurrence on $n > 1$:

$$T_a(n+1) = T_a(n) \cup (T_b(n) + 2^n) \text{ and } T_b(n+1) = T_b(n) \cup (T_a(n) + 2^n).$$

Notes

The present problem is a particular case of the so-called Tarry–Escott problem; see [6].

---

11   Conjugates and Rotations of Words

Two words x and y are conjugate if there exist two words u and v for which $x = uv$ and $y = vu$. They are also called rotations or cyclic shifts of one another. For instance, the word abaab = aba·ab is a conjugate of ababa = ab·aba. It is clear that conjugacy is an equivalence relation between words but it is not compatible with the product of words.

Below are the seven conjugates of aabaaba (left) and the three conjugates of aabaabaab (right).

```
a a b a a b a            a a b a a b a a b
  a b a a b a a            a b a a b a a b a
    b a a b a a a            b a a b a a b a a
      a a b a a a b
        a b a a a b a
          b a a a b a a
            a a a b a a b
```

> **Question.** Show that two non-empty words of the same length are conjugate if and only if their (primitive) roots are conjugate.

On the above example, aabaabaab $= (\text{aab})^3$ and baabaabaa $= (\text{baa})^3$ are conjugate, like their respective roots aab and baa.

A more surprising property of conjugate words is stated in the next question.

> **Question.** Show that two non-empty words x and y are conjugate if and only if $xz = zy$ for some word z.

On the above example (left), aabaaba and baabaaa are conjugate and aabaaba $\cdot$ aa = aa $\cdot$ baabaaa.

Solution

Assume words x and y of the same length have conjugate roots. Let uv be the root of x and vu be the root of y. Then $x = (uv)^k$ and $y = (vu)^k$ with $k > 0$, since they have the same length. Thus $x = u \cdot v(uv)^{k-1}$ and $y = v(uv)^{k-1} \cdot u$, which shows they are conjugate.

Conversely, assume x and y are conjugate and let u and v be such that $x = uv$ and $y = vu$. Let z be the root of x and $k > 0$ with $x = z^k$. Let also u' and v' be defined by $z = u'v'$, u' is a suffix of u and v' is a prefix of v.

z		z		z	
u				v	
u'	v'	u'	v'	u'	v'

Then, $y = vu = (v'u')^{k'} v'(u'v')^{k''} u'$, where $k' + k'' = k - 1$. This gives $y = (v'u')^k$ and shows that the root t of y satisfies $|t| \leq |u'v'| = |z|$ using Lemma 2. But since the roles of x and y are symmetric, this also proves $|z| \leq |t|$ and thus $|z| = |t|$ and $t = v'u'$. Therefore, the respective roots z and t of x and y are conjugate.

To answer the second question, let us first assume x and y are conjugate, that is $x = uv$ and $y = vu$. Then $xu = (uv)u = u(vu) = uy$, which proves the conclusion with $z = u$.

Conversely, assume $xz = zy$ for some word z. For any positive integer ℓ we get $x^\ell z = x^{\ell-1}zy = x^{\ell-2}zy^2 = \cdots = zy^\ell$. This is illustrated by the next diagram, expansion of the initial left square diagram associated with $xz = zy$, in which $\circ$ denotes the concatenation.

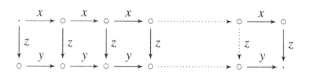

Considering the integer k that satisfies $(k-1)|x| \leq |z| < k|x|$, z is a proper prefix of x^k at least as long as x^{k-1} ($k = 3$ in the picture below).

x		x		x		x	
z				y			
u	v	u	v	u	v	u	v

Then, there exist two words u and v for which $x = uv$ and $z = x^{k-1}u$. It follows that $xz = (uv)^k u = zvu$, which implies $y = vu$ from the condition $xz = zy$. Therefore x and y are conjugate.

Notes

Conjugacy of words is intimately related to their periodicity as seen on page 3. More on conjugate words may be found in Lothaire [175].

12   Conjugate Palindromes

The problem is related to the two operations on words consisting of reversing a word and taking one of its conjugate. The operations are essentially incompatible in the sense that only a few conjugates of a word are also its reverse.

To examine the situation, we consider palindromes that are conjugates of each other. For example, the words abba and baab are both palindromes and conjugate of each other. On the contrary, the word aabaa has no other conjugate palindrome, that is to say, its conjugacy class contains only one palindrome.

Question. What is the maximal number of palindromes in the conjugacy class of a word?

[**Hint:** Consider the primitive root of two conjugate palindromes.]

The conjugacy class of abba, set {abba, bbaa, baab, aabb}, contains only two palindromes. This is also the case for the word (abba)^3 whose conjugacy class contains abbaab baabba and baabba abbaab, two palindromes. But the conjugacy class of (abba)^2 has only one palindrome among its four conjugates.

Solution

The preceding examples suggest a conjugacy class contains no more than two palindromes. Before showing it we prove an intermediate result.

Lemma 4 *If* $x \neq x^R$ *and* $xx^R = w^k$ *for a primitive word* w *and a positive integer* k, *then* k *is odd and* $w = uu^R$ *for some word* u.

Proof If k is even, $xx^R = (w^{k/2})^2$ and then $x = x^R$, a contradiction. So k is odd and then $|w|$ is even. Let $w = uv$ with $|u| = |v|$. Since u is a prefix of x and v is a suffix of x^R, we get $v = u^R$, as expected.   ∎

For two non-empty words x and y, assume the conjugate words xy and yx are distinct palindromes. We have both $xy = (xy)^R = y^R x^R$ and $yx = (yx)^R = x^R y^R$.

To prove that no more than two palindromes can be conjugate we first show that $xy = (uu^R)^k$ and $yx = (u^R u)^k$, where k is a positive integer and u is a word for which uu^R is primitive. There are two cases according to x and y having the same length or not.

If $|x| = |y|$, we have $y = x^R$, which implies $xy = xx^R$ and $yx = x^R x$. In addition, $x \neq x^R$ because of the hypothesis $xy \neq yx$. Using the result of Lemma 4, the primitive root of xy is of the form uu^R and $xy = (uu^R)^k$ for some odd integer.

If $|x| \neq |y|$, w.l.o.g. we assume $|x| < |y|$ (see picture). Then, x is a proper border of y^R and x^R is a proper border of y, which implies that xx^R is a proper border of xy. The word $z = (x^R)^{-1}y$ is also a border of xy. Then the word xy has two periods $|xx^R|$ and $|z|$ that satisfy the Periodicity Lemma condition. Thus $q = \gcd(|xx^R|, |z|)$ is also a period of xy and divides its length. Considering the primitive root w of xy, the latter word is of the form w^k, $k > 1$, where $p = |w|$ is a divisor of q. Using Lemma 4 again, the primitive root is of the form uu^R, with $u \neq u^R$ because it is primitive. Then $xy = (uu^R)^k$, where k is an odd integer.

Whether x and y have the same length or not, we get the same conclusion. To achieve the proof we just have to consider the conjugacy class of a palindrome $(uu^R)^k$ where uu^R is primitive. Such a class contains another palindrome, namely $(u^R u)^k$.

Since conjugates of $(u^R u)^k$ are of the form $(st)^k$ where st is a conjugate of uu^R, applying the above argument again, the inequalities $u \neq u^R$ and $s \neq u^R$ would lead to a contradiction with the primitivity of uu^R. This achieves the proof that a conjugacy class contains no more than two palindromes.

Notes
The result of this problem is by Guo et al. [133] and the present proof is adapted from their article.

13   Many Words with Many Palindromes

The problem deals with the number of words containing as many palindrome factors as possible. A word w is called *palindrome rich* if it contains $|w|$ distinct non-empty palindromes as factors, including single-letter palindromes.

Example. The words `poor`, `rich` and `abac` are rich, while the words `maximal` and `abca` are not. Indeed, the set of palindromes occurring in `abac` is $\{a, aba, b, c\}$, while it is $\{a, b, c\}$ for `abca`.

Let $Rich_k(n)$ denote the number of rich words of length n over an alphabet of size k.

Note that each position on a word is the (starting) position of the rightmost occurrence of a palindrome that it contains at most once. This is due to the fact that a second shorter palindrome sharing the position would be a proper suffix of the longer palindrome and then would occur later, a contradiction. This implies the following fact.

Observation. There are at most $|w|$ palindromes, factors of a word w.

The most interesting case to discuss is that of binary words, that is, $k = 2$, because we have

$$\begin{cases} Rich_2(n) = 2^n & \text{for } n < 8, \\ Rich_2(n) < 2^n & \text{for } n \geq 8. \end{cases}$$

Question. Show that $Rich_2(2n)$ grows exponentially; that is, there is a positive constant c for which $Rich_2(2n) \geq 2^{cn}$.

[**Hint:** Use the fact that the number of partitions of integers grows exponentially.]

Solution

Consider all partitions of the number n into different positive integers:

$$n = n_1 + n_2 + \cdots + n_k \text{ and } n_1 < n_2 < \cdots < n_k.$$

For each such partition $\pi = (n_1, n_2, \ldots, n_k)$ let us consider the word w_π of length $n + k - 1$ defined as follows:

$$w_\pi = \mathrm{a}^{n_1} \mathrm{ba}^{n_2} \mathrm{b} \ldots \mathrm{ba}^{n_k}.$$

It is fairly easy to see that the word w_π is palindrome rich.

The figure below displays non-unary palindromes occurring in the word $\mathrm{aba^2ba^3ba^5ba^6}$ of length 21 associated with the partition of 17 $(1, 2, 3, 5, 6)$. In addition to the 14 palindromes shown in the picture, the word contains the unary palindromes a, aa, aaa, aaaa, aaaaa, aaaaaa and b for a total of 21 palindromes.

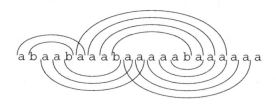

Appending b^{n-k+1} to w_π produces the word $v_\pi = w_\pi \mathrm{b}^{n-k+1}$ of length $2n$ that contains the additional palindromes $\mathrm{ba}^{n_k}\mathrm{b}$, b^2, b^3, $\ldots$, b^{n-k+1}. Then v_π is also rich. It is known that the number of partitions of an integer n into pairwise distinct positive integers grows exponentially with n. Hence $Rich_2(2n)$ also grows exponentially with n.

Notes

The problem is based on the survey by Glen et al. [130] on the palindromic richness of words.

14   Short Superword of Permutations

The goal of the problem is to show that a certain set of patterns can be packed into a single word in a space-economic way. This can be viewed as a compression technique for the specific set.

The present patterns called n-permutations are drawn from the alphabet of natural numbers. They are words on the alphabet $\{1, 2, \ldots, n\}$ in which every number from $\{1, 2, \ldots, n\}$ appears exactly once. The aim is to build words, called n-superwords, which contain all the n-permutations as factors.

For $n = 2$ the word 121 is a shortest 2-superword, since it contains the two 2-permutations 12 and 21. For $n = 3$, 123121321 is a shortest 3-superword. The six 3-permutations appear in it in the order

$$\pi_1 = 123, \pi_2 = 231, \pi_3 = 312, \pi_4 = 213, \pi_5 = 132, \pi_6 = 321.$$

Note how is the structure of 123121321: each occurrence of letter 3 is flanked by two occurrences of a 2-permutation.

The two examples of superwords are of respective lengths $\alpha_2 = 3$ and $\alpha_3 = 9$, where $\alpha_n = \sum_{i=1}^{n} i!$. But it is not clear whether a shortest n-superword is of length α_n for $n \geq 4$.

The problem consists in constructing a short n-superword, which may not be of minimal length.

Question. Show how to construct an n-superword of length α_n for each natural number n.

[**Hint:** Use this above remark on the structure of 123121321 to build an n-superword from an $(n-1)$-superword.]

Solution
The construction is done iteratively, starting with the base case $n = 2$ (or $n = 3$), as follows.

Let w_{n-1} be an $(n-1)$-superword of length α_{n-1}. The $(n-1)$-permutations are considered in their order of appearance along w_{n-1}. Let i_k be the ending position on w_{n-1} of the first occurrence of the kth $(n-1)$-permutation in w_{n-1}. This means that there are exactly $k - 1$ distinct $(n - 1)$-permutations with an ending position $i < i_k$ (some $(n - 1)$-permutations can repeat).

The n-superword w_n is built by inserting some n-permutations in w_{n-1}. The selected n-permutations are all the words $n \cdot \pi_k$ where π_k, $1 \leq k \leq (n - 1)!$, is the kth $(n - 1)$-permutation occurring in w_{n-1}. All these words are inserted simultaneously immediately after their respective position i_k in w_{n-1}.

From the definition of i_k, insertions generate factors of the form $\pi_k \cdot n \cdot \pi_k$ in w_n for each $(n-1)$-permutation π_k.

Example. Building w_4 from $w_3 = $ 123121321. The ending positions on w_3 of the six 3-permutations π_i above are

$$i_1 = 2,\, i_2 = 3,\, i_3 = 4,\, i_4 = 6,\, i_5 = 7,\, i_6 = 8.$$

The insertion of the six 4-permutations of the form $4 \cdot \pi_i$ produces the following 4-superword of length $\alpha_4 = 33$:

$$1234123142312431213421324132143214321,$$

in which occurrences of 4 are emphasised.

The length of the word w_n is α_n. Since there are $(n-1)!$ insertions of words of length n, the length of the resulting word w_n is $|w_{n-1}| + (n-1)!\, n = \sum_{i=1}^{n} i! = \alpha_n$, as required.

All n-permutations are factors of the word w_n. A n-permutations occurring in w_n is of the form $u \cdot n \cdot v$, where uv is a word of length $n-1$ that does not contain the letter n. This permutation occurs inside the factor $vu \cdot n \cdot vu$ of w_n, where $vu = \pi_k$ for some $(n-1)$-permutation π_k. Since by construction all words of the form $\pi_k \cdot n \cdot \pi_k$ appear in w_n all n-permutations appear in w_n. This answers the question.

Notes

It was conjectured that α_n is the minimal length of the shortest n-superwords. The conjecture was confirmed for $n = 4$ and $n = 5$ by Johnston [152] but was disproved for $n = 6$ by Houston [143].

15   Short Supersequence of Permutations

The problem deals with the idea of storing efficiently a set of patterns into a word. Contrary to the definition of a superword, in this problem patterns are stored as subsequences of a word called a supersequence.

The present patterns called n-permutations are drawn from the alphabet $\{1, 2, \ldots, n\}$. They are words in which every number from $\{1, 2, \ldots, n\}$ appears exactly once. The aim is to build words, called n-supersequences, that contain all n-permutations as subsequences.

For $n = 3$ the word 1213212 of length 7 is a shortest 3-supersequence. For $n = 4$ the word 123412314321 of length 12 is a shortest 4-supersequence. These two supersequences are of lengths $n^2 - 2n + 4$ (for $n = 3, 4$). Observe that for $n = 4$ our 4-supersequence has length 12 while a shortest 4-superword, obviously longer, is of length 33 (see Problem 14).

A simple way to produce an n-supersequence is to consider a word of the form π^n for any n-permutation π, or of the form $\pi_1 \pi_2 \pi_3 \ldots \pi_n$ where π_is are any n-permutations. It is clear they contain all the $n!$ n-permutations as subsequences but their length is n^2, far from optimal.

The aim of the problem is to show how to construct a moderately short n-supersequence, which may not be of minimal length.

Question. Show how to construct an n-supersequence of length $n^2 - 2n + 4$ for each natural number n.

[**Hint:** Starting from a straight n-supersequence of length n^2, show how to tune it to get the required length.]

Solution

To get the result, the n-supersequence $x = \pi_1 \pi_2 \pi_3 \ldots \pi_n$ as above is shortened in two steps.

Length $n^2 - n + 1$. The length of x is reduced by selecting permutations of the form $n \cdot \rho_i$, for $i = 1, \ldots, n - 1$, where ρ_i is an $(n - 1)$-permutation, and by considering the word

$$y = n \cdot \rho_1 \cdot n \cdot \rho_2 \cdot n \cdots n \cdot \rho_{n-1} \cdot n.$$

This obviously shortens the n-supersequence by $n - 1$ letters and gives the expected length.

Length $n^2 - 2n + 4$. Now the construction technique becomes slightly more tricky. The main idea is to choose more carefully the $(n - 1)$-permutations ρ_i of y.

Having solutions for $n \leq 4$ we develop a solution for $n \geq 5$. To do so, let γ_1, γ_2 and γ_3 be three $(n-1)$-permutations of respective forms $3 \cdot \gamma_1' \cdot 2$, $1 \cdot \gamma_2' \cdot 3$ and $2 \cdot \gamma_3' \cdot 1$, where γ_1' is a permutation of $\{1, 2, \ldots, n-1\} \setminus \{2, 3\}$ and similarly for the other γ's.

We first concatenate in an alternative way $n-1$ blocks of type γ_i and then insert n between them, which gives successively

$$\gamma_1 \cdot \gamma_2 \cdot \gamma_3 \cdot \gamma_1 \cdot \gamma_2 \cdot \gamma_3 \ldots,$$

$$w = n \cdot \gamma_1 \cdot n \cdot \gamma_2 \cdot n \cdot \gamma_3 \cdot n \cdots n,$$

$$w = n \cdot 3 \cdot \gamma_1' \cdot 2 \cdot n \cdot 1 \cdot \gamma_2' \cdot 3 \cdot n \cdot 2 \cdot \gamma_3' \cdot 1 \cdot n \ldots n.$$

It follows from the previous case that this is an n-supersequence and that its length is $n^2 - n + 1$.

The main step of the technique eventually consists in removing $n - 3$ letters in w, which gives the required length $n^2 - n + 1 - (n - 3) = n^2 - 2n + 4$. This is done by removing the letter i from each γ_i' occurring in w, except from their first and last occurrences, to produce the word z.

The word z is an n-supersequence. Observe that the removal of letter i from the block γ_i', for $i = 1, 2, 3$, is compensated by the presence of i to the left and to the right of γ_i beyond the letter n. Then an argument similar to the one applied to the above word y proves that z is an n-supersequence.

It achieves the construction of an n-supersequence of length $n^2 - 2n + 4$.

Example. We illustrate the construction by the case $n = 6$. Let $\gamma_1 = 31452$, $\gamma_2 = 12453$ and $\gamma_3 = 23451$ be the selected 5-permutations. Let also γ_i^{Rem} be the word γ_i after removal of letter i.

Considering the sequence

$$w = 6 \cdot \gamma_1 \cdot 6 \cdot \gamma_2 \cdot 6 \cdot \gamma_3 \cdot 6 \cdot \gamma_1 \cdot 6 \cdot \gamma_2 \cdot 6,$$

the required 6-supersequence is obtained by removing the letter i from each block γ_i, except from the first and last blocks, which produces

$$z = 6 \cdot \gamma_1 \cdot 6 \cdot \gamma_2^{\text{Rem}} \cdot 6 \cdot \gamma_3^{\text{Rem}} \cdot 6 \cdot \gamma_1^{\text{Rem}} \cdot 6 \cdot \gamma_2 \cdot 6;$$

that is

$$z = 6\ 31452\ 6\ 1453\ 6\ 2451\ 6\ 3452\ 6\ 12453\ 6.$$

Notes

The above method is a version of the construction by Mohanty [191]. It is known that the present construction gives a shortest supersequence of length

$n^2 - 2n + 4$ for $2 < n \le 7$. However, for $n \ge 10$ the construction by Zalinescu [242] gives supersequences of length $n^2 - 2n + 3$. The exact general formula for the smallest length of n-supersequences is still unknown; it is only known so far that it is $n^2 - o(n^2)$.

16   Skolem Words

A Skolem word of order n, for a positive integer n, is a word over the alphabet $A_n = \{1, 2, \ldots, n\}$ satisfying, for each $i \in A_n$, the properties:

(i) The letter i appears exactly twice in the word,

(ii) Consecutive occurrences of i are at distance i.

Skolem words have a definition very similar to that of Langford words (Problem 17) but the small change in the distance makes a big difference.

If igi is a factor of a Skolem word, the gap word g does not contain the letter i and $|g| = i - 1$. For example, 11 is an obvious Skolem word of order 1, 23243114 a Skolem word of order 4 and 4511435232 is a Skolem word of order 5. But a mere checking shows there is no Skolem word of order 2 or of order 3.

> **Question.** Discuss for which positive integer n there exists a Skolem word of order n and design an algorithm to build it when possible.

[**Hint:** Discuss according to n modulo 4.]

Solution
We examine different cases depending on n modulo 4.

Case $n = 4k$. The word 23243114 is an example of a Skolem word of order 4. Let $n = 4k$ for $k > 1$. The following procedure builds a Skolem word of order n.

The basic bricks of the construction are the two words w_{even} and w_{odd}. The first is made of the increasing sequence of even numbers in A_n and the second of the increasing sequence of odd numbers in $A_n \setminus \{n - 1\}$ (the largest odd number is discarded).

Algorithm SKOLEM produces the expected word.

SKOLEM(n multiple of 4 larger than 4)

1   $(c,d) \leftarrow (n/2 - 1, n - 1)$
2   $w_{odd} \leftarrow 1\ 3 \cdots n - 3 \triangleright$ no letter $n - 1$ in w_{odd}
3   $\alpha \cdot c \cdot \beta \cdot 1\ 1 \cdot \beta^R \cdot c \cdot \alpha^R \leftarrow$ decomposition of $w_{odd}^R w_{odd}$
4   $v \leftarrow \alpha \cdot 1\ 1 \cdot \beta \cdot c \cdot d \cdot \beta^R \cdot \alpha^R \cdot c$
5   $w_{even} \leftarrow 2\ 4 \cdots n$
6   **return** $v \cdot w_{even}^R \cdot d \cdot w_{even}$

The instruction at line 3 factorises the two ends of the word $w_{odd}^R w_{odd}$ around letter c.

Example. For $n = 12$ the algorithm computes successively, from the words $w_{odd} = 1\ 3\ 5\ 7\ 9$ and $w_{even} = 2\ 4\ 6\ 8\ 10\ 12$, the decomposition of $w_{odd}^R w_{odd}$ with $c = 5$

$$9\ 7 \cdot 5 \cdot 3 \cdot 1\ 1 \cdot 3 \cdot 5 \cdot 7\ 9,$$

where $\alpha = 9\ 7$ and $\beta = 3$; then

$$v = 9\ 7 \cdot 1\ 1 \cdot 3 \cdot 5 \cdot 11 \cdot 3 \cdot 7\ 9 \cdot 5$$

and eventually produces the Skolem word of order 12:

$$9\ 7\ 1\ 1\ 3\ 5\ \mathbf{11}\ 3\ 7\ 9\ 5\ 12\ 10\ 8\ 6\ 4\ 2\ \mathbf{11}\ 2\ 4\ 6\ 8\ 10\ 12,$$

in which $d = 11$ is emphasised.

Why does it work? First note that property (i) is satisfied. Then it is clear that occurrences of each letter in $u = w_{odd}^R w_{odd}$, in v and in the suffix $w_{even}^R \cdot d \cdot w_{even}$ of the output are at correct distances.

So it remains to show property (ii) holds for letters c and d. Inside v the distance between the occurrences of c is $|\alpha| + |\beta| + 1$, the number of odd numbers different from 1 and c; that is, $n/2 - 2$, as required.

The distance between the two occurrences of letter d in the output is $|\alpha| + |\beta| + 1 + |w_{even}|$, that is, $|A_n \setminus \{1,d\}| = n - 2$, as required as well.

Therefore SKOLEM(n) is a Skolem word of order n.

Case $n = 4k + 1$. This case works essentially in the same way as the previous case, except that d is set to n and c is set to $\lfloor n/2 \rfloor - 1$. Let w_{even} be, as before, the increasing sequence of even numbers in A_n and let w_{odd} be the increasing sequence of odd numbers in $A_n \setminus \{n\}$ (the largest odd number is discarded).

With this instance of length n, Algorithm SKOLEM produces the expected word. Observe that in the first case v and the output contain the factor $c \cdot d$ while in the present case they contain the factor $d \cdot c$.

SKOLEM(n in the form $4k + 1$ larger than 4)

1 $(c,d) \leftarrow (\lfloor n/2 \rfloor - 1, n)$
2 $w_{\text{odd}} \leftarrow 1\ 3 \cdots n - 2 \triangleright$ no letter n in w_{odd}
3 $\alpha \cdot c \cdot \beta \cdot 1\ 1 \cdot \beta^{\text{R}} \cdot c \cdot \alpha^{\text{R}} \leftarrow$ decomposition of $w_{\text{odd}}^{\text{R}} w_{\text{odd}}$
4 $v \leftarrow \alpha \cdot 1\ 1 \cdot \beta \cdot d \cdot c \cdot \beta^{\text{R}} \cdot \alpha^{\text{R}} \cdot c$
5 $w_{\text{even}} \leftarrow 2\ 4 \cdots n - 1$
6 **return** $v \cdot w_{\text{even}}^{\text{R}} \cdot d \cdot w_{\text{even}}$

Example. For $n = 13$ the algorithm computes successively, from the words $w_{\text{odd}} = 1\ 3\ 5\ 7\ 9\ 11$ and $w_{\text{even}} = 2\ 4\ 6\ 8\ 10\ 12$, the decomposition of $w_{\text{odd}}^{\text{R}} w_{\text{odd}}$ with $\lfloor n/2 \rfloor - 1 = c = 5$:

$$11\ 9\ 7 \cdot \mathbf{5} \cdot\ 3 \cdot 1\ 1 \cdot 3 \cdot \mathbf{5} \cdot 7\ 9\ 11,$$

where $\alpha = 11\ 9\ 7$ and $\beta = 3$; then

$$v = 11\ 9\ 7\ \mathbf{1}\ \mathbf{1}\ 3\ \mathbf{13}\ \mathbf{5}\ 3\ 7\ 9\ 11\ \mathbf{5}$$

and eventually produces the Skolem word of order 13:

$$v = 11\ 9\ 7\ 1\ 1\ 3\ \mathbf{13}\ \mathbf{5}\ 3\ 7\ 9\ 11\ \mathbf{5}\ 12\ 10\ 8\ 6\ 4\ 2\ \mathbf{13}\ 2\ 4\ 6\ 8\ 10\ 12,$$

in which $c = 5$ and $d = 13$ are emphasised.

Impossibility of other cases. Let $odd(n)$ be the number of odd natural numbers not exceeding n.

Observation. If there is a Skolem word of order n, we have the equality $odd(n) \bmod 2 = n \bmod 2$.

To prove the observation we consider sums modulo 2, called 2-sums, of positions on a Skolem word w of order n. First, the 2-sum of all positions on w is $n \bmod 2$. Second, let us pair positions of the same letter i to compute the sum. If i is even the (two) positions of its occurrences have the same parity, so their contribution to the 2-sum is null. But if i is odd the corresponding positions have different parities. Hence the 2-sum of positions is $odd(n) \bmod 2$. Consequently we have $odd(n) \bmod 2 = n \bmod 2$, as stated.

The impossibility of having Skolem words for $n = 4k+2$ and for $n = 4k+3$ follows directly from the observation, since $odd(n) \bmod 2 \neq n \bmod 2$ in these cases.

To conclude, Skolem words exist only if n is of the form $4k$ or $4k + 1$.

Notes

Words considered in the problem have been introduced by Skolem [227].

---

17   Langford Words

A Langford word of order n, for a positive integer n, is a word over the alphabet $A_n = \{1, 2, \ldots, n\}$ satisfying, for each $i \in A_n$, the properties:

(i)   Letter i appears exactly twice in the word,

(ii)   Consecutive occurrences of i are at distance $i + 1$.

Langford words have a definition very similar to that of Skolem words (Problem 16) but the small change in the distance makes a big difference.

If igi is a factor of a Langford word the gap word g does not contain the letter i and $|g| = i$. For example, 312132 is a Langford word of order 3 and 41312432 a Langford word of order 4.

> **Question.** Discuss for which positive integer n there exists a Langford word of order n and show how to build it when possible.

[**Hint:** Discuss according to n modulo 4.]

Solution

We examine different cases depending on n modulo 4.

Case $n = 4k + 3$. The above example shows a Langford word of order 3. For $n \geq 7$, that is, $k > 0$, let $X_n = \{2k + 1, n - 1, n\}$ and $A'_n = A_n \setminus X_n$. Let both w_{even} be the increasing sequence of even numbers in A'_n and w_{odd} be the increasing sequence of odd numbers in A'_n.

Note that A'_n has $4k$ elements, then exactly $2k$ even letters and $2k$ odd letters. Both w_{even} and w_{odd} can be split into halves: $w_{\text{even}} = p_1 \cdot p_2$, where $|p_1| = |p_2| = k$, and $w_{\text{odd}} = p_3 \cdot p_4$, where $|p_3| = |p_4| = k$.

To get a solution let start with the following word that is almost a Langford word:

$$u = p_2^R \, p_3^R * p_3 * p_2 * p_4^R \, p_1^R * * p_1 * p_4,$$

where $*$ stands for a missing letter to be inserted. It is clear that the distance between the two occurrences of each $i \in A'_n$ equals $i + 1$.

Now it is enough to substitute twice the remaining elements of A_n to $*$, which is done in the order

$$4k + 2, \ 4k + 3, \ 2k + 1, \ 4k + 2, \ 2k + 1, \ 4k + 3.$$

Since each p_j has length k, it is straightforward to compute the distances between copies of inserted elements from $\{2k+1, n-1, n\}$ and see they comply with property (ii), producing a Langford word of order n.

Example. Let $n = 11 = 4 \times 2 + 3, k = 2$. We have $X_{11} = \{5, 10, 11\}$ and $A'_{11} = \{1, 2, 3, 4, 6, 7, 8, 9\}$; then $p_1 = 2 \ 4, p_2 = 6 \ 8, p_3 = 1 \ 3$ and $p_4 = 7 \ 9$. The first step produces

$$u = 8 \ 6 \ 3 \ 1 * 1 \ 3 * 6 \ 8 * 9 \ 7 \ 4 \ 2 * * 2 \ 4 * 7 \ 9,$$

which leads to the Langford word of order 11

$$8 \ 6 \ 3 \ 1 \ \mathbf{10} \ 1 \ 3 \ \mathbf{11} \ 6 \ 8 \ 5 \ 9 \ 7 \ 4 \ 2 \ \mathbf{10} \ 5 \ 2 \ 4 \ \mathbf{11} \ 7 \ 9,$$

in which $2k + 1 = 5, n - 1 = 10$ and $n = 11$ are emphasised.

Case $n = 4k$. An example of Langford word of order 4 is shown above. Then let $n = 4k+4$, with $k > 0$. This case is similar to the previous case. A solution u associated with $4k + 3$ is first built. Then a few changes are made to insert in it the largest element n. It is done by substituting it for the first copy of $2k+1$, an element that is moved to the end of the word and becomes its second occurrence. The second copy of n is placed after it.

To say it differently, insertions inside the word u associated with $4k + 3$ are done in the order

$$4k + 2, \ 4k + 3, \ n, \ 4k + 2, \ 2k + 1, \ 4k + 3, \ 2k + 1, \ n,$$

where the last two letters are appended at the end of the word.

Distances between elements smaller than n are not changed and the distance between occurrences of the largest element $n = 4k+4$ is as required, producing a Langford word of order n.

Impossibility of other cases. Any Langford word w over A_{n-1} can be transformed into a Skolem word over A_n by adding 1 to all elements in w

and by inserting at the beginning the two copies of letter 1. For example, the Langford word 312132 is so transformed into the Skolem word 11423243.

It is known that Skolem words do not exist for n of the forms $4k + 2$ nor $4k + 3$ (see Problem 16). The same observation works for Langford words and proves none exist when n is of the forms $4k + 1$ or $4k + 2$.

To conclude, a Langford word exists only when n is of the form $4k + 4$ or $4k + 3$ ($k \geq 0$).

Notes

There are various notions of Langford words. For example, property (i) can be dropped. In this case Berstel [32] showed that the associated words are square free.

---

18   From Lyndon Words to de Bruijn Words

The combinatorial result of the problem provides the basis for an efficient online construction of de Bruijn words.

A binary word (on the alphabet $\{0, 1\}$) is a de Bruijn word of order (rank or span) k if it contains cyclically each binary word of length k exactly once as a factor. The word is of length 2^k. There is a surprising relation between these words and the lexicographic ordering, which shows once more that ordering words is a powerful tool in text algorithms.

A Lyndon word is a primitive word that is the (lexicographically) smallest word in its conjugacy equivalence class.

Let p be a prime number and $\mathcal{L}_p = (L_0, L_1, \ldots, L_m)$ the sorted sequence of binary Lyndon words of length p or 1. Let also

$$\mathbf{b}_p = L_0 \cdot L_1 \cdots L_m$$

be the concatenation of words in $\mathcal{L}_p$.

For example, the sorted list of Lyndon words of length 5 or 1 is

$$\mathcal{L}_5 = (0, 00001, 00011, 00101, 00111, 01011, 01111, 1)$$

and the concatenation of its words is

$$\mathbf{b}_5 = 0 \ 00001 \ 00011 \ 00101 \ 00111 \ 01011 \ 01111 \ 1.$$

It is the lexicographically smallest de Bruijn word of order 5 and has length $32 = 2^5$.

> **Question.** For a prime number p, show that the word $\mathbf{b}_p$ is a de Bruijn word of order p.

Solution
The number of binary Lyndon words of length p in $\mathcal{L}_p$ is $(2^p - 2)/p$ (see Problem 1). Therefore the length of $\mathbf{b}_p$ is $p(2^p - 2)/p + 2 = 2^p$. Then to show it is a de Bruijn word we just have to prove that each word w of length p appears cyclically in $\mathbf{b}_p$.

Let us start with a preliminary observation. For a word x in $\mathcal{L}_p$, $x \neq 1$, let $next(x)$ denote the word following x in the sequence.

Observation. If $|x| = |next(x)| = p$, $x = uv$ and v contains an occurrence of 0, then u is a prefix of $next(x)$.

Proof   Assume, to the contrary, that $next(x) = u'v'$ with $|u| = |u'| = t$ and $u' \neq u$. Then $u < u'$ due to the order of elements in $\mathcal{L}_p$. However, the word $u \cdot 1^{n-t}$ is a Lyndon word that is lexicographically between uv and $u'v'$, which contradicts $next(x) = u'v'$. Thus u is a prefix of $next(x)$.   ∎

Lyndon words of length p are all factors of $\mathbf{b}_p$ by construction. Words 0^p and 1^p are respectively prefix and suffix of $\mathbf{b}_p$. Words of length p in 1^+0^+ occur cyclically at the last $p - 1$ positions of $\mathbf{b}_p$. Thus it remains to prove that words of length p which are not Lyndon words and do not belong to 1^*0^* appear (non-cyclically) in $\mathbf{b}_p$. Let w be such a word and L_i be its Lyndon conjugate; then

$$w = vu \ \text{and} \ L_i = uv$$

for v and u non-empty words because $w \neq L_i$.

There are two cases to consider whether v contains an occurrence of 0 or not.

Case v contains 0. Then u is a prefix of $L_{i+1} = next(L_i)$ from the observation. Hence $w = vu$ is a factor of $L_i L_{i+1}$.

Case v does not contain 0. Then $v = 1^t$, for some $t > 0$. Let L_j be the first word in $\mathcal{L}_p$ prefixed by u and let $L_{j-1} = u'v'$ with $|v'| = t$. Then v' cannot contain the letter 0, because otherwise $u' = u$ and L_j would not be the first word in $\mathcal{L}_p$ prefixed by u. Consequently $v' = 1' = v$ and the concatenation $L_{j-1}L_j = u' \cdot v \cdot u \cdots$ contains vu as a factor.

In both cases w has an occurrence in $\mathbf{b}_p$. This concludes the proof that $\mathbf{b}_p$ is a de Bruijn word.

Notes

The list $\mathcal{L}_p$ can be generated online using only $O(p)$ memory space. The above construction then leads to an online generation of a de Bruijn word, using only a window of size $O(p)$ for storing the last computed letters of the word.

When the order k of de Bruijn words is not a prime number, a similar construction applies. In that case, the sorted list $\mathcal{L}_k$ is composed of Lyndon words whose length divides k. The concatenation of these sorted words gives in fact the lexicographically smallest de Bruijn word of order k over the given alphabet. The algorithm was initially developed by Fredricksen and Maiorana [120]. See also [192] for a simplified complete proof of the general case.

3 Pattern Matching

19 Border Table

The border table, as well as the prefix table in Problem 22, are basic tools for building efficient algorithms on words. They are used mostly for searching texts online for various types of given patterns.

The **border table** of a non-empty word x is defined on the lengths ℓ, $\ell = 0, \ldots, |x|$, of its prefixes both by $border[0] = -1$ and, for $\ell > 0$, by $border[\ell] = |Border(x[0 \ldots \ell - 1])|$. Here is the border table of the word abaababaaba:

i		0	1	2	3	4	5	6	7	8	9	10
$x[i]$		a	b	a	a	b	a	b	a	a	b	a
ℓ	0	1	2	3	4	5	6	7	8	9	10	11
$border[\ell]$	-1	0	0	1	1	2	3	2	3	4	5	6

> **Question.** Prove that Algorithm BORDERS correctly computes the border table of a non-empty word x and executes a maximum of $2|x| - 3$ letter comparisons when $|x| > 1$.

BORDERS(x non-empty word)

```
1   border[0] ← −1
2   for i ← 0 to |x| − 1 do
3       ℓ ← border[i]
4       while ℓ ≥ 0 and x[ℓ] ≠ x[i] do
5           ℓ ← border[ℓ]
6       border[i + 1] ← ℓ + 1
7   return border
```

Example. Let us consider the prefix $u = $ abaababa of the above word. Its border is $v = $ aba of length $3 = border[8]$. The next letter a extends the border, that is, $Border(u\mathrm{a}) = v\mathrm{a}$.

```
a b a a b a b a
  v           v
```

If the next letter c is not a, the border of uc is the border of vc, which sketches the proof of the recurrence relation, for u a word and c a letter:

$$Border(uc) = \begin{cases} Border(u)c & \text{if } Border(u)c \text{ is a prefix of } u, \\ Border(Border(u)c) & \text{otherwise.} \end{cases}$$

> **Question.** Show how to detect the non-primitive prefixes of a word using its border table.

Solution

The proof of correctness relies on the above recurrence relation. It can be restated by saying that the second longest border of a word u, if it exists, is the border of its border.

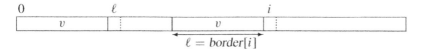

Correctness of Algorithm BORDERS. First note that $border[0]$ is set up correctly.

Instructions in the for loop, lines 3–6, compute $border[i + 1]$ from all the other values $border[i']$, $i' = 0, \ldots, i$. During the execution of the while loop, ℓ runs through lengths of the borders of $x[0 .. i - 1]$ from the longest to the shortest.

If the while stops and $\ell = -1$, no border can be extended by the letter $x[i]$; then the next border is empty, that is, $border[i + 1] = 0$, as done. Otherwise, the loop stops the first time a match is found providing the longest border of $x[0 .. i - 1]$, of length ℓ, extensible by letter $x[i]$. Then $border[i + 1] = \ell + 1$, as done again. This ends the proof.

Running time of Algorithm BORDERS. Note it is sufficient to establish the bound to prove the linear running time. To do it we show that the value of $2i - \ell$ increases by at least 1 after each letter comparison. Indeed, i and ℓ are both incremented after a positive comparison and ℓ is decreased by at least 1 with i unchanged after a negative comparison.

When $|x| > 1$, the value of $2i - \ell$ runs from 2, for the first comparison with $i = 1$ and $\ell = 0$, to at most $2|x| - 2$ during the last comparison with $i = |x| - 1$ and $\ell \geq 0$. The overall number of comparisons is thus bounded by $2|x| - 3$, as stated. The bound of $2|x| - 3$ is reached by any string x of the form $a^{|x|-1}b$, where a and b are different letters.

Non-primitive prefixes. By definition, a non-primitive word u is of the form w^k for some non-empty word w and an integer $k > 1$. It means $|u| = k|w|$; that is, the period $|w|$ of u divides its length $|u|$. Therefore the detection of a non-primitive prefix of length i of x from the border table of x can be done by checking if the exponent $i/(i - border[i])$ of the prefix is an integer greater than 1.

Notes

The use of border tables for matching words is a classical topic in textbooks like [74, 96, 134, 194, 228]. The initial design is by Morris and Pratt (see [162]).

Since $|u| - border[|u|]$ is the smallest period of u, the border table of a word can be transformed into the table of periods of its prefixes. A striking solution for computing this latter table for a Lyndon word is shown in Problem 42.

20   Shortest Covers

The notion of cover tries to capture the regularity of a word. It goes beyond the possible periodicity of the word by considering an a priori shorter factor that covers the whole word. Period words are specific covers that occur consecutively in the word while general covers may have overlapping occurrences. In that sense the notion of cover generalises the notion of period. More accurately, a cover u of a word x is a border of x whose consecutive occurrence positions are at maximum distance $|u|$.

Example. The word $u = $ aba is a cover of the word $x = $ abaababa. Indeed, the sorted list of starting positions of occurrences of u in x is $pos(\text{aba}, \text{abaababa}) = (0, 3, 5)$ and the maximum distance consecutive positions of the list is $MaxGap(\{0, 3, 5\}) = 3 \leq |u|$. The word u is the shortest cover of x.

The shortest cover of abaababaaaba is the whole word, which is always a trivial cover of itself. When this condition holds the word is said to be *super-primitive*. It is also primitive.

The **cover table**, denoted by *cover*, associated with a word x is defined on length ℓ of its prefixes as follows: $cover[\ell]$ is the smallest length of covers of $x[0 .. \ell - 1]$. Here is the cover table of the word ababababaaba.

i		0	1	2	3	4	5	6	7	8	9
$x[i]$		a	b	a	b	a	b	a	a	b	a
ℓ	0	1	2	3	4	5	6	7	8	9	10
$cover[\ell]$	0	1	2	3	2	3	2	3	8	9	3

Question. Design a linear-time algorithm computing the shortest cover of each prefix of a word.

[**Hint:** Use the border table of the word.]

Solution

The present solution, an online algorithm to compute the cover table of a word x, relies on a key observation. (The border table of a word is treated in Problem 19.)

Observation. The only candidate for a non-trivial shortest cover of $x[0 \mathinner{..} j-1]$ is the shortest cover $u = x[0 \mathinner{..} \ell-1]$ of $v = x[0 \mathinner{..} border[j]-1]$, which is the (longest) border of $x[0 \mathinner{..} j-1]$ (see picture). This is because any non-trivial cover of $x[0 \mathinner{..} j-1]$ is a cover, possibly trivial, of its border.

In addition, the algorithm makes a crucial use of a supplementary table *range*: $range[\ell]$ is the length of the longest prefix of $x[0 \mathinner{..} j-1]$ covered by $x[0 \mathinner{..} \ell-1]$ (prefix v is covered by u on the picture). The next observation explains the role of the table *range*.

Observation. If $u = x[0 \mathinner{..} \ell-1]$ is a cover of the border of $x[0 \mathinner{..} j-1]$ and $range[\ell]$ is as large as the period of $x[0 \mathinner{..} j-1]$, u is a cover of $x[0 \mathinner{..} j-1]$.

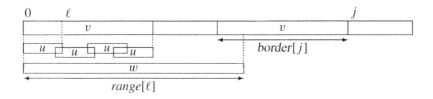

Algorithm SHORTESTCOVERS implements the observations.

SHORTESTCOVERS(x non-empty word)

```
1   border ← BORDERS(x)
2   for j ← 0 to |x| do
3       (cover[j], range[j]) ← (j, j)
4   for j ← 2 to |x| do
5       ℓ ← cover[border[j]]
6       if ℓ > 0 and (range[ℓ] ≥ j − border[j]) then
7           (cover[j], range[ℓ]) ← (ℓ, j)
8   return cover
```

After a run of Algorithm SHORTESTCOVERS on the above example abababaaba, the tables get their final values:

j	0	1	2	3	4	5	6	7	8	9	10
border[j]	-1	0	0	1	2	3	4	5	1	2	3
range[j]	0	1	6	10	4	5	6	7	8	9	10
cover[j]	0	1	2	3	2	3	2	3	8	9	3

Note that super-primitive prefixes are those whose length j satisfies $cover[j] = j$.

Following the computation of the table *border*, the instruction at lines 3 initialises trivially tables *cover* and *range*. Instructions at lines 4–7 compute *cover*[j] and update *range*. The condition ($range[\ell] \geq j - border[j]$) at line 6 checks, according to the second observation, whether ℓ is actually the length of the shortest cover of $x[0 .. j - 1]$. This completes the proof of correctness.

Since Algorithm BORDERS runs in linear time, this is also the case for Algorithm SHORTESTCOVERS.

Notes
The present algorithm was designed by Breslauer in [43] to test the super-primitivity of words.

---

21   Short Borders

The problem deals with a special type of border table of a word. It is adapted to search texts for Zimin patterns containing word variables (see Problem 43). It shows the notion of border table is powerful when tuned for searching online for various types of patterns.

A border of a non-empty word x is any word that is both a proper prefix and a suffix of it. A border is said to be *short* if its length is smaller than $|x|/2$. The notations *Border*(x) and *ShortBorder*(x) stand for the longest border of x and for its longest short border, respectively. Any of these borders can be the empty word.

For example, borders of $x =$ abababab are ε, ab, abab and ababab. Only ε and ab are short, *Border*(x) = ababab and *ShortBorder*(x) = ab.

In some algorithms the notion of a short border is more appropriate when known for all the prefixes of a word. Let *shbord* denote the **short-border table** of prefixes of a non-empty word x. It is defined on prefix lengths ℓ, $0 < \ell \le |x|$, by

$$shbord[\ell] = |ShortBorder(x[0 .. \ell - 1])|$$

(by convention $shbord[0] = -1$). Below are the tables for the word abaababaaba. They differ at positions $\ell = 6, 10, 11$.

i		0	1	2	3	4	5	6	7	8	9	10
$x[i]$		a	b	a	a	b	a	b	a	a	b	a
ℓ	0	1	2	3	4	5	6	7	8	9	10	11
$border[\ell]$	−1	0	0	1	1	2	3	2	3	4	5	6
$shbord[\ell]$	−1	0	0	1	1	2	1	2	3	4	2	3

Question. Design a linear-time algorithm computing the table *shbord* of a non-empty word.

Solution
A straightforward solution would be to compute the table *shbord* from the table *border* of the word without looking at the word itself. But this is likely to yield a quadratic execution time on examples like a^k or $(ab)^k$.

Instead, Algorithm SHORTBORDERS, which still uses the table of borders, is a modification of Algorithm BORDERS that computes this table (see Problem 19). Then it also runs in linear time. It tries to enlarge the previous short border and when the extension is too long uses the table of borders to switch to a shorter border.

SHORTBORDERS(x non-empty word)
```
1  border ← BORDERS(x)
2  shbord[0] ← −1
3  for i ← 0 to |x| − 1 do
4      ℓ ← shbord[i]
5      while (ℓ ≥ 0 and x[ℓ] ≠ x[i]) or (2ℓ + 1 ≥ i) do
6          ℓ ← border[ℓ]
7      shbord[i + 1] ← ℓ + 1
8  return shbord
```

The correctness of Algorithm SHORTBORDERS follows from the fact that the next short border is an extension of the previous short border of $u = x[0 .. i-1]$ by the single symbol $x[i]$, or is an extension of a shorter border of u.

Since the number of executions of the instruction at line 6 is bounded by the number of increments of ℓ, the overall running time is $O(|x|)$, as expected.

Notes

The motivation to introduce and compute the table *shbord* is its essential implication in the computation of Zimin types of words and their crucial use in algorithms fast searching for a given Zimin pattern (containing variables) in words (without variables) (Problem 43).

22 Prefix Table

The prefix table, like the border table of Problem 19, is a basic tool for building efficient algorithms on words. It is used mostly when searching texts for various types of given patterns.

Let x be a non-empty string. The **prefix table** of x is defined on its positions $i, i = 0, \ldots, |x| - 1$, by: $pref[i]$ is the length of the longest prefix of x starting at position i. Obviously $pref[0] = |x|$.

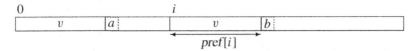

$$pref[i]$$

Here is the prefix table of the word abaababaaba:

i	0	1	2	3	4	5	6	7	8	9	10
$x[i]$	a	b	a	a	b	a	b	a	a	b	a
$pref[i]$	11	0	1	3	0	6	0	1	3	0	1

Question. Show that Algorithm PREFIXES computes in linear time the prefix table of its input word x and executes no more than $2|x| - 2$ letter comparisons.

PREFIXES(x non-empty word)

```
 1   pref[0] ← |x|
 2   g ← 0
 3   for i ← 1 to |x| − 1 do
 4       if i < g and pref[i − f] ≠ g − i then
 5           pref[i] ← min{pref[i − f], g − i}
 6       else (f, g) ← (i, max{g, i})
 7           while g < |x| and x[g] = x[g − f] do
 8               g ← g + 1
 9           pref[f] ← g − f
10   return pref
```

The key idea in Algorithm PREFIXES that computes the table sequentially from left to right is to benefit from what has been computed before the current position.

When $v = x[f \mathinner{.\,.} g − 1]$ is a prefix of x and position i is between f and g (see picture), the first step for computing $pref[i]$ is to check whether or not its value can be deduced from the work done on the prefix occurrence of v, that is, at position $i − f$ on x. This saves enough work to get a linear-time algorithm.

Solution

Correctness of PREFIXES. Let us first clarify the role of variables f and g. At some point during a run of the algorithm, the position g is the farthest position to the right where a (negative) letter comparison happened. More accurately, for a given position i, $g = \max\{j + pref[j] : 0 < j < i\}$. And the associated position f satisfies $f + pref[f] = g$.

During the first pass in the for loop, f and g are set as well as is $pref[i] = pref[f]$ in accordance with their definitions by mere letter comparisons, which gives the invariant of the loop.

To show the invariant is maintained during other passes in the for loop, we examine what instructions at lines 4–9 do.

If $i < g$ and $pref[i − f] < g − i$ it is clear that $pref[i] = pref[i − f]$; see the above picture. If $i < g$ and $pref[i − f] > g − i$ the longest prefix of x starting at position $i − f$ is of the form $v' x[g − f] v''$, where v' is a suffix of

$x[i - f \mathrel{..} g - f - 1] = x[f \mathrel{..} g - 1]$. Then, since $x[g] \neq x[g - f]$, v' is the longest prefix of x starting at i, that is, $pref[i] = g - i$. Therefore, when $i < g$ and $pref[i - f] \neq g - i$, the instruction at line 5 sets correctly the value of $pref[i]$ without changing the invariant.

When the condition at line 4 does not hold, as in the first pass, the value of $pref[i]$ is set correctly by letter comparisons and the invariant is satisfied after that pass. This ends the proof of correctness.

Running time of PREFIXES. The running time depends essentially on the number of letter comparisons at line 7. There is at most one negative comparison for each value of i because this stops the execution of the while loop, that is, at most $|x| - 1$. There is at most one positive comparison for each value of g because it increases the value of g that never decreases, that is, at most $|x| - 1$ again. The total number of letter comparisons is thus no more that $2|x| - 2$, which shows that the overall running time is $O(|x|)$.

Notes
Prefix tables, as well as border tables in Problem 19, are basic notions on words to design algorithms on texts, presented sometimes implicitly in textbooks like [74, 96, 134, 194, 228]. Algorithm PREFIXES is called the Z algorithm in [134, page 9].

23   Border Table to the Maximal Suffix

The maximal suffix of a word, its alphabetically greatest suffix, helps designing optimal text searches and periodicity tests. The problem introduces a computation of it based on the border table algorithm.

Question. Show that the following version of the border table computation correctly returns the starting position on the input word of its maximal suffix and that it runs in linear time.

MAXSUFFIXPOS(x non-empty word)

```
1   ms ← 0
2   border[0] ← −1
3   for i ← 0 to |x| − 1 do
4       ℓ ← border[i − ms]
5       while ℓ ≥ 0 and x[ms + ℓ] ≠ x[i] do
6           if x[ms + ℓ] < x[i] then
7               ms ← i − ℓ
8           ℓ ← border[ℓ]
9       border[i − ms + 1] ← ℓ + 1
10  return ms
```

Example. The word $x = $ abcbcacbc has **maximal suffix** MaxSuffix(x) = cbcacbc whose longest border is $v = $ cbc. A next letter is to be compared with the letter following the prefix cbc of the maximal suffix.

The following pictures show how the maximal suffix evolves according to the appended letter a, b, c or d. Note that if the periodicity of the maximal suffix changes, the maximal suffix is of the form va where v is a border of the initial maximal suffix and a is the new letter.

> **Question.** Show how to find the alphabetically largest conjugate (rotation) of a word.

Solution

The online algorithm is based on the above remark on the border of the previous maximal suffix. The role of instructions inside the for loop is simultaneously to update the starting position of the maximal suffix and to compute the length of its border. Note that without instruction at lines 6–7, the variable ms remains null and the algorithm computes the table *border* of the whole word x.

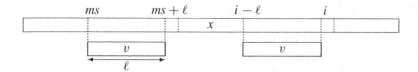

Correctness of MaxSuffixPos. The proof is done by showing the following invariant holds after executing instructions inside the for loop, lines 4–9: ms is the starting position of the maximal suffix of $x[0 .. i - 1]$ and $border[i - ms]$ is the border length of this suffix of length $i - ms$.

After the initial instructions and the first pass in the loop for $i = 0$, we get $ms = 0$ and $border[1] = 0$, the correct result for the word $x[0]$.

By induction, other passes start by setting ℓ to the border length of $x[ms .. i - 1]$. The fact that the border length of $x[ms .. i]$ is correctly computed follows the same argument as in the construction of the border tables in Problem 19 about the iteration of $border$ at line 8. In short, when the while loop stops ms was updated at line 7 each time the border v of the current maximal suffix satisfies $vx[ms + \ell] < ux[i]$, which effectively locates the maximal suffix of $x[ms .. i]$.

Running time of MaxSuffixPos. This is the same running time as for the computation of the border table (see Problem 19), that is, $O(|x|)$, since instruction at lines 6–7 takes constant time.

Largest conjugate. Let $ms = \text{MaxSuffixPos}(y)$, where $y = xx$. Then the largest conjugate of x is $y[ms .. ms + |x| - 1]$. Modular arithmetic on indices can be used to avoid duplicating x.

Notes
The above algorithm is adapted from the computation of the smallest rotation of a circular word by Booth [39].

Two other solutions for the computation of the maximal suffix of a word are shown in Problems 38 and 40. They also run in linear time but with the advantage of requiring only constant extra memory space. The second additionally reports the period of the maximal suffix.

24   Periodicity Test

The detection of periodicities in words is an essential question to cope with when designing text searching or text compression methods. The goal is to test the periodicity of a word in a space-economical way.

A word x is said to be **periodic** if its (smallest) period is no more than half its length, $per(x) \leq |x|/2$. Equivalently, x is periodic if it is of the form $u^k v$ for two words u and v and an integer k, u non-empty, v a proper prefix of u and $k \geq 2$.

Checking the property is straightforward from the border or prefix tables of x. The goal here is to do it still in linear time but with only constant extra space (in addition to input). The idea is to use the function MAXSUFFIXPOS of Problem 40 that gives the position and period of the maximal suffix of x.

The examples below illustrate variations of the period of a word according to its maximal suffix. The maximal suffix starts at position ms and is in the form $u^k v$ (here $k = 1$), where $u = x[ms \mathinner{.\,.} ms + p - 1]$, p is its period and v is a proper prefix of u.

First, $x = $ abababbaababbaab. The prefix aba of x preceding the maximal suffix uv is a suffix of u. Then x is periodic with period 6.

```
    ms
a b a b b a a b a b b a a b
    └──────u──────┘└───v───┘
◄──────────────────►
```

Second, $x = $ ababbaaabbaababbaa. The prefix of x preceding uv is longer than u. The period of x is $11 > |uv|$ and x is not periodic.

```
          ms
a b a b b a a a b b a a b a b b a a
          └──────u──────┘└───v───┘
    ◄──────────────────────►
```

Third, $x = $ baabbaababbaab. The prefix of x preceding uv is shorter than u but not a suffix of it. The period of x is $10 > |x| - |v|$ and x is not periodic.

```
    ms
b a a b b a a b a b b a a b
    └──────u──────┘└───v───┘
◄──────────────────►
```

Question. Show that the periodicity of a word x can be tested with less than $|x|/2$ letter comparisons if the starting position and the period of its maximal suffix are given.

Solution

Let ms be the starting position and p be the period of the maximal suffix of x. The solution consists in checking the condition at line 2 below, which takes less than $|x|/2$ comparisons and answers the question.

PERIODIC(x non empty word)

1   $(ms, p) \leftarrow$ MAXSUFFIXPP(x)

2   **if** $ms < |x|/2$ and $p \leq |x|/2$

        and $x[0 .. ms - 1]$ suffix of $x[ms .. ms + p - 1]$ **then**

3   **return** TRUE

4   **else return** FALSE

It is clear that if the condition holds x is periodic with period p and if $ms \geq |x|/2$ or $p > |x|/2$ the word is not periodic.

Let $x = yz$, where $y = x[0 .. ms - 1]$, $z = x[ms .. |x| - 1] = u^k v$ is the maximal suffix, u the prefix period of z, v a proper prefix of u and $k > 0$. Assume y is not a suffix of u.

We first consider the case where $|y| \geq |u|$ and show that $per(x) > |z|$. If not (above picture), a second occurrence of y in x overlaps some occurrence of u. Let w be their overlap, suffix of y and prefix of u (or v) and then of z. Let $z = wz'$. Both wz and z' are suffixes of x smaller than z. But $wz < z = wz'$ implies $z < z'$, a contradiction. In this situation, we have $per(x) > |z|$ and $per(x) > |y|$ (see Problem 41), which yields $2per(x) > |y| + |z|$ and proves that x is not periodic.

In the second case $|y| < |u|$ and we first show $per(x) > \min\{|z|, |x| - |v|\}$. If not and $per(x) \leq |z|$ we get the same conclusion as above. We then consider by contradiction that $per(x) \leq |x| - |v|$. In fact we have $per(x) < |x| - |v|$ because y is not suffix of u. Thus u (strictly) overlaps itself (picture below). A contradiction because u is border-free (see Problem 40 for example). In this situation, we have $per(x) > |x| - |v|$ and also trivially $per(x) > |v|$ then $2per(x) > |x|$, which shows that x is not periodic. This ends the proof of correctness of PERIODIC.

Notes

Algorithm PERIODIC tests the periodicity of x but does not compute its period. In fact it is possible to compute the period with the same time and space complexities using the time–space optimal string matching in [69]. The time–space optimal algorithm by Galil and Seiferas [124] (see [97]) can certainly be tuned to yield the same result as well.

---

25   Strict Borders

When used for searching texts online, the border table of a pattern is better replaced by the notion introduced in this problem. The effect is to improve the behaviour of searches as shown in Problem 26.

The **strict-border table** of a non-empty word x is defined on the lengths ℓ, $\ell = 0, \ldots, |x|$, of its prefixes by: $stbord[0] = -1$, $stbord[|x|] = border[|x|]$ and, for $0 < \ell < |x|$, $stbord[\ell]$ is the greatest t satisfying

- $-1 \le t < \ell$ and
- $(x[0..t-1]$ is a border of $x[0..\ell-1]$ and $x[t] \ne x[\ell])$ or $t = -1$.

Word $x[0..stbord[\ell] - 1]$ is the strict border of prefix $x[0..\ell - 1]$ of x. It exists only if $stbord[\ell] \ne -1$.

Here are border and strict-border tables of the word abaababaaba:

i		0	1	2	3	4	5	6	7	8	9	10
$x[i]$		a	b	a	a	b	a	b	a	a	b	a
ℓ	0	1	2	3	4	5	6	7	8	9	10	11
$border[\ell]$	-1	0	0	1	1	2	3	2	3	4	5	6
$stbord[\ell]$	-1	0	-1	1	0	-1	3	-1	1	0	-1	6

Question. Design a linear-time algorithm computing the table *stbord* without using the table *border* or any other additional table.

Solution

First notice that the table *stbord* can be used to compute the table *border*. It consists just in substituting *stbord* to *border* in the instruction at line 5 of Algorithm BORDERS (see Problem 19), which gives

BORDERS(x non-empty word)
1   $border[0] \leftarrow -1$
2   **for** $i \leftarrow 0$ **to** $|x| - 1$ **do**
3       $\ell \leftarrow border[i]$
4   **while** $\ell \geq 0$ and $x[i] \neq x[\ell]$ **do**
5           $\ell \leftarrow stbord[\ell]$
6       $border[i + 1] \leftarrow \ell + 1$
7   **return** *border*

This accelerates the computation of the table on examples like $a^n b$.

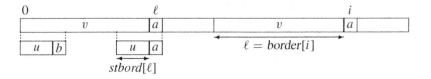

Observation. The computation of the table of strict borders is based on the following property. If $\ell = border[i]$ for some i, $0 \leq i \leq |x|$, then

$$stbord[i] = \begin{cases} \ell & \text{if } i = 0 \text{ or } i = |x| \text{ or } x[i] \neq x[\ell], \\ stbord[\ell] & \text{else } (0 < i < |x| \text{ and } x[i] = x[\ell]). \end{cases}$$

Indeed, if the first condition is met the border of $x[0 \mathinner{..} i - 1]$ complies with the definition of a strict border; then $stbord[i] = border[i]$. If not (see picture), the situation is the same as when computing the strict border of $x[0 \mathinner{..} \ell]$, then $stbord[i] = stbord[\ell]$.

STRICTBORDERS(x non-empty word)

```
1   stbord[0] ← −1
2   ℓ ← 0
3   for i ← 1 to |x| − 1 do
4        ▷ here ℓ = border[i]
5        if x[i] = x[ℓ] then
6             stbord[i] ← stbord[ℓ]
7        else stbord[i] ← ℓ
8             do   ℓ ← stbord[ℓ]
9             while ℓ ≥ 0 and x[i] ≠ x[ℓ]
10       ℓ ← ℓ + 1
11  stbord[|x|] ← ℓ
12  return stbord
```

Algorithm STRICTBORDERS solves the problem. The instructions at lines 5–7 implement the observation. Instructions at lines 8–9 correspond to those at lines 4–5 in Algorithm BORDERS and serve to compute the length ℓ of the border of $x[0 .. i + 1]$. The correctness follows from these remarks and the linear running time follows from that of Algorithm BORDERS.

Notes

The table *stbord* is part of the design of the string-matching algorithm by Knuth, Morris and Pratt [162], which improves on the initial algorithm by Morris and Pratt (see [74, chapter 2]). For this online algorithm the improvement is on the delay between processing two consecutive symbols of the searched text (see Problem 26). A further improvement on the delay is provided by String matching automata (see Problem 27).

---

26   Delay of Sequential String Matching

Algorithm KMP encapsulates a key feature (the use of a border table or the like) for the design of string-matching algorithms processing the text sequentially. Its concept is used for various types of patterns after appropriate preprocessing.

Algorithm KMP searches a text for occurrences of a pattern x. After preprocessing x it treats the text in an online manner and outputs found occurrences. It runs in linear time executing no more letter comparisons than twice the text length. In the version below, it just outputs '1' each time an occurrence of x is found in the text and outputs '0' otherwise.

The algorithm runs in linear time but not in real time due to the internal while loop of the algorithm dealing with a symbol of the text and that can take some time. This is called the *delay* of the algorithm. The goal of the problem is to bound the delay, precisely defined as the maximum number of comparisons executed at line 4 on the letter a of the input *text*.

KMP(x, *text* non-empty words)

```
1   stbord ← STRICTBORDERS(x)
2   i ← 0
3   for each letter a of text, sequentially do
4       while (i = |x|) or (i ≥ 0 and a ≠ x[i]) do
5           i ← stbord[i]
6       i ← i + 1
7       if i = |x| then output 1 else output 0
```

If the table *border* (see Problem 19) of x is used in the algorithm instead of its table *stbord* (see Problem 25), the delay is $|x|$ in the worst-case. For example, if $x = a^m$ is aligned with a factor $a^{m-1}b$ of the text, the letter b is compared to all the letters of x. But with the table *stbord* the delay becomes logarithmic.

Question. Show the delay of Algorithm KMP is $\Theta(\log |x|)$ when searching for a word x.

[**Hint:** Consider interlocked periods and apply the Periodicity Lemma.]

Solution

Delay lower bound. The worst-case delay $\Omega(\log|x|)$ is reached, for example, when x is a prefix of a Fibonacci word.

Let x ($|x| > 2$) be such a word and let k be the integer for which $F_{k+2} \le |x| + 1 < F_{k+3}$. The pattern x is a prefix of f_{k+1} (of length F_{k+3}) of the form $uabv$, where $uab = f_k$ for some letters $a, b \in \{a, b\}$. When ua is aligned with a factor uc of *text* and $c \notin \{a, b\}$, letter c is compared k times unsuccessfully alternatively to a and to b. Since k is of the order of $\log F_{k+2}$, then of the order of $\log|x|$, this gives the lower bound.

Example. Let $x = $ abaababaabaababa, prefix of f_6 ($|f_6| = F_8$). We have $F_7 = 13$, $|x| + 1 = 17$, $F_8 = 21$. When the prefix abaababaabaa is aligned with the factor abaababaabac of the searched text, exactly $k = 5$ comparisons are done by Algorithm KMP before dealing with the letter following c (see picture).

Delay upper bound. For a position i on x let k be the largest integer for which both $stbord^{k-1}[i]$ is defined and $stbord^k[i]$ is not. We show that the integer k is an upper bound on the number of comparisons between $x[i]$ and a letter of the text.

Let us first show that if $stbord^2[i]$ is defined the prefix $u = x[0..i-1]$ satisfies $|u| \ge stbord[i] + stbord^2[i] + 2$. Since $stbord[i]$ and $stbord^2[i]$ are borders of $x[0..i-1]$, $p = |u| - stbord[i]$ and $q = |u| - stbord^2[i]$ are periods of u. By contradiction, if $|u| < stbord[i] + stbord^2[i] + 2$ then $p + q - 1 \le |u|$. Thus, by the Periodicity Lemma, $q - p$ is also a period of u. This implies that $x[stbord^2[i]] = x[stbord[i]]$, letters at distance $q - p$ in u, which is a contradiction with the definition of *stbord*.

The inequality enables to show, by recurrence, that $|u| \ge F_{k+2} - 2$. Thus $|x| + 1 \ge |u| + 2 \ge F_{k+2}$. From the classical inequality $F_{n+2} \ge \Phi^n$ we get the delay upper bound of $O(\log_\Phi |x|)$.

Lower and upper bounds answer the question.

Notes

The proof of the problem can be found in [162] (see also [74]). The algorithm by Simon [225] and by Hancart [136] reduces even more the upper bound on the delay to $\min\{\log_2 |x|, |alph(x)|\}$ using sparse matching automata (see Problem 27).

---

27 Sparse Matching Automaton

The most standard method to locate given patterns in a text processed sequentially is to use a pattern-matching automaton. Border tables used in Algorithm KMP may be viewed as implementations of such an automaton. The aim of the problem is to show another implementation technique that eventually improves searches. Searches using this implementation run at least as fast as Algorithm KMP, then run in linear time executing no more letter comparisons than twice the text length.

The pattern-matching or **string-matching automaton** $\mathcal{M}(x)$ of a word x drawn from the alphabet A is the minimal deterministic automaton accepting words ending with x. It accepts the language A^*x and has $|x| + 1$ states, $0, 1, \ldots, |x|$, the initial state 0 and its only accepting state $|x|$. Its transition table δ is defined, for a state i and a letter a, by

$$\delta(i,a) = \max\{s + 1 : -1 \leq s \leq i \text{ and } x[0..s] \text{ suffix of } x[0..i-1] \cdot a\}.$$

Observe that the size of the table is $\Omega(|x|^2)$ when the alphabet of x is as large as its length. But the table is very sparse, since most of its values are null.

Below is the string-matching automaton of abaab of length 5 on the alphabet $\{a, b\}$. Labelled arcs represent non-null values in the transition table. There are five forward arcs (on the main line) and four backward arcs. All other undrawn arcs have 0 as the target state. Were the alphabet to contain a third letter, all arcs labelled with it would also have 0 as the target state.

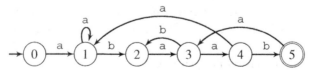

Question. Show that the table δ associated with the string-matching automaton of a word of length n has at most $2n$ non-zero entries and that the bound is tight.

Solution

In the automaton $\mathcal{M}(x)$, there are n forward arcs corresponding to $\delta(i,a) = i + 1$. The other arcs are backward arcs when $0 < \delta(i,a) \le i$. Showing that there are at most n backward arcs answers the question.

Observation. An entry $\delta(i,a) = t$ associated with a backward arc satisfies $x[t] = a$, $x[i] \ne a$ and $x[0\mathinner{\ldotp\ldotp}t-1] = x[i-t\mathinner{\ldotp\ldotp}i-1]$. Then since the latter word is a border of length t of $x[0\mathinner{\ldotp\ldotp}i-1]$, $i-t$ is a period (not necessarily the smallest) of $x[0\mathinner{\ldotp\ldotp}i-1]$ denoted by $p(i,a)$.

For the above example, associated with the backward arcs we have $p(1,\mathsf{a}) = 1$, $p(3,\mathsf{b}) = 2$, $p(4,\mathsf{a}) = 4$ and $p(5,\mathsf{a}) = 3$. Note that $p(4,\mathsf{a}) = 4$ is not the smallest period of $x[0\mathinner{\ldotp\ldotp}3] = \mathsf{abaa}$.

To prove the bound on the number of backward arcs we first show that p is a one-to-one function between backward arcs and periods of prefixes of x.

Let $\delta(i,a) = t+1$ with $0 \le t < i$, $\delta(j,b) = t'$ with $0 \le t' < j$. We assume $p(i,a) = p(j,b)$; that is, $i - t = j - t'$, and prove that $(i,a) = (j,b)$.

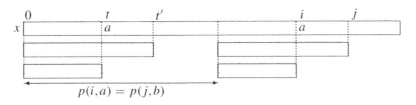

Indeed, if $i = j$ we get $t = t'$ and then $a = x[t] = x[t'] = b$; thus $(i,a) = (j,b)$. And otherwise, if for example $i < j$ like in the picture, since $i - t = p(i,a) = p(j,b)$ is a period of $x[0\mathinner{\ldotp\ldotp}j-1]$, we immediately get $x[t] = x[t + (i - t)] = x[i]$, which contradicts the definition of t.

Consequently p is a one-to-one function and since its values range from 1 to n, the number of backward arcs is no more than n, which achieves the first part of the proof.

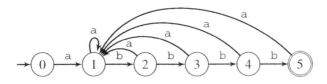

The bound in the statement is tight because the string-matching automaton of the word ab^{n-1} has exactly n backward arcs in addition to its n forward arcs.

Notes

The sparsity of the transition table of string-matching automata was observed by Simon [225]. The complete analysis is by Hancart [136] (see [74, chapter 2]), who showed how to use it for improving the string-matching algorithm by Knuth, Morris and Pratt [162]. The sparsity of the automaton does not extend to the similar automaton for a finite set of words.

The above result also applies to an analogue table used in the string-matching algorithm by Boyer and Moore (see [74, 98, 134]).

---

28   Comparison-Effective String Matching

When the access to textual data is through equality comparisons between symbols only, it is appropriate to reduce their number during searches for patterns. For example, Algorithm KMP (in Problem 26) executes in the worst case $2|y| - 1$ letter comparisons to find occurrences of a preprocessed pattern x in a text y. The same result holds when the search uses a string-matching automaton with an appropriate implementation.

The problem shows that the number of letter comparisons can easily be reduced to only $|y|$ comparisons for simple patterns. A similar approach, sketched at the end of the solution, leads to a maximum of $\frac{3}{2}|y|$ letter comparisons for general patterns.

> **Question.** Design an algorithm searching a text y for all occurrences of a two-letter pattern x and using at most $|y|$ comparisons in the equality model.

[**Hint:** Distinguish whether the two letters are identical or not.]

Solution

We consider two cases, whether the pattern x is of the form aa or ab for two letters a and b with $a \neq b$.

In the first case, Algorithm KMP executes exactly $|y|$ comparisons whichever border table is used. Note that a straightforward naive approach is likely to execute close to $2|y|$ comparisons.

In the second case, when $x = ab$ with $a \neq b$, the search is done with the following algorithm.

SEARCH-FOR-AB-IN(y word, a and b different letters)

```
1   j ← 1
2   while j < |y| do
3       if y[j] = b then
4           if y[j − 1] = a then
5               ab occurs at position j − 1 on y
6           j ← j + 2
7       else j ← j + 1
```

The algorithm can be viewed as a recursive algorithm:

find the smallest position $j > 0$ for which $y[j] = b$,
check if $y[j − 1] = a$,
then recursively search for ab in $y[j + 1 .. |y| − 1]$.

Note that computing j during the first step of the recursive version takes exactly j comparisons since there is no comparison on $y[0]$.

We prove that Algorithm SEARCH-FOR-AB-IN makes at most $|y|$ symbol comparisons by induction on the length of y. Assume we found the first occurrence of b at position ℓ on y. This is done with ℓ comparisons. Then accounting for the comparison $y[\ell − 1] = a$ gives a total of $\ell + 1$ comparisons to deal with $y[0 .. \ell]$ of length $\ell + 1$.

Since the same steps are applied to $y[\ell + 1 .. |y| − 1]$, by the inductive assumption the algorithm executes at most $|y| − \ell − 1 = |y[\ell + 1 .. |y| − 1]|$ more comparisons. Together we get at most $|y|$ comparisons as expected. This proves the inductive claim and completes the proof.

General patterns. To apply a similar technique for a general non-empty pattern x, this one is split as $x = a^k bu$, where u is a word, a and b are different letters and $k > 0$. The algorithm consists in searching for bu in the text (scanning it from left to right) and, whenever it makes sense, in checking if a^k occurs immediately before occurrences of bu. The search for bu can use, for example, the Morris-Pratt algorithm (Algorithm KMP with the table *border* instead of *stbord* in Problem 26). There are several versions implementing this method. However, it is quite technical and details are not included here.

Notes

The first string-matching algorithm achieving a $\frac{3}{2}n$ ($n = |y|$) upper bound on letter comparisons is by Apostolico and Crochemore [14]. It has been improved to a $\frac{4}{3}n - \frac{1}{3}m$ comparisons bound by Galil and Giancarlo [123]. A tight upper bound of $n + \frac{8}{3(m+1)}(n - m)$ comparisons, where $m = |x|$, is proved by Cole and Hariharan in [60].

Under the additional constraint that searches operate strictly online on the text, the exact upper bound (obviously larger than above best bounds) on letter comparisons is $(2 - \frac{1}{m})n$ by Hancart [136] and by Breslauer et al. [44].

29   Strict Border Table of the Fibonacci Word

The border table *border* (see Problem 19) of the infinite Fibonacci word **f** has a simple structure but values in its strict border table *stbord* (see Problem 25) look chaotic at first glance. The problem examines a simple relation between the two tables, which helps to quickly compute any individual value of the table *stbord*.

Below are tables of periods, borders and strict borders related to a prefix of Fibonacci word. Values at index ℓ correspond to the prefix $\mathbf{f}[0\,.\,.\,\ell - 1]$ of length ℓ.

i		0	1	2	3	4	5	6	7	8	9	10
$x[i]$		a	b	a	a	b	a	b	a	a	b	a
ℓ	0	1	2	3	4	5	6	7	8	9	10	11
$period[\ell]$		1	2	2	3	3	3	5	5	5	5	5
$border[\ell]$	−1	0	0	1	1	2	3	2	3	4	5	6
$stbord[\ell]$	−1	0	−1	1	0	−1	3	−1	1	0	−1	6

Question. Show how to compute in logarithmic time the nth element of the strict border table of the infinite Fibonacci word **f**.

[**Hint:** Examine positions where tables *border* and *stbord* match.]

Solution

Positions ℓ on tables *border* and *stbord* pointing to the same entry are essential for the computation of *stbord*[ℓ]. Other values in *stbord* can be computed from them.

The table *period* of periods of prefixes of $\mathbf{f}$ (defined for $\ell > 0$ by *period*[ℓ] = $per(\mathbf{f}[0 .. \ell-1]) = \ell-border[\ell]$) has an extremely simple structure, encapsuled in the following observation.

Observation. Values in the table *period* of Fibonacci word can be seen as the word

$$1\,2\,2\,3\,3\,3\,5\,5\,5\,5\,5\,8\cdots = 1^1\,2^2\,3^3\,5^5\,8^8\,13^{13}\,21^{21}\cdots$$

composed of a concatenation of runs. Runs are all unary runs of a Fibonacci number with exponent equal to the same number and starting with $F_2 = 1$.

Notice that, for $\ell > 0$, the equality *stbord*[ℓ] = *border*[ℓ] holds exactly at positions where the periodicity breaks, that is, at the end of a unary run. Let H be the increasing sequence of these (positive) positions. Hence, due to the observation on the structure of periods, the positions in H are

$$1,\ 1+2,\ 1+2+3,\ 1+2+3+5,\ 1+2+3+5+8,\ldots$$

and it is rather straightforward to see that

$$H = (1,3,6,11,19,32,\ldots) = (n > 0 : n + 2 \text{ is a Fibonacci number}).$$

The relation between tables *border* and *stbord* (shown in Problem 25) can then be reformulated as

$$stbord[\ell] = \begin{cases} border[\ell] & \text{if } \ell \in H, \\ stbord[border[\ell]] & \text{otherwise.} \end{cases}$$

The formula translates immediately into Algorithm FIBSTRICTBORDERS that computes *stbord*[n] corresponding to the prefix of length n of the Fibonacci word. In the algorithm, the computation of *border*[n] = $n - period[n]$ is fast due to the structure of the sequence of periods. Testing if $n + 2$ is a Fibonacci number can be done by keeping the greatest two Fibonacci numbers not larger than $n + 2$. When going to smaller values in the recursion, the two Fibonacci numbers follow naturally.

FIBSTRICTBORDERS(n natural number)

1   **if** $n = 0$ **then**
2   **return** -1
3   **elseif** $n + 2$ is a Fibonacci number **then**
4   **return** $n - period[n]$
5   **else return** FIBSTRICTBORDERS($n - period[n]$)

The following observation is the argument used to prove the running time of the algorithm.

Observation. $period[n]/n \geq \lim_{n \to \infty} \frac{F_{n-2}}{F_n} \geq \frac{1}{3}$.

As a consequence $n - period[n] \leq \frac{2}{3}n$, which implies that the depth of the recursion is logarithmic. Consequently the total running time of the algorithm is also logarithmic with respect to n.

---

30   Words with Singleton Variables

The problem shows the flexibility of the border table notion and of the fast algorithm computing this table. Having such a table is a valuable element to design efficient pattern matching, searching here for patterns with a variable.

We consider words over the alphabet $A = \{a, b, \ldots\}$ in which letters are considered as singleton variables, that is, each letter represents a distinct unknown letter of the alphabet.

Two words u and v are said to be equivalent, denoted as $u \equiv v$, if there is a bijective letter-to-letter morphism $h : alph(u)^* \to alph(v)^*$ for which $h(u) = v$. For example aacbaba $\equiv$ bbdabab through the morphism h on A^* to itself defined by $h(a) = b$, $h(b) = a$, $h(c) = d$ and $h(d) = c$. When $alph(u) = alph(v)$ and $u \equiv v$ the words become equal after permuting their letters.

The pattern-matching problem is naturally redefined as follows: given a pattern word x and a text y, check if a factor z of y is equivalent to x: $z \equiv x$. For example, the pattern $x =$ aacbaba occurs in $y =$ babbdababbacb because its factor $z =$ bbdabab is equivalent to x.

> **Question.** Assume the alphabet is sortable in linear time. Design a linear-time algorithm that searches a text for a pattern with singleton variables.

[**Hint:** Design a notion of border table adequate to the problem.]

Solution

The solution is based on the notion of a **varying border table**. It is denoted by *vbord* and defined, for a parameter m and a non-empty word $w = w[0 .. n-1]$, on the lengths $\ell = 0, \ldots, n$ of its prefixes as follows: $vbord[0] = -1$ and, for $0 < j \leq n$, $vbord[j]$ is

$$\max\{t : 0 \leq t < \min\{j, m+1\} \text{ and } w[0 .. t-1] \equiv w[j-t+1 .. j]\}.$$

In other words, $vbord[j]$ is the length ℓ of a longest proper suffix of length at most m of $w[1 .. j]$ that is equivalent to its prefix of length ℓ. The reason for the restriction to length m appears when matching a pattern of length m.

Here is the table *vbord* for $w = $ abaababbabba and $m = 4$:

i		0	1	2	3	4	5	6	7	8	9	10	11
$w[i]$		a	b	a	a	b	a	b	b	a	b	b	a
ℓ	0	1	2	3	4	5	6	7	8	9	10	11	12
$vbord[\ell]$	-1	0	1	2	1	2	3	3	4	2	3	4	2

In the algorithm that builds *vbord* another table named *pred* is used and defined, for $0 \leq i < n$, by

$$pred[i] = \max\{t : t < i \text{ and } w[i] = w[t]\} \cup \{-1\}.$$

For example, if $w = $ abcaabac we get $pred = [-1, -1, -1, 0, 3, 1, 4, 2]$.

Observation 1. Table *pred* can be computed in linear time.

Let ∇_m denote the following predicate: $\nabla_m(i, \ell) = \text{TRUE}$ if and only if

$$(pred[\ell] \geq 0 \ \& \ i = pred[i] + k) \text{ or } (pred[\ell] = -1 \ \& \ pred[i] < i - \ell),$$

where $k = \ell - pred[\ell]$.

The proof of the next technical simple fact is left to the reader.

Observation 2. Assume $w[0 .. \ell - 1] \equiv w[i - \ell .. i - 1]$ and $\ell < m$. Then $w[0 .. \ell] \equiv w[i - \ell .. i] \iff \nabla_m(i, \ell)$.

In the classical algorithm computing border tables (see Problem 19) we can replace the test for symbols inequality by ∇_m. In this way we get the following linear-time algorithm computing the varying border table. Its correctness follows from Observation 2.

VARBORDERS(x non-empty word)

1 $vbord[0] \leftarrow -1$
2 **for** $i \leftarrow 0$ **to** $|x| - 1$ **do**
3       $\ell \leftarrow vbord[i]$
4   **while** $\ell \geq 0$ and **not** $\nabla_m(i, \ell)$ **do**
5            $\ell \leftarrow vbord[\ell]$
6   **if** $\ell < m$ **then**
7            $vbord[i + 1] \leftarrow \ell + 1$
8   **else** $vbord[i + 1] \leftarrow vbord[\ell + 1]$
9 **return** $vbord$

How it is related to pattern matching. The pattern-matching question, searching a text y for occurrences of the pattern x of length m, is solved with table $vbord$. This varying border table is built for the word $w = xy$ and parameter m. Then

$$x \equiv y[i - m + 1 .. i] \Longleftrightarrow vbord[m + i - 1] = m.$$

Hence searching y for pattern x with singleton variables reduces to the computation of the table $vbord$.

Notes
The problem here is a simplified version of the so-called parameterised pattern matching; see [24]. In this more general problem some symbols stands for singleton variables and some symbols are just constant letters. This is the subject of Problem 32.

31   Order-Preserving Patterns

Searching time series or list of values for patterns representing specific fluctuations of the values requires a redefinition of the notion of pattern. The question is to deal with the recognition of peaks, breakdowns, double-dip recessions or more features on expenses, rates or the like.

In the problem we consider words drawn from a linear-sortable alphabet Σ of integers. Two words u and v of the same length over Σ are said to be *order-equivalent*, written $u \approx v$, if

$$u[i] < u[j] \Longleftrightarrow v[i] < v[j]$$

for all pairs of positions i, j on the words. For example,

$$5\ 2\ 9\ 4\ 3 \approx 6\ 1\ 7\ 5\ 2,$$

which shows in particular their central value is the largest in both words.

The order-preserving pattern-matching problem is naturally defined as follows: given a pattern $x \in \Sigma^*$ and a text $y \in \Sigma^*$, check if x is order-equivalent to some factor of y. For example, word $5\ 2\ 9\ 4\ 3$ appears equivalently at position 1 on

$$4\ \underline{6\ 1\ 7\ 5\ 2}\ 9\ 8\ 3$$

but nowhere else. For instance, it does not appear at position 4 because $5 < 8$, while in the pattern the corresponding values satisfy $5 > 4$.

For simplicity we assume that letters in each considered word are pairwise distinct (words are permutations of their set of letters).

Question. Design a linear-time algorithm for the order-preserving pattern-matching.

[**Hint:** Design a notion of border table adequate to the problem.]

Solution

The present solution is based on the notion of an ***OP-border table***. For the non-empty word $w = w[0 \mathinner{.\,.} n - 1] \in \Sigma^*$, the table *opbord* is defined by $opbord[0] = -1$ and, for $0 < \ell \le n$, by $opbord[\ell] = t$, where $t < \ell$ is the largest integer for which $w[0 \mathinner{.\,.} t - 1] \approx w[\ell - t + 1 \mathinner{.\,.} \ell]$.

Below is table *opbord* associated with $w = 1\ 3\ 2\ 7\ 11\ 8\ 12\ 9$.

i	0	1	2	3	4	5	6	7
$w[i]$		1	3	2	7	11	8	12	9
ℓ	0	1	2	3	4	5	6	7	8
$opbord[\ell]$	-1	0	1	1	2	2	3	4	3

Two additional tables associated with w are defined to deal with the problem:

$$LMax[i] = j, \text{ where } w[j] = \max\{w[k] : k < i \text{ and } w[k] \leq w[i]\}$$

and $LMax[i] = -1$ if there no such $w[j]$,

$$LMin[i] = j, \text{ where } w[j] = \min\{w[k] : k < i \text{ and } w[k] \geq w[i]\}$$

and $LMin[i] = -1$ if there no such $w[j]$.

Observation 1. Both tables $LMax$ and $LMin$ can be computed in linear time.

Let us redefine the predicate ∇ (introduced in Problem 30) as follows:

$$\nabla_n(i, \ell) = 1 \Longleftrightarrow w[p] \leq w[i] \leq w[q],$$

where $p = LMax[\ell]$ and $q = LMin[\ell]$ (if p or q equals -1 then the respective inequality is satisfied in the vacuum).

We leave to the reader the simple but technical proof of the following fact (see Notes).

Observation 2. Assume $w[0 .. \ell - 1] \approx w[i - \ell .. i - 1]$ and $\ell < n$. Then

$$w[0 .. \ell] \approx w[i - \ell .. i] \Longleftrightarrow \nabla_n(i, \ell).$$

Pattern matching. To conclude, the algorithm to check if w is order-equivalent to some factor of a text is the same as for matching a pattern with singleton variables in Problem 30 except that the predicate ∇ is the predicate defined above.

Notes

The present algorithm is a version of the order-preserving pattern matching by Kubica et al. in [170], where Observation 2 is proved (see also [54, 139, 160]). The problem together with the possibility of mismatches is treated by Gawrychowski and Uznanski in [129]. Suffix trees for order-preserving indexing are introduced in [81].

32   Parameterised Matching

The problem considers a more general and more complex version of Problem 30 where some symbols are unknown and some others are fixed constant symbols. Searching texts for a fixed pattern is rather restrictive in some contexts, and parameterised string matching provides an efficient solution in several applications by introducing variables in patterns. The problem was initially stated to detect code duplicates in which, for example, identifiers are substituted for the original names.

Let A and V be two disjoint alphabets: A is the alphabet of constant letters and V is the alphabet of variable letters. We assume that no alphabet contains integers. A word over $A \cup V$ is called a **parameterised word** or a p-word. Two p-words x and y are said to match or p-match if x can be transformed into y by applying a one-to-one mapping on symbols of V occurring in x.

For example, with $A = \{a,b,c\}$ and $V = \{t,u,v,w\}$, $aubvaub$ and $awbuawb$ p-match by mapping u to w and v to u. But $aubvaub$ and $avbwazb$ do not p-match, since u should be mapped to both v and z.

The parameterised pattern matching problem can be stated as follows: given a pattern $x \in (A \cup V)^*$ and a text $y \in (A \cup V)^*$ find all the p-occurrences of x in y, that is, find all the positions j on y, $0 \le j \le |y| - |x|$, for which x and $y[j \mathinner{.\,.} j + |x| - 1]$ p-match.

For instance, with $y = azbuazbzavbwavb$ the pattern $x = aubvaub$ occurs at position 0 by mapping u to z and v to u and at position 8 by mapping u to v and v to w.

> **Question.** Design an algorithm that solves the parameterised pattern matching problem and runs in linear time for a fixed alphabet.

Solution
The problem can be solved by adapting Algorithm KMP (see Problem 26) after a careful encoding of variables.

For a word $x \in (A \cup V)^*$ let $prev(x)$ be the word $z \in (A \cup \mathbf{N})^*$ defined, for a position i on x, by

$$
z[i] = \begin{cases} x[i] & \text{if } x[i] \in A \\ 0 & \text{if } x[i] \in V \text{ not in } x[0 \mathinner{.\,.} i - 1]. \\ i - \max\{j < i : x[j] = x[i]\} & \text{if } x[i] \in V \end{cases}
$$

For instance, $prev(aubvaub) = a0b0a4b$. The word $prev(x)$ can be computed in time $O(|x| \times \min\{\log |x|, \log |V|\})$ and $O(|x|)$ space, which reduces to $O(|x|)$ time and $O(|V|)$ space if V is a fixed alphabet.

Let $z_i = z[i .. |z| - 1]$ be a suffix of $z \in (A \cup \mathbf{N})^*$. Then, *shorten*$(z_i)$ is the word s defined, for $0 \le j \le |z_i| - 1$, by $s[j] = z_i[j]$ if $z_i[j] \le j$, and by $s[j] = 0$ otherwise. For instance, with $z = $ a0b0a4b, $z_3 = $ 0a4b and *shorten*$(z_3) = $ 0a0b.

Observation. Let $z = prev(x)$. Letter $x[i] \in V$ p-matches the letter $y[j] \in V$ in y if one of the two conditions holds:

* $z[i] = 0$.
* $z[i] \ne 0$ and $y[j - z[i]] = y[j]$.

Due to the observation, p-matching x at a position j on y takes no long than $O(|x|)$ time. Mimicking Algorithm KMP with a ***parameterised-border table*** *pbord* gives a linear-time solution. For $x \in (A \cup V)^*$, it is defined by *pbord*$[0] = -1$ and, for $1 \le i \le |x|$, *pbord*$[i] = j$, where $j < i$ is the largest integer for which $prev(x[0 .. j - 1])$ is a suffix of *shorten*$(prev(x[i - j .. i - 1]))$. Tables *prev* and *pbord* for $x = $ aubvaub:

i	0	1	2	3	4	5	6	7
$x[i]$	a	u	b	v	a	u	b	
$prev(x)[i]$	a	0	b	0	a	4	b	
$pbord[i]$	-1	0	0	0	0	1	2	3

Given *pbord* for the p-word x, the next algorithm reports all positions of an occurrence of x in the word y.

PARAMETERISEDMATCHING$(x, y \in (A \cup V)^*)$

```
1   z ← prev(x)
2   i ← 0
3   for j ← 0 to |y| − 1 do
4       while i ≥ 0 and not ((x[i], y[j] ∈ A and x[i] = y[j])
                or (x[i], y[j] ∈ V and
                (z[i] = 0 or y[j − z[i]] = y[j]))) do
5           i ← pbord[i]
6       i ← i + 1
7       if i = |x| then
8           report an occurrence of x at position j − |x| + 1
9           i ← pbord[i]
```

The proofs of correctness and of the complexity analysis of PARAMETERI-SEDMATCHING are similar to the ones of Algorithm KMP. And the parameterised border table *pbord* can be computed by adapting Algorithm BORDERS that computes the usual border table (see Problem 19).

Notes
Parameterised pattern matching was first formalised by B. Baker [23, 24]. She introduced a solution based on Suffix trees for the offline version of the problem. A first solution for the online version was given in [11]. The present solution was first published in [145] together with a solution for online multiple parameterised pattern matching. The reader can refer to the survey that appeared in [188].

33   Good-Suffix Table

The Boyer–Moore algorithm (BM in Problem 34) applies the sliding window strategy on the text to locate occurrences of a pattern. It requires a pattern preprocessing to accelerate the search.

At a given step, the algorithm compares the pattern and a window on the text by computing their longest common suffix u. If $u = x$ a match occurs. Otherwise, in the generic situation, pattern $x[0..m-1]$ is aligned with the window, factor $y[j-m+1..j]$ of the text, au is a suffix of x and bu a suffix of the window, for different letters a and b.

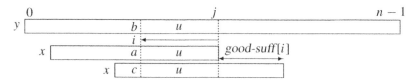

To continue the search, Algorithm BM slides the window according to the period of x in case of a match or otherwise to the factor bu of the text to

avoid positions of the window where no occurrence of x is possible. To do
so it uses the **good-suffix table** *good-suff* defined for a position i on x and
$u = x[i + 1 .. m - 1]$ by

$$good\text{-}suff[i] = \min\{|v| : x \text{ suffix of } uv \text{ or } cuv \text{ suffix of } x, c \neq x[i]\}.$$

The condition 'cuv suffix of x' with $c \neq a = x[i]$ ensures that when letter
c is aligned with letter $b = y[j - m + 1 + i]$ after sliding the window, the same
mismatch does not re-occur immediately (see picture). From the definition note
that $good\text{-}suff[0] = per(x)$.

> **Question.** Design a linear-time algorithm for computing the good suffix
> table of a word.

[**Hint:** Use the reverse table of prefixes of x^R.]

Solution
The solution uses the table of suffixes of x, *suff*, symmetric of the table of pre-
fixes (see Problem 22), defined for a position i by $suff[i] = |lcs(x[0 .. i], x)|$,
where *lcs* denotes the **longest common suffix** between x and $x[0 .. i]$.

Example. Tables *suff* and *good-suff* of baacababa are

i	0	1	2	3	4	5	6	7	8
$x[i]$	b	a	a	c	a	b	a	b	a
$suff[i]$	0	2	1	0	1	0	3	0	9
$good\text{-}suff[i]$	7	7	7	7	7	2	7	4	1

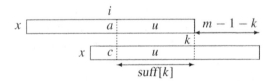

Observation. Tables *good-suff* and *suff* are closely related (see picture, in
which $i = m - 1 - suff[k]$): $good\text{-}suff[m - 1 - suff[k]] \leq m - 1 - k$.

Then the computation of table *good-suff* is a mere application of the
inequality and done by Algorithm GoodSuffixes. The get the smallest value
of $m - 1 - k$, *suff* is scanned in increasing order of positions k (lines 8–9) after
the table is filled in by periods of x (lines 3–7).

GOODSUFFIXES(x non-empty word, *suff* its table of suffixes)

```
 1   m ← |x|
 2   p ← 0
 3   for k ← m − 2 to −1 do
 4       if k = −1 or suff[k] = k + 1 then
 5           while p < m − 1 − k do
 6               good-suff[p] ← m − 1 − k
 7               p ← p + 1
 8   for k ← 0 to m − 2 do
 9       good-suff[m − 1 − suff[k]] ← m − 1 − k
10   return good-suff
```

The overall computation takes $O(|x|)$ time, since the table *suff* can be computed in linear time (like table *pref* in Problem 22) and the above algorithm also runs in linear time when *suff* is given.

Notes

Table *good-suff* is often associated with a heuristics to account for the mismatch letter b as proposed by Boyer and Moore [41] (see also [162]). In fact this can be done for most string-matching methods.

The first exact algorithm for computing the good suffix table was designed by Rytter [212].

Table *good-suff* is the essential element of Algorithm BM. However, its above definition does not accurately use the mismatch letter b. This can be done using techniques related to sparse matching automata (see Problem 27) within space $O(|x|)$ independently of the alphabet size.

Table *suff* is used in a more efficient variant of Algorithm BM by Apostolico and Giancarlo [16] for which the maximal number of letter comparisons is $1.5|y|$ (see [89]).

34   Worst Case of the Boyer–Moore Algorithm

Boyer–Moore string matching is based on a technique that leads to the fastest searching algorithms for fixed patterns. Its main feature is to scan the pattern backward when aligned with a factor of the searched text. A typical pattern preprocessing is shown in Problem 33.

When locating a fixed pattern x of length m in a text y of length n, in the generic situation x is aligned with a factor (the window) of y ending at position j (see picture). The algorithm computes the longest common suffix (*lcs*) between x and the factor of y, and, after possibly reporting an occurrence, slides the window towards the end of y based on the preprocessing and on information collected during the scan, without missing an occurrence of x. Algorithm BM implements the method with table *good-suff* of Problem 33:

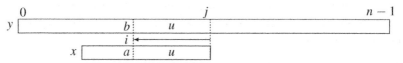

BM(x, y non-empty words, m, n their lengths)

```
1   j ← m − 1
2   while j < n do
3       i ← m − 1 − |lcs(x, y[j − m + 1 .. j])|
4       if i < 0 then
5           report an occurrence of x at position j − m + 1 on y
6           j ← j + per(x)   ▷ per(x) = good-suff[0]
7       else j ← j + good-suff[i]
```

After position j on y is treated, if an occurrence of x is found the algorithm slides naturally the window at distance $per(x)$. If no occurrence is found, the distance $good\text{-}suff[i]$ depends on the factor bu of y (it depends on au of x in Problem 33). Value $per(x)$ and array $good\text{-}suff$ are preprocessed before the search.

> **Question.** Give examples of a non-periodic pattern and of a text y for which Algorithm BM performs close to $3|y|$ letter comparisons at line 3 for computing the longest common suffix.

Solution

Let $x = \mathrm{a}^{k-1}\mathrm{ba}^{k-1}$ and $y = \mathrm{a}^{k-1}(\mathrm{aba}^{k-1})^{\ell}$ with $k \geq 2$. Then $m = 2k - 1$ and $n = \ell(k + 1) + (k - 1)$.

Example. Let $k = 5$ and $\ell = 4$ when considering the pattern a^4ba^4 of length 9 and the text $a^4(aba^4)^4$ of length 28. The picture illustrates the beginning of the search, which overall executes $4 \times 13 = 52$ letter comparisons.

Consider the position $j = (k - 3) + p(k + 1)$ on y with $p \geq 1$. We have $y[j - m + 1 .. j] = a^kba^{k-2}$ and $|lcs(x, y[j - m + 1 .. j])| = k - 2$ computed with $k - 1$ letter comparisons. The window slide length is $good\text{-}suff[m - k - 1] = 1$, updating j to $(k - 2) + p(k + 1)$, and $y[j - m + 1 .. j]$ becomes $a^{k-1}ba^{k-1}$. This time $|lcs(x, y[j - m + 1 .. j])| = m$ computed with m letter comparisons and the next slide length is $per(x) = k$, producing $j = (k - 3) + (p + 1)(k + 1)$.

The two steps require $k - 1 + m = 3k - 2$ comparisons and lead to a similar situation from which the same process repeats on each of the $\ell - 1$ first occurrences of the factor aba^{k-1} (of length $k + 1$) of y. On the last occurrence $(k - 1) + (k + 1) = 2k$ comparisons are performed and on the prefix of length $k - 1$ of y, $k - 2$ comparisons are performed. Overall, Algorithm BM with these inputs x and y executes $\frac{3k-2}{k+1}(n - k + 1) = \left(n - \frac{m-1}{2}\right)\left(3 - \frac{10}{m+3}\right)$ comparisons, as expected.

Notes

Boyer–Moore string matching is from [41] (see also [162]). The proof of the $3n$ comparison bound for searching for an aperiodic pattern in a text of length n is by Cole [59]. Detailed descriptions and variants of the Boyer–Moore algorithm can be found in classical textbooks on string algorithms [74, 96, 98, 134, 228].

35   Turbo-BM Algorithm

The problem shows how a very light modification of Boyer–Moore string matching produces a much faster algorithm when the method is used to locate all the pattern occurrences in a text, like Algorithm BM in Problem 34 does. The initial design of the Boyer–Moore algorithm was to find the first pattern occurrence. It is known that for that goal it runs in linear time according to the searched text length. But it has a quadratic worst-case running time to report all pattern occurrences, especially for periodic patterns. This is due to its amnesic aspect when it slides the window to the next position.

The goal of Algorithm TURBO-BM is to get a linear-time search by adapting the Boyer–Moore search algorithm, Algorithm BM, without changing its pattern preprocessing, table *good-suff*. Only constant extra space is added and used during the search.

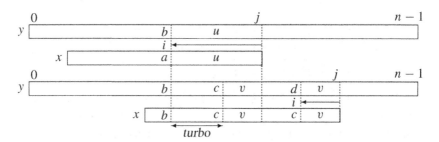

Algorithm TURBO-BM uses the lengths $mem = |u|$ of the previous suffix match u and $\ell = |v|$ of the current suffix match v to compute $\max\{good\text{-}suff[i], |u| - |v|\}$.

In the example below, the first match $u = $ bababa of length 6 leads to a slide of length $4 = good\text{-}suff[4]$. After sliding the window, the new match $v = $ a alone would give a slide of length $1 = good\text{-}suff[9]$. But the **turbo-shift** applies and produces a slide of length $turbo = 6 - 1 = 5$.

```
y    b a b a b b b a b a b a a b a a . . . . .
x    b b a b a b a b a b a
                 |_____|
                      u

y    b a b a b b b a b a b a a b a a . . . . .
x          b b a b a b a b a b a
             |_____| |___|
                      u          v
```

Question. Show that Algorithm TURBO-BM correctly reports all occurrences of the pattern x in y.

TURBO-BM(x, y non-empty words, m, n their lengths)

1   $(j, mem) \leftarrow (m - 1, 0)$

2   **while** $j < n$ **do**

3   ▷ jumping over memory if $mem > 0$

4        $i \leftarrow m - 1 - |lcs(x, y[j - m + 1 .. j])|$

5   **if** $i < 0$ **then**

6   report an occurrence of x at position $j - m + 1$ on y

7             $(shift, \ell) \leftarrow (per(x), m - per(x))$

8   **else** $(shift, \ell) \leftarrow (good\text{-}suff[i], m - i - 1)$

9        $turbo \leftarrow mem - (m - i - 1)$

10   **if** $turbo > shift$ **then**

11            $(j, mem) \leftarrow (j + turbo, 0)$

12   **else** $(j, mem) \leftarrow (j + shift, \ell)$

Solution

Based on the proof of correctness of the original algorithm, that of Algorithm TURBO-BM depends on the fact that no occurrence of the pattern x in y is missed when the window is slid by $turbo$ positions (line 11).

Indeed, when line 11 executes, $turbo > 1$ because $turbo > shift \geq 1$. Then cv is a (proper) suffix of u in x and in y, since the occurrences of u are aligned (see picture). The suffix $uzcv$ of x, z a word and c a letter, has period $|zcv|$ because u is a suffix of x. It is aligned with the factor $uz'dv$ of y, where z' is a word and d a letter. But since $c \neq d$, $|zcv|$ is not a period of the latter factor.

Therefore, the suffix $uzcv$ of x cannot cover both letters c and d occurring in y, which shows the ending position of the next possible occurrence of x in y is at least at position $j + turbo$ as required.

Notes

Several solutions have been proposed to cope with the quadratic-time behaviour of the Boyer–Moore algorithm. The first solution is by Galil [122] who showed a linear-time variant. Another solution by Apostolico and Giancarlo [16] requires extra memory space, linear in the pattern length, during both the preprocessing and the search steps and executes no more than $1.5n$ letter comparisons [89].

Algorithm TURBO-BM [70] is certainly the lightest improvement of the original algorithm. Not only does it provide a linear-time solution but also executes no more than $2n$ letter comparisons during the search step (see [74, 96]) at the cost of a constant extra memory space.

36   String Matching with Don't Cares

Words in the problem are drawn from the alphabet of positive integers with an extra letter ∗. Letter ∗, called a don't care (or joker), stands for any other letter of the alphabet and matches any letter including itself.

Matching strings with don't cares consists in searching a text y for all occurrences of a pattern x, assuming the two words contain don't care symbols. Let $m = |x|$ and $n = |y|$.

Example. ab∗b occurs in abaaba∗cbcb at positions 3 and 5 only.

Contrary to several other string-matching algorithms, solutions to the present problem often use arithmetic operations for convolution: given sequences B and C of length at most n compute the sequence A of length $2n$ defined, for $0 \le i \le 2n - 1$, by

$$A[i] = \sum_{j=0}^{n-1} B[j] \cdot C[i + j].$$

It is assumed that each elementary arithmetic operation executes in constant time and that convolution of sequences of length n can be done in $O(n \log n)$ time.

Question. Show how string matching with don't cares can be reduced in linear time to the convolution problem.

Solution
After changing the don't care symbol to zero, we define the sequence $A[0 .. n - m]$ by: $A[i] = \sum_{j=0}^{m-1} x[j] \cdot y[i + j] \cdot (x[j] - y[i + j])^2$, which is

$$\sum_{j=0}^{m-1} x[j]^3 y[i + j] - 2 \sum_{j=0}^{m-1} x[j]^2 y[i + j]^2 + \sum_{j=0}^{m-1} x[j] \cdot y[i + j]^3.$$

The computation can then be done with three instances of convolution, running overall in $O(n \log n)$ time. The relation between A and the question stands in the next observation.

Observation. $A[i] = 0$ if and only if pattern x occurs at position i on y.

Indeed $A[i]$ is null if and only if each term $x[j] \cdot y[i + j] \cdot (x[j] - y[i + j])^2$ is null, which means that either $x[j]$ or $y[i + 1]$ (originally equal to the don't care symbol) are null or both are equal. This corresponds to a match of letters and proves the correctness of the reduction algorithm.

Notes

Convolution adapted to string matching has been introduced by Masek and Paterson in [186]. The present simplification is from [58].

---

37   Cyclic Equivalence

Two words are cyclically equivalent if one is a conjugate (rotation) of the other. Testing their equivalence appears in some string matching questions but also in graph algorithms, for example, for checking the isomorphism of directed labelled graphs, in which the test applies to graph cycles.

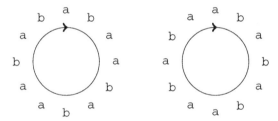

The picture shows equivalent words drawn cyclically. The following algorithm tests cyclic equivalence using the alphabet ordering.

CYCLICEQUIVALENCE(u, v non-empty words of length n)

```
 1   (x, i, y, j) ← (uu, 0, vv, 0)
 2   while i < n and j < n do
 3       k ← 0
 4       while k < n and x[i + k] = y[j + k] do
 5           k ← k + 1
 6       if k = n then
 7           return TRUE
 8       if x[i + k] > y[j + k] then
 9           i ← i + k + 1
10       else j ← j + k + 1
11   return FALSE
```

Question. Show that Algorithm CYCLICEQUIVALENCE checks if two words are cyclically equivalent and runs in linear time with constant extra space.

[**Hint:** Consider Lyndon conjugates.]

When the alphabet has no clear ordering, it is useful to have a solution based on simpler types of symbol comparisons.

Question. How would you test the cyclic equivalence of two strings with no ordering, that is, using only $=/\neq$ letter comparisons?

Solution

Let us run Algorithm CYCLICEQUIVALENCE on words $u =$ abbab and $v =$ babab and look how pairs of indices (i, j) on $x = uu$ and $y = vv$ respectively evolve.

$$
\begin{array}{ccccccccccc}
 & 0 & 1 & 2 & 3 & 4 & 5 & 6 & 7 & 8 & 9 \\
x = uu & a & b & b & a & b & a & b & b & a & b \\
y = vv & b & a & b & a & b & b & a & b & a & b
\end{array}
$$

Starting from the pair of indices $(i, j) = (0,0)$, after the first execution of instructions in the main while loop the pair becomes $(0,1)$ because $x[0] < y[0]$. The algorithm then compares factor $x[0..2] =$ abb of x with factor $y[1..3] =$ aba of y, producing the next pair $(3,1)$ because $x[2] > y[3]$. Eventually, in the next pass of the loop it detects that u and v are conjugate.

Commenting on the algorithm's run, note that indices i and j bump on the starting positions on x and y of the Lyndon conjugate ababb of the cyclically equivalent words u and v. (If u or v are not primitive, the argument applies to their roots.) The dramatic increase of i at line 9 or of j at line 10 intuitively comes from that property of Lyndon words: if wa is a prefix of a Lyndon word and letter a is smaller than letter b then wb is a Lyndon word. A consequence is that wb is border free. Therefore matching wa can resume right after an occurrence of wb. This is illustrated in particular when comparing aba and abb in the example.

Analysis of CYCLICEQUIVALENCE. Let $u^{(k)}$ be the kth conjugate (kth rotation or kth-shift) of u, $k = 0, 1, \ldots, n - 1$. For $x = uu$, $u^{(k)} = x[k..k+n-1]$. Similarly for $y = vv$, $v^{(k)} = y[k..k+n-1]$.

Let $D(u)$ and $D(v)$ be the set of positions on x and on y respectively:

$$D(u) = \{k : 0 \le k < n \text{ and } u^{(k)} > v^{(j)} \text{ for some } j\},$$

$$D(v) = \{k : 0 \le k < n \text{ and } v^{(k)} > u^{(i)} \text{ for some } i\}.$$

The algorithm's correctness relies on the invariant of the main while loop: $[0 . . i - 1] \subseteq D(u)$ and $[0 . . j - 1] \subseteq D(v)$, which is easy to check because, for example, if we have $x[i + k] > y[j + k]$ at line 8, we have $x[i . . i + k] > y[j . . j + k]$, $x[i + 1 . . i + k] > y[j + 1 . . j + k]$, etc.

If the algorithm returns TRUE then $u^{(i)} = v^{(j)}$ and the two words are conjugate. If it returns FALSE, we have either $i = n$ or $j = n$. W.l.o.g., assuming $i = n$ we get $D(u) = [1 . . n]$. This means that every cyclic conjugate of u has a smaller conjugate of v. So the words cannot have the same smallest conjugate, which implies they are not conjugate.

The number of symbol comparisons is clearly linear. The largest number of comparisons is for conjugate words of the form $u = \mathrm{b}^k \mathrm{ab}^\ell$ and $v = \mathrm{b}^\ell \mathrm{ab}^k$. This implies linear running time. Modular arithmetic on indices can be used to avoid duplicating u and v, then reducing the extra space to a constant amount.

No ordering. A solution to solve the question without considering any ordering on the alphabet is to use a string-matching technique with this feature or the border table. For example, the border table of $u \# vv$, where $\#$ is a letter that does not occur in uv, allows locating u in vv. An occurrence exists if and only if u and v of the same length are conjugate.

Using a time–space optimal string-matching algorithms gives an overall algorithm sharing the features of CYCLICEQUIVALENCE but that is far less simple and elegant than it.

Notes

The design of Algorithm CYCLICEQUIVALENCE borrows ideas from the circular lists equivalence algorithm by Shiloach [223].

A less direct approach to solve cyclic equivalence is to use the function MAXSUFFIXPOS (see Problems 38 and 40). After computing indices $i = $ MAXSUFFIXPOS(uu) and $j = $ MAXSUFFIXPOS(vv) that identify the maximal suffixes MaxSuffix(uu) and MaxSuffix(vv), the solution consists in testing the equality of their prefixes of length $|u| = |v|$.

The table *Lyn* (see Problem 87) can also be used but yields a less efficient technique.

Time–space optimal string-matching algorithms may be found in [94, 97, 124].

38   Simple Maximal Suffix Computation

The maximal suffix of a word is its alphabetically greatest suffix. The notion is a key element in some combinatorial aspects of words (e.g. related to runs or critical positions) but also in the development of string-matching algorithms (e.g. the two-way algorithm used in some C libraries such as glibc and FreeBSD's lib). The algorithm presented in this problem is tricky but simpler than the one in Problem 40. Both work in place, that is, need only constant space to work in addition to their input (contrary to the solution in Problem 23), which makes their implementation straightforward.

For a non-empty word x, Algorithm MAXSUFFIXPOS computes the starting position of MaxSuffix(x), **maximal suffix** of x. For example, MAXSUFFIXPOS(bbabbbba) = 3 position of suffix bbbba of the input.

Note the similarity between MAXSUFFIXPOS and Algorithm CYCLIC-EQUIVALENCE in Problem 37 and the similarity of its pseudo-code with that of the other version in Problem 40.

MAXSUFFIXPOS(x non-empty word)

```
 1   (i, j) ← (0, 1)
 2   while j < |x| do
 3        ▷ note the invariant i < j
 4        k ← 0
 5        while j + k < |x| and x[i + k] = x[j + k] do
 6             k ← k + 1
 7        if j + k = |x| or x[i + k] > x[j + k] then
 8             j ← j + k + 1
 9        else i ← i + k + 1
10        if i ≥ j then
11             j ← i + 1
12   return i
```

Question. Show that Algorithm MAXSUFFIXPOS computes the position on a word of its maximal suffix and that it runs in linear time with constant extra space.

Solution

Let us run Algorithm MAXSUFFIXPOS on word x = bbabbbba, which is duplicated on the picture below to better show values of indices, i on the top row and j on the bottom row.

```
      0   1   2   3   4   5   6   7   8
x     b   b   a   b   b   b   b   b   a

x     b   b   a   b   b   b   b   b   a
```

The first pair (i, j) of indices on x is $(0, 1)$, leading $x[0 .. 1]$ = bb to be compared to $x[1 .. 2]$ = ba. This produces the next pair $(0, 3)$. Then the comparison between $x[0 .. 2]$ = bba and $x[3 .. 5]$ = bbb leads to increase i to 3 and additionally j to 4 to avoid equality. Eventually, j moves to 9, which causes the main loop and the procedure to stop. The algorithm returns position 3 of the maximal suffix bbbbba of bbabbbba.

Correctness of MAXSUFFIXPOS. The proof is just sketched, since its elements may be found in Problem 40. The proof relies on the following invariant of the main iteration (while loop):

in the interval $[0 .. j - 1]$ the position i is the only candidate as starting position of the maximal suffix of $x[0 .. j - 1]$. In other words if $t \neq i$ and $t < j$ then t is not a starting position of the maximal suffix.

Hence, at the end j is not less than $|x|$ and i is the only possible position in the interval $[0 .. |x| - 1]$ (all positions of x) starting the maximal suffix. Consequently i is the required output.

Notes

The present Algorithm MAXSUFFIXPOS is a version of the algorithm by Adamczyk and Rytter [1].

The algorithm, after a simple cosmetic modification, also computes the shortest period of the maximal suffix as its other pseudo-code in Problem 40 does. Indeed, it is $i - j'$, where j' is the penultimate value of j (the last value of j is $|x|$, out of the range).

39   Self-Maximal Words

The notion of a *self-maximal word*, word that is the alphabetically greatest among its suffixes, is somehow dual to the notion of Lyndon word, word that is smaller than all its proper non-empty suffixes. The former words appear naturally when locating critical positions on a word (see Problem 41) and in string-matching algorithms based on them.

Algorithm SELFMAXIMAL checks if its input word x is self-maximal, that is, if $x = \text{MaxSuffix}(x)$. It processes the word in real time since the instruction in the for loop executes in constant time.

SELFMAXIMAL(x non-empty word)

1   $p \leftarrow 1$
2   **for** $i \leftarrow 1$ **to** $|x| - 1$ **do**
3   **if** $x[i] > x[i - p]$ **then**
4   **return** FALSE
5   **elseif** $x[i] < x[i - p]$ **then**
6             $p \leftarrow i + 1$
7   **return** TRUE

Example. The word $\text{cbcbacbcbacbc} = (\text{cbcba})^2\text{cbc}$ is self-maximal as well as its prefix period cbcba that is additionally border free. Its suffix cbcbacbc is essentially the only suffix competing with it as the greatest suffix. A letter a appended to it is then to be compared to the letter following the prefix occurrence of cbcbacbc.

```
        ┌────────────────┐
c b c b a c b c b a c b c a
└───u────┘└───u────┘└─v─┘
```

> **Question.** Prove that the above really simple algorithm correctly tests if its input word is greater than all its proper suffixes.

The next picture illustrates the role of variables in SELFMAXIMAL.

0		p		$i - p$		i	
u		u		u		v	a
v	b	v	b	v	b	v	a

> **Question.** Upgrade the above algorithm to SMPREFIX that computes the longest self-maximal prefix of a word.

Solution

A note before starting the proofs. Let y be a non-empty self-maximal word that is also border free, that is, $per(y) = |y|$. Then any proper non-empty suffix z of y satisfies $z \ll y$ (i.e., $z = ras$ and $y = rbt$ with letter a smaller than letter b). Therefore $zs' \ll yt'$ for any words s' and t'.

Correctness of SELFMAXIMAL. Consider the invariant of the for loop: $u = x[0..p-1]$ is a non-empty self-maximal and border-free word, $x[0..i-1] = u^e v$, where $e > 0$ and v a proper prefix of u.

The invariant holds at the start of the loop because $u = x[0]$, $e = 1$ and v is the empty word. If the invariant holds at line 7, $x = u^e v$ and then x is self-maximal, as expected, with period $p = |u|$.

It remains to show that instructions within the loop do not change the invariant validity. We have three cases to consider according to the result of the letter comparison.

If $x[i] > x[i-p]$, x is not self-maximal, since its factor $x[p..i-1]x[i] = x[0..i-p-1]x[i]$ is greater than its prefix $x[0..i-p-1]x[i-p]$. If $x[i] = x[i-p]$, the invariant still holds, possibly with $e+1$ and $v = \varepsilon$.

The case in which $x[i] < x[i-p]$ provides the key feature of the algorithm: $x[0..i]$ becomes border free in addition to being self-maximal. To show it, let $a = x[i]$ and $b = x[i-p]$ with $a < b$. First consider suffixes of the form $v'a$ of va. Since vb is a prefix of the self-maximal u, $v'b \leq u < x[p..i]$, and since $v'a < v'b$ we get $v'a < x[p..i]$. Second, suffixes $x'a$ starting at positions $j < e|u|$ that are not multiple of p are prefixed by a proper suffix u' of u. Referring to the above note, we have $u' \ll u$, which implies $x'a \ll u^e va = x[p..i]$. Third, the remaining suffixes $x'a$ to consider start at positions of the form $p, 2p, \ldots, ep$. All x' are also prefixes of u^e and followed by the letter b. Therefore $x'a < x'b < x[p..i]$. This completes the proof.

Algorithm SMPREFIX. Its design follows closely that of SELFMAXIMAL and its correctness readily comes from the above proof.

SMPREFIX(x non-empty word)

```
1   p ← 1
2   for i ← 1 to |x| − 1 do
3       if x[i] > x[i − p] then
4           return x[0 .. p − 1]
5       elseif x[i] < x[i − p] then
6           p ← i + 1
7   return x[0 .. |x| − 1]
```

Notes

Algorithm SELFMAXIMAL is adapted from the Lyndon factorisation algorithm by Duval [105] and reduced to exhibit its key feature.

---

40   Maximal Suffix and Its Period

The maximal suffix of a word is its alphabetically greatest suffix. The problem follows Problem 38 and presents another pseudo-code for computing a maximal suffix. As the other it processes its input in linear time using only constant extra space.

MAXSUFFIXPP(x non-empty word)

```
1   (ms, j, p, k) ← (0, 1, 1, 0)
2   while j + k < |x| do
3       if x[j + k] > x[ms + k] then
4           (ms, j, p, k) ← (j, j + 1, 1, 0)
5       elseif x[j + k] < x[ms + k] then
6           (j, p, k) ← (j + k + 1, j − ms, 0)
7       elseif k = p − 1 then
8           (j, k) ← (j + k + 1, 0)
9       else k ← k + 1
10  return (ms, p)
```

> **Question.** Show that Algorithm MAXSUFFIXPP computes the starting position and the period of the maximal suffix of its input word.

Example. $(\texttt{cbcba})^3\texttt{cbc} = \text{MaxSuffix}(\texttt{aba}(\texttt{cbcba})^3\texttt{cbc})$. A next letter is to be compared to the letter following prefix $\texttt{cbc}$ of the maximal suffix.

```
ms                              j
a b a c b c b a c b c b a c b c b a c b c
    └─── u ───┘└─── u ───┘└─── u ───┘└─ v ─┘
```

The pictures display the three possibilities corresponding to the execution of instructions at lines 4, 6 and 8 respectively.

```
                              ms j
a b a c b c b a c b c b a c b c b a c b c c
                                        └u┘
```
```
ms                                          j
a b a c b c b a c b c b a c b c b a c b c a
└──────────────── u ────────────────┘
```
```
ms                              j
a b a c b c b a c b c b a c b c b a c b c b
    └─── u ───┘└─── u ───┘└─── u ───┘└─ v ─┘
```

> **Question.** Show how to test the primitivity of a word in linear time and constant extra space.

Solution

Correctness of Algorithm MAXSUFFIXPP. Up to a change of variables the structure of MAXSUFFIXPP and its proof follow that of the algorithms in Problem 39. Here, ms stands for the starting position of $\text{MaxSuffix}(x[0 .. j + k - 1]) = u^e v$ with u self-maximal and border free, $e > 0$ and v a proper prefix of u. The picture illustrates the role of variables i, j and k. The letter $x[j + k]$ is compared to $x[ms + k] = x[j + k - p]$.

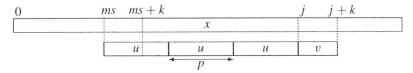

Lines 3–4 correspond to the case when the candidate starting position ms of the maximal suffix has to be updated. Position j becomes the next candidate because suffix $x[j .. j + k]$ is larger than suffixes of $x[ms .. j + k]$ starting before j. And the process restarts from that position forgetting what has been done beyond j.

Lines 5–6 deal with the key feature. The word $x[ms \mathbin{..} j+k]$ is self-maximal and border free of period $j + k - ms + 1$, its length.

Eventually, lines 7–9 manage the incrementation of k, possibly updating j to keep k smaller than p.

Complexity of Algorithm MAXSUFFIXPP. Its memory space requirement is clear. Its running time is less obvious to evaluate due to its oblivious element at line 4. But it suffices to consider the value of the expression $ms + j + k$.

At line 4, ms is incremented by at least p, j by 1 and k decremented by at most $p - 1$, while p is unchanged; thus the value is strictly incremented. At line 6, j is incremented by $k + 1$ before k becomes null, leading again to a strict incrementation of the value. At lines 8–9, $j + k$ is incremented by 1 and ms unchanged, yielding the same conclusion.

Since $ms + j + k$ runs from 1 to at most $2|x| + 1$, this shows that the algorithm stops and performs no more than $2|x|$ letter comparisons.

Primitivity test. Let $ms = \text{MAXSUFFIXPP}(x)$ and p be the period of MaxSuffix(x). It is known that $ms < p$ (see Problem 41). Let k be the largest integer for which $j = ms + kp \le |x|$. Then testing primitivity amounts to check if $x[j \mathbin{..} n - 1]x[0 \mathbin{..} ms - 1] = x[ms \mathbin{..} ms + p - 1]$.

Notes

Algorithm MAXSUFFIXPP is by Crochemore and Perrin in [94], where it is used for the preprocessing of a time–space optimal string matching, known as the two-way algorithm.

Relaxing the constant extra space aspect of the algorithm with a border table improves the running time of the technique but keeps the asymptotic behaviour unchanged in the worst case.

41   Critical Position of a Word

The existence of critical positions on a word is a wonderful tool for combinatorial analyses and also for the design of text algorithms. One of its striking application is the two-way string matching implemented in some C libraries.

Let x be a non-empty word and $\ell per(i)$ denote the **local period** at i on x, $i = 0, \ldots, |x|$, length of the shortest non-empty word w that is

$$\text{suffix of } A^*x[0 \mathinner{.\,.} i-1] \text{ and prefix of } x[i \mathinner{.\,.} |x|-1]A^*.$$

In lay terms this roughly means the shortest non-empty square ww centred at position i has period $\ell per(i)$. For the word baababababba of period 8 we have $\ell per(1) = |\text{aab}| = 3$, $\ell per(6) = |\text{ab}| = 2$, $\ell per(10) = |\text{a}| = 1$ and $\ell per(7) = |\text{bbaababa}| = 8$. Some squares overflow the word to the right, to the left or to both.

Note that $\ell per(i) \leq per(x)$ for any i. If $\ell per(i) = per(x)$, i is called a **critical position**. When $x = u \cdot v$ its factorisation is said to be critical if $\ell per(|u|) = per(x)$.

Let $\mathrm{MaxSuffix}(\leq, x)$ and $ms = \mathrm{MaxSuffixPos}(\leq, x)$ be the respective greatest suffix of x and its position according to the alphabet ordering $\leq$.

Question. Let $x = yz$ where $z = \mathrm{MaxSuffix}(\leq, x)$. Show that $|y| < per(x)$, that is $\mathrm{MaxSuffixPos}(\leq, x) < per(x)$.

Algorithm CRITICALPOS computes a critical position in linear time and constant extra space following Problems 38 and 40.

CRITICALPOS(x non-empty word)

1   $i \leftarrow \mathrm{MaxSuffixPos}(\leq, x)$
2   $j \leftarrow \mathrm{MaxSuffixPos}(\leq^{-1}, x)$
3   **return** $\max\{i, j\}$

Applied to $x = $ baababababba, $\mathrm{MaxSuffixPos}(\leq, x) = 7$ is a critical position and, for this example, $\mathrm{MaxSuffixPos}(\leq^{-1}, x) = 1$ is not.

Question. Show that Algorithm CRITICALPOS computes a critical position on its non-empty input word.

[**Hint:** Note the intersection of the two word orderings is the prefix ordering and use the duality between borders and periods.]

Solution

Answer to the first question. By contradiction assume $y \geq per(x)$ and let w be the suffix of y of length $per(x)$. Due to the periodicity, either w is a prefix of z or z is a suffix of w.

Case 1: If $z = ww'$, by its definition $www' < ww'$, then $ww' < w'$, a contradiction with the same definition.

Case 2: If $w = zz'$, $zz'z$ is a suffix of x, then $z < zz'z$, a contradiction with the definition of z.

Answer to the second question. The case of the alphabet of x reduced to one letter is easily solved because any position is critical. Then we consider both that x contains at least two different letters and w.l.o.g. that $i > j$ and show that i is a critical position.

Let w be the shortest non-empty square centred at i, that is, $|w| = \ell per(i)$. From the first question we know that y is a proper suffix of w.

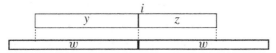

Case 1: Assume z is a prefix of w. Then $|w| = per(x)$ because x being factor of ww has period $|w| = \ell per(i)$ that cannot be larger than $per(x)$. Thus i is a critical position.

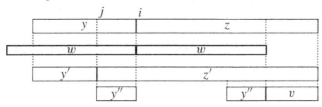

Case 2: Assume $z = wv$ for a non-empty word v. Then $v < z$ by definition of z. Let $x = y'z'$, where $z' = \text{MaxSuffix}(\leq^{-1}, x)$ and y'' the non-empty word for which $y = y'y''$ and $z' = y''z$. Since $y''v$ is a suffix of x, it is smaller than $z' = y''z$ according to the ordering induced by $\leq^{-1}$, and thus v is smaller than z according to the same ordering. Referring to the hint, v being smaller than z according to both orderings is a prefix of z, then a border of it. Therefore $|w|$ is a period of z and consequently also of $x = yz$. Then as in the previous case i is a critical position.

This concludes the proof.

Notes

The Critical Factorisation Theorem, the existence of a critical position on any non-empty word, is due to Cesari, Duval and Vincent [49, 105] (see Lothaire [175, chapter 8]).

The present proof appears in [96, 98] and is by Crochemore and Perrin [94], where it is part of the design of the two-way string-matching algorithm, which is time–space optimal. It is extended to a real-time algorithm by Breslauer et al. in [45].

---

42   Periods of Lyndon Word Prefixes

A Lyndon word is a non-empty self-minimal word, that is, it is alphabetically smaller than all its non-empty proper suffixes. The dual self-maximal words share some of their features. Lyndon words have useful properties for the design of matching algorithms and for the analysis of methods such as testing the cyclic equivalence of two words (Problem 37). The present problem deals with a remarkable simple solution to compute their prefix periods.

Let *period* denote the table of periods of prefixes of the word x. It is defined on non-empty prefix lengths ℓ, $\ell = 1, \ldots, |x|$ by

$$period[\ell] = \text{smallest period of } x[0 \mathinner{..} \ell - 1].$$

For the word $x = \text{aabababba}$ we get

i	0	1	2	3	4	5	6	7	8
$x[i]$	a	a	b	a	b	a	b	b	a
ℓ	1	2	3	4	5	6	7	8	9
$period[\ell]$	1	1	3	3	5	5	7	8	8

Question. Show that Algorithm PREFIXPERIODS correctly computes the table of periods of prefixes of a Lyndon word.

PREFIXPERIODS(*x* Lyndon word)

```
1   period[1] ← 1
2   p ← 1
3   for ℓ ← 2 to |x| do
4       if x[ℓ − 1] ≠ x[ℓ − 1 − p] then
5           p ← ℓ
6       period[ℓ] ← p
7   return period
```

Question. What changes are to be made to PREFIXPERIODS to compute the prefix periods of a self-maximal word?

Question. Show that testing if a word is a Lyndon word can be done in linear time with only constant extra space.

[**Hint:** Tune Algorithm PREFIXPERIODS.]

Solution

The solutions are very similar to those of Problem 39 although the notions of self-maximality and self-minimality are not strictly symmetric.

Adapting proofs in Problem 39, it is rather straightforward to prove that non-empty prefixes of a Lyndon word are of the form $u^e v$, where u is a Lyndon word and v is a proper prefix of u.

Correctness of PREFIXPERIODS. In Algorithm PREFIXPERIODS the variable p stores the period of the prefix $x[0 \mathinner{.\,.} \ell - 2]$. As recalled, the prefix is of the form $u^e v$ with $p = |u|$. The variable p is updated within the for loop. The comparison at line 4 is to check if the periodicity p continues, in which case p is also the period of $x[0 \mathinner{.\,.} \ell - 1]$ as done by the assignment at line 6. If the comparison is negative, we cannot have $x[\ell-1] < x[\ell-1-p]$ because the suffix $vx[\ell - 1 - p]$ would be smaller than x, a contradiction with the fact that x is a Lyndon word. Thus, in that case, $x[\ell - 1] > x[\ell - 1 - p]$; this is the key feature mentioned in the solutions of Problem 39 and for which $x[0 \mathinner{.\,.} \ell - 1]$ is border free, then of period ℓ, as done by the assignment at line 5.

Periods of self-maximal prefixes. When the input to PREFIXPERIODS is self-maximal, without any change the algorithm computes its table of prefixes periods. The above argument is still valid after exchanging '<' and '>' essentially because the key feature also applies.

Lyndon test. Algorithm LYNDON adapts the above algorithm and is like Algorithm SELFMAXIMAL (Problem 39) after exchanging '<' and '>'. An extra check is required to verify the whole word is border free.

LYNDON(x non-empty word)

```
1   p ← 1
2   for ℓ ← 2 to |x| do
3       if x[ℓ − 1] < x[ℓ − 1 − p] then
4           return FALSE
5       elseif x[ℓ − 1] > x[ℓ − 1 − p] then
6           p ← ℓ
7   if p = |x| then
8       return TRUE
9   else return FALSE
```

Prefixes of lengths 1, 3, 5, 7 and 8 of aabababba are Lyndon words. The word itself is not because it has border a.

At line 7, if $|x|$ is a multiple of p, x is a necklace; otherwise it is a prefix of a necklace.

---

43   Searching Zimin Words

The problem considers patterns that are words with variables. Besides the alphabet $A = \{a, b, \ldots\}$ of constant letters, variables are from the (disjoint) alphabet $V = \{\alpha_1, \alpha_2, \ldots\}$.

A pattern $P \in V^*$ is said to match a word $w \in A^*$ if $w = \psi(P)$, where $\psi : alph(P)^+ \rightarrow A^+$ is a morphism. **Zimin words** Z_n, $n \geq 0$, play a crucial role in pattern avoidability questions (see Problem 93). They are defined by

$$Z_0 = \varepsilon \text{ and } Z_n = Z_{n-1} \cdot \alpha_n \cdot Z_{n-1}.$$

For example, $Z_1 = \alpha_1$, $Z_2 = \alpha_1\alpha_2\alpha_1$ and $Z_3 = \alpha_1\alpha_2\alpha_1\alpha_3\alpha_1\alpha_2\alpha_1$.

The **Zimin type** of a word w is the greatest natural integer k for which $w = \psi(Z_k)$, where ψ is some morphism. The type is always defined since the empty word has type 0 and the type of a non-empty word is at least 1. For example, the Zimin type of $w = $ adbadccccadbad is 3 because it is the image of Z_3 by the morphism ψ defined by

$$\begin{cases} \psi(\alpha_1) = \text{ad}, \\ \psi(\alpha_2) = \text{b}, \\ \psi(\alpha_3) = \text{cccc}. \end{cases}$$

Question. Show how to compute in linear time Zimin types of all prefixes of a given word.

[**Hint:** Consider short borders of prefixes.]

Question. Show how to check in quadratic time if a given Zimin pattern occurs in a word.

[**Hint:** Consider Zimin types of words.]

Solution

Computing Zimin types. The computation of Zimin types of prefixes of $w \in A^+$ is done online on w as follows. Let $Ztype[i]$ be the type of the prefix of length i if w. We have $Ztype[0] = 0$. For other values, it is enough to prove they are computed iteratively via the equality

$$Ztype[i] = Ztype[j] + 1,$$

where $j = |ShortBorder(w[0..i-1])|$.

Letting $z = w[0..i-1]$ and $u = ShortBorder(z)$ we have $z = uvu$ for two words u and v, $v \neq \varepsilon$. By definition of $Ztype[j]$ the word u is the image of $Z_{Ztype[j]}$ by a morphism $\psi : \{\alpha_1, \alpha_2, \dots, \alpha_{Ztype[j]}\}^+ \to A^+$. Extending the morphism by setting $\psi(\alpha_{Ztype[j]} + 1) = v$ shows that the Zimin type of z is at least $Ztype[j] + 1$. It remains to show that no border of z shorter than u can give a higher value.

Let $u'v'u'$ be a factorisation of z for which $Ztype[|u'|] = Ztype[|z|] - 1$ and assume by contradiction that u' is shorter than u with $Ztype[|u'|] > Ztype[|u|]$. Since then $Ztype[|u|] > 0$, $Ztype[|u'|] > 1$ which implies that $u' = u''v''u''$ for words such that $v'' \neq \varepsilon$ and $Ztype[|u''|] = Ztype[|u'|] - 1$. Then $Ztype[|u''|] = Ztype[|z|] - 2$. But since u'' is also a border of z, $Ztype[|z|] = Ztype[|u''|] + 1$, a contradiction.

The algorithm computing short borders of prefixes (Problem 21) infers the solution.

Matching a Zimin pattern. The following fact reduces the question to the computation of Zimin types.

Fact. The prefix $w[0 . . i - 1]$ of w matches a Zimin pattern Z_k if and only if $Ztype[i] \geq k$.

Indeed if a word is a morphic image of Z_j for some $j \geq k$ it is also a morphic image of Z_k.

The solution comes readily. The table $Ztype$ is computed for each suffix z of w, which allows to detect prefixes of z that match Z_k. And if Z_k occurs in w it will be detected that way.

MATCHINGZIMINPATTERN(w non-empty word, k positive integer)

```
1  for s ← 0 to |w| − 1 do
2      Ztype[0] ← 0
3      for i ← s to |w| − 1 do
4          compute Ztype[i − s + 1] on w[s . . |w| − 1]
5          if Ztype[i − s + 1] ≥ k then
6              return TRUE
7  return FALSE
```

The computation at line 4 uses the linear-time algorithm from the previous question. Therefore the whole test takes $O(|w|^2)$ running time as expected.

Note that a simple modification of the algorithm can produce the largest integer k for which Z_k occurs in the input word.

Notes

A more interesting question is the reverse pattern matching with variables, that is, to check if a given word with variables occurs in a given Zimin pattern. The problem is known to be in the NP class of complexity, but it is not known if it belongs to the NP-hard class.

44   Searching Irregular 2D Patterns

Let P be a given (potentially) irregular two-dimensional (2D) pattern. By *irregular* is meant that P is not necessarily a rectangle, it can be of any shape. The aim is to find all occurrences of P in a 2D $n \times n'$ text T of total size $N = nn'$.

The figure shows an irregular pattern P. It fits in a 3×3 box and has 2 occurrences in T, one of them is shown.

Question. Show that two-dimensional pattern matching of irregular 2D-patterns can be done in $O(N \log N)$ time.

Solution
The solution is to linearise the problem. Let P be a non-rectangular pattern that fits into an $m \times m'$ box. Assume w.l.o.g. that the first and last column, as well as the first and last row of this box, contain an element of P. Otherwise rows or columns are removed.

Text T is linearised into T' by concatenating its rows. The transformation of P is more subtle. First P is inserted into the $m \times m'$ box whose elements that are not of P (empty slots) are changed to $*$. Rows of this box are concatenated, inserting between the rows the word of $n' - m'$ symbols $*$. This way P is linearised to P'.

Example. For P in the figure, rows of the 3×3 box are $* b *, a a b$, and $a * b$, and $P' = * b * * * a a b * * a * b$.

The basic property of the transformation is that occurrences of P in T correspond to occurrences of word P' in word T', where P' contains don't care symbols.

Consequently all occurrences of P can be found using the method of Problem 36. The total running time of the solution then becomes $O(N \log N)$.

Notes
The running time can be reduced to $O(N \log(\max(m, m')))$. The linearisation method presented here is used in [10].

4   Efficient Data Structures

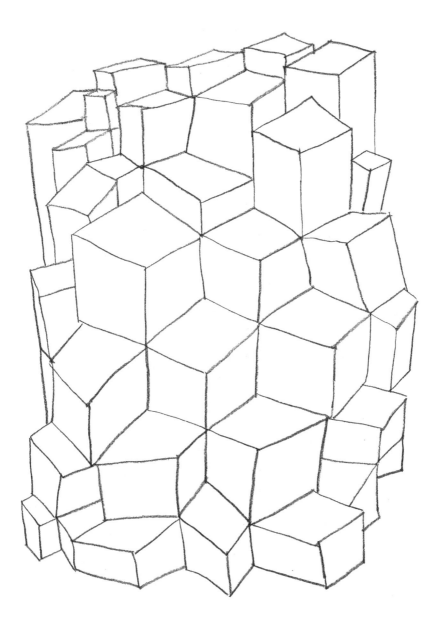

45   List Algorithm for Shortest Cover

A cover of a non-empty word x is one of its factors whose occurrences cover all positions on x. As such it is a repetitive element akin to a repetition. The problem shows how to compute the shortest cover of a word using its prefix table *pref*, instead of its border table as in Problem 20. The algorithm is simpler but uses linear extra memory space.

For each length ℓ of a prefix of x, let $L(\ell) = (i : pref[i] = \ell)$. Algorithm SHORTESTCOVER computes the length of the shortest cover of its input.

SHORTESTCOVER(x non-empty word)

1    $L \leftarrow (0, 1, \ldots, |x|)$
2   **for** $\ell \leftarrow 0$ **to** $|x| - 1$ **do**
3   remove elements of $L(\ell - 1)$ from L
4   **if** $maxgap(L) \leq \ell$ **then**
5   **return** ℓ

Simulating a run on $x = $ abababaaba, positions in the list L for $\ell = 1$, $2, 3$ are shown on the last lines. The associated values of $maxgap(L)$ are respectively 2, 3 and 3. The condition of line 4 is first met when $\ell = 3$, giving the shortest cover aba $= x[0 .. 2]$.

i	0	1	2	3	4	5	6	7	8	9	
$x[i]$	a	b	a	b	a	b	a	a	b	a	
$pref[i]$	10	0	5	0	3	0	1	3	0	1	
$L - L[0]$	0		2		4		6	7		9	10
$L - L[\leq 1]$	0		2		4			7			10
$L - L[\leq 2]$	0		2		4			7			10

Question. Show that Algorithm SHORTESTCOVER computes the length of the shortest cover of its input and if properly implemented runs in linear time.

Solution

The correctness of SHORTESTCOVER is clear: it removes positions with small *pref* values, since their prefixes are too short and can be ignored. Eventually the condition is satisfied when $\ell = |x|$.

If lists L and $L[\ell]$ are implemented, for example, by double-linked sorted lists, removing an element and updating *maxgap* simultaneously takes constant time per element. The overall running time is then linear, since each element is removed at most once from L and the total size of disjoint lists $L[\ell]$ is $|x| + 1$.

46   Computing Longest Common Prefixes

The Suffix array of a non-empty word y is a light and efficient solution for text indexing. It consists in using a binary search procedure to locate patterns inside y. To do so the suffixes of y are first sorted in lexicographic order, producing a table SA that lists the starting positions of the sorted suffixes.

But this standard technique is not sufficient to get a powerful search method. This is why the table SA is adjoined to a second table LCP that gives the length of **longest common prefixes** between consecutive suffixes in the sorted list (some more values easy to deduce are also needed). Using both tables, searching y for a word x is then achieved in time $O(|x| + \log|y|)$ instead of a straightforward $O(|x|\log|y|)$ time without the table LCP. Here is the Suffix array of abaabababbabbb:

j	0	1	2	3	4	5	6	7	8	9	10	11	12	13	
$y[j]$	a	b	a	a	b	a	b	a	b	b	a	b	b	b	
Rank r	0	1	2	3	4	5	6	7	8	9	10	11	12	13	14
SA[r]	2	0	3	5	7	10	13	1	4	6	9	12	8	11	
LCP[r]	0	1	3	4	2	3	0	1	2	3	4	1	2	2	0

where $\text{LCP}[r] = |\text{lcp}(y[\text{SA}[r-1]\mathinner{..}|y|-1], y[\text{SA}[r]\mathinner{..}|y|-1])|$.

> **Question.** Given the table SA for the word y, show that Algorithm LCP computes the associated table LCP in linear time.

Lcp(y non-empty word)

```
 1   for r ← 0 to |y| − 1 do
 2       Rank[SA[r]] ← r
 3   ℓ ← 0
 4   for j ← 0 to |y| − 1 do
 5       ℓ ← max{0, ℓ − 1}
 6       if Rank[j] > 0 then
 7           while max{j + ℓ, SA[Rank[j] − 1] + ℓ} < |y| and
                  y[j + ℓ] = y[SA[Rank[j] − 1] + ℓ] do
 8               ℓ ← ℓ + 1
 9       else ℓ ← 0
10       LCP[Rank[j]] ← ℓ
11   LCP[|y|] ← 0
12   return LCP
```

Note the solution is counterintuitive, since it looks natural to compute the values LCP[r] sequentially, that is, by processing suffixes in the increasing order of their ranks. But this does not readily produce a linear-time algorithm. Instead, Algorithm Lcp processes the suffixes from the longest to the shortest, which is its key feature and is more efficient.

Solution

The correctness of the algorithm relies on the inequality

$$\text{LCP}[\text{Rank}[j-1]] - 1 \le \text{LCP}[\text{Rank}[j]]$$

illustrated by the picture below.

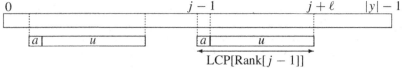

Assume $\ell = \text{LCP}[\text{Rank}[j-1]]$ has just been computed and the longest common prefix associated with position $j - 1$ is au for a letter a and a word u, that is, $\text{LCP}[\text{Rank}[j-1]] = |au|$. Then the longest common prefix associated with position j cannot be shorter than u. Therefore comparisons to compute $\text{LCP}[\text{Rank}[j]]$ by extending u can start at position $j + \ell$. This is what the algorithm does at lines 7–8. Line 5 rules out the case when the longest common prefix is empty.

As written the computation requires the table Rank, inverse of the table SA, which is computed at lines 1–2. It is used to retrieve the suffix immediately before the suffix $y[j .. |y| - 1]$ in the sorted list of all suffixes.

As for the running time of the procedure, it mostly depends on the number of tests at line 7. If the letters match, the value of $j + \ell$ increases and never decreases later. So, there are no more than $|y|$ such cases. There is at most one mismatch for each value of the variable j, then again no more than $|y|$ such cases. This proves the algorithm runs in linear time and executes no more than $2|y|$ letter comparisons.

Notes
The solution presented here is by Kasai et al. [155]. See also [74], where it is shown how to compute table SA in linear time on a linear-sortable alphabet.

47   Suffix Array to Suffix Tree

The goal of the problem is to transform the Suffix array of a word x into its Suffix tree. Despite the fact that both data structures infer essentially the same types of indexing operations, some come more readily from the Suffix tree structure.

The interest in designing a linear-time algorithm to do it is interesting when the alphabet is linearly sortable. Indeed, with this hypothesis, there are many linear-time algorithms to build the Suffix array of a word, although there is mostly one method to build its Suffix tree in the same time. Moreover, techniques used for the former construction are way easier to develop.

Here are tables SA and LCP of the Suffix array of `aacab`:

r	SA	LCP	
0	0	0	aacab
1	3	1	ab
2	1	1	acab
3	4	0	b
4	2	0	cab

Table SA stores the starting position of non-empty suffixes according to their rank r in lexicographic order. Suffixes themselves are not part of the structure. Table LCP$[r]$ gives the longest common prefix between rank-r and rank-$(r-1)$ suffixes.

> **Question.** Show how to build the Suffix tree of a word in linear time given its Suffix array.

The pictures below illustrate three first steps of a possible Suffix tree construction for the example aacab. The first picture is when suffixes aacab, ab and acab have been treated. Labels of nodes are their word depth and labels of arcs are in the form (i, j) (on the left) representing factors $x[i \mathbin{..} j-1]$ (on the right) of the word x. Doubly circled nodes are terminal states and thick paths show last inserted suffixes.

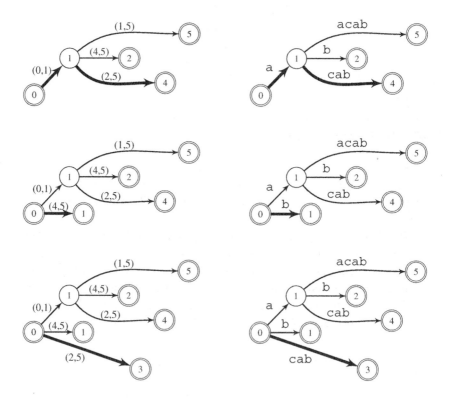

Solution

SARRAY2STREE(Suffix array of a non-empty word x)

```
 1   ▷ (SA, LCP) Suffix array of x
 2   (q, d[q]) ← (NEW-TERMINAL-STATE(), 0)
 3   INITIAL ← q
 4   S ← ∅
 5   PUSH(S, (q, 0, 0, q))
 6   for r ← 0 to |x| − 1 do
 7       do  (p, i, j, q) ← POP(S)
 8       while LCP[r] < d[p]
 9       if LCP[r] = d[q] then
10           PUSH(S, (p, i, j, q))
11           s ← q
12       elseif LCP[r] = d[p] then
13           s ← q
14       else (s, d[s]) ← (NEW-STATE(), LCP[r])
15           SPLIT(p, i, i + LCP[r] − d[p], s, i + LCP[r] − d[p], j, q)
16           PUSH(S, (p, i, i + LCP[r] − d[p], s))
17       (t, d[t]) ← (NEW-TERMINAL-STATE(), |x| − SA[r])
18       (s, SA[r] + LCP[r], |x|, t) ← NEW-ARC()
19       PUSH(S, (s, SA[r] + LCP[r], |x|, t))
20   return (INITIAL, nodes and arcs)
```

Algorithm SARRAY2STREE processes the suffixes of the underlying word in alphabetic order, that is, according to table SA, and inserts them in the tree. Recall that arcs are labelled as explained above to ensure the linear space of the whole structure. Table LCP is used in conjunction with the depth of nodes $d[\ ]$ (displayed on nodes in the above pictures). At a given step a stack S stores the arcs along the path associated with the last inserted suffix (thick path in pictures). The operation SPLIT (line 15) inserts a node s at the middle of an arc and re-labels the resulting arcs accordingly.

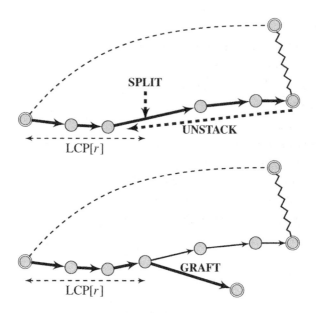

Instructions in the for loop, illustrated by the above pictures, consist of three main steps: **UNSTACK**, an optional **SPLIT** and **GRAFT**. Step **UNSTACK** is realised by the while loop at lines 7–8. Then, the found arc is split at lines 14–15 if necessary, that is, if the split operation has to be done in the middle of the arc, not at one extremity. Eventually a new arc is grafted at lines 17–18. Meanwhile new arcs along the path labelled by the current suffix are pushed on the stack.

The correctness of the algorithm can be elaborated from the given indications. For the running time, mostly the analysis of the while loop, the value relies on the time to traverse the tree, which is realised with the help of the stack. Since the size of the tree is linear according to the word length the algorithm runs in linear time. Note there is no condition on the word alphabet.

Notes

The first algorithm to build a Suffix tree in linear time on a linearly sortable alphabet was developed by Farach [110]. The present algorithm provides another solution from any Suffix array construction having the same characteristics. The historically first such construction was by Kärkkäinen and Sanders [153, 154] (see [74]), then by Ko and Aluru [163] and by Kim et al. [159], followed by several others.

48   Linear Suffix Trie

The Suffix trie of a word can be of quadratic size according to the word length. On the contrary, its Suffix tree requires only a linear amount of space for its storage, but the space should include the word itself.

The goal is to design a Suffix trie with edges labelled by single letters and that can be stored in linear space without the word itself. This is done by adding extra nodes and a few elements to the Suffix tree.

A node of the Suffix trie of y is identified to the factor of y that labels the path from the root to the node. Nodes in the linear Suffix trie $\mathcal{LST}(y)$ that are not in the Suffix tree $\mathcal{ST}(y)$ are of the form au, where a is a letter and u is a node of $\mathcal{ST}(y)$. That is, denoting by s the suffix link of the tree, $s(au) = u$. When nodes are added to $\mathcal{ST}(y)$ to create $\mathcal{LST}(y)$ edges are relabelled accordingly.

> **Question.** Show the number of extra nodes added to the Suffix tree of a word y to create its linear Suffix trie is less than $|y|$.

Labels of edges in $\mathcal{LST}(y)$ are reduced to the first letter of the corresponding factor as follows. If v, $|v| > 1$, labels the edge from u to uv in $\mathcal{ST}(y)$, the label of the associated edge in $\mathcal{LST}(y)$ is the first letter of v and the node uv is marked with the $+$ sign to indicate the actual label is longer.

> **Question.** Design an algorithm that checks if x occurs in y using the linear Suffix trie $\mathcal{LST}(y)$ and runs in time $O(|x|)$ on a fixed alphabet.

[**Hint:** Edge labels can be recovered using suffix links.]

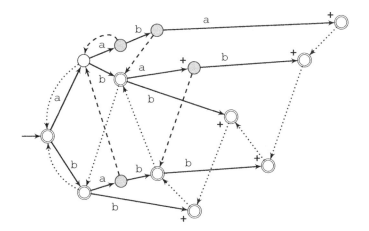

The above picture illustrates the linear Suffix trie of aababbab. White-coloured nodes are those of its Suffix tree (below with explicit edge labels), doubly circled when they are suffixes. Dotted edges form the suffix links of the Suffix tree. Grey-coloured nodes are the extra nodes with the dashed edges for the suffix links from them.

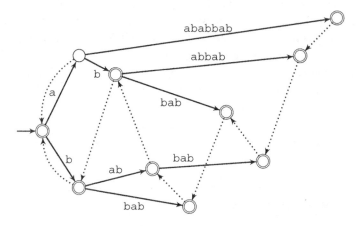

Solution

Few extra nodes. To answer the first question let u be a node of $\mathcal{LST}(y)$ that is not in $\mathcal{ST}(y)$. By definition $s(u)$ is a node of $\mathcal{ST}(y)$. Any proper suffix of u is of the form $s^k(u)$, which means it is also a node of $\mathcal{ST}(y)$. Therefore, two distinct nodes like u cannot share the same right position and there are no more than $|y|$ such nodes.

Note that a word whose letters are pairwise distinct has exactly $|y| - 1$ extra nodes. If a letter has two occurrences (two distinct right positions) at least, it is a node of $\mathcal{ST}(y)$, then there are no more than $|y| - 2$ extra nodes. Overall the number of extra nodes is less than $|y|$.

On the example of $\mathcal{LST}(\text{aababbab})$, the right positions of added nodes (grey-coloured in the picture) are 1 for aa, 2 for aab, 4 for abab, 3 and 6 for ba.

Searching $\mathcal{LST}(y)$. Checking if x is a factor of y is done by calling SEARCH($root, x$), where $root$ is the root of $\mathcal{LST}(y)$. The main point, dealing with uncomplete edges, that is, edges whose target has a + sign, relies mostly on the following observation.

Observation. Let au, a a letter, be a node of $\mathcal{LST}(y)$. If auv is also a node then uv is as well. This means that if v can be read from au in the tree, it can also be read from $s(au) = u$. (The converse does not hold.)

This leads to the sketch of Algorithm SEARCH that returns TRUE if ux is a factor of y.

SEARCH(u node of $\mathcal{LST}(y)$, x a word)

1   if $x = \varepsilon$ then
2   return TRUE
3   elseif no label of edges from u is $x[0]$ then
4   return FALSE
5   else let (u,uv) be the edge whose label v is $x[0]$
6   if uv has no $+$ sign then
7   return SEARCH($uv,x[1..|x|-1]$)
8   elseif SEARCH($s(u),v$) then
9   return SEARCH($uv,v^{-1}x$)
10   else return FALSE

A straight implementation of the above scheme may not run in linear time due to non-explicit labels of some edges. To cope with it another suffix link, denoted by $\bar{s}$, is used.

First note that for any edge (u,uv) of $\mathcal{LST}(y)$ the pair $(s^k(u),s^k(uv))$ is defined for $0 \le k \le |u|$ but nodes $s^k(u)$ and $s^k(uv)$ may not be connected by a single edge. The suffix link $\bar{s}$ is defined on edges of $\mathcal{LST}(y)$ corresponding to edges of the Suffix tree having a label longer than a unique letter. If (u,uv) if such an edge of $\mathcal{LST}(y)$, that is, $|v| > 1$, $\bar{s}(u,uv) = (s^k(u),s^k(uv))$, where k is the smallest integer for which nodes $s^k(u)$ and $s^k(uv)$ are not connected by an edge. This definition is valid because all words of length 1 are nodes of $\mathcal{LST}(y)$ (not necessarily of $\mathcal{ST}(y)$). Note $\bar{s}$ can be computed in time proportional to the number of edges of $\mathcal{LST}(y)$.

Using $\bar{s}$ the implementation runs in linear time. Indeed, each time $\bar{s}(u,uv)$ is used to find the explicit label v of the edge, a letter of v is recovered. Then it cannot be used more than $|v|$ times, which yields a linear amortised running time. On a general alphabet A the implementation runs in time $O(|x|\log|A|)$.

Notes

The linear Suffix trie of a word and the associated searching techniques are described in [71]. The linear Suffix trie can be built by a mere post-processing of the Suffix tree of the word.

Hendrian et al. designed a right-to-left online construction of $\mathcal{LST}(y)$ running in time $O(|y|\log|A|)$ in [140]. They also produced a left-to-right online construction running in time $O(|y|(\log|A| + \log|y|/\log\log|y|))$.

49   Ternary Search Trie

Ternary search tries provide an efficient data structure to store and search a set
of words. It figures a clever implementation of the trie of the set in the same
way as the Suffix array does for the set of suffixes of a word.

Searching a trie for a pattern starts at the initial state (the root) and proceeds
down following the matching arcs until the end of the pattern is met or until
no arc matches the current letter. When the alphabet is large, representing arcs
outgoing a state can lead to either a waste of space because many arcs have no
target, or to a waste of time if linear lists are used. The goal of ternary search
tries is to represent them by binary search trees on the outgoing letters.

To do so, each node of the trie has three outgoing arcs: left and right (up
and down on the picture) for the binary search tree at the current trie node, and
a middle arc to the next trie node. Below are the ternary search trie (left) and
the trie (right) of the set
{large, long, pattern, sequence, short, string}.

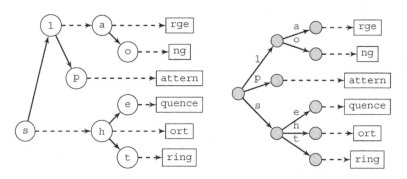

> **Question.** Describe the data structure to implement a ternary search trie
> storing a set of n words and show how to search it for a word of length m.
> Analyse the running time.

[**Hint:** Note the analogy with searching a Suffix array.]

Notice on the above example that the binary search tree corresponding to
the arcs outgoing the initial node of the trie has its root labelled s and not the
middle letter p. Indeed, to make the search more efficient binary search trees
are weight balanced. The weight corresponds to the number of elements in the
subtree. This is why the s starting letter of the majority of words is chosen for
the root of the binary search tree.

Solution

The data structure of a ternary search tree T is composed of nodes linked in a tree manner. Each node q stores three pointers to other nodes, denoted by $q.left$, $q.right$ and $q.mid$, which have the functions described above. Some nodes are terminal (no outgoing arc). Each node also stores in $q.val$ either a suffix of a word in T if q is terminal or a letter.

TST-SEARCH(T a TST and x a non-empty word)

```
 1   q ← initial node of T
 2   for i ← 0 to |x| − 1 do
 3       if q is a terminal node then
 4           if x[i .. |x| − 1] = q.val then
 5               return TRUE
 6           else return FALSE
 7       q ← BST-SEARCH((q, x[i]))
 8       if q undefined then
 9           return FALSE
10       q ← q.mid
11   return FALSE      ▷ x prefix of a word in T
```

The BST search at line 7 is done in the subtree rooted at q using only the pointers *left* and *right*, and the field *val* compared to $x[i]$.

Let $n > 0$ be the number of words stored in T. A rough worst-case analysis shows the running time is $O(|x|\log n)$. But the role of the TST search is analogous to the binary search in a Suffix array to locate the current letter $x[i]$, leading to a tighter $O(|x| + \log n)$ time. More accurately, each negative letter comparison done during the TST search reduces the interval of words to be searched, which gives $O(\log n)$ such comparisons. And each positive comparison ends instructions in the for loop, thus a total of $O(|x|)$ such comparisons. Then overall there are $O(|x| + \log n)$ comparisons, including those at line 4, which is representative of the running time.

Notes

The notion of a ternary search trie is by Bentley and Sedgewick [31]. Clément et al. [57] give a thorough analysis of the structure according to several probabilistic conditions.

Applied to the suffixes of a word, the ternary search trie is the data structure that corresponds to algorithms associated with the Suffix array of the word.

50   Longest Common Factor of Two Words

The problem deals with common factors of two words. It serves as a basis to compare texts and extends to applications such as bio-sequence alignment or plagiarism detection.

Let $LCF(x, y)$ denote the maximal length of factors that appear in two given words x and y drawn from the alphabet A. A straightforward solution to compute it is to build the common Suffix tree of x and y. Nodes are prefixes of their suffixes. A deepest node whose subtree contains both suffixes of x and suffixes of y gives the answer, its depth. This can also be done with the Suffix tree of $x\#y$, where $\#$ is a letter that does not appear in x nor in y.

The time to compute the tree is $O(|xy| \log |A|)$, or $O(|xy|)$ on linearly sortable alphabets (see Problem 47), and the required space is $O(|xy|)$.

Below is the common Suffix tree of $x = \text{aabaa}$ and $y = \text{babab}$. Grey (resp. white) doubly circled nodes are non-empty suffixes of x (resp. y). The node aba gives $LCF(\text{aabaa}, \text{babab}) = |\text{aba}| = 3$.

i	0	1	2	3	4		j	0	1	2	3	4
$x[i]$	a	a	b	a	a		$y[j]$	b	a	b	a	b

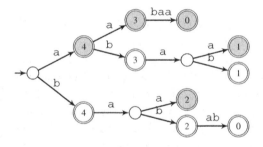

The goal of the problem is to reduce the size of the data structure to that of only one word, contrary to the above solution.

Question. Design an algorithm to compute $LCF(x, y)$ using the Suffix automaton (or the Suffix tree) of only one word. Analyse the time and space complexity of the whole computation.

[**Hint:** Use the indexing structure as a search machine.]

Solution

We assume $|x| \le |y|$ and consider the Suffix automaton $\mathcal{S}(x)$ of x. Its size is known to be $O(|x|)$ independently of the alphabet. In addition to its states and labelled arcs, the automaton is equipped with two functions defined on states: failure link *fail* and maximal depth L. For a state q associated with a non-empty word v (i.e., $q = goto$(initial, v)), $fail[v]$ is the state $p \neq q$ associated with the longest possible suffix u of v. And $L[q]$ is the maximal length of words associated with q.

Below is the Suffix automaton of the example word aabaa with the failure links (dotted arcs) on its states.

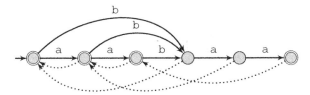

Algorithm LCF solves the question by using $S(x)$ as a search engine.

LCF($S(x)$ Suffix automaton of x, y non-empty word)

```
 1   (m, ℓ, q) ← (0, 0, initial state of S(x))
 2   for j ← 0 to |y| − 1 do
 3       if goto(q, y[j]) defined then
 4           (ℓ, q) ← (ℓ + 1, goto(q, y[j]))
 5       else do  q ← fail[q]
 6           while q defined and goto(q, y[j]) undefined
 7           if q defined then
 8               (ℓ, q) ← (L[q] + 1, goto(q, y[j]))
 9           else (ℓ, q) ← (0, initial state of S(x))
10       m ← max{m, ℓ}
11   return m
```

At each step, the algorithm computes the length ℓ of the longest match between a factor of x and a suffix of $y[0 \mathinner{.\,.} j]$. To do so, it proceeds like string-matching algorithms based on the use of a failure link. The only details specific to the algorithm is the faculty to reset properly the length ℓ to $L[q] + 1$ after following a series of links (see notes).

As for the whole running time, it is linear on a linearly sorted alphabet. Indeed, building the Suffix automaton of x can be done in linear time; and the above algorithm also runs in the same time because any computation of $goto(q, y[j])$ leads to an increase of either the variable j or the expression $j - \ell$, quantities that vary from 0 to $|y|$.

Note that, in fact, the algorithm finds the longest factor of x that ends at any position on y.

Notes

The method developed in the problem is by Crochemore [68] (see also [74, Chapter 6]. A similar method using a Suffix tree is by Hartman and Rodeh [138]. The technique adapts to locate a conjugate of x inside y with the Suffix automaton of xx.

---

51   Subsequence Automaton

Subsequences (or subwords) occurring in a word are useful elements to filter series of texts or to compare them. The basic data structure for developing applications related to subsequences is an automaton accepting them due to its reasonable size.

For a non-empty word y, let $\mathcal{SM}(y)$ be the minimal (deterministic) automaton accepting the subsequences of y. It is also called the Deterministic Acyclic Subsequence Graph (DASG). Below is the subsequence automaton of abcabba. All its states are terminal and it accepts the set

$$\{a, b, c, aa, ab, ac, ba, bb, bc, ca, cb, aaa, aab, aba, abb, abc, \ldots\}.$$

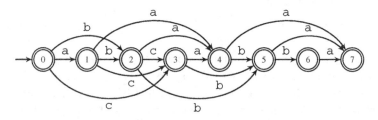

Question. Show how to build the subsequence automaton of a word and analyse the time and space complexity of the construction according to the size of the automaton.

Subsequence automata are an essential structure to find words that discriminate two words because they provide a direct access to all their subsequences.

A word u distinguishes two distinct words y and z if it is a subsequence of only one of them, that is, if it is in the symmetric difference of their associated sets of subsequences.

Question. Show how to compute a shortest subsequence distinguishing two different words y and z with the help of their automata $\mathcal{SM}(y)$ and $\mathcal{SM}(z)$.

To design the algorithm it is interesting to note the following property of the subsequence automaton of y: if there is a path from state 0 to state i labelled by the word u, then $y[0 .. i - 1]$ is the shortest prefix of y containing u as a subsequence.

Solution
Subsequence automaton construction. States of automaton $\mathcal{SM}(y)$ are $0, 1, \ldots, |y|$ and its transition table is goto. Let us assume that the alphabet of the word y is fixed, of size σ, and that it indexes a table t storing states. Algorithm DASG below processes y online. When its non-empty prefix w has just been processed, $t[a] - 1$ is the rightmost position on w of letter a. Equivalently, it is also the rightmost state target of an arc labelled by letter a.

DASG(y)

```
1   for each letter a ∈ alph(y) do
2        t[a] ← 0
3   for i ← 0 to |y| − 1 do
4        for j ← t[y[i]] to i do
5             goto(j, y[i]) ← i + 1
6        t[y[i]] ← i + 1
```

Since the automaton is deterministic, its number of arcs is less than $\sigma |y|$. In fact it is no more than $\sigma |y| - \sigma(\sigma - 1)/2$. Therefore the instruction at line 5 is executed less than $\sigma |y|$ times, which shows that the running time is $O(\sigma |y|)$. The extra space used by table t is $O(\sigma)$.

If the alphabet is not fixed, letters occurring in y can be first sorted in $O(alph(y) \log alph(y))$ time to get the above hypothesis. This adds to the total running time.

Distinguishing words. To find the shortest subsequence distinguishing two different words, one can use the general algorithm to test the equivalence of two deterministic finite automata. The algorithm is a standard application of the UNION-FIND data structure and runs in time $O(n \log^* n)$, where n is the smaller length of the two words.

Notes

The notion of a subsequence automaton was first introduced by Baeza-Yates [21] and later on called a DASG by Troníček and Melichar [231]. Baeza-Yates's construction processes the word from right to left contrary to the above algorithm. The extension of the automaton to a finite set of words can be found in [21, 100]. The size of a DASG is analysed in [232].

Testing the equivalence of deterministic automata is by Hopcroft and Karp (1971), see [4], as an application of the UNION-FIND data structure. Another description and analysis of the structure appears in [63].

52   Codicity Test

Sets of words, especially binary words, are used to encode information. They may be related to transmission protocols, to data compression or mere texts. Streams of data need to be parsed according to the set to retrieve the original information. Parsing is a simple operation when codewords have the same length, like ASCII and UTF-32 codes for characters, and gives a unique factorisation of encoded data.

A code is a set of words that features a uniquely decipherable property. The question of having a unique parsing concerns mostly variable-length codes. The goal of the problem is to test whether a set of words is a code.

More precisely, a set $C = \{w_1, w_2, \ldots, w_n\}$ of words drawn from an alphabet A is a code if for every two sequences (noted as words) $i_1 i_2 \ldots i_k$ and $j_1 j_2 \ldots j_\ell$ of indices from $\{1, 2, \ldots, n\}$ we have

$$i_1 i_2 \ldots i_k \neq j_1 j_2 \ldots j_\ell \Rightarrow w_{i_1} w_{i_2} \ldots w_{i_k} \neq w_{j_1} w_{j_2} \ldots w_{j_\ell}.$$

In other words, if we define the morphism h from $\{1, 2, \ldots, n\}^*$ to A^* by $h(i) = w_i$, for $i \in \{1, 2, \ldots .n\}$, the condition means h is injective.

The set $C_0 = \{\text{ab}, \text{abba}, \text{baccab}, \text{cc}\}$ is not a code because the word abbaccab $\in C_0^*$ has two factorisations, ab $\cdot$ baccab and abba $\cdot$ cc $\cdot$ ab, on the words of C_0. On the contrary, the set $C_1 = \{\text{ab}, \text{bacc}, \text{cc}\}$ is a code because a word in C_1^* can start by only one word in C_1. It is said to be a prefix code (no $u \in C$ is a proper prefix of $v \in C$).

To test if $C_2 = \{\text{ab}, \text{abba}, \text{baaabad}, \text{aa}, \text{badcc}, \text{cc}, \text{dccbad}, \text{badba}\}$ is a code we can try to build a word in C_2^* with a double factorisation. Here is a sequence of attempts:

At each step we get a remainder, namely ba, aabad, bad and cc, that we try to eliminate. Eventually we get a double factorisation because the last remainder is the empty word. Then C_2 is not a code.

The size N of the codicity testing problem for a finite set of words is the total length $\|C\|$ of all words of C.

Question. Design an algorithm that checks if a finite set C of words is a code and that runs in time $O(N^2)$.

Solution

To solve the question, testing the codicity of C is transformed into a problem on a graph $G(C)$. Nodes of $G(C)$ are the remainders of attempts at a double factorisation, and as such are suffixes of words in C (including the empty word).

Nodes of $G(C)$ are defined in a width-first manner. Initial nodes at level 0 are those of the form $u^{-1}v$ for two distinct words $u, v \in C$. Their set may be empty if C is a prefix code. Then nodes at level $k + 1$ are words of $C^{-1}D_k \cup D_k^{-1}C$, where D_k are nodes at level k. The set of nodes includes the empty word called the sink. There is an edge in $G(C)$ from u to v when $v = z^{-1}u$ or when $v = u^{-1}z$, for $z \in C$.

The picture below shows the graph $G(C_2)$ in which there is only one initial node and where columns correspond to node levels. The set C_2 is not a code because there is a path from the initial node to the sink. The middle such path corresponds to the above double factorisation. In fact, there is an infinity of words with a double factorisation due to the loop in the graph.

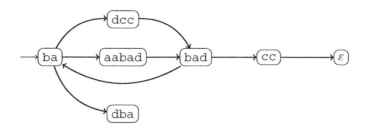

Observation. The set C is a code if and only if there is no path in $G(C)$ from an initial node to the sink.

The size of graph $G(C)$ is $O(N^2)$, since nodes are suffixes of words in C. Therefore the observation leads to an effective test of codicity. And since building the graph and exploring it can be done in time proportional to the size of the graph the solution runs in $O(N^2)$ time.

Notes

The algorithm to test the codicity of a finite set of words has been invented by Sardinas and Paterson [217]. A formal proof of the observation appears in [175, chapter 1] and in [36, chapter 1].

The algorithm can be implemented with the trie of the set, equipped with appropriate links, to obtain a $O(nN)$ running time, where n is the maximal length of words; see [15].

53 LPF Table

The problem deals with yet another table on words called abusively the *longest previous factor* table. It is a useful tool to factorise words for data compression (see Problem 97) and more generally to design efficient algorithms for finding repeats in texts.

For a non-empty word y, its table LPF stores lengths of repeating factors. More precisely, for a position j on y, LPF$[j]$ is the maximal length of factors that starts both at position j and at a previous (i.e., smaller) position. Here is the table for abaababbbabbb.

j	0	1	2	3	4	5	6	7	8	9	10	11	12	13
$y[j]$	a	b	a	a	b	a	b	a	b	b	a	b	b	b
LPF[j]	0	0	1	3	2	4	3	2	1	4	3	2	2	1

The next algorithm computes the table LPF for its input word y. It utilises the Suffix array of y and the table Rank that gives ranks of its suffixes in lexicographic order. Tables *prev* and *next* are links for a list representation of suffix ranks.

LPF(y non-empty word)

```
 1   for r ← 0 to |y| − 1 do
 2       (prev[r], next[r]) ← (r − 1, r + 1)
 3   for j ← |y| − 1 downto 0 do
 4       r ← Rank[j]
 5       LPF[j] ← max{LCP[r], LCP[next[r]]}
 6       LCP[next[r]] ← min{LCP[r], LCP[next[r]]}
 7       if prev[r] ≥ 0 then
 8           next[prev[r]] ← next[r]
 9       if next[r] < |y| then
10           prev[next[r]] ← prev[r]
11   return LPF
```

Question. Show that Algorithm LPF correctly computes the table LPF and works in linear time.

Looking accurately at the algorithm proves more than what it is designed for: lengths in LPF form a permutation of lengths in LCP.

Question. Show both that values in the LPF table are permuted from values in the LCP table and that the LCP table can be transformed into the LPF table.

Solution

The analysis of Algorithm LPF becomes obvious when the Suffix array of its input is displayed graphically. The Suffix array of abaabababbbabbb and the ranks of its suffixes are as follows.

j	0	1	2	3	4	5	6	7	8	9	10	11	12	13	
$y[j]$	a	b	a	a	b	a	b	a	b	b	a	b	b	b	
$\text{Rank}[j]$	1	7	0	2	8	3	9	4	12	10	5	13	11	6	
r	0	1	2	3	4	5	6	7	8	9	10	11	12	13	14
$SA[r]$	2	0	3	5	7	10	13	1	4	6	9	12	8	11	
$LCP[r]$	0	1	3	4	2	3	0	1	2	3	4	1	2	2	0

The display (below top) shows a graphic representation of the Suffix array of the above word. Positions are displayed according to their ranks (x-axis) and of their values (y-axis). The link between positions at ranks $r-1$ and r is labelled by $LCP[r]$.

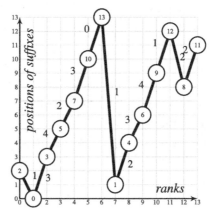

Observation. The LCP length between the position at rank $r-1$ (resp. r) and any position of higher (resp. smaller) rank is not larger than $LCP[r]$.

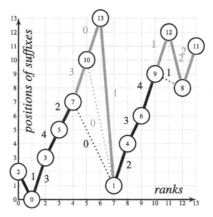

A straight consequence of the observation gives the clue of the technique. When the position j at rank r occurs at a peak on the graphic, its associated

LPF length is the larger value of LCP[r] and LCP[$r + 1$]. And the LCP length between its previous and next positions is the smaller of the two values. This is exactly the role of comparisons at lines 5–6.

It also explains why positions are treated from the largest to the smallest because then each position appears at a graphic peak in turn.

Next instructions of LPF manage the list of positions like a doubly linked list thanks to *prev* and *next*. The role of instructions at lines 8 and 10 is to remove the position j, of rank r, from the list.

The picture (above bottom) illustrates the situation just after positions 13 to 10 (in grey) have been treated. Dotted links are still labelled by LCP values.

This shows Algorithm Lᴘꜰ correctly computes the sought LPF table.

Solution to the second question. The above argument also shows that the values in the LPF table are permuted values of those in the LCP table of the Suffix array of y.

To transform the LCP table into the LPF table of the input, lines 5–6 of Algorithm Lᴘꜰ are changed to:

5   **if** LCP[r] < LCP[$next[r]$] **then**

6       $(\ell, \text{LCP}[r], \text{LCP}[next[r]]) \leftarrow (\text{LCP}[r], \text{LCP}[next[r]], \ell)$

where line 6 exchanges two values of the table. The algorithm produces the table LCP′ corresponding to LPF, since LPF[SA[r]] = LCP′[r], or equivalently LPF[j] = LCP′[Rank[j]]. Sorting pairs (SA[r], LCP′[r]) according to their first component produces values of the table LPF as their second component.

r	0	1	2	3	4	5	6	7	8	9	10	11	12	13	14
SA[r]	2	0	3	5	7	10	13	1	4	6	9	12	8	11	
LCP′[r]	1	0	3	4	2	3	1	0	2	3	4	2	1	2	0

In the example, the algorithm produces the above table LCP′ from which we deduce for example LPF[2] = 1 (corresponding to the second occurrence of a) because 2 and 1 are aligned at rank $r = 0$.

Notes

The first linear-time algorithm for computing the LPF table of a word from its Suffix array appears in [76]. More efficient algorithms are designed in [78], where it is shown the computation can be done time–space optimally with an algorithm that runs in linear time with only $O(\sqrt{|y|})$ extra memory space used for a stack.

Three variants of the LPF table are presented in [87] with their corresponding construction algorithms; see also [50, 52, 99].

54   Sorting Suffixes of Thue–Morse Words

Thue–Morse words with their special structure provide examples in which some algorithms running in linear time or more can be optimised to run in logarithmic time instead. The problem shows such an example related to the Suffix array of words.

The infinite Thue–Morse word results from the iteration of the Thue–Morse morphism μ from $\{0, 1\}^*$ to itself defined by

$$\begin{cases} \mu(0) = 01 \\ \mu(1) = 10 \end{cases}$$

The Thue–Morse word τ_n is $\mu^n(0)$, for a natural integer n. This type of description of Thue–Morse words is suitable to describe recursively the array SA_n that lists the starting positions of non-empty suffixes of τ_n sorted according to the lexicographic order of the suffixes. For example, $\tau_3 = \mathtt{01101001}$ and $\mathrm{SA}_3 = [5, 6, 3, 0, 7, 4, 2, 1]$.

Question. Given integers n and k, $0 \le k < n$, show how to compute $\mathrm{SA}_n[k]$ in time $O(n)$ for the word τ_n of length 2^n.

Solution
Let us start with two observations on word τ_n.

Observation 1. Let i be an even position on τ_n. Then $\tau_n[i] \ne \tau_n[i+1]$.

For $c \in \{0, 1\}$, I_{odd}^c, resp. I_{even}^c, is the set of odd, resp. even, positions i for which $\tau_n[i] = c$. The justification of Observation 2, in which suf_i is $\tau_n[i \,.\,.\, 2^n - 1]$, follows from Observation 1.

Observation 2.
(a) If $i \in I_{\mathrm{odd}}^0$, $j \in I_{\mathrm{even}}^0$ and $suf_i \ne \mathtt{01}$, then $suf_i < suf_j$.
(b) If $i \in I_{\mathrm{even}}^1$, $j \in I_{\mathrm{odd}}^1$ and $suf_j \ne \mathtt{1}$, then $suf_i < suf_j$.
An alternative formulation of Observation 2 is

$$I_{\mathrm{odd}}^0 < I_{\mathrm{even}}^0 < I_{\mathrm{even}}^1 < I_{\mathrm{odd}}^1.$$

For a sequence S of integers and two integers p and q, $p \cdot S$ and $S + q$ denote the sequences of elements of S multiplied by p and increased by q respectively. For example, $2 \cdot [1, 2, 3] = [2, 4, 6]$ and $[1, 2, 3] + 3 = [4, 5, 6]$.

The solution is split into two parts according to the parity of n.

The case of even n**.** When n is an even integer the table SA_n is related to SA_{n-1} in the following way. Let α and β be the two halves of SA_{n-1} ($\text{SA}_{n-1} = [\alpha, \beta]$); then

$$(*) \quad \text{SA}_n = [2 \cdot \beta + 1, 2 \cdot \alpha, 2 \cdot \beta, 2 \cdot \alpha + 1].$$

Proof Let $sorted(X)$, for a set X of suffix starting positions on a word, denote the sorted list of positions according to the lexicographic order of the suffixes. Let also

$$\gamma_1 = sorted(I^0_{\text{odd}}), \quad \gamma_2 = sorted(I^0_{\text{even}}),$$

$$\gamma_3 = sorted(I^1_{\text{even}}), \quad \gamma_3 = sorted(I^1_{\text{odd}}).$$

Then, due to Observation 2, $\text{SA}_n = [\gamma_1, \gamma_2, \gamma_3, \gamma_4]$.

Fortunately, for even n we do not have bad suffixes 01 nor 1 in τ_n. We can use the morphic representation of Thue–Morse words. First observe that the morphism μ preserves the lexicographic order ($u < v \Leftrightarrow \mu(u) < \mu(v)$). Each suffix at position i on τ_{n-1} is mapped by μ to a suffix at position $2i$ on τ_n. Hence $2 \cdot \text{SA}_{n-1} = [2 \cdot \alpha, 2 \cdot \beta]$ is the sequence of sorted suffixes at even positions in τ_n.

Then due to the previous observation $\text{SA}_n = [\gamma_1, \gamma_2, \gamma_3, \gamma_4]$, where γ_1 corresponds to sorted suffixes starting at second positions of suffixes associated with $2 \cdot \beta$. Similarly for γ_4 and $2 \cdot \alpha$. Therefore we get $\text{SA}_n = [2 \cdot \beta + 1, 2 \cdot \alpha, 2 \cdot \beta, 2 \cdot \alpha + 1]$, as required. ∎

Computing SA_4 **from** SA_3**.** $\text{SA}_3 = [5, 6, 3, 0, 7, 4, 2, 1]$ is composed of $\alpha = [5, 6, 3, 0]$ and $\beta = [7, 4, 2, 1]$. We have $2 \cdot \beta = [14, 8, 4, 2]$, $2 \cdot \beta + 1 = [15, 9, 5, 3]$, $2 \cdot \alpha = [10, 12, 6, 0]$ and $2 \cdot \alpha + 1 = [11, 13, 7, 1]$, which gives

$$\text{SA}_4 = [15, 9, 5, 3, \ 10, 12, 6, 0, \ 14, 8, 4, 2, \ 11, 13, 7, 1].$$

The case of odd n**.** When n is odd we can also apply the formula $(*)$ except that the *bad* suffixes 01 and 1 should be *specially* placed at their correct places: the suffix 1 should be placed in front of all other suffixes starting with 1. The suffix 01 should be placed immediately after the whole sequence of suffixes starting with 00. Hence the correction reduces to the computation of the number $p(n)$ of occurrences of 00 in τ_n.

The numbers $p(n)$ for $n = 2, 3, \ldots, 10$ are $0, 1, 2, 5, 10, 21, 42, 85, 170$. These numbers satisfy the recurrence

$$(**) \quad p(1) = 0, \ p(2k + 1) = 4 \cdot p(2k - 1) + 1, \ p(2k + 2) = 2 \cdot p(2k + 1).$$

Consequently $p(2k + 1) = (4^k - 1)/3$.

Computing SA_5 **from** SA_4**.** To do it, first apply the transformation (∗) to get the four blocks:

$$29, 17, 9, 5, 23, 27, 15, 3 \qquad \mathbf{30}, 18, 10, 6, 20, 24, 12, 0,$$

$$28, 16, 8, 4, 22, 26, 14, 2 \qquad \mathbf{31}, 19, 11, 7, 21, 25, 13, 1.$$

The bad suffixes 01 and 1 start at positions 30, 31. The number 31 should be moved after the 5th element 23, since $p(5) = 5$. The number 31 corresponding to a one-letter suffix should be moved to the beginning of the third quarter (it is the smallest suffix starting with letter 1). We get the final value of the suffix table SA_5 by concatenating:

$$29, 17, 9, 5, 23, \mathbf{30}, 27, 15 \qquad 3, 18, 10, 6, 20, 24, 12, 0,$$

$$\mathbf{31}, 28, 16, 8, 4, 22, 26, 14 \qquad 2, 19, 11, 7, 21, 25, 13, 1.$$

Conclusion. To answer the question, computing quickly $SA_n[k]$, let us summarise how it can be done:

- Identify in which quarter of SA_n the number k is located.
- Reduce the problem to the computation of $SA_{n-1}[j]$, where the corresponding position j (around half of k) is computed using the formula (∗) backwards.
- If n is odd, take into account the relocation of the two *bad* suffixes in SA_n. The value of $p(n)$ given by (∗∗) is used for the relocation.
- Iterate such reductions until coming to a constant-sized table.

Altogether $O(n)$ steps are sufficient to compute $SA_n[k]$, which is logarithmic with respect to the size of the table SA_n.

Notes

It seems there is a possible different approach using a compact factor automaton for Thue–Morse words, as described in [204]. However, this leads to an even more complicated solution.

55   Bare Suffix Tree

Suffix trees provide a data structure for indexing texts. Optimal-time constructions of them suffer from a rather high memory requirement, larger than
for Suffix arrays with the same usage. The problem deals with a moderately
efficient but not completely naive and very simple construction of Suffix trees.

The Suffix tree T of a word x ending with a unique end marker is the
compacted trie of suffixes of x. A leaf corresponds to a suffix and an internal
node to a factor having at least two occurrences followed by different letters.
Each edge is labelled by a factor $x[i .. j]$ of x, represented by the pair (i, j).
Its word-length is $|x[i .. j]| = j - i + 1$. The word-length of a path in T is the
sum of word-lengths of its edges, while the length of the path is its number of
edges. Let $depth(T)$ be the maximum length of a path in T from the root to a
leaf. Let l_i be the leaf ending the branch labelled by $x[i .. n - 1]$.

> **Question.** Design a construction of the Suffix tree T of a word x using no
> additional array and running in time $O(|x| depth(T))$ on a fixed-size alphabet.

Solution
The main scheme of the solution is to insert iteratively the suffixes in the tree,
from the longest to the shortest suffix of x.

Let T_{i-1} denote the compacted trie of suffixes starting at positions
$0, 1, \ldots, i - 1$ on x. We show how to update T_{i-1} to get the tree T_i.

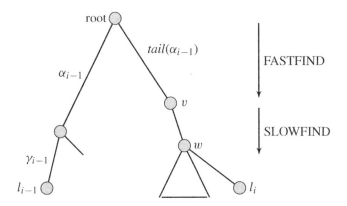

The ith suffix can be split into $\alpha_i \gamma_i$ where $\alpha_i = x[i .. i + d_i - 1])$ and $\gamma_i = x[i + d_i .. n - 1]$. The word α_i is the path-label from the root to $w = parent(l_i)$ (see picture). In particular $\alpha_i = \varepsilon$ if $parent(l_i) = root$.

When a is the first letter of the word au, $tail(au) = u$. Note the word $\alpha_k \neq \varepsilon$ has an occurrence starting at k and at some smaller position. Consequently $tail(\alpha_k)$ has occurrences at $k + 1$ and at a smaller position. This implies the following crucial fact.

Observation. Assume $\alpha_{i-1} \neq \varepsilon$. Then there is a path in T_{i-1} spelling the word $tail(\alpha_{i-1})\gamma_{i-1}$ (see picture). In other words, a great part of the suffix $x[i \mathinner{\ldotp\ldotp} n]$ that is being inserted is already present in the tree.

The algorithm uses two types of tree traversal:

- *FastFind*(α) assumes that α is present in the current tree (as a path-label). It finds the node v by spelling the word α. If the spelling ends in the middle of an edge-label, the node v is created.

  The traversal is guided by the length d of α. It uses the edges of the tree as *shortcuts*, reading only the first symbol and the length of each edge. The cost of the traversal is $O(depth(T))$.

- *SlowFind*(v, γ) finds the lowest descendant w of v in the current tree following the path labelled by the longest possible prefix β of γ. As above, node w may have to be created.

  The traversal goes symbol by symbol, updating the value of d. Its cost is $O(|\beta|)$.

The whole algorithm starts with the tree composed of a single edge labelled by the whole word $x[0 \mathinner{\ldotp\ldotp} n - 1]$ and executes the following scheme for suffixes at positions $i = 1, 2, \ldots, n - 1$.

One iteration, from T_{i-1} to T_i:

if $\alpha_{i-1} = \varepsilon$ then $v \leftarrow root$ else $v \leftarrow$ *FastFind*$(tail(\alpha_{i-1}))$,
$w \leftarrow$ *SlowFind*(v, γ_{i-1}),
a new leaf l_i and new edge $w \rightarrow l_i$ are created.

Running time of the algorithm. There are $n - 1$ iterations. In each iteration the cost of *FastFind* is $O(depth(T))$. The total cost of *SlowFind*s is $O(n)$, since each of their single moves decreases the length of the word γ_i. Altogether the time cost is $O(n \cdot depth(T))$.

Note the algorithm requires no additional array as required.

Notes

The algorithm described here is a simplified version of McCreight's Suffix tree construction [187] that runs on linear time but requires additional arrays to work. The present variant is slightly slower but significantly simpler than

McCreight's algorithm. It can be viewed as a first step towards understanding the complete algorithm. Moreover, for many types of words, the coefficient *depth*(T) is logarithmic.

Ukkonen's algorithm [234] can be modified in a similar way, which gives another simple but not naive construction of Suffix trees.

56   Comparing Suffixes of a Fibonacci Word

The structure of Fibonacci words like that of Thue–Morse words, is an example of a situation in which some algorithms can be optimised to run in logarithmic time with respect to the length of words. The problem is concerned with a fast lexicographic comparison between two suffixes of a finite Fibonacci word, which shows such a phenomenon.

We deal with a slightly shortened version of Fibonacci words to simplify arguments. Let g_n be the nth Fibonacci word fib_n with the last two letters deleted, that is, $g_n = fib_n\{a,b\}^{-2}$, for $n \geq 2$. Let also $suf(k,n)$ be the kth suffix $g_n[k \mathbin{..} |g_n| - 1]$ of g_n. For example, $g_2 = a$, $g_3 = aba$, $g_4 = abaaba$, $g_5 = abaababaaba$ and $suf(3,5) = ababaaba$.

The comparison between suffixes of g_n is efficiently reduced to the comparison of their compact representation of logarithmic length implied by their logarithmic-size decomposition (property below). Factors of the decomposition are the reverse $R_n = fib_n^R$ of Fibonacci words. The first factors are $R_0 = a$, $R_1 = ba$, $R_2 = aba$ and $R_3 = baaba$. Observe that $R_{n+2} = R_{n+1}R_n$ and R_n starts with the letter a if and only if n is even.

Property. For $n > 2$, $suf(k,n)$ uniquely factorises as $R_{i_0} R_{i_1} \dots R_{i_m}$, where $i_0 \in \{0,1\}$ and $i_t \in \{i_{t-1} + 1, i_{t-1} + 2\}$ for $t = 1, \dots, m$.

Related to the factorisation let $\mathcal{R}_n(k) = (i_0, i_1, \dots, i_m)$. For example, $suf(3,5) = ababaaba = R_0 \cdot R_1 \cdot R_3 = a \cdot ba \cdot baaba$ and $\mathcal{R}_5(3) = (0,1,3)$.

Question. (A) Show how to compare any two suffixes of $g_n = fib_n\{a,b\}^{-2}$ in time $O((\log |fib_n|)^2)$.

(B) Improve the running time to $O(\log |fib_n|)$.

[**Hint:** For (A) use the algorithm of Problem 6.]

Solution

Associated with $\mathcal{R}_n(k) = (i_0, i_1, \ldots, i_m)$ let

$$\Psi_n(k) = first(R_{i_0})first(R_{i_1}) \ldots first(R_{i_m}),$$

where $first(w)$ denotes the first letter of w. It can be verified that

Observation. $suf(p,n) < suf(q,n) \iff \Psi_n(p) < \Psi_n(q)$.

Example. For $g_5 = $ abaababaaba, we have $suf(3,5) = $ a $\cdot$ ba $\cdot$ baaba $= R_0 R_1 R_3$ and $suf(5,5) = $ a $\cdot$ ba $\cdot$ aba $= R_0 R_1 R_2$. Then $\Psi_5(3) = $ abb and $\Psi_5(5) = $ aba. Therefore $suf(5,5) < suf(3,5)$, since aba $<$ abb.

The observation reduces the problem to the fast computation of the decomposition in the above property and of the function $\mathcal{R}$.

Point (A). $\mathcal{R}_n(k)$ can be computed as follows, scanning the suffix $suf(n,k)$ from left to right. If $g_n[k] = $ a we know that $i_0 = 0$; otherwise $i_0 = 1$. Then in each iteration $t > 0$ the current position on g_n is increased by the length $F_{i_{t-1}+2} = |R_{i_{t-1}}|$ to point to the next letter of g_n. Depending on this letter we know whether $i_t = i_{t-1} + 1$ or $i_t = i_{t-1} + 2$. In this way $\mathcal{R}_n(k) = (i_0, i_1, \ldots, i_m)$ is computed and the process has a logarithmic number of iterations.

Accessing each letter in g_n is done in time $O(\log |fib_n|)$ using the algorithm of Problem 6.

Overall this gives an algorithm running in time $O((\log |fib_n|)^2)$ and solves (A).

Point (B). It does not come as a surprise that Fibonacci words are closely related to the Fibonacci numeration system (see Problem 6). Here we show they are related to a dual version of this system in the context of lexicographic sorting.

Lazy Fibonacci numeration system. Let $LazyFib(k)$ be the lazy Fibonacci representation of the natural number k, starting with least significant digits. In this system a natural number N is represented in a unique way as the sequence of bits $(b_0, b_1, b_2, \ldots)$ for which $N = \sum b_i F_{i+2}$, where F_js are consecutive Fibonacci numbers, and in which no two consecutive zeros appear. This corresponds to the condition $i_{t+1} \in \{i_t + 1, i_t + 2\}$ stated in the factorisation property.

For example, $LazyFib(9) = (1\ 0\ 1\ 1)$ and $LazyFib(23) = (0\ 1\ 1\ 1\ 0\ 1)$, since $9 = F_2 + F_4 + F_5$ and $23 = F_3 + F_4 + F_5 + F_7$.

Fast computation of the decomposition. Let $(b_0, b_1, b_2, \ldots)$ be the representation of the length $|suf(k,n)|$ in the lazy Fibonacci system. Then $\mathcal{R}_n(k) = (i_0, i_1, \ldots, i_m)$, where i_js are the positions of bit 1 in $(b_0, b_1, b_2, \ldots)$.

Since the lazy Fibonacci representation can be computed in logarithmic time with respect to the length of fib_n, this solves (B).

Notes

The proof of the factorisation property can be found in [213, 238].

If we want to compare two suffixes of length larger than 2 of standard (not shortened) Fibonacci words fib_n then the same function Ψ can be used if n is odd. But if n is even we have to replace $\Psi(k)$ by $\Psi(k) \cdot$ b. It is also known that for even n the table SA of the Suffix array of Fibonacci words contains an arithmetic progression (modulo the length of the array) and this gives an alternative comparison test for the case of an even n.

The lazy Fibonacci system allows computation in logarithmic time of the rank of the kth suffix (its position in SA) of a Fibonacci word.

57   Avoidability of Binary Words

Some patterns occur in all long enough words. They are said to be unavoidable. The notion obviously depends on the alphabet size and in the problem we consider binary patterns.

A word w is said to avoid a set X of words if no factor of w belongs to X. The set X is said to be avoidable if there is an infinite word avoiding it, or equivalently on a finite alphabet, if there are infinitely many words avoiding it. The goal is to test if a set of words drawn from the binary alphabet $B = \{a, b\}$ is avoidable.

For example, $\{aa, abab, bb\}$ cannot be avoided by a word of length at least 5. On the contrary, $\{aa, bb\}$ is avoided by the infinite word $(ab)^\infty$.

To design the test we define two reductions on a set $X \subseteq B^+$.

reduce1 (remove super-word): If $x, y \in X$ and x is a factor of y remove y from X.

reduce2 (chop last letter): If x is a suffix of $y \neq \varepsilon$ and $x\bar{a}, ya \in X$ substitute y for ya in X (the bar morphism exchanges a and b).

AVOIDABLE(X non-empty set of binary words)

1   **while** reduce1 or reduce2 are applicable to X **do**

2       $X \leftarrow$ reduce1(X) or reduce2(X)

3   **if** $X \neq \{a, b\}$ **return** TRUE **else return** FALSE

Example. Set $X = \{aaa, aba, bb\}$ is unavoidable because the sequence of reductions yields B (changed words are underlined): $\{aaa, \underline{aba}, bb\} \rightarrow \{\underline{aaa}, ab, bb\} \rightarrow \{aa, \underline{ab}, bb\} \rightarrow \{\underline{aa}, a, bb\} \rightarrow \{a, \underline{bb}\} \rightarrow$ B.

Question. Show that a set X of binary words is avoidable if and only if AVOIDABLE(X) = TRUE.

Question. Show that a set $X \subseteq B^{\leq n}$ is avoidable if and only if it is avoided by a word of length larger than $2^{n-1} + n - 2$ and that the bound is optimal.

Solution

Correctness of AVOIDABLE. It is a consequence of the following two properties.

Property 1. If $Y =$ reduce1(X) or $Y =$ reduce2(X), X is avoidable if and only if Y is avoidable.

Proof It is clear that a word that avoids Y also avoids X. To prove the converse, let w be an infinite word avoiding X. We show that w also avoids Y. This is obvious if $Y =$ reduce1(X). If $Y =$ reduce2(X), there are two words $x\bar{a}, ya \in X$, x a suffix of y and $Y = X \setminus \{ya\} \cup \{y\}$.

It is then enough to show that w avoids y. If not, yb is a factor of w. Letter b cannot be a because w avoids ya. But it cannot be $\bar{a}$ either because w avoids $x\bar{a}$ suffix of $y\bar{a}$. Then y is not a factor of w. ∎

Property 2. If no reduction is applicable to X and $X \neq$ B, X is avoidable.

Proof To show the conclusion we construct incrementally an infinite word w avoiding X. Let v be a finite word avoiding X (v can be just a letter because $X \neq$ B). We claim that v can be extended by a single letter to va that also avoids X. Indeed, if it cannot, there are two suffixes x and y of v for which

$x\bar{a} \in X$ and $ya \in X$. Since one of the words is a suffix of the other, reduction2 applies to X, in contradiction of the hypothesis. Hence v can be extended eventually to an infinite word w, avoiding X.   ∎

Length bound on avoiding words. The next property is used to answer the second question.

Property 3. $X \subseteq \mathsf{B}^{\leq n}$ is avoidable if and only if it is avoided by a word having a border in B^{n-1}.

In fact, if X is avoidable, an infinite word avoiding it has a factor satisfying the condition. Conversely, let $w = uv = v'u$, avoiding X with $u \in \mathsf{B}^{n-1}$. Since $uv^i = v'uv^{i-1} = \cdots = v'^i u$, $i > 0$, it is clear that any length-n factor of uv^i is a factor of w. Therefore uv^∞ also avoids X.

To answer the second question, just the converse of the if-and-only-if needs to be proved. If a word of length larger than $2^{n-1} + n - 2$ avoids X it contains at least two occurrences of some word in B^{n-1} and thus a factor as in property 3 that avoids X. Therefore X is avoidable.

The optimality of the bound relies on de Bruijn (binary) words of order $n - 1$. Such a word w contains exactly one occurrence of each word in B^{n-1} and has length $2^{n-1} + n - 2$. The word avoids the set X of length-n words that are not factors of it. This achieves the proof, since X is unavoidable.

Notes

Algorithm AVOIDABLE is certainly not the most efficient algorithm to test set avoidability in the binary case but it is probably the simplest one. References on the subject may be found in [175]. The solution of the second question is from [90].

58   Avoiding a Set of Words

For a finite set F of words on a finite alphabet A, $F \subseteq A^*$, let $L(F) \subseteq A^*$ be the language of words that avoids F; that is, no word in F appears in words of $L(F)$. The aim is to build an automaton accepting $L(F)$.

Note that if w avoids u it also avoids any word u is a factor of. Thus we can consider that F is an anti-factorial (factor code) language: no word in F is a proper factor of another word in F. On the contrary, $F(L)$ is a factorial language: any factor of a word in $F(L)$ is in $F(L)$.

Examples. For $F_0 = \{aa, bb\} \subseteq \{a, b\}^*$ we get $L(F_0) = (ab)^* \cup (ba)^*$. For $F_1 = \{aaa, bbab, bbb\} \subseteq \{a, b, c\}^*$ we have $(ab)^* \subseteq L(F_1)$ as well as $(bbaa)^* \subseteq L(F_1)$ and $c^* \subseteq L(F_1)$.

> **Question.** Show that $L(F)$ is recognised by a finite automaton and design an algorithm to build, from the trie of F, a deterministic automaton that accepts it.

[**Hint:** Use the Aho–Corasick technique.]

The set F is said to be unavoidable if no infinite word avoids it (see Problem 57). For example, the set F_1 is avoidable on the alphabet $\{a, b\}$ because it is avoided by the infinite word $(ab)^\infty$.

> **Question.** Show how to test if the set F is unavoidable.

Solution

Assume F is non-empty and anti-factorial (in particular it does not contain the empty word) and consider the automaton accepting $A^* F A^*$, words having a factor in F. States of the automaton are (or can be identified with) the prefixes of words in F. Indeed, any such prefix can be extended to produce a word of F and these latter words form sink states. Below left is an automaton accepting $\{a, b\}^* F_1 \{a, b\}^*$, in which doubly circled nodes correspond to words with a factor in F_1.

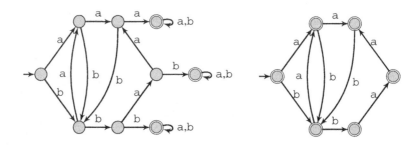

The language $L(F) = A^* \setminus A^* F A^*$, the complement of $A^* F A^*$, is accepted by the automaton accepting $A^* F A^*$ after exchanging the role of terminal and non-terminal nodes. This shows $L(F)$ is accepted by a finite automaton. Above right is an automaton accepting $L(F_1)$.

Algorithm AVOIDING follows closely the construction of the dictionary matching automaton of F and eventually reverses the status of states and deletes useless states.

AVOIDING(trie of F, alphabet A)

```
 1   q_0 ← initial state (root) of the trie
 2   Q ← ∅        ▷ empty queue
 3   for each letter a ∈ A do
 4       if goto(q_0, a) undefined then
 5           add arc (q_0, a, q_0)
 6       else append (goto(q_0, a), q_0) to Q
 7   while Q not empty do
 8       remove (p, r) from Q
 9       if r terminal then
10           set p a terminal state
11       for each letter a ∈ A do
12           s ← goto(r, a)
13           if goto(p, a) undefined then
14               add arc (p, a, s)
15           else append (goto(p, a), s) to Q
16   remove all terminal states and their associated arcs
17   set all remaining states as terminal states
18   return transformed automaton
```

The algorithm runs in time $O(|A| \sum \{|w| : w \in F\})$ with an appropriate implementation of the goto function. But instead of setting all possible arcs out of each state, a failure link can be created from state p to state r when (p, r) is in the queue. This is the usual technique to implement this type of automaton, reducing its size to $O(\sum \{|w| : w \in F\})$.

To test if F is unavoidable, it remains to check if the graph formed by nodes of the output automaton contains a cycle. This can be done in linear time with a topological sorting algorithm. The above right automaton contains a cycle, which shows again that F_1 is unavoidable.

Notes

The construction of a dictionary-matching automaton, also called an Aho–Corasick automaton is by Aho and Corasick [3] and described in most textbooks on text algorithms. The automaton is usually implemented with a notion of failure links to save space.

---

59   Minimal Unique Factors

The topic of this problem has the same flavour as the notion of minimal absent words. It can also be used to identify, to filter or to distinguish files. But the corresponding algorithms and the underlying combinatorial properties are simpler.

A ***minimal unique factor*** of a word x is a factor that occurs once in x and whose proper factors are repeats, that is, have at least two occurrences in x. A minimal unique factor $x[i \mathinner{.\,.} j]$ is stored in the table *MinUniq* by setting $MinUniq[j] = i$.

Example. Minimal unique factors of $x = $ abaabba are aba $= x[0 \mathinner{.\,.} 2]$, aa $= x[2 \mathinner{.\,.} 3]$ and bb $= x[4 \mathinner{.\,.} 5]$, and $MinUniq[2] = 0$, $MinUniq[3] = 2$ and $MinUniq[5] = 4$ (other values are set to -1).

$$
\begin{array}{c c c c c c c c}
 & 0 & 1 & 2 & 3 & 4 & 5 & 6 \\
x & \text{a} & \text{b} & \text{a} & \text{a} & \text{b} & \text{b} & \text{a}
\end{array}
$$

Algorithm MinUnique applies to a singleton-free word (each letter appear at least twice in it).

MinUnique(non-empty singleton-free word x)

1    $(SA, LCP) \leftarrow$ Suffix array of x
2   **for** $i \leftarrow 0$ **to** $|x|$ **do**
3        $MinUniq[i] \leftarrow -1$
4   **for** $r \leftarrow 0$ **to** $|x| - 1$ **do**
5        $\ell \leftarrow \max\{LCP[r], LCP[r + 1]\}$
6        $MinUniq[SA[r] + \ell] \leftarrow \max\{MinUniq[SA[r] + \ell], SA[r]\}$
7   **return** $MinUniq[0 \mathinner{.\,.} |x| - 1]$

> **Question.** Show that the algorithm MINUNIQUE computes the table *MinUniq* associated with its singleton-free input word x.

There is a duality between minimal unique factors and maximal occurrences of repeats in the word x.

> **Question.** Show that a minimal unique factor induces two maximal occurrences of repeats in a singleton-free word.

> **Question.** How many minimal unique factors are there in a de Bruijn word of order k?

Solution

Sketch of the proof of correctness. The notion of minimal unique factor of a word is close to the notion of identifier of a position on the word. The identifier of a position i on $x\#$ (# is an end-marker) is the shortest prefix of $x\#[i \mathbin{..} |x|]$ that occurs exactly once in $x\#$. Then if the factor ua with letter a is the identifier of i, u occurs at least twice in x, corresponding to length ℓ computed at line 5 in MINUNIQUE.

The algorithm implicitly uses identifiers because a minimal unique factor is the shortest identifier among all those ending at a given position, say j. This is done at line 6, where $j = SA[r] + \ell$ and *MinUniq*[j] is updated accordingly.

The computation of minimal unique factors of abaabba is illustrated below. The value *MinUniq*[7] $= 6$ is discarded when there is no end-marker. When $r = 3$, *MinUniq*[5] is set to 3, which is eventually updated to 4 when $r = 6$. The three non-negative values, 0, 2 and 4, correspond to factors given before.

r	0	1	2	3	4	5	6	7
$SA[r]$	6	2	0	3	5	1	4	
$LCP[r]$	0	1	1	2	0	2	1	0
j	0	1	2	3	4	5	6	7
MinUniq[j]	-1	-1	-1	-1	-1	-1	-1	-1
			0	2		3		6
						4		

Maximal repeats. A minimal unique factor in the singleton-free word x is of the form aub, for a word u and letters a, b, because it cannot be reduced to a single letter. Then au and ub both occur at least twice in x, that is, are repeats. The occurrence of au (determined by the occurrence of aub) can be extended to the left to a maximal occurrence of a repeat. Similarly, the occurrence of ub can be extended to the right to a maximal occurrence of a repeat. This answers the second question.

De Bruijn words. In a de Bruijn word of order k on the alphabet A, each word of length k appears exactly once. Shorter words are repeats. Then there are exactly $|A|^k$ minimal unique factors in the de Bruijn word whose length is $|A|^k + k - 1$.

Notes
The elements in this problem are by Ilie and Smyth [148]. The computation of shortest unique factors is treated in [233]. The computation of minimal unique factors in a sliding window is discussed in [189].

The computation of identifiers is a straight application of Suffix trees (see [98, chapter 5]). Minimal unique factors can be left-extended to produce all identifiers of the word positions.

In genomics, a minimal unique factor, called a marker, has a known location on a chromosome and is used to identify individuals or species.

---

60 Minimal Absent Words

Words that do not occur in files provide a useful technique to discard or discriminate files. They act like the set of factors of a file but admit a more compact trie representation as factor codes.

A word w, $|w| > 1$, is said to be absent or forbidden in a word x if it does not occur in x. It is said to be minimal with this property if in addition both $w[0 .. |w| - 2]$ and $w[1 .. |w| - 1]$ do occur in x.

Minimal absent words of ababbba are aa, abba, baba, bbab and bbbb. In their trie below, they are each associated with a leaf (double-circled) because no minimal absent word is a factor of another one.

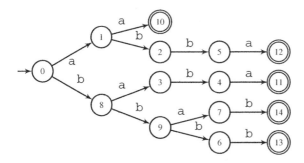

A natural method to compute the minimal words absent in x is to start with its Factor automaton $\mathcal{F}(x)$, smallest deterministic automaton accepting all its factors. Each factor is spelt out along a path starting from the initial state and all states are terminal. Below is the Factor automaton of abababba with its failure links (dotted edges).

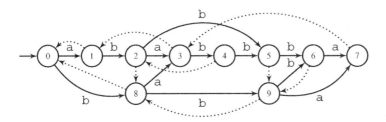

Question. Design a linear-time algorithm to compute the trie of minimal absent words of a word x from its Factor automaton $\mathcal{F}(x)$.

[**Hint:** Use failure links of the automaton.]

Question. Design a linear-time algorithm to recover the Factor automaton of a word x from the trie of its minimal absent words.

[**Hint:** Use the Aho–Corasick technique.]

Solution

Computing minimal absent words. The algorithm below works on the Factor automaton $\mathcal{F}(x)$ of its input. The automaton on the alphabet A comprises a set of states Q with initial state i and the transition function goto, represented by arcs on the above picture. The algorithm detects absent words by considering undefined arcs.

The algorithm traverses the automaton in a width-first way to ensure the minimality of an absent words. It checks at line 3 if some proper suffix of a candidate is not already absent using the failure link of the automaton (a by-product of efficient algorithms that build the automaton). The link refers to the longest suffix of the word associated with another state. The algorithm transform the automaton by adding new states and computing the new transition function $goto'$.

MINIMALABSENTWORDS(x non-empty word)

1 $(Q, A, i, Q, goto) \leftarrow \mathcal{F}(x)$ Factor automaton of x
   and its failure function *fail*

2 **for** each $p \in Q$ in width-first traversal from i and each $a \in A$ **do**

3   **if** $goto(p, a)$ undefined and $goto(fail(p), a)$ defined **then**

4          $goto'(p, a) \leftarrow$ new final state

5   **elseif** $goto(p, a) = q$ and q not already reached **then**

6          $goto'(p, a) \leftarrow q$

7 **return** $(Q \cup \{\text{new final states}\}, A, i, \{\text{new final states}\}, goto')$

Applied to the above example ababbba, the algorithm produces the trie of minimal absent words, drawn differently below to show the similarity with the automaton structure.

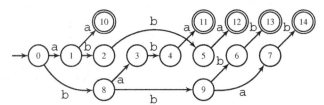

Running times. The construction of the Factor automaton of a word is known to be achievable in linear time, mostly due to the fact that the size of the structure is linear according to the length of the word independently of the alphabet size. The rest of instructions in the algorithm clearly takes $O(|A| \times |x|)$ time if the goto function and the failure links are implemented in arrays.

Computing a Factor automaton. From the trie $(Q, A, i, T', goto')$ of minimal absent words of a single word x, the algorithm below builds its Factor automaton. The construction relies on the failure link *fail* on states of the trie. The process is similar to the construction of a dictionary-matching machine that builds the automaton accepting all words in which appear a word from a finite set.

FACTORAUTOMATON($(Q, A, i, T', goto')$ trie of minimal absent words)

1   **for** each $a \in A$ **do**
2   **if** $goto'(i,a)$ defined and not in T' **then**
3           $goto(i,a) \leftarrow goto'(i,a)$
4           $fail(goto(i,a)) \leftarrow i$
5   **for** each $p \in Q \setminus \{i\}$ in width-first traversal and each $a \in A$ **do**
6   **if** $goto'(p,a)$ defined **then**
7           $goto(p,a) \leftarrow goto'(p,a)$
8           $fail(goto(p,a)) \leftarrow goto(fail(p),a)$
9   **elseif** p not in T' **then**
10          $goto(p,a) \leftarrow goto(fail(p),a)$
11 **return** $(Q \setminus T', A, i, Q \setminus T', goto)$

The next picture displays the Factor automaton of ababbba, drawn differently to show the relation with the first picture of the trie.

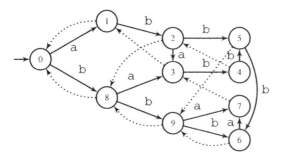

Notes

The notion of a minimal absent or forbidden word was introduced by Béal et al. in [28]. The design and analysis of the present algorithms are in [92]. An extension to regular languages appears in [30].

The linear-time construction of a Factor automaton appears in [67]. It can be obtained by minimising the DAWG introduced by Blumer et al. (see [38]) or the Suffix automaton (see [74, 96, 98]).

The second algorithm is similar to the construction of a pattern-matching machine by Aho and Corasick [3]. Applied to the trie of minimal absent words of several words, the method does not always produce a (minimal) Factor automaton.

Antidictionaries, sets of absent words, are used in the data compression method in [93]; see more in [198–200] and references therein. Computation in a sliding window is discussed in [75, 189].

Absent words are also used in bioinformatics to detect avoided patterns in genomic sequences or to help build phylogenies; see, for example, [51, 224].

61   Greedy Superstring

A superstring of a set of words can be used to store the set in a compact way. Formally, a common superstring of a set X of words is a word z in which all elements of X occur as factors, that is, $X \subseteq Fact(z)$. The shortest common superstring of X is denoted by SCS(X).

The greedy paradigm leads to a simple algorithm that produces a fairly good approximation of SCS(X). The goal of the problem is to show an efficient implementation of the method.

For two words u and v, $Overlap(u, v)$ is the longest suffix of u that is a prefix of v. If $w = Overlap(u, v)$, $u = u'w$ and $v = wv'$, $u \otimes v$ is defined as the word $u'wv'$. Note that SCS(u, v) is either $u \otimes v$ or $v \otimes u$. Also note that a word in X factor of another word in X can be discarded without changing SCS(X). Then X is supposed to be factor free.

GREEDYSCS(X non-empty factor-free set of words)
1   **if** $|X| = 1$ **then**
2   **return** $x \in X$
3   **else** let $x, y \in X, x \neq y$, with $|Overlap(x, y)|$ maximal
4   **return** GREEDYSCS$(X \setminus \{x, y\} \cup \{x \otimes y\})$

Question. For a set X of words drawn from the alphabet $\{1, 2, \ldots, n\}$ show how to implement the algorithm so that GREEDYSCS(X) runs in time $O(\Sigma\{|x| : x \in X\})$.

Example. The superstring `fbdiachbgegeakhiacbd` is produced by
GREEDYSCS from the set {`egeakh`, `fbdiac`, `hbgege`, `iacbd`, `bdiach`}.

```
                              i a c b d
                    e g e a k h
                  h b g e g e
          b d i a c h
          f b d i a c
          f b d i a c h b g e g e a k h i a c b d
```

Solution

The overlap between two words u and v is the border of the word $v\#u$, where
$\#$ does not occur in the words. Hence, methods for computing borders in linear
time (e.g. in Problem 19) lead to a direct implementation running in time
$O(n \cdot |X|)$, where $n = \Sigma\{|x| : x \in X\}$. We show how to design a $O(n)$-time
implementation.

If words in the above example are denoted by x_1, x_2, x_3, x_4 and x_5 the
superstring produced by the algorithm is $x_2 \otimes x_5 \otimes x_3 \otimes x_1 \otimes x_4$. It is identified
by the corresponding permutation $(2, 5, 3, 1, 4)$ of word indices.

Let us first design an iterative version of the algorithm that produces the
permutation of word indices associated with the sought superstring. It is
implemented as a doubly linked list whose elements are linked by the tables
prev and *next*, and that starts at some index. During the computation, for a
(partial) list starting with index p and ending with q we have $head[q] = p$ and
$tail[p] = q$.

Here is the scheme of an iterative version of the algorithm.

ITERGREEDY($\{x_1, x_2, \ldots, x_m\}$ non-empty factor-free set of words)

```
1   for i ← 1 to m do
2       (prev[i], next[i]) ← (i, i)
3       (head[i], tail[i]) ← (i, i)
4   for m − 1 times do
5       let i, j, next[i] = i, prev[j] = j, head[i] ≠ j
            with |Overlap(x_i, x_j)| maximal
6       (next[i], prev[j]) ← (j, i)
7       head[tail[j]] ← head[i]
8       tail[head[i]] ← tail[j]
9   let i with prev[i] = i
10  return (i, next)
```

Condition $next[i] = i$ on line 5 ensures that i is the tail of its list, and similarly condition $prev[j] = j$ that j is the head of its list. Condition $head[i] \neq j$ attests that i and j are on different lists, which instructions at line 6 concatenate. The next instructions update heads and tails.

From the output $(i, next)$, the permutation of indices associated with the superstring of $\{x_1, x_2, \ldots, x_m\}$ is i, $next[i]$, $next[next[i]]$, etc.

Algorithm ITERGREEDY is made efficient by introducing several useful data structures *Last* and *First*: for each $u \in Pref(\{x_1, \ldots, x_m\})$

- *Last(u)* is the list of indices of words in $\{x_1, \ldots, x_m\}$ having u as a suffix,
- *First(u)* is the list of indices of words in $\{x_1, \ldots, x_m\}$ having u as a prefix.

In addition, for each index of a word we keep all its locations in the lists to be able to delete it from the lists. Let $n = \Sigma_{i=1}^{m} |x_i|$.

Observation. The total length of all lists is $O(n)$. .
Indeed, index i is on the list *First(u)*, for each proper prefix u of w_i. Hence it is on $|w_i|$ lists, which sums up to $O(n)$ globally. The same holds for *Last*.

Algorithm ITERGREEDY rewrites as Algorithm EFFIGREEDY that processes all potential overlaps u in order of decreasing length, and merges words having such overlaps if they are eligible for merge. Testing eligibility is done as in Algorithm ITERGREEDY.

EFFIGREEDY($\{x_1, x_2, \ldots, x_m\}$ non-empty factor-free set of words)

```
1   for i ← 1 to m do
2       (head[i], tail[i]) ← (i, i)
3   for each u ∈ Pref({x₁, …, xₘ}) in decreasing length order do
4       for each i ∈ Last(u) do
5           let j be the first element of First(u) with j ≠ head[i]
6           ▷ it is the first or second element, or NIL
7           if j ≠ NIL then   ▷ u is an overlap of xᵢ and xⱼ
8               remove j from all lists First
9               remove i from all lists Last
10              next[i] ← j
11              head[tail[j]] ← head[i]
12              tail[head[i]] ← tail[j]
13  let i word index for which i ≠ next[j] for all j = 1, …, m
14  return (i, next)
```

Algorithm EFFIGREEDY runs in time $O(n)$ if all lists are preprocessed, since their total size is $O(n)$.

The preprocessing of *Pref* and of other lists is done with the trie of the set $\{x_1, x_2, \ldots, x_m\}$ and with a Suffix tree. The only tricky part is the computation of lists *Last(u)*. To do it, let $\mathcal{T}'$ be the Suffix tree of $x_1\#_1 x_2\#_2 \ldots x_m\#_m$, where $\#_i$ are new distinct symbols. Then for each word x_i, $\mathcal{T}'$ is traversed symbol by symbol along the path labelled by x_i and, for each prefix u of x_i, if the corresponding node in $\mathcal{T}'$ has k outgoing edges whose labels start with $\#_{i_1}, \ldots, \#_{i_k}$ respectively then indices $i_1, \ldots, i_k$ are inserted into *Last(u)*. This results in a $O(n)$ preprocessing time if the alphabet is linearly sortable.

Notes

Computing a shortest common superstring is a problem known to be NP-complete. Our version of Algorithm GREEDYSCS derives from the algorithm by Tarhio and Ukkonen in [230].

One of the most interesting conjectures on the subject is whether GREEDYSCS produces a 2-approximation of a shortest common superstring of the input. This is true for words of length 3 and is quite possibly always true.

62   Shortest Common Superstring of Short Words

A common superstring of a set X of words is a word in which all elements of X occur as factors. Computing a shortest common superstring (SCS) is an NP-complete problem but there are simple cases that can be solved efficiently, like the special case discussed in the problem.

For example, 1 2 6 3 9 2 3 7 5 7 is a shortest common superstring for the set of seven words $\{1\,2, 2\,3, 2\,6, 5\,7, 6\,3, 7\,5, 9\,2\}$.

> **Question.** Show how to compute in linear time the length of a shortest common superstring of a set X of words of length 2 over an integer alphabet.

[**Hint:** Transform the question into a problem on graphs.]

Solution

The problem translates into a question on (directed) graphs as follows. From the set X we consider the graph G whose vertices are letters (integers) and whose edges correspond to words in X. The picture corresponds to the above example.

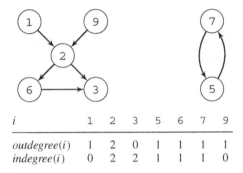

i	1	2	3	5	6	7	9
$outdegree(i)$	1	2	0	1	1	1	1
$indegree(i)$	0	2	2	1	1	1	0

A directed graph is said to be weakly connected if every two nodes are connected by an undirected path, after discarding edge orientations. The observation sketches the road map to build a shortest superstring.

Observation. Let G be a weakly connected graph associated to a set of length-2 words and let Z be the smallest set of (directed) edges to be added to G so that it contains an Eulerian cycle. Then the length of a shortest superstring for X is $|X| + 1$ if Z is empty and $|X| + |Z|$ otherwise.

The problem switches to the question of building an appropriate set Z to get an Eulerian graph. Recall that a directed graph is Eulerian if it is weakly connected and each vertex v is balanced, that is, $indegree(v) = outdegree(v)$. Each weakly connected component of the graph G is processed separately. So to start we can assume that G itself is weakly connected.

To add a minimum number of directed edges to make each vertex v balanced we proceed as follows. If $D(v) = outdegree(v) - indegree(v) > 0$, $D(v)$ incoming edges are added to v; if $D(v) < 0$, $D(v)$ outgoing edges are added from v. The point is that when adding an edge it is always from a vertex that needs an outgoing edge to a vertex that requires an incoming edge. Since each edge contribute to both an incoming edge and an outgoing edge, we cannot be left with only one vertex v with $D(v) \neq 0$ and the process continues until all vertices are balanced. This implies also that the total number of added edges is exactly $|Z| = \frac{1}{2} \sum_v |D(v)|$.

Computing Z is done easily using the tables *outdegree* and *indegree* and runs in linear time. Worst cases are when no two words of X overlap. When the transformed graph has an Eulerian cycle, deleting one of the added edges

$v \to w$ provides an Eulerian path from w to v. If the original graph is already Eulerian, a path starting from any vertex and ending to it gives a solution. Paths corresponds to shortest superstrings.

Finally, if the graph G is not weakly connected, each weakly connected component is treated as above and the resulting words are concatenated to get a shortest superstring.

On the above example, only two edges, $3 \to 1$ and $3 \to 9$, are added to the left component, giving the new tables:

i	1	2	3	5	6	7	9
$outdegree(i)$	1	2	2	1	1	1	1
$indegree(i)$	1	2	2	1	1	1	1

Removing the first added edge give the word 1 2 6 3 9 2 3 for the first component and 7 5 7 for the second component. The resulting superstring is 1 2 6 3 9 2 3 7 5 7.

Notes

The method presented in the problem is by Gallant et al. [126]. If the input set consists of words of length 3 the problem becomes NP-complete.

---

63   Counting Factors by Length

Let $fact_x[\ell]$ denote the number of (distinct) factors of length ℓ occurring in a word x.

> **Question.** Show how to compute in linear time all numbers $fact_x[\ell]$, $\ell = 1, \dots, |x|$, related to a word x, assuming a constant-size alphabet.

[**Hint:** Exploit the Suffix tree of the word.]

Solution

Let $T = \mathcal{ST}(x)$ be the Suffix tree of x. Recall its internal nodes are factors of x having at least two occurrences in x. They are followed either by at least two different letters or possibly by just one letter when one occurrence is a suffix occurrence.

With a non-root node v of T whose parent is node u is associated the interval of lengths

$$I_v = [|u| + 1 .. |v|].$$

Observation. $fact_x[\ell]$ is the number of intervals I_v containing the number ℓ.

Indeed, each non-root node v of the Suffix tree corresponds to a set of factors sharing the same set of occurrences. Their lengths are distinct and form the interval I_v. Hence the total number of (distinct) factors of length ℓ is the number of all intervals I_v containing ℓ.

The observation reduces the problem to an *interval covering problem*: given a family $\mathcal{I}(x)$ of subintervals of $[1 .. |x|]$ compute the number of intervals containing ℓ, for each ℓ, $1 \le \ell \le |x|$.

NumbersOfFactors($\mathcal{I}(x)$ for a non-empty word x)

```
1   Count[1 .. |x| + 1] ← [0, 0, ..., 0]
2   for each [i .. j] ∈ I(x) do
3       Count[i] ← Count[i] + 1
4       Count[j + 1] ← Count[j + 1] − 1
5   prefix_sum ← 0
6   for ℓ ← 1 to n do
7       prefix_sum ← prefix_sum + Count[ℓ]
8       fact_x[ℓ] ← prefix_sum
9   return fact_x
```

Algorithm NumbersOfFactors computes $fact_x$ from the family $\mathcal{I}(x)$ of intervals defined from the Suffix tree of x. To do it, an auxiliary array $Count[1 .. n + 1]$ that initially contains null values is used.

Example. Let $x =$ abaababaaba. The intervals in $\mathcal{I}(x)$ are labels of nodes in the picture below showing the Suffix tree of x. The algorithm computes the table $Count = [2, 1, 1, 1, 0, 0, 0, -1, -1, -1, -1]$ (discarding the value at position $|x| + 1$) and outputs the sequence of prefix sums of the table $Count$:

$$fact_x = [2, 3, 4, 5, 5, 5, 5, 4, 3, 2, 1].$$

For instance, the value $fact_x[3] = 4$ corresponds to the four factors of length 3 occurring in x: aab, aba, baa and bab.

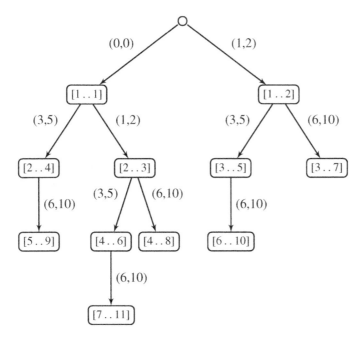

It is clear Algorithm NUMBERSOFFACTORS runs in linear time mainly because the number of nodes in the Suffix tree of x is $O(|x|)$.

Notes

An alternative algorithm can be achieved using the Factor automaton of x. In the automaton each non-initial state v is labelled by the interval $[s(v) .. l(v)]$, where $s(v)$ and $l(v)$ are respectively the length of the shortest and of the longest path from the root to v.

64   Counting Factors Covering a Position

A factor of a word x covers a position k on x if it has an occurrence $x[i \mathinner{.\,.} j]$ that satisfies $i \leq k \leq j$.

Let $\mathcal{C}(x,k)$ denote the number of (distinct) factors of x covering the position k and let $\mathcal{N}(x,k)$ denote the number of factors having an occurrence that does not cover k.

Question. Show how to compute in linear time $\mathcal{C}(x,k)$ and $\mathcal{N}(x,k)$ for a given position k on x, assuming a constant-size alphabet.

Solution
Nodes of the Suffix tree $\mathcal{ST}(w)$ of a word w are factors of w. For an edge (u,v) of the tree let $weight(v) = |v| - |u|$, the length of its label.

Computing $\mathcal{N}(x,k)$. Let # be a letter that does not occur in x and let x' be the word obtained from x by changing its letter $x[k]$ to #. Then, using the Suffix tree $\mathcal{ST}(x')$ the number N of distinct factors of x' is computed as the sum of weights of all non-root nodes.

Observation. $\mathcal{N}(x,k) = N - M$, where M is the number of (distinct) factors of x' containing the letter #.

This leads to an evaluation of $\mathcal{N}(x,k)$ since $M = (k+1) \times (n-k)$.

Computing $\mathcal{C}(x,k)$. Assume x ends with special end-marker and each leaf of $\mathcal{ST}(x)$ is labelled with the starting position of the corresponding suffix of x. For each node v let $LeftLeaves(v,k)$ be the set of leaves i in the subtree rooted at v satisfying both $i \leq k$ and $k - i < |v|$.

Let V be the set of nodes v with a non-empty set $LeftLeaves(v,k)$. In other words, V is the set of nodes corresponding to factors covering the position k. For $v \in V$ let $Dist(v,k) = \min\{k - i : i \in LeftLeaves(v,k)\}$.

Observation. $\mathcal{C}(x,k) = \sum_{v \in V} \min\{|v| - Dist(v,k), weight(v)\}$.

Computing $\mathcal{C}(x,k)$ reduces to the computation of all $Dist(v,k)$, which is done during a bottom-up traversal of the Suffix tree.

On constant-size alphabets all computations run in linear time.

Notes
Interesting versions of the problem are when factors are to cover all positions of a set of positions. An attractor, a related notion introduced by Prezza [202] (see also [157, 183]), is a set K of positions on x whose factors have at least one occurrence covering an element of K. Attractors provide a framework to analyse dictionary text compressors and are used in [193] to develop universal compressed self-indexes.

65   Longest Common-Parity Factors

For a word $v \in \{0,1\}^+$ we denote by *parity(v)* the sum modulo 2 of letter 1 occurring in v. For two words $x, y \in \{0,1\}^+$ we denote by $lcpf(x,y)$, the **longest common-parity factor**, the maximal common length of two factors u and v of x and y respectively with *parity(u)* = *parity(v)*. Surprisingly this problem essentially amounts to computing all periods of words.

> **Question.** Show how to compute in linear time $lcpf(x,y)$ for two binary words x and y.

Solution

The solution uses a data structure called the *parity table*. For a word x, $Parity[\ell, x]$ is the set of distinct parities of factors of length ℓ of x. If two factors of length ℓ have different parities $Parity[\ell, x] = \{0, 1\}$.

Observation. The length $lcpf(x, y)$ derives from the parity tables of x and of y: $lcpf(x, y) = \max\{\ell : Parity[\ell, x] \cap Parity[\ell, y] \neq \emptyset\}$.

Fast computation of the table *Parity*. The problem reduces to the computation of *Parity*, which relies on the following simple fact.

Observation. $Parity[\ell, x] \neq \{0, 1\}$ if and only if ℓ is a period of x.

Indeed, if ℓ is a period of x then obviously the parity of all factors of length ℓ is the same. Conversely, assume all factors of length ℓ have the same parity. Then whenever the next sum is defined we get the equality $\sum_{j=i}^{i+\ell-1} x[j]$ (mod 2) $= \sum_{j=i+1}^{i+\ell} x[j]$ (mod 2), which implies $x[i + \ell] = x[i]$ and completes the proof.

All the periods of x are computed, for example, as by-products of the border table computation (see Problem 19). Next, when ℓ is a period of x, $Parity[\ell, x]$ is the parity of the prefix of length ℓ of x, which results from a prefix-sum computation for all ℓ's. If ℓ is not a period of x, by the observation, $Parity[\ell, x] = \{0, 1\}$. In this way the entire parity tables for x and y are computed in linear time, which gives a linear-time solution to compute $lcpf(x, y)$.

Notes

The problem extends to words on a larger alphabet $\{0, 1, \ldots, k-1\}$ considering sums modulo k. A similar algorithm gives a solution.

66   Word Square-Freeness with DBF

The *dictionary of Basic Factors* (*DBF* in short) is a useful elementary data structure to produce efficient algorithmic solutions to many problems on words. It is used here to test the square-freeness of a word.

The DBF of a word w consists of a logarithmic number of tables $Name_k$, $0 \le k \le \log|w|$. Tables are indexed by positions on w and $Name_k[j]$ intends to identify $w[j .. j + 2^k - 1]$, factor of length 2^k starting at position j on w. Identifiers have the following property, for $i \ne j$: $Name_k[i] = Name_k[j]$ if and only if

$$i + 2^k - 1, j + 2^k - 1 < |w| \text{ and } w[i .. i + 2^k - 1] = w[j .. j + 2^k - 1].$$

It is known that the DBF of w can be computed in time $O(|w| \log|w|)$.

To test the square-freeness of w, let $Pred_k$, $0 \le k < \log|w|$, denote the table indexed by positions on w and defined by

$$Pred_k[j] = \max\{i < j : Name_k[i] = Name_k[j]\} \cup \{-1\}$$

and let $Cand_w$ denote the set of pairs of positions $(i, 2j - i)$ on w, candidates for a square occurrence $w[i .. 2j - i - 1]$ in w:

$$Cand_w = \{(i, 2j - i) : 2j - i \le |w| \text{ and } i = Pred_k[j] \ne -1 \text{ for some } k\}.$$

Question. Show that a word w contains a square if $w[p .. q - 1]$ is a square for some $(p, q) \in Cand_w$. Deduce an algorithm checking if the word w is square-free in time $O(|w| \log|w|)$.

Example. Here are the tables *Pred* for the word $w = \texttt{abacbaca}$:

j	0	1	2	3	4	5	6	7
$x[j]$	a	b	a	c	b	a	c	a
$Pred_0[j]$	-1	-1	0	-1	1	2	3	5
$Pred_1[j]$	-1	-1	-1	-1	1	2	-1	
$Pred_2[j]$	-1	-1	-1	-1	-1			

The associated set $Cand_w$ is $\{(0, 4), (1, 7), (2, 8)\}$. Only the pair $(1, 7)$ corresponds to a square, namely $w[1 .. 6] = \texttt{bacbac}$.

Solution

To answer the first part of the question, let i be the starting position of an occurrence of a shortest square occurring in w. Let 2ℓ be its length and

$j = i + \ell$. The square factor is $w[i \mathinner{.\,.} i + 2\ell - 1]$ and $u = w[i \mathinner{.\,.} i + \ell - 1] = w[j \mathinner{.\,.} j + \ell - 1]$. Let us show that $(i, i + 2\ell)$ belongs to $Cand_w$, that is, $i = Pred_k[j]$ for some integer k.

Let k be the largest integer for which $2^k \le \ell$. As prefix of u we have $v = w[i \mathinner{.\,.} i + 2^k - 1] = w[j \mathinner{.\,.} j + 2^k - 1]$, that is, $Name_k[i] = Name_k[j]$.

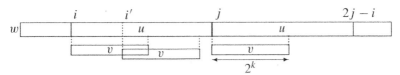

By contradiction, assume $i < Pred_k[j]$, that is, there is an occurrence of v starting at position $Pred_k[j]$ (i' on picture). This occurrence is distinct from the occurrences of v prefixes of u (see picture) and overlaps at least one of them due to its length. But this yields a shorter square, a contradiction. Thus $Pred_k[j] = i$, which means $(i, i + 2\ell) \in Cand_w$ as expected.

Algorithm SQUAREFREE applies the above property by searching $Cand_w$ for a pair of positions corresponding to a square.

SQUAREFREE(w non-empty word of length n, DBF of w)

```
1   for k ← 0 to ⌊log n⌋ do
2       compute Pred_k from DBF of w
3   compute Cand_w from Pred_k tables
4   for each pair (p,q) ∈ Cand_w do
5       k ← ⌊log(q − p)/2⌋
6       if Name_k[p] = Name_k[(p + q)/2] and
            Name_k[(p + q)/2 − 2^k] = Name_k[q − 2^k] then
7           return FALSE
8   return TRUE
```

Correctness of SQUAREFREE. The correctness of the algorithm is an extension of the previous proof that justifies the choice of k at line 5. Testing if a pair (p, q) corresponds to a square, that is, checking if the two factors $w[p \mathinner{.\,.} (p + q)/2 - 1]$ and $w[(p + q)/2 \mathinner{.\,.} q - 1]$ are equal, then amounts to checking both that their prefixes of length 2^k match and that their suffixes of length 2^k also match. This is exactly what is done at line 6 in the algorithm.

Running time of SQUAREFREE. For a given k the table $Pred_k$ can be computed in linear time, scanning the table $Name_k$ from left to right. Computing the set $Cand_w$ by traversing the $\lfloor \log |x| \rfloor$ tables $Pred$ takes $O(|x| \log |x|)$ time.

The same bound holds for lines 5-7 thanks to *Name* from the DBF structure. Thus SQUAREFREE runs in time $O(|x|\log|x|)$.

Notes
There are many algorithms testing the square-freeness of a word with similar running time. But this one is especially simple when the DBF structure is available. It is a version of an algorithm published in [84].

67   Generic Words of Factor Equations

The problem deals with an algorithm to build words from factor equations. A factor equation is of the form $w[p\mathbin{..}q]=w[p'\mathbin{..}q']$ and has length $q-p+1$. In short, the equation is written as a triple $(p,p',q-p+1)$.

We say that a word w of length n is a solution to a system of factor equations E if it satisfies each equation of the system. We are interested in generic solutions containing the largest number of different letters. Such a solution of length n can be used to describe all other solutions of the system. It is denoted by $\Psi(E,n)$ and defined up to a renaming of letters.

Example. For the system of equations

$$E = \{(2,3,1),\ (0,3,3),\ (3,5,3)\},$$

the generic solution $\Psi(E,8)$ is $w=\text{abaababa}$. Indeed, $w[2]=w[3]=\text{a}$, $w[0\mathbin{..}2]=w[3\mathbin{..}5]=\text{aba}$ and $w[3\mathbin{..}5]=w[5\mathbin{..}7]=\text{aba}$. In other words, we have an equivalence on the set of positions on w comprising two equivalence classes $\{0,2,3,5,7\}$ and $\{1,4,6\}$. It is the finest equivalence satisfying the equations in E. Note that $\Psi(E,11)=\text{abaababacde}$.

Question. Describe how to build a generic solution $\Psi(E,n)$ for a given system of factor equations E in time $O((n+m)\log n)$, where $m=|E|$.

[**Hint:** Use spanning forests to represent sets of equivalent positions.]

Solution

For $k \geq 0$, let E_k be the subset of equations of length ℓ, $2^{k-1} < \ell \leq 2^k$, in E. In particular, E_0 is its subset of equations of length 1.

Operation REDUCE. Let $k > 0$. For a set X of equations of length ℓ, $2^{k-1} < \ell \leq 2^k$, the operation REDUCE(X) produces an equivalent set of equations of shorter length as follows.

* **Split**. Each equation (p, p', ℓ) in X is replaced by two equations

$$(p, p', 2^{k-1}) \text{ and } (p + \ell - 2^{k-1}, p' + \ell - 2^{k-1}, 2^{k-1}).$$

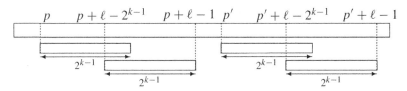

After the operation, X is transformed into an equivalent system of size $O(n + m)$ of equations of the same length.

* Then we create the graph G whose vertices are starting positions of equations of the same length 2^{k-1} and whose edges correspond to equations. If there is a cycle in G then we can remove one of its edges together with the corresponding equation without changing equivalence classes.

* **Shrink**. A spanning tree is built for each connected component of G. Trees form a spanning forest of the whole graph. Eventually, REDUCE(X) is the set of equations corresponding to edges of the spanning forest.

Key observation. Since there are $O(n)$ edges in the spanning forest, the size of the set of equations $|\text{REDUCE}(X)|$ is $O(n)$.

Main algorithm. The whole algorithm consists in applying a logarithmic number of iterations executing operation REDUCE. After each iteration the obtained equivalent system contains equations of much smaller length.

Eventually we get a system E_0 with equations of length 1, from which $\Psi(E_0, n) = \Psi(E, n)$ is easily computed in linear time.

Psi(E set of equations, n positive length)

1    $\triangleright E = \bigcup_{i=0}^{\lceil \log n \rceil} E_i$

2   **for** $k \leftarrow \lceil \log n \rceil$ **downto** 1 **do**

3        $E_{k-1} \leftarrow E_{k-1} \cup \text{REDUCE}(E_k)$

4        $\triangleright$ invariant: system $\bigcup_{i=0}^{k-1} E_i$ is equivalent to E

5   **return** $\Psi(E_0, n)$

The last system E_0 concerns only single positions and gives equivalence classes of positions. All positions in the same equivalence class are assigned the same letter, unique for the class. The resulting word is the required word $\Psi(E,n)$. Since the operation REDUCE runs in time $O(n + m)$, the whole algorithm runs in time $O((n + m)\log n)$, as expected.

Notes

The present algorithm is a version of the algorithm by Gawrychowski et al. presented in [127]. In fact, the algorithm is transformed in [127] into a linear-time algorithm using intricate data structures. It can be used to construct a word having a given set of runs, if there are any.

---

68   Searching an Infinite Word

The goal is to design an algorithm for matching a pattern in an infinite word. Since there is no answer for general infinite words, we restrict the question to a pure morphic word. It is an infinite word obtained by iterating a morphism θ from A^+ to itself, where $A = \{\text{a},\text{b}, \ldots\}$ is a finite alphabet. To do so, we assume that θ is prolongable over the letter a, that is, $\theta(\text{a}) = \text{a}u$ for $u \in A^+$. Then $\Theta = \theta^\infty(\text{a})$ exists and is $\text{a}u\theta(u)\theta^2(u)\ldots$. The infinite word Θ is a fixed point of θ, that is, $\theta(\Theta) = \Theta$.

To avoid trivial cases, like that of the morphism η defined by $\eta(\text{a}) = \text{ab}$, $\eta(\text{b}) = \text{c}$, $\eta(\text{c}) = \text{b}$ and $\eta(\text{d}) = \text{d}$ where the letter d is useless and the letter a appear only once in Θ, we assume that θ is irreducible. It means that any letter is accessible from any letter: for any distinct letters $c,d \in A$ the letter d appears in $\theta^k(c)$ for some integer k.

Thue–Morse morphism μ and Fibonacci morphism ϕ (see Chapter 1) are both irreducible morphisms.

Question. Show how to test if a morphism is irreducible.

Question. Design an algorithm to compute the set of factors of length m occurring in the infinite word $\Theta = \theta^\infty(\text{a})$, where θ is an irreducible morphism.

When the set of length-m factors of Θ is represented by a (deterministic) trie, testing if a pattern of length m appears in Θ becomes a mere top-down traversal of the trie.

Solution

To test the irreducibility of the morphism θ we build its accessibility graph on letters. Vertices of the graph are letters and, for any two different letters c and d, there is an arc from c to d if d appears in $\theta(c)$. Irreducibility holds if the graph contains a cycle going through all alphabet letters, which can be tested in polynomial time.

For example, the graph of the morphism ζ satisfies the property

$$\begin{cases} \zeta(\text{a}) = \text{ab} \\ \zeta(\text{b}) = \text{c} \\ \zeta(\text{c}) = \text{cad} \\ \zeta(\text{d}) = \text{a} \end{cases}$$

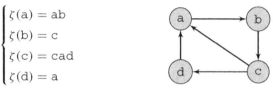

To solve the second question, one can extract length-m factors from words $\theta^k(\text{a})$ by iterating the morphism from a. Indeed it is rather clear that after a finite number of iterations all length-m factors are captured.

Instead, the algorithm below handles only words that are images by θ of factors of Θ having length at most m. Its correctness is a consequence of the irreducibility of the morphism because it implies that any factor of $\theta^k(\text{a})$ is a factor of $\theta^\ell(b)$ for any letter b and some integer ℓ.

The sought set of length-m factors of Θ is the set of length-m words stored in the trie T produced by the algorithm.

Factors(irreducible morphism θ, a $\in A$, positive integer m)

```
 1   initialise T to the empty trie
 2   Queue ← A
 3   while Queue not empty do
 4       v ← extract the first word in Queue
 5       w ← θ(v)
 6       for each length-m factor z of w do
 7           if z not in T then
 8               insert z into T  and  append z to Queue
 9       if |w| < m and w not in T then
10           insert w into T  and  append w to Queue
11   return T
```

Depending on the properties of the morphism, the algorithm can be tuned to get a faster execution. This is the case if, for example, the morphism is k-uniform: $|\theta(c)| = k$ for any letter c. Then only factors of length $\lfloor m/k \rfloor + 1$ need to be appended to the queue, which reduces dramatically the number of words put in the queue.

The insertion into the trie at line 8 can be implemented carefully to avoid useless operations. In fact, after inserting the factor $z = cy$ (for some letter c) it is natural to continue with the next factor of the form yd (for some letter d). If the trie is equipped with suffix links (same links as in a Suffix tree) the operation takes constant time (or at most $\log |A|$). Then the insertion of all factors z of w takes $O(|w|)$ time (or $O(|w| \log |A|)$).

Notes

A stronger hypothesis on the morphism is to be primitive, which means that there is an integer k for which the letter d appears in $\theta^k(c)$ for any $c, d \in A$ (k is independent of the pair of letters). For primitive morphisms there is another solution to the problem. It consists in considering return words in the infinite word x: a return word to a factor w of x is a shortest (non-empty) word r for which rw has border w and is a factor of x. Durand and Leroy [104] prove, for a primitive morphism θ, that there is a constant K for which both $|r| \leq K|w|$ and all length-m factors of Θ appear in factors of length $(K + 1)m$. Moreover they are able to bound the constant K by $\max\{\theta(c) : c \in A\}^{4|A|^2}$. This leads to another algorithm for finding the set of length-m factors of Θ.

69   Perfect Words

A word of length is called *dense* if it has the largest number of (distinct) factors among words of the same length on the same alphabet. A word is said to be *perfect* if all its prefixes are dense. Note that each prefix of a perfect word is also perfect.

Example. The word 0110 is dense but 0101 is not. The longest binary perfect words are 011001010 and its complement 100110101, they have length 9. However, on the ternary alphabet the word 0120022110 of length 10 is perfect.

There are only finitely many binary perfect words, but the situation changes dramatically for larger alphabets.

Question. Show how to construct in linear time a ternary perfect word of any given length. Prove also the existence of an infinite perfect ternary word.

[**Hint:** Consider Hamiltonian and Eulerian cycles in de Bruijn automata.]

Solution

Let $A = \{0,1,2\}$ be the alphabet and consider the length $\Delta_n = 3^n + n - 1$ of a de Bruijn word of order n over A. It is enough to show how to construct perfect words having these particular lengths, since their prefixes are perfect.

Any perfect ternary word of length Δ_n is a de Bruijn word. Hence the problem reduces to the construction of perfect de Bruijn words.

Our basic data structure is the de Bruijn graph G_n of order n (graph structure of de Bruijn automaton) over the alphabet A. Vertices of G_n are ternary words of length $n - 1$. The label of an Eulerian cycle is a circular de Bruijn word of order n, which produces a (linear) de Bruijn word of the same order when its prefix of length $n - 1$ is appended to it.

Our first goal is to extend such a de Bruijn word w of order n to a de Bruijn word of order $n + 1$. Let u be the border of length $n - 1$ of w and ua its prefix of length n. Let $\widehat{w} = wa$.

Observation. In the graph G_{n+1} whose vertices are the words of A^n, $\widehat{w}$ is the label of a Hamiltonian cycle, denoted $Cycle_n(\widehat{w})$, starting and ending at vertex ua, prefix of length n of w.

Example. The word $w = 0122002110$ is a de Bruijn word of order 2 on A. It is associated with the Eulerian cycle in G_2:
$$Cycle_1(w) = 0 \to 1 \to 2 \to 2 \to 0 \to 0 \to 2 \to 1 \to 1 \to 0.$$

Hence the word $\widehat{w} = \texttt{01220021101}$ corresponds to the Hamiltonian cycle H in G_3 (see picture where loops at nodes $\texttt{00}$, $\texttt{11}$ and $\texttt{22}$ are omitted for clarity):
$$Cycle_2(\widehat{w}) = \texttt{01} \to \texttt{12} \to \texttt{22} \to \texttt{20} \to \texttt{00} \to \texttt{02} \to \texttt{21} \to \texttt{11} \to \texttt{10} \to \texttt{01}.$$

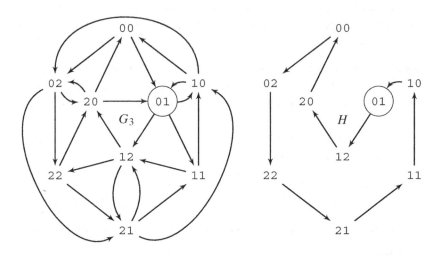

Drawing on the observation, the cycle is concatenated to a disjoint cycle to create an Eulerian cycle in G_{n+1} yielding a de Bruijn word of order $n + 1$ prefixed by w.

The next goal is to extend a perfect de Bruijn word of order n to a perfect de Bruijn word of order $n + 1$. To do so, we construct a sequence of perfect de Bruijn words $w_1, w_2, \ldots$ that satisfies: w_i is a prefix of w_{i+1}. The limit is then a perfect infinite word, as expected.

Let $EulerExt_n(h)$ be an Eulerian cycle in G_n extending a Hamiltonian cycle h in G_n, if this is possible. Let also $Word_n(e)$ be the word associated with an Eulerian cycle e in G_n.

PERFECTWORD(N positive length, $\{\texttt{0}, \texttt{1}, \texttt{2}\}$ alphabet)

1   $(w, n) \leftarrow (\texttt{012}, 1)$
2   **while** $|w| < N$ **do**
3       $n \leftarrow n + 1$
4       $h \leftarrow Cycle_n(\widehat{w})$
5       $e \leftarrow EulerExt_n(h)$
6       $w \leftarrow Word_n(e)$
7   **return** prefix of length N of w

Informal explanation of the construction. The word w_n after extending it by one letter to $\widehat{w_n}$ corresponds to a Hamiltonian cycle $h = Cycle_n(\widehat{w_n})$ in G_{n+1}. We extend it to an Eulerian cycle e in G_{n+1}, and finally we define w_{n+1} as the word representation of e. The interesting point in this construction is that we treat cycles as words and words as cycles, and, in the main step, for computing an Eulerian extension we use graph-theoretic tools rather than stringologic arguments.

Example. For the perfect word $w_2 = 0120022110$ of length 10 we have $\widehat{w_2} = 01200221101$, which corresponds in G_3 to the cycle H (see above picture):

$$01 \to 12 \to 20 \to 00 \to 02 \to 22 \to 21 \to 11 \to 10 \to 01.$$

H is extended to an Eulerian cycle E by concatenating it with the following Eulerian cycle in $G_3 - H$:

$$01 \to 11 \to 11 \to 12 \to 21 \to 12 \to 22 \to 22 \to 20 \to 02$$
$$\to 21 \to 10 \to 02 \to 20 \to 01 \to 10 \to 00 \to 00 \to 01.$$

Finally we get from E:

$$w_3 = Word(E) = 01200221101\,112122202102010001.$$

Before showing the word produced by the algorithm is perfect, we need to be sure it is possible to get an Eulerian cycle in $G_n - H$.

Lemma 5 *If H is a Hamiltonian cycle in G_n then after removing the edges of H the graph G_n remains Eulerian.*

Proof We use the following obvious but useful property of de Bruijn graphs shown schematically in the figure below: a special configuration of 3 edges implies the existence of the 4th edge. More formally:

   (∗) If $u \to v, u \to y, x \to v$ are edges of G_n then $x \to y$ is an edge.

We are to show that $G_n - H$ is Eulerian. Clearly each node of $G_n - H$ has the same in-degree and out-degree. Hence it is enough to show it is strongly connected. However, weak connectivity (disregarding directions of edges) is sufficient due to well-known property (a graph is regular when its vertices have the same degree).

Property. A regular weakly connected directed graph is also strongly connected.

Hence it is enough to show that, for any edge $u \to v \in H$, nodes u and v are weakly connected in $G_n - H$ (there is a path between them not using edges of H and disregarding directions of edges). Indeed, since each node has in-degree and out-degree 3, there are nodes x, x', y for which the edges

$$u \to y, \; x \to v, \; x' \to v$$

are in $G_n - H$. Now property ($*$) implies the existence in G_n of two additional edges $x \to y$ and $x' \to y$ (see the figure), and at least one of them is not in H. Removing directions of these edges, we deduce there is an undirected path from u to v, not using edges of H.

Consequently, $G_n - H$ is weakly connected and is Eulerian (as a directed graph), which completes the proof.   ∎

Correctness of PERFECTWORD. Let w_n be the value of w immediately before instruction at line 3. By induction, all the prefixes of length at most $|w_{n-1}|$ of w_n are dense since w_{n-1} is perfect. A longer prefix of w_n contains all words of length $n-1$ and no repeat of words of length n, since it is a prefix of a de Bruijn word. Consequently it is also dense. Hence each prefix of w_n is dense, so w_n is perfect.

Complexity. The algorithm runs in linear time since Eulerian cycles can be found in linear time, and in de Bruijn graphs finding a Hamiltonian cycle reduces to the computation of an Eulerian cycle.

Notes
Perfect words are also called *super complex* and their construction is presented in [237]. In case of binary words the notion of perfect words is weakened to semi-perfect words whose existence is shown in [206].

70   Dense Binary Words

A word is called *dense* if it has the largest number of (distinct) factors among words of the same length on the same alphabet.

Over an alphabet with at least three letters, generating dense words for any given length is solved by the generation of perfect words (see Problem 69). But the solution does not apply to binary words and the present problem shows how to deal efficiently with this case.

Question. Show how to construct in $O(N)$ time a dense binary word of any given length N.

[**Hint:** Consider Hamiltonian and Eulerian cycles in de Bruijn automata.]

Solution

Let $A = \{0,1\}$ be the alphabet. Let us fix N and let n be such that $\Delta_{n-1} < N \le \Delta_n$, where $\Delta_n = 2^n + n - 1$. Our basic data structure is the de Bruijn graph G_n of order n (graph structure of de Bruijn automaton) over the alphabet A. Vertices of G_n are binary words of length $n - 1$.

We say that a path π in G_n is an *Eulerian chain* if it contains all nodes of G_n, possibly many times, and no repeating edge. Let $Word_n(\pi)$ be the word associated with the Eulerian cycle π in G_n.

Property 1. When π is an Eulerian chain of length $N - (n-1)$ in G_n, $Word_n(\pi)$ is a dense word of length N.

Proof   Any binary word of length N, where $\Delta_{n-1} < N \le \Delta_n$, contains at most 2^{n-1} (distinct) factors of length $n - 1$ and at most $N - n + 1$ factors of length n. Hence a word achieving these bounds is dense. In particular, if π is an Eulerian chain, $Word_n(\pi)$ contains all words of length $n - 1$ and all its factors of length n are distinct since they correspond to distinct edges of the Eulerian chain in G_n. Consequently $Word_n(\pi)$ is dense.   ∎

Following property 1, the answer to the question lies in the next property.

Property 2. An Eulerian chain of a length $N - (n - 1)$ in G_n can be computed in linear time.

Proof   To do it we first compute a Hamiltonian cycle H of size 2^{n-1} in G_n, given by an Eulerian cycle of G_{n-1}. The graph $G_n - H$ consists of disjoint simple cycles $C_1, C_2, \ldots, C_r$, called *ear-cycles*. Then we choose a subset $C_1', C_2', \ldots, C_t'$ of ear-cycles for which $\sum_{i=1}^{t-1} |C_i'| < M \leq \sum_{i=1}^{t} |C_i'|$. Then we add a prefix subpath c_t' of C_t' to get

$$\sum_{i=1}^{t-1} |C_i'| + |c_t'| = M.$$

It is clear that $H \cup C_1' \cup C_2' \cup \cdots \cup C_{t-1}' \cup c_t'$ can be sequenced into an Eulerian chain of length M. It starts at any node of c_t', then goes around H and around each encountered ear-cycle C_i'. After coming back it traverses the path c_t'.   ∎

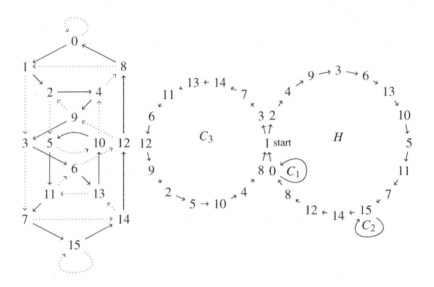

Example. The above picture displays G_5 (left) whose vertices are binary words of length 4, shown in decimal to shorten the display. The picture (right) shows the decomposition of G_5 into the edge-disjoint ear-cycles H, C_1, C_2 and C_3. Cycle H is the Hamiltonian cycle of length 16, C_1 and C_2 are loops and C_3 is the big ear-cycle of length 14. The three last ear-cycles cover the dotted edges (left) in G_5, those that are not in H.

To compute a dense binary word of length $N = 33$, we first construct an Eulerian chain π of length $21 = 25 - 4$. We can start at node 1, go around the Hamiltonian cycle additionally traversing the two loops, then come back to 1, and follow a path of 4 edges on the big ear-cycle C_3. In this case $t = 3$, C_1', C_2' are loops and $c_3' = 1 \rightarrow 3 \rightarrow 7 \rightarrow 14$. We get the path

$$\pi = (1, 2, 4, 9, 3, 6, 13, 10, 5, 11, 7, 15, 15, 14, 12, 8, 0, 0, 1, 3, 7, 14)$$

whose label is the binary word

$$0\,0\,1\,1\,0\,1\,0\,1\,1\,1\,1\,1\,0\,0\,0\,0\,0\,1\,1\,1\,0.$$

The final dense word of length 25 results by prepending to it the binary representation $0\,0\,0\,1$ of the first node 1:

$$Word_5(\pi) = 0\,0\,0\,1\,0\,0\,1\,1\,0\,1\,0\,1\,1\,1\,1\,1\,0\,0\,0\,0\,0\,1\,1\,1\,0.$$

Notes
The first efficient and quite different algorithm for constructing dense words was by Shallit [222]. Observe that in our example, for $n = 5$, the graph G_5 decomposes into four edge disjoint simple cycles: a Hamiltonian cycle H, two loops and one big ear-cycle of length $2^{n-1} - 2$. If we disregard the loops then G_5 is decomposed into two edge-disjoint simple cycles. In fact, such a special decomposition of any binary graph G_n, for $n > 3$, can be found using so-called *complementary* Hamiltonian cycles, see [206]. Nevertheless any other decomposition is sufficient to compute dense words.

---

71   Factor Oracle

The Factor oracle is an indexing structure similar to the Factor or Suffix automaton (or DAWG) of a word x. It is a deterministic automaton with $|x|+1$ states, the minimum number of states the Suffix automaton of x can have. This makes it a well-suited data structure in many applications that require a simple indexing structure and leads both to a space-economical data structure and to an efficient online construction. The drawback is that the oracle of x accepts slightly more words than the factors of x.

For a factor v of y, let $pocc(v, y)$ be the position on y following the first occurrence of v in y, that is, $pocc(v, y) = \min\{|z| : z = wv \text{ prefix of } y\}$. The following algorithm may be viewed as a definition of the Factor oracle $\mathcal{O}(x)$ of a word x. It computes the automaton in which Q is the set of states and E the set of labelled edges.

ORACLE(x non-empty word)

1   $(Q, E) \leftarrow (\{0, 1, \ldots, |x|\}, \emptyset)$
2   **for** $i \leftarrow 0$ **to** $|x| - 1$ **do**
3       $u \leftarrow$ shortest word recognised in state i
4   **for** $a \in A$ **do**
5   **if** $ua \in Fact(x[i - |u| .. |x| - 1])$ **then**
6               $E \leftarrow E \cup \{(i, a, pocc(ua, x[i - |u| .. |x| - 1]))\}$
7   **return** (Q, E)

Actually the structure has several interesting properties. Its $|x| + 1$ states are all terminal states. Every edge whose target is $i + 1$ is labelled by $x[i]$. There are $|x|$ edges of the form $(i, x[i], i + 1)$, called internal edges. Other edges, of the form $(j, x[i], i + 1)$ with $j < i$, are called external edges. The oracle can thus be represented by x and its set of external edges without their labels.

Example. The oracle $\mathcal{O}$(aabbaba) accepts all the factors of aabbaba but also abab, which is not. It is determined by its external unlabelled edges $(0, 3)$, $(1, 3)$ and $(3, 5)$.

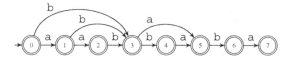

Question. Show that the Factor oracle of a word x has between $|x|$ and $2|x| - 1$ edges.

Solution

First note the bounds are met. Indeed, $\mathcal{O}(a^n)$ has n edges for any letter a, and $\mathcal{O}(x)$ has $2|x| - 1$ edges when the letters of x are pairwise distinct, that is, $|alph(x)| = |x|$.

Fact. Let u be a shortest word among the words recognised in state i of $\mathcal{O}(x)$. Then $i = pocc(u, x)$ and u is unique. Let $sh(i)$ denote it.

To answer the question, since there are $|x|$ internal edges, we have to show there are less than $|x|$ external edges. To do so, let us map each external edge of the form (i, a, j) with $i < j - 1$ to the proper non-empty suffix $sh(i)ax[j + 1 .. |x| - 1]$ of x. We show the mapping is injective.

Assume there are edges (i_1, a_1, j_1) and (i_2, a_2, j_2) with

$$sh(i_1)a_1x[j_1 + 1 .. |x| - 1] = sh(i_2)a_2x[j_2 + 1 .. |x| - 1]$$

and w.l.o.g. that $i_1 \leq i_2$.

- If $j_1 < j_2$ then $sh(i_1)a_1$ is a proper prefix of $sh(i_2)$. Setting $d = |sh(i_2)| - |sh(i_1)a_1|$ we get $j_1 = j_2 - d - 1$. An occurrence of $sh(i_2)$ ends in i_2 then an occurrence of $sh(i_1)a_1$ ends in $i_2 - d < j_2 - d - 1 = j_1$. But this is a contradiction with the construction of the Factor oracle of x.
- If $j_1 > j_2$ the word $sh(i_2)$ is a proper prefix of $sh(i_1)$. Consequently there is an occurrence of $sh(i_2)$ ending before $i_1 \leq i_2$, a contradiction again with the construction of the Factor oracle.

Therefore $j_1 = j_2$, which implies $a_1 = a_2$, $sh(i_1) = sh(i_2)$, $i_1 = i_2$ and eventually $(i_1, a_1, j_1) = (i_2, a_2, j_2)$.

Since the mapping is injective and since there are $|x| - 1$ proper non-empty suffixes of x, adding internal and external edges gives the maximum of $2|x| - 1$ edges in the Factor oracle, as expected.

> **Question.** Design an online construction of the Factor oracle of a word x running in linear time on a fixed alphabet with linear space.

[**Hint:** Use suffix links.]

Solution

Since the oracle is deterministic, let δ denote its transition function, that is, $\delta(i, a) = j \Leftrightarrow (i, a, j) \in E$. Let S be the suffix link defined on states as follows: $S[0] = -1$ and, for $1 \leq i \leq |x|$, $S[i] = \delta(0, u)$ where u is the longest (proper) suffix of $x[0 .. i]$ for which $\delta(0, u) < i$. For the above example we get

i	0	1	2	3	4	5	6	7
$x[i]$	a	a	b	b	a	b	a	
$S[i]$	-1	0	1	0	3	1	3	5

Fact. Let $k < i$ be a state on the suffix path of state i of the Factor oracle of $x[0 .. i]$. If $\delta(k, x[i+1])$ is defined then the same holds for all the states on the suffix path of k.

Following the fact, step i, for $0 \leq i \leq |x| - 1$, of the online construction of the Factor oracle makes a standard use of the suffix link and consists of

- adding state $i + 1$ and setting $\delta(i, x[i]) = i + 1$;
- following the suffix path of i to set $\delta(S^k[i], x[i]) = i + 1$ whenever necessary; and
- setting $S[i + 1]$.

The following algorithm implements this strategy.

ORACLEONLINE(x non-empty word)

```
1   (Q,δ,S[0]) ← ({0},undefined, − 1)
2   for i ← 0 to |x| − 1 do
3        Q ← Q ∪ {i + 1}
4        δ(i,x[i]) ← i + 1
5        j ← S[i]
6        while j > −1 and δ(j,x[i]) undefined do
7             δ(j,x[i]) ← i + 1
8             j ← S[j]
9        if j = −1 then
10            S[i + 1] ← 0
11       else S[i + 1] ← δ(j,x[i])
12  return (Q,δ)
```

The correctness of ORACLEONLINE comes mainly from the equality $(S[i], x[i], i + 1) = (S[i], x[i], S[i] + pocc(sh(S[i]), x[i − S[i] .. |x| − 1]))$.

The time linearity comes from the fact that at each iteration of the while loop of lines 6–8 an external transition is created and there can be only $|x| − 1$ such transitions in $\mathcal{O}(x)$. The loop of lines 2–11 runs exactly $|x| − 1$ times and all the other instructions take constant time.

The space linearity comes from the fact that the Factor oracle needs linear space, so does the array S.

Question. Show the Factor oracle $\mathcal{O}(x)$ can be used for locating all the occurrences of x in a text, despite the oracle may accept words that are not factors of x.

[**Hint:** The only word of length $|x|$ recognised by $\mathcal{O}(x)$ is x itself.]

Solution

A solution mimicking KMP algorithm is possible but a more time-efficient solution use the Boyer–Moore strategy. To do so, we use the Factor oracle of x^R, the reverse of x. A window of length $|x|$ slides along the text and when the whole window is accepted by the oracle a match is detected, since the window contains x as said in the hint.

When a mismatch occurs, that is, when a factor au of the text is not accepted by the oracle, au is not either a factor of x. Then a shift of length $|x − u|$ can be safely performed. The following algorithm implements this strategy. It outputs the starting positions of all the occurrences of x in y.

BACKWARDORACLEMATCHING(x, y non-empty words)
1   $(Q, \delta) \leftarrow$ ORACLEONLINE(x^R)
2   $j \leftarrow 0$
3   **while** $j \le |y| - |x|$ **do**
4       $(q, i) \leftarrow (0, |x| - 1)$
5   **while** $\delta(q, y[i + j])$ is defined **do**
6           $(q, i) \leftarrow (\delta(q, y[i + j]), i - 1)$
7   **if** $i < 0$ **then**
8   report an occurrence of x at position j on y
9           $j \leftarrow j + 1$
10   **else** $j \leftarrow j + i + 1$

Notes

The notion of Factor oracle and its use for text searching is by Allauzen et al. [5] (see also [79]). Improvements given in [109, 111] lead to the fastest string-matching algorithms in most common applications.

The exact characterisation of the language of words accepted by the Factor oracle is studied in [182] and its statistical properties are presented in [40].

The oracle is used to efficiently find repeats in words for designing data compression methods in [173].

The data structure is well suited for computer-assisted jazz improvisation in which states stand for notes as it has been adapted by Assayag and Dubnov [17]. See further developments of the associated OMax project at recherche.ircam.fr/equipes/repmus/OMax/.

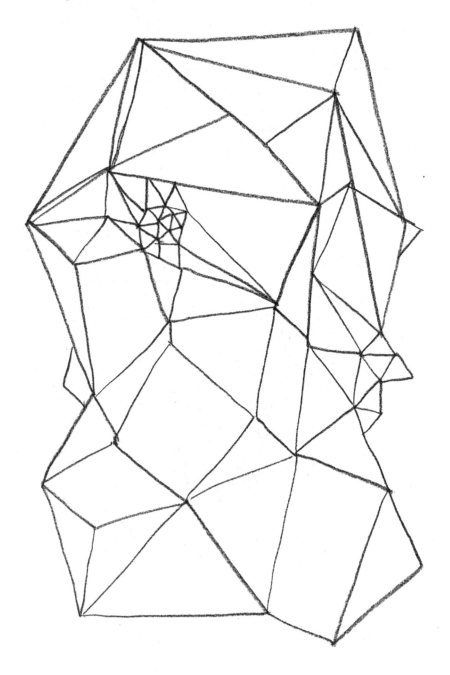

72   Three Square Prefixes

The combinatorial analysis of square prefixes of a word leads to several consequences useful to design algorithms related to periodicities.

Three non-empty words u, v and w satisfy the square-prefix condition if u^2 is a proper prefix of v^2 and v^2 a proper prefix of w^2. For example, when $u =$ abaab, $v =$ abaababa, $w =$ abaababaabaabab, the prefix condition is met:

abaababaab
abaababaabaababa
abaababaabaabababaababaabaabab

but u^2 is not a prefix of v nor v^2 a prefix of w, which otherwise would provide a trivial example.

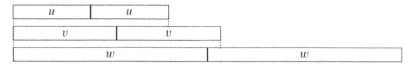

> **Question.** Show that if u^2, v^2 and w^2 satisfy the square-prefix condition and $|w| \le 2|u|$ then $u, v, w \in z^2 z^*$ for some word z.

The conclusion implies in particular that u is not primitive. In fact, this implication holds true if both the square-prefix condition and the inequality $|w| < |u| + |v|$ are met (Three-Square-Prefix Lemma). But the statement in the above question has a stronger conclusion that says we are essentially in the trivial situation where $w^2 = \mathtt{a}^k$ or the like.

> **Question.** Give infinitely many examples of word triples that satisfy the square-prefix condition and for which both $|u| + |v| = |w|$ and u is primitive.

The next question provides a consequence of the Three-Square-Prefix Lemma or of the first statement. The exact upper bound or even a tight bound on the concerned quantity is still unknown.

> **Question.** Show that less than $2|x|$ (distinct) primitively rooted squares can be factors of a word x.

Another direct consequence of the Three-Square-Prefix Lemma is that a word of length n has no more than $\log_\phi n$ prefixes that are primitively rooted squares. The golden mean Φ comes from the recurrence relation for Fibonacci numbers in the second question.

Solution

Assume that $|w| \le 2|u|$ as displayed in the picture.

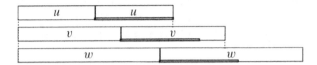

The condition in the first question implies that the three occurrences of u at positions $|u|$, $|v|$ and $|w|$ pairwise overlap. Thus the word u has periods $|v| - |u|$ and $|w| - |v|$ whose sum is no more than $|u|$, and then $q = \gcd(|v| - |u|, |w| - |v|)$ is also a period of u due to the Periodicity Lemma. The word $z = u[0 \mathinner{.\,.} p]$, where p is the (smallest) period of u, is a primitive word and as such occurs in u only at positions kp for $k = 0, \ldots, \lfloor |u|/p \rfloor$. Period p is also a divisor of q because $q < |u|/2$.

The word z occurs at position $|u|$ on w^2 and then at position $|u| + |v| - |w|$ on u. Since $|u| + |v| - |w|$ and $|w| - |v|$ are multiples of p, their sum $|u|$ is, and then u is an integer power of z; thus $u \in z^2 z^*$. The same holds for v and w because $|v| - |u|$ and $|w| - |v|$ are multiples of $p = |z|$.

The infinite word $\mathbf{s}$, limit of the sequence defined by $s_1 = \texttt{aab}$, $s_2 = \texttt{aabaaba}$ and $s_i = s_{i-1} s_{i-2}$ for $i \ge 3$, contains an infinity of prefix triples that answer the second question. The first triple lengths are $(3, 7, 10)$, $(7, 10, 17)$, $(10, 17, 27)$. The infinite Fibonacci word shows a similar behaviour.

To count the number of primitively rooted squares that are factors of a word x, assign to each its rightmost starting position on x. If ever a position i is assigned to three squares u^2, v^2 and w^2 like in the picture below, due to the statement of the first question, since u is primitive, the shortest square u^2 is a proper prefix of w. Then u^2 reoccurs at position $i + |w|$, which contradicts the fact that i is the rightmost starting position of u^2. Therefore, no more than two squares can be assigned to a given position. And since the last position of x is not considered, the total number of primitively rooted square factors is less than $2|x|$.

Notes

The Three-Square-Prefix Lemma and consequences are by Crochemore and Rytter [97] (see also [74, chapter 9] and [176, chapters 8 and 12]). The first statement and variations on the lemma are by Bai et al. [22].

The problem of counting square factors and the present result are by Fraenkel and Simpson [118]. Direct simple proofs are by Hickerson [141] and Ilie [146]. Slightly improved upper bounds are by Ilie [147] and by Deza et al. [103].

---

73   Tight Bounds on Occurrences of Powers

The problem considers lower bounds on the number of occurrences of integer powers occurring in a word.

An integer power is a word in the form u^k for some non-empty word u and some integer $k > 1$. The size of the set of square factors (Problem 72) and the number of runs (Problem 86) in a word are known to be linear in the length of the word. This contrasts with the number of occurrences of integer powers that does not satisfy this property.

To avoid trivial lower bounds we consider primitively rooted integer powers, that is, powers of the form u^k, where u is a primitive word (i.e., not itself a power).

To start with, let us consider the word a^n. Though it contains a quadratic number occurrences of squares, it contains exactly $n - 1$ occurrences of primitively rooted squares (underlined below).

```
0   1   2   3   4   5   6   7   8   9   10  11  12  13  14  15  16  17
a   a   a   a   a   a   a   a   a   a   a   a   a   a   a   a   a   a
```

But if a few occurrences of a are changed to b in the word (see below) the number of primitively rooted squares increases, although some occurrences of short squares disappear (when n is large enough).

Consider the sequence of words defined by

$$\begin{cases} x_0 = a^5b, \\ x_{i+1} = (x_i)^3b, & \text{for } i \geq 0. \end{cases}$$

Question. Show that x_i contains asymptotically $\Omega(|x_i| \log |x_i|)$ occurrences of primitively rooted squares.

In fact, the property on squares also holds for powers of any integer exponent $k \geq 2$.

Question. For a given integer $k \geq 2$, define a sequence of words y_i, for $i \geq 0$, containing asymptotically $\Omega(|y_i| \log |y_i|)$ occurrences of primitively rooted kth powers.

Notice the bound is tight due to the upper bound on square prefixes in Problem 72.

Solution

Consider the sequence of words x_i of length ℓ_i and let c_i be the number of occurrences of primitively rooted squares in x_i.

We have (looking at $(x_0)^3$ in the above picture and accounting for the suffix occurrence of bb in x_1)

$$\begin{cases} \ell_0 = 6, & c_0 = 4, \\ \ell_1 = 19, & c_1 = 20. \end{cases}$$

Note that all short squares appear in each occurrence of a^5b in x_1 and that a^5b itself is a primitive word. The same property holds true by induction for all squares occurring in x_i. This produces the recurrence relations, for $i > 0$

$$\begin{cases} \ell_1 = 19, & c_1 = \ell_1 + 1, \\ \ell_{i+1} = 3\ell_i + 1, & c_{i+1} = 3c_i + \ell_i + 2. \end{cases}$$

Then, asymptotically we get $\ell_{i+1} \approx 3^i \ell_1$, $c_{i+1} > 3^i c_1 + i3^{i-1}\ell_1$ and $i \approx \log |x_{i+1}|$, which proves the statement of the first question.

When k is the exponent of considered powers, for some positive integer m, we can define the sequence of words

$$\begin{cases} y_0 = \mathsf{a}^m \mathsf{b}, \\ y_{i+1} = (y_i)^{k+1}\mathsf{b}, \quad \text{for } i > 0, \end{cases}$$

which induces

$$\{ \ \ell_{i+1} = (k+1)\ell_i + 1, \quad c_{i+1} = (k+1)c_i + \ell_i + 2,$$

and also leads to an $\Omega(|y_i| \log |y_i|)$ lower bound on the number of occurrences of primitively rooted kth powers.

Notes
The lower bound on primitively rooted squares holds for Fibonacci words [64]. The proof uses the fact that Fibonacci words have no factors that are 4th powers. The bound has also been shown by Gusfield and Stoye [135].

The asymptotic lower bound for occurrences of kth power is shown in [72], which inspired the present proof.

---

74   Computing Runs on General Alphabets

The goal of the problem is to design an algorithm for computing runs in a word without any extra assumption on the alphabet. To say it differently, the algorithm should use the equality model on letters, that is, use only $=$/$\neq$ letter comparisons when necessary.

Problem 87 deals with computing runs on linear-sortable alphabets, a necessary condition to obtain a linear-time algorithm.

A run in a word x is a maximal periodicity or a maximal occurrence of a periodic factor of x. Formally, it is an interval of positions $[i \mathinner{..} j]$ for which the (smallest) period p of $x[i \mathinner{..} j]$ satisfies $2p \leq j - i + 1$, and both $x[i-1] \neq x[i+p-1]$ and $x[j+1] \neq x[j-p+1]$ when the inequalities make sense. The centre of run $[i \mathinner{..} j]$ is the position $i + p$.

To avoid reporting the same run twice, they can be filtered out according to their centre. To do so, we say that a run is right centred in the product uv of words if it starts at a position on u and has its centre on v. And we say it is left centred in uv if its centre is on u and it ends in v.

Question. Design a linear-time algorithm that finds right-centred runs occurring in a product uv of two words.

[**Hint:** Use prefix tables, see Problem 22.]

Question. Design an algorithm that computes all the runs in a word of length n in time $O(n \log n)$ in the equality model.

[**Hint:** Use a divide-and-conquer approach.]

Solution

To answer the first question, we can look for the sought runs in the increasing order of their periods. As shown in the picture, given a potential period p of a run, we just have to check how long the associated factor $v[0 .. p-1]$ matches to its left and to its right. These are longest common extensions (LCE) from two positions, for instance $r = lcp(v, v[p .. |v| - 1])$. If the sum of extension lengths is at least the period a run is detected.

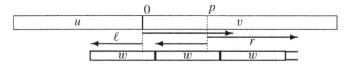

The length r of the right extension is simply given by the prefix table of v. The length ℓ of the left extension is computed similarly with the prefix table of $z = u^R \# v^R u^R$, where # does not appear in uv.

If the condition $\ell \leq p$ holds at line 6 in the algorithm below, the potential run is centred on v, as required. The *offset*, position on x of one of its factors, uv, is added to report runs as intervals of positions on x (instead of uv) in Algorithm RUNS below.

RIGHT-CENTRED-RUNS(u, v non-empty words, *offset*)

1   $pref_v \leftarrow$ PREFIXES(v)
2   $pref_z \leftarrow$ PREFIXES($u^R \# v^R u^R$)
3   **for** $p \leftarrow 1$ **to** $|v| - 1$ **do**
4       $r \leftarrow pref_v[p]$
5       $\ell \leftarrow pref_z[|u| + |v| - p + 1]$
6   **if** $\ell \leq p$ and $\ell + r \geq p$ **then**
7   Output run $[|u| - \ell .. |u| + p + r - 1] + $ *offset*

The design of LEFT-CENTRED-RUNS to compute runs of uv centred on u follows the same scheme and is done symmetrically.

The running time of both algorithms depends on the complexity to compute a prefix table. It is linear in the input length, as shown in Problem 22. Moreover, only $=/\neq$ comparisons are used during the calculation.

Eventually, to compute all runs in a word x, the process divides x into two words of similar length as in the algorithm below. Runs are obtained by calling $\text{Runs}(x, n, 0)$. As a consequence of the running times of the two previous algorithms, the whole computation runs in time $O(n \log n)$ in the comparison model.

$\text{Runs}(x$ non-empty word of length $n, \textit{offset})$

1   **if** $n > 1$ **then**
2        $(u, v) \leftarrow (x[0 \mathinner{.\,.} \lfloor n/2 \rfloor], x[\lfloor n/2 \rfloor + 1 \mathinner{.\,.} n - 1])$
3        $\text{Runs}(u, \lfloor n/2 \rfloor + 1, \textit{offset})$
4        $\text{Runs}(v, n - \lfloor n/2 \rfloor - 1, \textit{offset} + \lfloor n/2 \rfloor + 1)$
5        $\text{Right-Centred-Runs}(u, v, \textit{offset})$
6        $\text{Left-Centred-Runs}(u, v, \textit{offset})$

Note that some runs may be reported several times by the algorithm. This happens when a long run in the first half of the word overflows on the second half of it. Some filtering is needed to get a clean list of runs.

Notes

The present technique to compute runs is presented in [84] together with other solutions running in the same time according to the computational model. In this model, the algorithm is optimal due to a result by Main and Lorentz [179], who gave a $\Omega(n \log n)$ lower bound for the detection of a square in a word.

75   Testing Overlaps in a Binary Word

The goal of the problem is to design an efficient algorithm to test whether a binary word contains an overlap factor. An overlap is a factor whose exponent is larger than 2. A word contains an overlap if equivalently it has a factor of the form $auaua$, where a is a letter and u is a word.

The Thue–Morse word $\mu^{\infty}(a)$ is an example of an infinite overlap-free word. It is generated by the Thue–Morse morphism μ (defined by $\mu(a) = ab$ and $\mu(b) = ba$) that preserves overlap-freeness of words.

For a binary word x we define its decomposition $uyv = x$, formally a triple (u, y, v): $|u|$ is the smallest position on x of a longest factor y that belongs to $\{ab, ba\}^{+}$. The decomposition is called an RS-factorisation if $u, v \in \{\varepsilon, a, b, aa, bb\}$. RS-factorisations are transformed into words in $\{ab, ba\}^{*}$ by the partial functions f or g as follows (c and d are letters and the bar function exchanges letters a and b):

$$
f(uyv) = \begin{cases} y & \text{if } u = v = \varepsilon \\ \bar{c}cy & \text{if } u = c \text{ or } cc \text{ and } v = \varepsilon \\ yd\bar{d} & \text{if } u = \varepsilon \text{ and } v = d \text{ or } dd \\ \bar{c}cyd\bar{d} & \text{if } u = c \text{ or } cc \text{ and } v = d \text{ or } dd \end{cases}
$$

$$
g(uyv) = \begin{cases} y & \text{if } u = v = \varepsilon \\ \bar{c}cy & \text{if } u = c \text{ or } cc \text{ and } v = \varepsilon \\ yd\bar{d} & \text{if } u = \varepsilon \text{ or } c \text{ or } cc \text{ and } v = d \text{ or } dd \end{cases}
$$

OVERLAPFREE(x non-empty binary word)

1   **while** $|x| > 6$ **do** ▷ below c and d are letter variables
2       $uyv \leftarrow RS - factorisation(x)$
3   **if** uyv is not an RS-factorisation **then**
4   **return** FALSE
5   **if** $[u = cc$ and $(ccc$ or $cc\bar{c}cc\bar{c}c$ prefix of $uy)]$ or
            $[v = dd$ and $(ddd$ or $d\bar{d}dd\bar{d}d$ suffix of $uy)]$ **then**
6   **return** FALSE
7   **if** $(u = c$ or $u = cc)$ and $(v = d$ or $v = dd)$ and
            uyv is a square **then**
8           $x \leftarrow \mu^{-1}(g(uyv))$
9   **else** $x \leftarrow \mu^{-1}(f(uyv))$
10   **return** TRUE

> **Question.** Show that Algorithm OVERLAPFREE runs in linear time for testing if its binary input word is overlap free.

Solution

The proof of correctness of OVERLAPFREE is out of the scope of the problem but we give a few properties that are used to do it. The proof relies on the property of decomposition of overlap-free words used in the algorithm. To state it, let O and E be the sets

$O = \{\mathsf{aabb},\mathsf{bbaa},\mathsf{abaa},\mathsf{babb},\mathsf{aabab},\mathsf{bbaba}\},$

$E = \{\mathsf{abba},\mathsf{baab},\mathsf{baba},\mathsf{abab},\mathsf{aabaa},\mathsf{bbabb}\}.$

Let x be an overlap-free binary word. Then, if x has a prefix in O, $x[j] \neq x[j-1]$ for each odd position j satisfying $3 \leq j \leq |x| - 2$. And, if x has a prefix in E, $x[j] \neq x[j-1]$ for each even position j satisfying $4 \leq j \leq |x|-2$. Consequently, if the word is long enough, it has a long factor that belongs to $\{\mathsf{ab},\mathsf{ba}\}^+$. Namely, if $|x| > 6$, x uniquely factorises into uyv, where $u,v \in \{\varepsilon,\mathsf{a},\mathsf{b},\mathsf{aa},\mathsf{bb}\}$ and $y \in \{\mathsf{ab},\mathsf{ba}\}^+$.

Iterating the decomposition, the word x uniquely factorises into

$$u_1 u_2 \ldots u_r \cdot \mu^{r-1}(y) \cdot v_r \ldots v_2 v_1,$$

where $|y| < 7$ and $u_s, v_s \in \{\varepsilon, \mu^{s-1}(\mathsf{a}), \mu^{s-1}(\mathsf{b}), \mu^{s-1}(\mathsf{aa}), \mu^{s-1}(\mathsf{bb})\}$.

As for the running time of OVERLAPFREE, note that instructions in the while loop execute in time $O(|x|)$. Since the length of x is essentially halved at each step by the action of the Thue–Morse morphism, this results in a total linear-time execution of the loop. The last test is done on a word of length at most 6, and therefore takes constant time, which proves the whole algorithm runs in time $O(|x|)$.

Notes

Most properties of overlap-free words concerned by this problem have been shown by Restivo and Salemi [207], who deduced the polynomial growth of their number according to the length. The present algorithm is by Kfoury [158], who proved tighter properties on overlap-free words and eventually reduced slightly the previous bound on the number of overlap-free words of a given length.

The present algorithm gives a direct solution to the question. A more generic solution that requires more tools is given by Problem 87 with an algorithm that computes all runs in a word. To detect overlap-freeness with it, it suffices to check that the exponent of all runs is exactly 2 (it cannot be smaller by the run definition). The latter algorithm also runs in linear time on binary words.

76   Overlap-Free Game

The game relies on the notion of overlaps occurring in words. A word contains
an overlap (factor of exponent larger than 2) if one of its factors is of the form
$avava$ for a letter a and a word v.

The overlap-free game of length n is played between two players, Ann and
Ben, on the alphabet $A = \{0, 1, 2, 3\}$. Players extend an initially empty word
by alternately appending a letter to the word. The game ends when the length
of the emerging word is n.

We assume that Ben makes the first move and that n is even. Ann wins if
there is no overlap in the final word. Otherwise, Ben is the winner.

Ann's winning strategy. Let $d \in A$ be the letter Ann adds during the kth
move. If Ben just added the letter c, d is defined by

$$d = c \oplus \mathbf{f}[k],$$

where $x \oplus y = (x + y) \bmod 4$ and $\mathbf{f} = f^\infty(1)$ is the infinite square-free word
obtained by iterating the morphism f defined on $\{1, 2, 3\}^*$ by $f(1) = 123$,
$f(2) = 13$ and $f(3) = 2$ (see Problem 79). Word $\mathbf{f}$ and a series of moves
look like

$\mathbf{f}$	1		2		3		1		3		2		1		2	$\cdots$
moves	0	1	2	0	0	3	2	3	3	2	3	1	1	2	1	3	$\cdots$

> **Question.** Show that Ann always wins against Ben in the overlap-free game
> of any even length n when using Ann's strategy.

[**Hint:** The sum of letters of any odd-length factor of $\mathbf{f}$ is not divisible by 4.]

Solution
To answer the question we definitely use the fact the word $\mathbf{f}$ is square free but
also use here the crucial property stated in the hint.

Proof of the hint. Let $\alpha = |v|_1$, $\beta = |v|_2$ and $\gamma = |v|_3$ be the respective
number of occurrences of letters 1, 2 and 3 in v. Due to its morphic definition
the word $\mathbf{f}$ is composed of blocks 123, 13 and 2. Hence there is always a
single occurrence of 1 between any two (not adjacent) consecutive occurrences
of 3's. This implies $|\alpha - \gamma| \leq 1$.

If $|\alpha - \gamma| = 1$, $\alpha + 2\beta + 3\gamma$ is not divisible by 2 and consequently not
divisible by 4.

Otherwise $\alpha = \gamma$ and then β is odd because the length $\alpha + \beta + \gamma = |v|$ is
odd. This implies $2\beta \bmod 4 = 2$. Hence $\alpha \oplus 2\beta \oplus 3\gamma = 2\beta \bmod 4 = 2$, and
the sum of letters of v is not divisible by 4, which achieves the hint's proof.

Correctness of Ann's strategy. We prove it by contradiction. Assume that at some moment in the game the word w gets an overlap, which is then of the form $cvcvc$ for $c \in A$. Let us distinguish two cases.

Case $|cv|$ is even. Choosing either $u = cv$ or $u = vc$, the word w contains a square uu for which $|u|$ is even and its first letter is a Ben's move in the game. The square looks like

$$uu = b_1 a_1 b_2 a_2 \ldots b_k a_k \ b_1 a_1 b_2 a_2 \ldots b_k a_k,$$

where b_i's correspond to Ben's moves and a_i's to Ann's moves. Denoting $x \ominus y = (x - y) \bmod 4$, the word $e_1 e_2 \ldots e_k \ e_1 e_2 \ldots e_k$, where $e_i = (b_i \ominus a_i)$ is a square in $\mathbf{f}$. So this case is impossible because $\mathbf{f}$ is square free.

Case $|cv|$ is odd. As above, the word w contains a square uu for which $|u|$ is odd and its first letter corresponds to a Ben's move. Observe that $|u| > 1$, since the second letter is from Ann's move and is different from Ben's move.

We demonstrate the proof for $|u| = 7$, which clearly shows the pattern of the general proof. Let $u = b_1 a_1 \ b_2 a_2 \ b_3 a_3 \ b_4$, where b_i are Ben's moves and a_i's are Ann's moves. The square is of the form

$$uu = b_1 a_1 \ b_2 a_2 \ b_3 a_3 \ b_4 b_1 \ a_1 b_2 \ a_2 b_3 \ a_3 b_4.$$

Consequently $\mathbf{f}$ contains the factor $e_1 e_2 e_3 e_4 e_5 e_6 e_7$, where
$e_1 = a_1 \ominus b_1$, $e_2 = a_2 \ominus b_2$, $e_3 = a_3 \ominus b_3$, $e_4 = b_1 \ominus b_4$,
$e_5 = b_2 \ominus a_1$, $e_6 = b_3 \ominus a_2$, $e_7 = b_4 \ominus a_3$.
We get

$$e_1 \oplus e_2 \oplus e_3 \oplus e_4 \oplus e_5 \oplus e_6 \oplus e_7 \ = \ 0,$$

writing the sum as
$(a_1 \ominus b_1) \oplus (b_1 \ominus b_4) \oplus (b_4 \ominus a_3) \oplus (a_3 \ominus b_3) \oplus (b_3 \ominus a_2) \oplus (a_2 \ominus b_2) \oplus (b_2 \ominus a_1)$.
But this is impossible because from the hint the sum of letters of an odd-length factor of $\mathbf{f}$ is not divisible by 4.

To conclude, since no case is possible, w contains no overlap and Ann's strategy causes her to win.

Notes
The solution of the problem is a version of the Thue game strategy presented in [132]. Note Ben has a simple winning strategy if the game is played with only three letters and Ann sticks to a similar strategy.

77   Anchored Squares

When searching, in a divide-and-conquer way, a word for square factor it is natural to look for squares in the product of two square-free words. The problem deals with the latter question and extends to a square-freeness test running in $O(n \log n)$ time on a word of length n.

The method based on prefix tables (see Problem 74) achieves the same goal but requires tables of size $O(n)$ while the present solution needs only a few variables in addition to input.

Let y and z be two square-free words. Algorithm RIGHT tests if yz contains a square centred in z only. Other squares in the product can be found symmetrically.

The algorithm examines all possible periods of a square. Given a period p (see picture), the algorithm computes the longest common suffix $u' = z[j \mathinner{\ldotp\ldotp} p - 1]$ between y and $z[0 \mathinner{\ldotp\ldotp} p - 1]$. Then it checks if $z[0 \mathinner{\ldotp\ldotp} j - 1]$ occurs at position p on z, scanning z from the right position $k - 1$ of the potential square. If it is successful, a square is found.

RIGHT(y, z non-empty square-free strings)

```
1   (p, end) ← (|z|, |z|)
2   while p > 0 do
3       j ← min{q : z[q .. p − 1] suffix of y}
4       if j = 0 then
5           return TRUE
6       k ← p + j
7       if k < end then
8           end ← min{q : z[q .. k − 1] suffix of z[0 .. j − 1]}
9           if end = p then
10              return TRUE
11      p ← max{j − 1, ⌊p/2⌋}
12  return FALSE
```

> **Question.** Show both that Algorithm RIGHT returns true if and only if the word yz contains a square centred in z and that its running time is $O(|z|)$ with only constant extra space.

In Algorithm RIGHT the role of variable *end* and instructions at lines 7 and 11 are crucial to get the running time announced in the question. Note that it does not depend on the length of y.

Solution

Correctness of RIGHT. This relies on the next statement, whose combinatorial proof is left to the reader. It is illustrated by the following picture, in which $u' = z[j \mathinner{.\,.} p - 1]$ is the longest common suffix of y and $z[0 \mathinner{.\,.} p - 1]$ computed at line 3, and v' is the longest common suffix of $z[0 \mathinner{.\,.} j - 1]$ and $z[p \mathinner{.\,.} k - 1]$ possibly computed at line 8. A test in the algorithm can be added to discard an empty u', since it cannot lead to a square because z is square-free.

Lemma 6 *Let y and z be two square-free words and vuv be the shortest prefix of z for which u is a suffix of y. Let u' and v' be as described above, and w and w', $|w| = |w'|$, as in the picture.*

Assume that vu is a proper prefix of $wv'u'$. Then, vu is a proper prefix of wv' or $|vu| \le |wv'u'|/2$. The word vuv is also a prefix of $wv'u'w'$.

The correctness follows from the conclusion of the lemma after checking that u' and v' are correctly computed with indices j and *end* respectively. The next value of p assigned at line 11 applies the first conclusion of the lemma. The second conclusion is used at line 7 after the assignment of the variable k to skip a useless computation of v' when the condition is not met.

Running time of RIGHT. The worst-case running time of Algorithm RIGHT relies on the maximum number of letter comparisons, which we evaluate. Let p' and p'', $p' > p''$, be two consecutive values of the variable p during a run of the algorithm; that is, p' is the value of p when entering the while loop, and p'' is its value at the end of the loop execution.

If a test is added to discard an empty u' we have $p'' = p' - 1$ after 1 comparison. Otherwise we have $p'' = \max\{j' - 1, \lfloor p'/2 \rfloor\}$, where j' is the value of j after execution of line 3. If $j' - 1$ is the maximum, the number of comparisons at this line is $p' - p''$. Otherwise the number of comparisons is no more than $2(p' - p'')$. Summing up on all the executions of the loop we get no more than $2|z|$ letter comparisons at line 3.

Due to the role of the variable *end*, positive letter comparisons on letters of $z[p..end - 1]$ at line 8 are all at different positions on z, which gives a maximum of $|z|$ comparisons. Besides, there is at most one negative comparison for each value of p. Then no more than $2|z|$ letter comparisons at line 8. Therefore the total number of letter comparisons is no more than $4|z|$, yielding a $O(|z|)$ running time.

Notes

The bound on the number of letter comparisons performed by Algorithm RIGHT on words y and z is $2|z| - 1$ when y is a Zimin word (see Problem 43) and $z = \#y$ for a letter $\#$ not appearing in y, for example when $y =$ abacabadabacaba.

The first design of Algorithm RIGHT with the constant extra space feature is by Main and Lorentz [179]. The slight improvement given here appears in [66].

A solution to the question using prefix tables or analogue tables, like in Problem 74, is described in [74, 98]. The computation of j and of *end* in Algorithm RIGHT are often referred to as Longest Common Extensions (LCEs). They can be found in constant time after some preprocessing when the alphabet is linearly sortable; see, for example, the method designed by Fischer and Heun in [115]. This latter type of solution is used in Problem 87.

Solutions of the question with a dual Algorithm LEFT lead to an algorithm that tests the square-freeness of a word of length n and runs in $O(n \log n)$ time using only constant extra space. The optimality is proved in [179]. On a fixed-size alphabet, it also leads to a linear-time square-freeness test (see [67]) using a factorisation of the word similar to the factorisation by Lempel and Ziv described in Chapter 6.

Extension to the computation in $O(n \log n)$ time of runs occurring in a word of length n is treated in [84].

78 Almost Square-Free Words

Testing if a word that contains no short squares is square free can be done in a more efficient and simpler way than with the methods treating ordinary words. This is the object of the problem.

A word w is said to be *almost square free* if it does not contain any square factor of length smaller than $|w|/2$. Such words have a useful property stated in the observation, in which $Occ(z, w)$ denotes the set of starting positions of occurrences of z in the word w.

Observation 1. If z is a factor of length $|w|/8$ of an almost square-free word w, then z is non-periodic (its smallest period is larger than $|z|/2$), $|Occ(z, w)| < 8$ and $Occ(z, w)$ can be computed in linear time and constant space.

Under the hypothesis of the observation, the computation of $Occ(z, w)$ is realised, for example, by Algorithm NAIVESEARCH, a naive version of Algorithm KMP.

NAIVESEARCH(z, w non-empty words)
1 $(i, j) \leftarrow (0, 0)$
2 $Occ(z, w) \leftarrow \emptyset$
3 **while** $j \leq |w| - |z|$ **do**
4   **while** $i < |z|$ and $z[i] = w[j + i]$ **do**
5          $i \leftarrow i + 1$
6   **if** $i = |z|$ **then**
7          $Occ(z, w) \leftarrow Occ(z, w) \cup \{j\}$
8      $(j, i) \leftarrow (j + \max\{1, \lfloor i/2 \rfloor\}, 0)$
9 **return** $Occ(z, w)$

Question. Design an algorithm that checks in linear time with constant space if an almost square-free word w is square free, assuming for simplicity that $|w| = 2^k, k \geq 3$.

[**Hint:** Use a factorisation of w into short factors, and apply Algorithm NAIVESEARCH and Observation 1.]

Solution
The idea of the solution is to factorise w into short blocks that a large square cannot miss.

To do so, let $\ell = 2^{k-3}$ and $z_r = w[r \cdot \ell \mathinner{..} r \cdot \ell + \ell - 1]$ for $r = 0, 1, \ldots, 7$. Let also $Z = \{z_0, z_1, \ldots, z_7\}$.

Consider the operation *TestSquare*(p, q) that checks if there is a square of length $2(q - p)$ in w containing positions p, q, $p \leq q$. The operation is easily performed in time $O(n)$ and constant space using extensions to the left and to the right like in Problem 74. Based on the operation, the following fact is a straightforward observation.

Observation 2. If w is almost square free then it contains a square if and only if

$$\exists z \in Z\ \exists p, q \in Occ(z, w)\ TestSquare(p, q) = \text{True}.$$

We know that the sets Z and $Occ(z, w)$ are of constant size. Now the required algorithm is a direct implementation of Observation 1 and of Observation 2, using a constant number of executions of Algorithms NAIVESEARCH and TESTSQUARE (the latter implements *TestSquare*(p, q)). Since each of them works in linear time and constant space, this achieves the answer.

Notes

The above method easily extends to test if a word of length $n = 2^k$ that has no square factor of length smaller than 2^3 is square free. This yields an algorithm running in time $O(n \log n)$ and in constant space. The sketch is as follows. For each $m = 3, 4, \ldots, k$ in this order, the algorithm checks if overlapping segments of length 2^m are square free assuming that they are almost square free. The segments that overlap are chosen by intervals of length 2^{m-1}. As soon as a square is found the algorithm stops and reports its occurrence. Since for a given m the total length of segments is $O(n)$ this leads to an overall $O(n \log n)$ running time.

The presented algorithm is adapted from a method by Main and Lorentz [180].

79   Binary Words with Few Squares

The goal of the problem is to exhibit binary words containing the fewest number of (distinct) square factors.

A square is a word whose exponent is even; it is of the form $u^2 = uu$ for a non-empty word u. The longest words on the binary alphabet $\{0,1\}$ containing no square as factor are 010 and 101. But there are square-free infinite words on three-letter alphabets. One of them, on the alphabet $\{a,b,c\}$, is obtained by iterating the morphism f defined by

$$\begin{cases} f(a) = abc \\ f(b) = ac \\ f(c) = b, \end{cases}$$

which gives the infinite square-free word

$$\mathbf{f} = f^{\infty}(a) = abcacbabcbacabcacbacabcb\cdots$$

despite the fact that f does not preserve square-freeness of words, since $f(aba) = abcacabc$ that contains the square $(ca)^2$.

A cube is a word whose exponent is a multiple of 3.

> **Question.** Show that no infinite binary word contains less than 3 squares. Show that no infinite binary word that contains only 3 squares avoids cubes, that is, is cube free.

Let g be the morphism from $\{a,b,c\}^*$ to $\{0,1\}^*$ defined by

$$\begin{cases} g(a) = 01001110001101 \\ g(b) = 0011 \\ g(c) = 000111. \end{cases}$$

Note that $g(ab)$ contains the three squares, 0^2, 1^2 and 10^2, as well as the two cubes 0^3 and 1^3.

> **Question.** Show there are only three squares and two cubes occurring in $\mathbf{g} = g(f^{\infty}(a))$.

[**Hint:** Consider distances between consecutive occurrences of 000.]

Solution
Checking the first assertion is a mere verification on the trie of binary words. Similarly, a word containing exactly three squares and no cube has maximal length 12, which can be checked with the next trie.

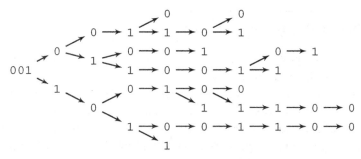

To prove the property of **g** we consider occurrences of 000 in it. In fact, distances between two consecutive occurrences are in {7, 11, 13, 17}:

$$g(\text{ac}) = 01001110\underline{000}1101\ \underline{000}111 \qquad\qquad 7$$
$$g(\text{abc}) = 01001110\underline{000}1101\ 0011\ \underline{000}111 \qquad 11$$
$$g(\text{ca}) = \underline{000}111\ 01001110\underline{000}1101 \qquad\qquad 13$$
$$g(\text{cba}) = \underline{000}111\ 0011\ 01001110\underline{000}1101 \qquad 17.$$

Factors of **g** containing few occurrences of 000 have a bounded length; then it can be checked directly they do not have more squares than expected. We show it holds for other factors by contradiction.

Assume **g** contains a (large enough) square w^2 with an even number of occurrences of 000. Let us consider the two consecutive occurrences on each side of the centre of the square and consider their distance is 7. This implies the centre of the square is in the occurrence of 1101 inside $g(\text{ac})$. Since the set $\{g(\text{a}), g(\text{b}), g(\text{c})\}$ is a prefix code, possibly taking a conjugate of the square yields that it is of the form $g(cvacva)$ for some word $v \in \{\text{a}, \text{b}, \text{c}\}^*$. This is a contradiction since $f^\infty(\text{a})$ is square free.

Cases in which the distance between consecutive occurrences of 000 is 11, 13 or 17 are dealt with similarly.

Assume now w^2 contains an odd number of occurrences of 000. Then w is of the form $0y00$ or symmetrically $00y0$ for a binary word y. Taking a conjugate as above produces a square in $f^\infty(\text{a})$, a contradiction.

Notes
The square-free word **f** is given with a different construction and a proof in Problem 80 after a translation with the alphabetic morphism α defined by $\alpha(1) = \text{c}$, $\alpha(2) = \text{b}$ and $\alpha(3) = \text{a}$.

The existence of an infinite binary word with only three squares and two cubes was initially proved by Fraenkel and Simpson [117]. Simpler proofs are by Rampersad et al. [205] and by Badkobeh [18] (see related questions in [19]). The present proof with the morphism *g* is from [18].

80   Building Long Square-Free Words

A word is square free if it does not contain any factor of the form uu for a non-empty word u. Generating long square-free words is meaningful only for alphabets of size at least three because the longest square-free words on a two-letter alphabet like {a, b} are aba and bab.

The goal of the problem is to design an algorithm generating long square-free words in an almost real-time way. Algorithm SQUAREFREEWORD does it using the function bin-parity(n) that denotes the parity (0 if even, 1 if odd) of the number of 1's in the binary representation of the natural number n. The delay between computing two outputs is proportional to the evaluation of that function.

SQUAREFREEWORD

```
1   prev ← 0
2   for n ← 1 to ∞ do
3        ▷ prev = max{i : i < n and bin-parity(i) = 0}
4        if bin-parity(n) = 0 then
5             output (n − prev)
6             prev ← n
```

The generated word α starts with: 3 2 1 3 1 2 3 2 1 2 3 1 $\cdots$.

Question. Show Algorithm SQUAREFREEWORD constructs arbitrarily long square-free words over the ternary alphabet {1, 2, 3}.

[**Hint:** The condition at line 4 holds only when n is the position of an occurrence of a in the Thue–Morse word **t**.]

Solution

The question is related to the overlap-freeness of the Thue–Morse word **t** (it contains no factor of the form $cucuc$ for a letter c and a word u). Running Algorithm SQUAREFREEWORD up to $n = 18$ gives the output 321312321. Assigning letter a to position n if the condition at line 4 holds and letter b if not, we get the table below, where the third row gives the output $n - prev(n)$ if the condition holds, associated with the current value of n.

0	1	2	3	4	5	6	7	8	9	10	11	12	13	14	15	16	17	18
a	b	b	a	b	a	a	b	b	a	a	b	a	b	b	a	b	a	a
3			2		1	3			1	2		3			2		1	

The algorithm exploits the following definition of **t**: $\mathbf{t}[n] = $ a if and only if bin-parity$(n) = 0$. This equality is easily derived from other definitions of **t** in Chapter 1.

Word α. The square-freeness of the word α computed by Algorithm SQUARE-FREEWORD relies on the fact that **t** is overlap free.

Let τ be the morphism from $\{1, 2, 3\}^*$ to $\{a, b\}^*$ defined by $\tau(1) = $ a, $\tau(2) = $ ab and $\tau(3) = $ abb. Note that **t** factorises uniquely on the suffix code $\{a, ab, abb\}$. Algorithm SQUAREFREEWORD outputs i when the factor $\tau(i)$a is virtually detected in **t**.

Assume by contradiction that the output word contains a (non-empty) square factor uu. Then $\tau(uu)$ appears in **t**. But since both $u = $ av for a word v and the occurrence of $\tau(uu)$ is immediately followed by letter a, **t** contains the overlap avava, a contradiction. Therefore the output word α is square free.

Note that $a = h^\infty(3)$, where the morphism h, analogue to f in Problem 79, is defined by: $h(3) = 321, h(2) = 31$ and $h(1) = 2$.

Notes

A proof of the Thue–Morse word overlap-freeness may be found in [175, chapter 2]. The correctness of SQUAREFREEWORD also follows combinatorial proofs from the same chapter.

We give three alternative constructions of infinite square-free words β, γ, δ, omitting technical proofs:

- $\beta[i] = $ c if $\mathbf{t}[i] = \mathbf{t}[i + 1]$ and $\beta[i] = \mathbf{t}[i]$ otherwise.
- $\gamma[i] = $ c if $\mathbf{t}[i - 1] = \mathbf{t}[i]$ and $\gamma[i] = \mathbf{t}[i]$ otherwise.
- $\delta[0] = 0$ and, for $n > 0$, $\delta[n]$ is
  $\min\{k \geq 0 : k \neq \delta[\lfloor n/2 \rfloor]$ and $\delta[0 .. n - 1] \cdot k$ is square free$\}$.
  The word δ can be computed using the following formula:
      if $h(n) = 1$ **then** $\delta[n] = 0$
      else if bin-parity$(n) = 1$ **then** $\delta[n] = 1$
      else $\delta[n] = 2$,
  where, for $n > 0$, $h(n)$ is the parity of the length of the block of 0's at the end of the binary representation of n.

Despite different constructions the four defined words α, β, γ and δ are essentially almost the same (after renaming letters and in some cases removing the first letter). The number of square-free words of length n over a ternary alphabet, $sqf(n)$, is known to grow exponentially with n, as proved by Brandenburg [42] and later tuned by several authors. The first values of $sqf(n)$ are listed in the table:

n	1	2	3	4	5	6	7	8	9	10	11	12	13
$sqf(n)$	3	6	12	18	30	42	60	78	108	144	204	264	342

n		14	15	16	17	18	19	20	21	22	23	24
$sqf(n)$		456	618	798	1044	1392	1830	2388	3180	4146	5418	7032

In contrast, the number of overlap-free binary words of length n over a binary alphabet only grows polynomially, as shown by Restivo and Salemi [207] (see Problem 75).

---

81   Testing Morphism Square-Freeness

Square-free morphisms are word morphisms that preserve word square-freeness. These morphisms provide a useful method to generate by iteration square free words. The problem aim is to give an effective characterisation of square-free morphisms, which yields a linear-time test according to the morphism length on a fixed-size alphabet.

A square free morphism h satisfies: $h(x)$ is square free when x is. We also say h is k-square free if the condition is satisfied for $|x| \leq k$. In general k-square-freeness does not imply square-freeness. For example, h_1 is a shortest square-free morphism from $\{a, b, c\}^*$ to itself, but h_2 from $\{a, b, c\}^*$ to $\{a, b, c, d, e\}^*$ is not square free although it is 4-square free.

$$\begin{cases} h_1(a) = \mathsf{abcab} \\ h_1(b) = \mathsf{acabcb} \\ h_1(c) = \mathsf{acbcacb} \end{cases} \qquad \begin{cases} h_2(a) = \mathsf{deabcbda} \\ h_2(b) = \mathsf{b} \\ h_2(c) = \mathsf{c}. \end{cases}$$

The following characterisation is based on the notion of pre-square. Let z be a factor of $h(a)$, $a \in A$. Its occurrence at position i is called a pre-square if there is a word y for which ay (resp. ya) is square free and z^2 occurs in $h(ay)$ at position i (resp. in $h(ya)$ with centre i). It is clear that if some $h(a)$ has a pre-square h is not a square-free morphism. The converse holds up to an additional condition.

Question. Show that a morphism h is square free if and only if it is 3-square free and no $h(a)$, $a \in A$, contains a pre-square factor.

[**Hint:** Discuss cases using the picture below that displays a square z^2 in $h(x)$, where $x = x[0 .. m]$.]

Question. Show that for uniform morphisms 3-square-freeness implies square-freeness, and for morphisms on 3-letter alphabets 5-square-freeness implies square-freeness.

Solution

Pre-square condition. To prove the statement in the first question we only have to show that a non-square-free morphism breaks one of the two conditions because the converse is obvious.

$h(x[0])$	$h(x[1 .. j - 1])$	$h(x[j])$	$h(x[j + 1 .. m - 1])$	$h(x[m])$
		z		z	
α : $\bar{\alpha}$	u	β : $\bar{\beta}$	v	γ : $\bar{\gamma}$

Let $x = x[0 .. m]$, for which $h(x)$ contains a square z^2. Possibly chopping letters at the ends of x, we may assume the occurrence of z^2 starts in $h(x[0])$ and ends in $h(x[m])$ (see picture).

Note that if $h(a)$ is a prefix or a suffix of $h(b)$, $a \neq b$, the morphism is not even 2-square free. Therefore we can assume $\{h(a) : a \in A\}$ is a (uniquely decipherable) prefix and suffix code.

Let α, $\bar{\alpha}$, β, $\bar{\beta}$, γ and $\bar{\gamma}$ be as displayed in the picture.

First, if $\bar{\alpha} = \bar{\beta}$, by prefix codicity $x[1 .. j - 1] = x[j + 1 .. m - 1]$, and then $\beta = \gamma$. Since x is square free, $x[0] \neq x[j]$ and $x[j] \neq x[m]$. Thus $x[0]x[j]x[m]$ is square free but $h(x[0]x[j]x[m])$ contains $(\bar{\alpha}\beta)^2$: h is not 3-square free.

Assume w.l.o.g. in the next cases that $\bar{\alpha}\delta = \bar{\beta}$ for $\delta \neq \varepsilon$.

Second, if $x[1] \neq x[j]$, let i be the smallest index for which δ is a prefix of $h(x[1 .. i])$. Then $x[j]x[1 .. i]$ is square free but $h(x[j]x[1 .. i])$ contains δ^2: there is a pre-square in $h(x[j])$.

Third, if $x[1] = x[j]$, $h(x[j])$ follows $\bar{\alpha}$ in z then $h(x[j .. m])$ starts with $(\beta\bar{\alpha})^2$: there is a pre-square in $h(x[j])$.

Considering symmetric cases as above ends the proof.

Uniform morphism. When the morphism is uniform, it can just be remarked that the pre-square condition of the first statement is equivalent to the 2-square-free property, which is implied by the 3-square-free condition.

From a 3-letter alphabet. Let A be a 3-letter alphabet. Assume there is a pre-square in $h(a)$, $a \in A$, and that y extends the pre-square into a square in $h(ay)$. Possibly chopping a suffix of y, the letter a can only reappear as its last letter. The word ay being square free on 3 letters, ya^{-1} is square free on 2 letters, which implies its length is at most 3. Therefore $|ay| \leq 5$, which resorts to the 5-square-free condition on h.

Example h_2 shows the bound 5 is optimal.

Notes

A square-free morphism h provides an interesting tool to generate an infinite square-free words: if $h(a)$ is of the form ay for some letter a and a non-empty word y, iterating h from a gives the square-free infinite word $h^\infty(a)$. Note, however, the morphism f of Problem 79 is not square-free but $f^\infty(a)$ is. More is presented by Berstel and Reutenauer in Lothaire [175, chapter 2]; see also [35].

The full proof of the first statement appears in [65] together with some consequences of the result.

---

82   Number of Square Factors in Labelled Trees

It is known that the number of (distinct) square factors in a given word is linear (see Problem 72). Unfortunately, the property does not hold for edge-labelled trees.

The problem shows a surprising lower bound based on relatively simple example trees.

> **Question.** Prove that an edge-labelled binary tree of size n can contain $\Omega(n^{4/3})$ (distinct) square factors.

[**Hint:** Consider comb trees.]

Solution

Denote by $\mathsf{sq}(T)$ the number of square factors along the branches of an edge-labelled tree T. To prove the result we consider a special family of very simple trees, called combs, that achieves the largest possible number of squares in asymptotic terms.

A *comb* is a labelled tree that consists of a path called the *spine* with at most one *branch* attached to each node of the spine. All spine-edges are labelled by the letter a. Each branch is a path whose label starts with letter b followed by a number of a's. In the graphical example below the comb contains 14 square factors:

- $a^2, (aa)^2, (aaa)^2$,
- all cyclic rotations of: $(ab)^2, (aab)^2$ and $(aaab)^2$,
- and the squares $(abaaa)^2$ and $(aaaba)^2$.

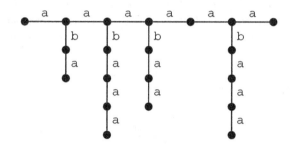

We show that there exists a family T_m of special combs that satisfy $sq(T_m) = \Omega(|T_m|^{4/3})$. From this result one easily obtains $sq(T) = \Omega(n^{4/3})$ for a tree T of size n.

We consider the integer $m = k^2$ and define the set

$$Z_m = \{1, \ldots, k\} \cup \{i.k : 1 \le i \le k\}.$$

For example, $Z_9 = \{1, 2, 3, 6, 9\}$.

Observation. For each integer d, $0 < d < m$, there exist $i, j \in Z_m$ for which $i - j = d$.

Proof Each number d, $0 < d < m$, has a unique representation in the form $p\sqrt{m} - q$ where $0 < p, q \le \sqrt{m}$. Choosing $i = p\sqrt{m}$ and $j = q$ gives the conclusion. ∎

The special comb T_m is then defined as follows: T_m consists of a spine of length $m - 1$ with vertices numbered from 1 to m and labelled by a^{m-1} and of branches labelled by ba^m attached to each vertex $j \in Z_m$ of the spine. The picture displays the special comb T_9 associated with $Z_9 = \{1, 2, 3, 6, 9\}$, with its spine and its five branches.

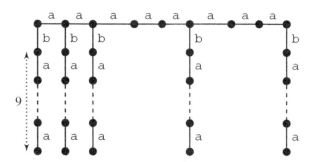

Fact. Each tree T_m satisfies $\mathsf{sq}(T_m) = \Omega(|T_m|^{4/3})$.

Proof   The above observation implies that for every d, $0 < d < m$, there are two nodes i, j of degree 3 on the spine with $i - j = d$. Thus, T_m contains all squares of the form $(a^i b a^{d-i})^2$ for $0 \le i \le d$.

Altogether this gives $\Omega(m^2)$ different squares. Since $m = k^2$, the size of T_m, its number of nodes, is $k(m + 2) + (k - 1)(k + m + 1) = O(m\sqrt{m})$. Therefore, the number of squares in T_m is $\Omega(|T_m|^{4/3})$.   ∎

Notes
The above result is optimal because the upper bound on the number of squares in labelled trees of size n is $O(n^{4/3})$. The combinatorial proof of this bound is much harder and can be found in [82].

83   Counting Squares in Combs in Linear Time

A comb is a labelled tree that consists of a path called the *spine* with at most
one *branch* attached to each node of the spine. All spine-edges are labelled
with the letter a. Each branch is a path whose label starts with the letter b
followed by a number of a's.

The number of (distinct) squares occurring on branches of a comb T can be
superlinear (see Problem 82) but despite the lower bound it is possible to count
them in linear time according to the tree size. This is the goal of the problem.
This is done with a careful encoding of squares due to their global structure.

> **Question.** Show how to compute in linear time the number of (distinct)
> square factors on branches of a binary comb.

Solution

We focus only on non-unary squares because it is clear that the number of
unary squares (of period 1) in any labelled tree can be computed in linear time.

To get the expected running time a special encoding of all squares is
required. It is based on admissible pairs of nodes of the spine. Such a pair
(i, j) is called *admissible* if $d \le p + q$, where d is the distance between i and
j ($|(j - i)|$) and p, q are the numbers of occurrences of a's on the branches
outgoing from i and from j respectively.

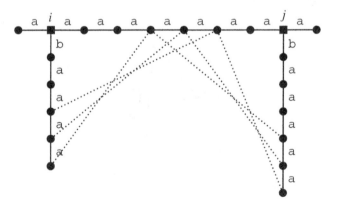

An *essential part* of a comb corresponds to an admissible pair of nodes (i, j)
on the spine, the edges between them, and the two outgoing branches whose
labels start with the letter b. All squares in each such essential part can be seen
as a *package* of squares (set of conjugates of a single factor) represented by an
interval.

The above picture shows an admissible pair (i, j) with $d = 7$, $p = 4$ and $q = 5$. The non-unary squares generated by the essential part of the tree corresponding to this pair are $(a^2ba^5)^2$, $(a^3ba^4)^2$ and $(a^4ba^3)^2$ illustrated by the dotted lines.

More generally the set of squares corresponding to a pair (i, j) is of the form $\{a^kba^ka^{d-k}ba^{d-k} : k \in [i', j'])\}$, where $[i', j'] \subseteq [i, j]$. The set can then be represented by the pair $(d, [i', j'])$. In the above example $(7, [2, 4])$ represents the set of squares $\{(a^2ba^5)^2, (a^3ba^4)^2, (a^4ba^3)^2\}$.

Fact. The number of admissible pairs in a comb T is linear according to the comb size.

Proof Observe that if (i, j) is an admissible pair with distance d and p, q the numbers of a's on the branches outgoing from i and j, then $d \leq 2 \max\{p, q\}$. Hence for a given node on the spine it is enough to consider nodes on the spine at distance at most k to the left and to the right from this node, where k is the number of a's on the branch outgoing from this node.

The total number of considered nodes is thus bounded by the total length of outgoing branches, which is $O(|T|)$.   ∎

Fact. The number of (distinct) square factors in a comb T can be computed in linear time.

Proof To achieve linear running time, we group admissible pairs into sets associated with the same distance d between the nodes of pair. For each pair (i, j) the set of squares generated by this pair corresponds to an interval. These intervals (for distinct pairs) are not necessarily disjoint; however, we can make a union of all intervals in linear time. The resulting set is again a union of intervals and its total size can be easily computed. The sets of squares corresponding to distinct groups are disjoint. We sum the numbers for each group and get the final result. This completes the proof.   ∎

Despite the fact that we can have super-linearly many distinct squares, in addition to unary squares, all of the other squares can be reported as a union of linearly many disjoint sets of the form

$$\{a^kba^ka^{d-k}ba^{d-k} : k \in [i', j']\}.$$

Notes
The present algorithm is adapted from the algorithm by Kociumaka et al. [164]. So far it is not known if squares can be counted in linear time for general trees.

84   Cubic Runs

Cubic runs constitute a particular case of runs for which bounds are easier to evaluate. As runs they encompass different types of periodic factors in a word but to a lesser extent.

A **cubic run** in a word x is a maximal periodicity in x whose length is at least three times its period. More accurately, it is an interval $[i \mathbin{..} j]$ of positions on x whose associated factor $u = x[i \mathbin{..} j]$ satisfies $|u| \geq 3per(u)$ and that is not extensible to the left nor to the right with the same period. Cubic runs in aaaabaabaabababbbbb are underlined in the picture.

We consider an ordering $<$ on the alphabet and define special positions of a run $[i \mathbin{..} j]$ in x as follows. Let p be the period of $x[i \mathbin{..} j]$ and let w be the alphabetically smallest conjugate (rotation) of $x[i \mathbin{..} i + p - 1]$. Then k is a special position of the run if $x[i \mathbin{..} j]$ contains a square ww centred at k. Special positions are shown in boldface in the above picture.

Question. Show that a cubic run has at least one special position and that two different cubic runs share no special position.

[**Hint:** Use the fact that the smallest conjugate of a primitive word, a Lyndon word, is border free.]

Question. Show both that the number of cubic runs in a word of length n is smaller than $n/2$ and that, for infinitely many n, it is at least $0.4n$.

[**Hint:** Consider the inverse alphabet ordering $<^{-1}$ and count cubic runs in words $x_m = (u^2 a^3 v^2 b^3 w^2 c^3)^m$, where $u = a^3 b^3$, $v = b^3 c^3$ and $w = c^3 a^3$.]

Solution

At least one special position in each cubic run. Let $[i \mathbin{..} j]$ be a cubic run, $p = per(x[i \mathbin{..} j])$ and w the smallest conjugate of $x[i \mathbin{..} i + p - 1]$.

If $p = 1$ it is clear that all positions in the run except the first position are special, which shows there are at least two special positions for this type of cubic run.

If $p > 1$ the square $x[i .. i + 2p - 1]$ contains at least one occurrence of w, which is followed immediately by another occurrence of w in the run. Therefore there is at least 1 special position in this type of cubic run.

Different cubic runs share no special position. Assume some position k is the centre of occurrences of ww and of $w'w'$ associated with two different cubic runs. Due to the maximality condition, the runs, being different, have different periods. If for example w' is the shorter it is then a border of w. But since w is primitive (due to the definition of p) and a smallest conjugate, it is a Lyndon word, which is known to be border free, a contradiction. Thus two different cubic runs cannot share a special position.

Less than $n/2$ cubic runs. We have already seen that cubic runs with period 1 have at least two special positions. For the other cubic runs first note the associated prefix period contains at least two different letters. Then a second special position can be found using the inverse alphabet ordering (or the greatest conjugate of the prefix period) and, as above, this position is not shared by any other run.

Since position 0 on x cannot be special, the total number of special positions in a word of length n is less than n, which implies less than $n/2$ cubic runs.

Lower bound. Observe that for any $m > 0$, the word x_m contains at least $18m - 1$ cubic runs:

$$x_m = (\mathrm{a^3b^3a^3b^3} \ \mathrm{a^3} \ \mathrm{b^3c^3b^3c^3} \ \mathrm{b^3} \ \mathrm{c^3a^3c^3a^3} \ \mathrm{c^3})^m.$$

Indeed, there are $15m$ cubic runs of period 1 whose associated factors are $\mathrm{a^3}$, $\mathrm{b^3}$ or $\mathrm{c^3}$; $2m$ cubic runs of period 6 with factors $(\mathrm{a^3b^3})^3$ and $(\mathrm{b^3c^3})^3$; and $m - 1$ cubic runs of the form $(\mathrm{c^3a^3})^3$.

Note that for $m > 2$ the whole word x_m forms an additional cubic run. Hence, in this case the word x_m has length $45m$ and contains at least $18m$ cubic runs. Thus, for $m > 2$, the number of cubic runs in x_m is not less than $0.4|x_m| = 0.4n$.

Notes
Slightly improved lower and upper bounds on the number of cubic runs in a word are shown in [85, 86].

Using an argument similar to the one above, Harju and Kärki in [137] introduced the notion of frame, square whose root is border-free, and derive upper and lower bounds on the number of frames in binary words, bounds that are close to the above bounds.

85   Short Square and Local Period

The notion of local periods in words provides a more accurate structure of its repetitiveness than its global period. The notion is central to that of critical positions (see Problem 41) and their applications.

Finding the local period at a given position i on a word x is the question of the problem. The local period $\ell per(i)$ is the period of a shortest non-empty square ww centred at position i and possibly overflowing x to the left or to the right (or both).

Question. Show how to compute all non-empty squares centred at a given position i on x in time $O(|x|)$.

```
0   1   2   3   4   5   6   7   8   9   10  11  12  13
b   a   a   b   a   a   b   a   b   a   a   b   a   a
```

For $x = $ baabaababaabaa, squares centred at 7 are $(abaab)^2$, $(ab)^2$ and the empty square. There is no non-empty square centred at 6 or 9, for example.

Question. If there exists a shortest non-empty square of period p centred at position i on x, show how to find it in time $O(p)$.

[**Hint:** Double the length of the search area.]

Here are a few local periods for the above example word: $\ell per(7) = 2$ period of $(ab)^2$, $\ell per(1) = 3$ period of $(aab)^2$, $\ell per(6) = 8$ period of $(babaabaa)^2$ and $\ell per(9) = 5$ period of $(aabab)^2$.

Question. Design an algorithm to compute the local period p at position i on x in time $O(p)$.

[**Hint:** Mind the situation where there is no square centred at i.]

Solution

Squares Let $u = x[0 \mathinner{\ldotp\ldotp} i-1]$, $v = x[i \mathinner{\ldotp\ldotp} |x|-1]$ and # a letter not in x.

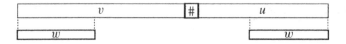

The borders w of $v\#u$ produce the squares centred at i on x. If the mere concatenation vu is used instead of $v\#u$, only its borders no longer than $\min\{|u|, |v|\}$ produce the sought squares.

Thus squares can be found with the border table of $v\#u$ whose computation take linear time (see Problem 19) like the whole process.

Shortest square. Given a length ℓ, $0 < \ell \le \min\{|u|, |v|\}$, a square of period p no more than ℓ can be found as above considering borders of $x[i \mathinner{\ldotp\ldotp} i + \ell - 1]\#x[i - \ell \mathinner{\ldotp\ldotp} i - 1]$ instead of $v\#u$. Running ℓ from 1 to at most $4p$ allows the detection of a square of period p.

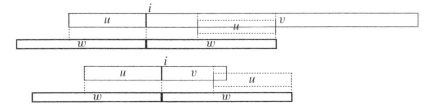

The whole process takes time

$$O(\Sigma\{\ell : \ell = 1, 2, 4, \ldots, 2^e, \text{ with } p \le 2^e < 2p\}) = O(p).$$

Local period. If there is a non-empty square centred at i, the local period at i is the period of the shortest such square.

If there is no non-empty square centred at i, the square ww whose period is the local period at i may overflow to the left or to the right (or both). The picture below shows overflows to the left.

To detect an overflow to the left, v is searched online for u with, for example, Algorithm KMP whose output is to be adapted to cope with the situation displayed in the bottom picture. This produces a potential local period p_1. Checking symmetrically for an overflow to the right by searching u^R for v^R gives another potential local period p_2. Eventually the sought local period is the minimum of the two.

The whole computation then runs in time $O(p)$, which answers the question.

Notes

The computation of a border table is treated in Problem 19 and works on general alphabets, similarly to Algorithm KMP described in Problem 26. See also textbooks on Stringology [74, 96, 98, 134, 228] and other textbooks on algorithms.

On fixed-size alphabets the computation of all local periods of a word can be done in linear time [106] using a factorisation of the word similar to its Lempel–Ziv factorisation; see Chapter 6.

---

86   The Number of Runs

A *run* is a maximal periodicity occurring in a word. Formally, a run in x is an interval $[i \mathbin{..} j]$ of positions on x whose associated factor $x[i \mathbin{..} j]$ is periodic (i.e., its smallest period p satisfies $2p \le |x[i \mathbin{..} j]| = (j - i + 1)$) and the periodicity does not extend to the right nor to the left (i.e., $x[i - 1 \mathbin{..} j]$ and $x[i \mathbin{..} j + 1]$ have larger periods when defined). The eight runs in abaababbababb are underlined in the picture.

```
0   1   2   3   4   5   6   7   8   9   10  11  12
a   b   a   a   b   a   b   b   a   b   a   b   b
```

We consider an ordering $<$ on a word alphabet and the corresponding lexicographic ordering denoted $<$ as well. We also consider the lexicographic ordering $\stackrel{\sim}{<}$, called the reverse ordering, inferred by the inverse alphabet ordering $<^{-1}$. Each run $[i \mathbin{..} j]$ is associated with its greatest suffix according to one of the two orderings as follows. Let $p = per(x[i \mathbin{..} j])$. If $j + 1 < n$ and $x[j + 1] > x[j - p + 1]$ we assign to the run the position k for which $x[k \mathbin{..} j]$ is the greatest proper suffix of $x[i \mathbin{..} j]$ according to $<$. Otherwise, k is the starting position of the greatest proper suffix of $x[i \mathbin{..} j]$ according to $\stackrel{\sim}{<}$. The position k assigned this way to a run is called its **special position**. These positions are intimately linked to Lyndon words (defined in Chapter 1), subject of the first question. The thick lines below show the greatest suffixes associated with runs in abaababbababb.

Question. Show that, if the special position k of a run of period p is defined according to $\widetilde{<}$ (resp. $<$), $x[k \mathinner{\ldotp\ldotp} k + p - 1]$ is the longest Lyndon factor of x starting at position k according to $<$ (resp. $\widetilde{<}$).

[**Hint:** The special position k of a run $[i \mathinner{\ldotp\ldotp} j]$ of period p satisfies $k \leq i + p$; see Problem 40.]

Question. Show two distinct runs have no special position in common and deduce that the number of runs in a word is smaller than its length.

Solution

Special position. Let $[i \mathinner{\ldotp\ldotp} j]$ be a run of period p with special position k. To answer the first question, note that $x[k \mathinner{\ldotp\ldotp} k + p - 1]$ is a Lyndon word because it is smaller than all its proper suffixes according to $<$. Consider a longer factor $x[k \mathinner{\ldotp\ldotp} j']$ for $k + p \leq j' \leq j$. It has period p which is smaller than its length; equivalently it is not border free, which shows it is not a Lyndon word for any of the two orderings.

There is nothing else to prove if $j + 1 = |x|$. Assume then that $j' > j$ and $a = x[j + 1]$. The picture displays the greatest suffix of $x[i \mathinner{\ldotp\ldotp} j]$ according to $\widetilde{<}$, that is, $x[k \mathinner{\ldotp\ldotp} j] = u^e v$ of period $|u|$ in which v is a proper prefix of u. Since $x[j + 1] < x[j - p + 1]$, we get $x[k + p \mathinner{\ldotp\ldotp} j + 1] < x[k \mathinner{\ldotp\ldotp} j - p + 1]$, which leads to $x[k + p \mathinner{\ldotp\ldotp} j'] < x[k \mathinner{\ldotp\ldotp} j']$ and shows that $x[k \mathinner{\ldotp\ldotp} j']$ is not a Lyndon word according to $<$.

Therefore, $x[k \mathinner{\ldotp\ldotp} k + p - 1]$ is the longest Lyndon factor of x starting at position k. Note the roles of the two orderings are perfectly symmetric.

Number of runs. Let us answer the second question by contradiction, assuming two runs share the same special position k. The position cannot be defined with the same ordering for the two runs due to the above result. Being defined by the two different orderings, the only possibility is that only one run has period 1. But then $x[k - 1] = x[k]$, which is impossible for the special position k on a non-unary run.

Since position 0 cannot be a special position, at most $n - 1$ positions can be special positions of runs in a word of length n. The previous result then implies that there are less that n runs, as stated.

Notes

The concept of a run, also called a maximal periodicity or the maximal occurrence of a repetition, coined by Iliopoulos et al. [149] when analysing repetitions in Fibonacci words, has been introduced to represent in a succinct manner all occurrences of repetitions in a word. It is known that there are only $O(n)$ of them in a word of length n from Kolpakov and Kucherov [167], who proved it in a non-constructive way.

The first explicit bound was later on provided by Rytter [214]. Several improvements on the upper bound can be found in [77, 80, 102, 203]. Kolpakov and Kucherov conjectured that this number is in fact smaller than n, which has been proved by Bannai et al. [26]. The present proof, very similar to their proof, appears in [91]. Fischer et al. [116] gave a tighter upper bound of $22n/23$ on the number of runs.

With the above notations, remark that if $k + 2p \leq j$, $k + p$ can also be considered a special position with the same property. In particular, a run whose associated word starts with a cube has at least two special positions. This gives an upper bound of $n/2$ for the maximum number of cubic runs in a word of length n (see Problem 84 and more in [25] and [86]).

---

87   Computing Runs on Sorted Alphabet

The aim of the problem is to show that all runs (maximal periodicities) in a word drawn from a linearly sortable alphabet can be computed in linear time.

The solution is based on the results of Problem 86, where it is shown that a run possesses a special position from which starts a longest Lyndon factor of the whole word. Tracking the longest Lyndon factors has to be done according to the alphabet ordering $<$ but also to its inverse $<^{-1}$. When a longest Lyndon factor is located, simple extensions from two positions to the right and to the left (like in Problem 74) can confirm the starting position of the Lyndon factor is a special position of a run whose period is the length of the Lyndon factor.

To do so we first define the **Lyndon table** *Lyn* of a (non-empty) word x. For a position i on x, $i = 0, \ldots, |x| - 1$, $Lyn[i]$ is the length of the longest Lyndon factor starting at i:

$$Lyn[i] = \max\{\ell : x[i \mathinner{.\,.} i + \ell - 1] \text{ is a Lyndon word}\}.$$

i	0	1	2	3	4	5	6	7	8	9	10	11	12	13	14	15
$x[i]$	a	b	b	a	b	a	b	a	a	b	a	b	b	a	b	a
$Lyn[i]$	3	1	1	2	1	2	1	8	5	1	3	1	1	2	1	1

> **Question.** Show that Algorithm LONGESTLYNDON correctly computes the table *Lyn*.

LONGESTLYNDON(x non-empty word of length n)

1   **for** $i \leftarrow n - 1$ **downto** 0 **do**
2       $(Lyn[i], j) \leftarrow (1, i + 1)$
3   **while** $j < n$ **and** $x[i \mathinner{.\,.} j - 1] < x[j \mathinner{.\,.} j + Lyn[j] - 1]$ **do**
4           $(Lyn[i], j) \leftarrow (Lyn[i] + Lyn[j], j + Lyn[j])$
5   **return** *Lyn*

> **Question.** Extend Algorithm LONGESTLYNDON to compute all runs occurring in a word.

[**Hint:** Use the longest common extensions like in Problem 74.]

> **Question.** What is the total running time of the algorithm if a comparison of two factors is done with the help of the ranks of their associated suffixes in the alphabetic order and if the longest common extension techniques are used?

Solution

Proofs rely on the following well-known properties of Lyndon words that may be found in [175]. First, if u and v are Lyndon words and $u < v$ then uv is also a Lyndon word (and $u < uv < v$). Second, each non-empty word factorises uniquely as $u_0 u_1 u_2 \cdots$, where each u_i is a Lyndon word and $u_0 \geq u_1 \geq u_2 \geq \cdots$. In addition, u_0 is the longest Lyndon prefix of the word. The factorisation can be computed using the *Lyn* table of the word to jump from a factor to the next one. But the table contains more information than the factorisation.

The factorisation of the above example word abbababaababbaba is abb · ab · ab · aababbab · a, corresponding to the subsequence 3, 2, 2, 8, 1 of values in its Lyndon table.

Correctness of LONGESTLYNDON. The invariant of the for loop, when processing position i, is: $Lyn[k]$ is computed for $k = i + 1, \ldots, n - 1$ and $u[i + 1 .. j - 1] \cdot u[j .. j + Lyn[j] - 1] \cdots$, where $j = i + 1 + Lyn[i + 1]$, is the Lyndon factorisation of $x[i + 1 .. n - 1]$.

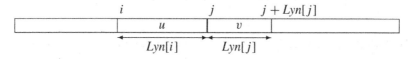

The current factor u starting at position i, initially $x[i]$, is compared to its next factor v. If $u < v$, u is replaced by uv and the comparison continues with the successor of uv. The while loop stops when the current factor u becomes no smaller than its next factor. It is clear when the loop stops that u is the longest Lyndon factor starting at i and then $Lyn[i] = |u|$. It is also clear that we get the Lyndon factorisation of $x[i .. n - 1]$, which achieves the proof of the invariant and of the correctness of LONGESTLYNDON.

Computing runs. To compute all runs in the word x, we just check for each position i if it is the special position of a run whose word period is $x[i .. i + Lyn[i] - 1]$. This is done by computing lengths ℓ and r of longest common extensions (LCEs) of the period to the left and to the right and by checking if $\ell + r \geq Lyn[i]$. If the inequality holds a run is reported.

RUNS(x non-empty word of length n)

```
1   for i ← n − 1 downto 0 do
2       (Lyn[i], j) ← (1, i + 1)
3       while j < n and x[i .. j − 1] < x[j .. j + Lyn[j] − 1] do
4           (Lyn[i], j) ← (Lyn[i] + Lyn[j], j + Lyn[j])
5       ℓ ← |lcs(x[0 .. i − 1], x[0 .. i + Lyn[i] − 1])|
6       r ← |lcp(x[i .. |x| − 1], x[i + Lyn[i] .. |x| − 1])|
7       if ℓ + r ≥ Lyn[i] then
8           output run [i − ℓ .. i + Lyn[i] + r − 1]
```

More precisely, ℓ is the length of the longest common suffix of $x[0 .. i - 1]$ and $x[0 .. i + Lyn[i] - 1]$, while r is the length of the longest common prefix of $x[i .. |x| - 1]$ and $x[i + Lyn[i] .. |x| - 1]$. They are set to null if $i = 0$ and if $i + Lyn[i] = n$ respectively.

The above process has to be repeated for the ordering $\bar{<}$ associated with the inverse alphabet ordering.

Running time of RUNS. First note that the number of word comparisons performed at line 3 by RUNS is less than $2|x|$. Indeed there is at most one negative comparison at each step. And there are less than $|x|$ positive comparisons because each reduces the number of factors of the Lyndon factorisation of x. Therefore, to get a linear-time algorithm we have to discuss how to compare words and to compute LCE.

Comparison of words at line 3 of algorithms can be realised using ranks of suffixes due to the next property.

Property. Let u be a Lyndon word and $v \cdot v_1 \cdot v_2 \ldots v_m$ be the Lyndon factorisation of a word w. Then $u < v$ if and only if $uw < w$.

Proof Assume $u < v$. If $u \ll v$ then $uw \ll vv_1v_2 \ldots v_m = w$. Otherwise u is a proper prefix v. Let $e > 0$ be the largest integer for which $v = u^e z$. Since v is a Lyndon word, z is not empty and we have $u^e < z$. Since u is not a prefix of z (by definition of e) nor z a prefix of u (because v is border free) we have $u \ll z$. This implies $u^{e+1} \ll u^e z = v$ and then $uw < w$.

Conversely, assume $v \leq u$. If $v \ll u$ we obviously have $w < uw$. It remains to consider the situation where v is a prefix of u. If it is a proper prefix, u writes vz for a non-empty word z. We have $v < z$ because u is a Lyndon word. The word z cannot be a prefix of $t = v_1 v_2 \cdots v_m$ because v would not be the longest Lyndon prefix of w, a contradiction with a property of the factorisation. Thus, either $t \leq z$ or $z \ll t$. In the first case, if t is a prefix of z, $w = vt$ is a prefix of u and then of uw, that is, $w < uw$. In the second case, for some suffix z' of z and some factor v_k of t we have $z' \ll v_k$. The factorisation implies $v_k \leq v$. Therefore, the suffix z' of u is smaller than its prefix v, a contradiction with the fact that u is a Lyndon word. ∎

For each starting position i of a suffix of x, $i = 0, \ldots, |x| - 1$, let $Rank[i]$ be the rank of the suffix $x[i \ldots |x| - 1]$ in the increasing alphabetic list of all non-empty suffixes of x (ranks range from 0 to $|x| - 1$).

Due to the property, the inequality $x[i \ldots j - 1] < x[j \ldots j + Lyn[j] - 1]$ at line 3 of the two previous algorithms rewrites $Rank[i] < Rank[j]$.

i	0	1	2	3	4	5	6	7	8	9	10	11	12	13	14	15
$x[i]$	a	b	b	a	b	a	b	a	a	b	a	b	b	a	b	a
$Lyn[i]$	3	1	1	2	1	2	1	8	5	1	3	1	1	2	1	1
$Rank[i]$	7	15	12	4	11	3	9	1	5	13	6	14	10	2	8	0

Note the Lyndon factorisation can be recovered by following the longest decreasing sequence of ranks from the first rank. It is $(7,4,3,1,0)$ in the above example, corresponding to positions $(0,3,5,7,15)$ on x and its factorisation abb · ab · ab · aababbbab · a.

As for the running time, when the table Rank of suffix ranks is precomputed, the comparison of words at line 3 can be realised in constant time. It is known that the table of ranks, inverse of the sorted list of suffixes (Suffix array), can be computed in linear time under the hypothesis that the alphabet is linearly sortable.

Instructions at lines 5–6 can executed as LCE queries and as such computed in constant time after a linear-time preprocessing under the same hypothesis (see, e.g., [115]). Therefore the whole algorithm RUNS works in linear time when the alphabet is linearly sortable.

Notes

Algorithm LONGESTLYNDON can be slightly changed to compute the Lyndon forest of a word. The forest comprises the list of Lyndon trees corresponding to factors of the Lyndon factorisation of the word.

The Lyndon tree of a Lyndon word is associated recursively with the (right) standard factorisation of a Lyndon word w not reduced to a single letter: w can be written uv, where v is chosen either as the smallest proper non-empty suffix of w or as the longest proper Lyndon suffix of w, which yields the same suffix. The word u is then also a Lyndon word and $u < v$ (see [175]).

The structure of a Lyndon tree has been shown to be the same as that of the Cartesian tree of ranks of suffixes by Hohlweg and Reutenauer [142]. Algorithm LONGESTLYNDON proceeds like a right-to-left construction of a Cartesian tree (https://en.wikipedia.org/wiki/Cartesian_tree).

The relation between Suffix arrays and Lyndon factorisations is examined by Mantaci et al. in [184]

Franek et al. ([119]) present several algorithms to compute the Lyndon table.

The reader can refer to the review by Fischer and Heun [115] concerning LCE queries. More advanced techniques to implement them over a general alphabet and to compute runs can be found in [83, 128] and references therein.

88   Periodicity and Factor Complexity

The property stated in the problem provides a useful condition to detect the periodicity of infinite words.

An infinite word x (indices run through natural numbers) is said to be ultimately periodic or simply u-periodic if it can be written yz^∞ for some (finite) words y and z, $z \neq \varepsilon$.

Let $F_x(n)$ denote the number of (distinct) factors of length n occurring in the infinite word x. The function F_x is called the factor (or subword) complexity function of x.

Question. Show that an infinite word x is u-periodic if and only if F_x is bounded by a constant.

Solution

If x is u-periodic it can be written yz^∞, where z is primitive and either y is empty or y and z end with two distinct letters. With this normalised representation of x, we get $F_x(n) = |yz|$ for every length $n \geq |yz|$, which shows that F_x is bounded by a constant.

Conversely, assume that F_x is bounded by an integer constant $m > 0$. Since $F_x(\ell) \leq F_x(\ell+1)$ for every length ℓ, the bound implies that $F_x(n) = F_x(n+1)$ for some length n. This implies that all occurrences of each length-n factor v are followed by the same letter b_v in x. Consequently, we can consider the next factor function *next* defined on non-empty factors u of length $n + 1$ as follows: $next(u) = vb_v$ where $u = av$ for a letter a.

Let w be the prefix of length n of the infinite word x. There exist p and s such that $next^s(w) = next^{s+p}(w)$, since there are only finitely many factors of length n. Thus, x is u-periodic with period p starting from position s. This completes the proof.

Notes

The u-periodicity of x is also equivalent to the condition $F_x(n) \leq n$ for some length n.

The set of boundary infinite words x for which $F_x(n) = n + 1$, for every n, is known as the set of infinite Sturmian words. They are non-u-periodic infinite words with the minimal factor complexity. In particular, the infinite Fibonacci word has this property.

More on the subject is in the book by Allouche and Shallit [7] and in the tutorial by Berstel and Karhumäki [34].

89 Periodicity of Morphic Words

The problem shows that it is possible to test whether an infinite word generated by a (finite) morphism is periodic.

An infinite morphic word is obtained by iterating a morphism θ from A^+ to itself, where $A = \{a, b, \ldots\}$ is a finite alphabet. To do so, we assume that θ is prolongable over the letter a, that is, $\theta(a) = au$ for $u \in A^+$. Then $\Theta = \theta^\infty(a)$ exists and is $au\theta(u)\theta^2(u)\cdots$. The infinite word Θ is a fixed point of θ, that is, $\theta(\Theta) = \Theta$.

The infinite word Θ is periodic if it can be written z^∞ for some (finite) words z, $z \neq \varepsilon$.

To avoid unnecessary complications we assume that the morphism θ is both irreducible, which means that any letter is accessible from any letter (for any $c, d \in A$ the letter d appears in $\theta^k(c)$ for some integer k), and is elementary, which means it is not the product $\eta \circ \zeta$ of two morphisms $\zeta : A^+ \longrightarrow B^+$ and $\eta : B^+ \longrightarrow A^+$, where B is an alphabet smaller than A. The second condition implies that θ is injective on A^* and on A^∞.

Question. For an irreducible and elementary morphism θ prolongable over letter a, design an algorithm that checks if $\Theta = \theta^\infty(a)$ is periodic and that runs in time $O(\Sigma\{|\theta(b)| : b \in A\})$.

[**Hint:** Θ is periodic if and only if it has no bispecial letter, that is, occurrences of each letter in Θ are all followed by a unique letter.]

The morphism ρ defined by $\rho(a) = ab$, $\rho(b) = ca$ and $\rho(c) = bc$ complies with the conditions and produces the periodic word $\rho^\infty(a) = abcabcabc\cdots = (abc)^\infty$. None of the letter is bispecial.

On the contrary, Fibonacci morphism ϕ, defined by $\phi(a) = ab$ and $\phi(b) = a$, also satisfies the conditions but generates the non- (ultimately) periodic Fibonacci word $\phi^\infty(a) = abaababa\cdots$. In it letter a is bispecial, since its occurrences are followed either by a or by b, while occurrences of letter b are all followed by a.

Solution

The decision algorithm builds on the combinatorial property: Θ is periodic if and only if it has no bispecial letter. Intuitively, if Θ has an infinite number of bispecial factors, its factor complexity is not bounded and it is not ultimately periodic (see Problem 88).

If the condition holds, that is, if Θ contains no bispecial letter, each letter is fully determined by the letter occurring before it. And since all letters of the alphabet appear in Θ the period word corresponds to a permutation of the alphabet. Thus the period of Θ is $|A|$.

Conversely, let us assume that Θ contains a bispecial letter and prove it is not periodic.

Let b be a bispecial letter, that is, bc and bd appear in Θ, for two distinct letters c and d. Due to the irreducibility of θ, the letter a appears in $\theta^k(b)$ for some k. Since θ is injective, $\theta^k(bc) \neq \theta^k(bd)$. Let i and j be starting positions of $\theta^k(bc)$ and $\theta^k(bd)$ on Θ. Since θ is injective on A^∞, $\Theta[i .. \infty) \neq \Theta[j .. \infty)$. Their longest common prefix v is then bispecial and contains the letter a.

We show more generally that for any bispecial factor v of Θ, v containing the letter a, there exists a longer factor with the same property.

Let i and j be two positions on Θ with $\Theta[i .. i + m] = vc$ and $\Theta[j .. j + m] = vd$, and c and d be distinct letters. Let $y = \Theta[i .. \infty)$ and $z = \Theta[j .. \infty)$. Then, again from the injectivity of θ on A^∞, we get $\theta(y) \neq \theta(z)$. Let $\theta(v)u$ be the longest common prefix of $\theta(y)$ and $\theta(z)$. So there exist two letters e and f, $e \neq f$, for which $\theta(v)ue$ and $\theta(v)uf$ are factors of Θ. Since v contains a, $|\theta(v)u| > |v|$.

Repeating the argument, we get an infinite sequence of bispecial factors of Θ. For each such v of length n we have $F_\Theta(n + 1) > F_\Theta(n)$ ($F_\Theta(n)$ is the number of factors of length n occurring in Θ) because any (length-n) word has a prolongation in Θ and v has two. This implies that $\lim_{i \to \infty} F_\Theta(i) = \infty$ and shows (see Problem 88) that Θ is not periodic, not even ultimately periodic.

The algorithm derived from the combinatorial property consists in testing if Θ contains a bispecial letter, which can be implemented to run in time $O(\Sigma\{|\theta(b)| : b \in A\})$.

Notes

The present proof of the combinatorial property is derived from the original proof by Pansiot [201] and can be found in the book by Kůrka [171, chapter 4]. The notion of an elementary morphism is from Rozenberg and Salomaa [209]. The decidability of the ultimate periodicity for non-elementary morphic words is also proved in [201].

A common property on morphisms is primitivity, an analogue to primitivity of integer matrices, a property stronger than irreducibility (the exponent k is the same for all pairs of letters). But a weaker condition can lead to the same conclusion, like when all letters appear in $\theta^k(a)$ for some $k > 0$. With such a condition, the above proof applies to the following morphism ξ that is not irreducible and produces $\Xi = \xi^\infty(a) = abcdabcd \cdots = (abcd)^\infty$. The same word is produced by the irreducible morphism ψ.

$$\begin{cases} \xi(a) = abcda \\ \xi(b) = b \\ \xi(c) = c \\ \xi(d) = d \end{cases} \qquad \begin{cases} \psi(a) = abcd \\ \psi(b) = b \\ \psi(c) = c \\ \psi(d) = dabcd \end{cases}$$

More on the topic appears in the section 'Shift Spaces' of [8].

90   Simple Anti-powers

A dual notion of periodicity or local periodicity is that of anti-powers, which is introduced in the problem.

A word $u \in \{1, 2, \ldots, k\}^{+}$ is an anti-power if each of its letters appear exactly once in it. It is a permutation of a subset of the alphabet, that is, $alph(u) = |u|$.

> **Question.** Show how to locate in time $O(n)$ anti-powers of length k occurring in a word $x \in \{1, 2, \ldots, k\}^n$.

For example, 13542 and 54231 occur in 341354231332 $\in$ $\{1, 2, \ldots, 5\}^{+}$ at positions 2 and 4 and are its only anti-powers of length 5.

Solution

The problem can be extended to locate the longest anti-power ending at any position j on x. To do so, let $antip[j]$ be

$$\max\{|u| : u \text{ antipower suffix of } x[0 .. j]\}.$$

The table corresponding to the word 341354231332 shows its two anti-powers of length 5 13542 and 54231 ending respectively at positions 6 and 8 since $antip[6] = antip[8] = 5$.

j	0	1	2	3	4	5	6	7	8	9	10	11
$x[j]$	3	4	1	3	5	4	2	3	1	3	3	2
$antip[j]$	1	2	3	3	4	4	5	4	5	2	1	2

The computation of table *antip* associated with x solves the question because an anti-power of length k ends at position j on x if $antip[j] = k$. Algorithm ANTIPOWERS computes *antip* for a word in $\{1, 2, \ldots, k\}^+$.

ANTIPOWERS($x \in \{1, 2, \ldots, k\}^+$)

```
1   for each a ∈ {1,2,...,k} do
2       pp[a] ← −1
3   pp[x[0]] ← 0
4   antip[0] ← 1
5   for j ← 1 to |x| − 1 do
6       a ← x[j]
7       if j − pp[a] > antip[j − 1] then
8           antip[j] ← antip[j − 1] + 1
9       else antip[j] ← j − pp[a]
10      pp[a] ← j
11  return antip
```

Algorithm ANTIPOWERS computes the table sequentially and uses an auxiliary array *pp* to do it. The array indexed by letters stores at a given step the previous position *pp*[*a*] of occurrences of each letter *a* met so far.

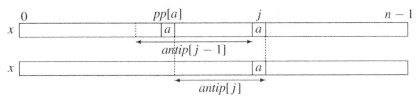

The correctness of ANTIPOWERS is rather straightforward. Indeed, if the current letter a at position j does not occur in the longest anti-power ending at position $j - 1$, the length of the anti-power ending at j is one unit more (line 8). Otherwise, as illustrated by the picture, $x[pp[a] + 1 .. j - 1]$ is an anti-power not containing a, which gives the length $j - pp[a]$ of the longest anti-power ending at j (line 9).

It is clear that the running time of ANTIPOWERS is $O(n)$.

Notes

The notion of an anti-power introduced by Fici et al. [113] refers to a word that is a concatenation of blocks of the same length but pairwise distinct. Authors show that every infinite word contains anti-powers of any anti-exponent (number of block). In [20], Badkobeh et al. design an optimal algorithm to locate these anti-powers with a specified anti-exponent. The above algorithm is the first step of their solution. See also [165].

---

91   Palindromic Concatenation of Palindromes

Palindromes constitute another type of regularity different from periodicity. They appear naturally in data folding when the process requires segments of data to be matched like in some genomic sequences. The problem deals with palindromes occurring in a product of palindromes.

Given a finite set of words X, computing the number of all palindromes in X^2 can be easily done in $n \cdot |X|$ time, where n is the total length of words in X. However, there is a much simpler and more efficient method when X is itself a set of palindromes.

> **Question.** Given a finite set X of binary palindromes whose total length is n, design an algorithm computing the number of (distinct) palindromes in X^2 and running in time $O(n + |X|^2)$.

[**Hint:** When x and y are palindromes, xy is also a palindrome if and only if $xy = yx$.]

Solution
The algorithm below is based on the crucial combinatorial property stated in the hint. Let us start proving it.

Let x and y be palindromes. If xy is a palindrome then we have $x \cdot y = (x \cdot y)^R = y^R \cdot x^R = y \cdot x$.

Conversely, if $xy = yx$ then x and y have the same primitive root (consequence of Lemma 2), which is also palindromic. Consequently it follows that $xy = (xy)^R$.

From the property, the algorithm reduces to considering words in X that have the same primitive root. We execute the following algorithm:

- Compute the root of each word.

- After roots are lexicographically sorted, split them into groups with the same root.

- In each group Y, compute the number of palindromes in Y^2. As the roots are the same we only need to compute the size of the set $\{|u| + |v| : u, v \in Y\}$, which can be done in $O(|Y|^2)$ time.

The last step can be performed in time $|Y|^2$ for each group, and altogether in time $O(|X|^2)$ since the sum of sizes of Y's is $|X|$. Sorting and computing the roots takes $O(n)$ time on a fixed-size alphabet. Consequently the algorithm works in the required $O(n + |X|^2)$ time.

Notes
The problem appeared in the 13th Polish Olympiad in Informatics, 2006.

92   Palindrome Trees

The notion of a *palindrome forest* $\mathcal{P}(x)$ provides a structural representation of all palindromes occurring in a word x. The data structure is used to perform different operations on the set of palindromic factors, such as to access efficiently to the longest palindrome ending at a given position on x or to count the number of occurrences of each palindrome in x.

The forest consists of a collection of trees in which each represents all palindromic factors in a similar way as a Suffix tree represents all factors. Suffix links are also part of the structure to get an efficient construction. However, palindrome forests are simpler than Suffix trees, since each edge is labelled by a single letter.

Each node of $\mathcal{P}(x)$ is a palindrome occurring in x. From a node z, there is an edge $z \xrightarrow{a} aza$ labelled by the letter a if aza is a palindrome in x. The empty word ε is the root of the tree for even palindromes. And each letter occurring in w is the root of a tree for odd palindromes having the letter at their centre. The picture shows the forest $\mathcal{P}(\text{ababbababaab})$ that comprises three palindrome trees.

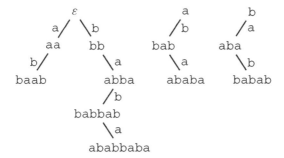

Each node of the trees can be represented by an interval $[i \mathbin{..} j]$ of positions corresponding to an occurrence of the palindrome $x[i \mathbin{..} j]$. The palindrome is also fully determined by the path from the root to the node.

> **Question.** Assume the alphabet is of constant size. Show how to construct the palindrome forest of a word in linear time according to the word length.

[**Hint:** Use suffix links.]

Solution

Algorithm PALINDROMEFOREST builds the palindrome forest of its input word x. The main trick of the construction is to augment the structure with suffix links defined as follows. For a non-empty palindrome u its suffix link points to the longest palindrome that is a proper suffix of u. It is denoted by $palsuf(u)$ and may be the empty word. A suf-ancestor of u is any node accessible from u, including u itself, by iterating suffix links.

Assume u is a palindromic suffix of $x[0 \mathinner{.\,.} i - 1]$. Let $upward(u, x[i])$ be either the lowest suf-ancestor v of u for which $x[i]vx[i]$ is a suffix of $w[0 \mathinner{.\,.} i]$ or the empty word ε.

To build the forest of x, the algorithm processes the word online. Initially, the forest consists of the roots of its trees, that is, nodes ε and a, for letters a occurring in x. Suffix links on nodes are maintained during the process, and the variable u of the algorithm stores the longest palindrome that is a suffix of the prefix of x read so far.

Inside the main for loop, the computation of the next value of u that includes the current letter $x[i]$ is done with the crucial help of *upward* at lines 4–7. The rest of the step at lines 9–15 consists in updating the forest in case a new node has to be added.

PALINDROMEFOREST(x non-empty word)

1   initialise the forest $\mathcal{P}$
2   $u \leftarrow x[0]$
3   **for** $i \leftarrow 1$ **to** $|x| - 1$ **do**
4       $v \leftarrow upward(u, x[i])$
5   **if** $v = \varepsilon$ and $x[i - 1] \neq x[i]$ **then**
6           $u \leftarrow x[i]$
7   **else** $u \leftarrow x[i]vx[i]$
8   **if** $u \notin \mathcal{P}$ **then**
9   add node u and edge $v \xrightarrow{x[i]} u$ to $\mathcal{P}$
10          $v \leftarrow upward(palsuf(v), x[i])$
11   **if** $v = \varepsilon$ **then**
12   **if** $x[i - 1] \neq x[i]$ **then**
13                  $palsuf(u) \leftarrow x[i]$
14   **else** $palsuf(u) \leftarrow \varepsilon$
15   **else** $palsuf(u) \leftarrow x[i]vx[i]$
16 **return** $\mathcal{P}$

The algorithm works in linear time mostly because the number of steps in computing *upward* shortens proportionally the depth of u and of *palsuf*(v) in the forest. In addition, each of these two depths increases by at most one unit in each iteration.

Notes

The tree structure of palindromes has been investigated by Rubinchik and Shur in [210], where it is called an *eertree*. It has been later used in the design of several algorithms related to palindromes.

93   Unavoidable Patterns

Patterns of the problem are defined with a specific alphabet of variables in addition to the finite alphabet $A = \{a, b, \ldots\}$. Variables are from the infinite alphabet $V = \{\alpha_1, \alpha_2, \ldots\}$. A pattern is a word whose letters are variables. A typical pattern is $\alpha_1 \alpha_1$: it appears in a word that contains a square. The aim of the problem is to produce unavoidable patterns.

A word $w \in A^+$ is said to contain a pattern $P \in V^*$ if $\psi(P)$ is a factor w for some morphism $\psi : alph(P)^+ \to A^+$. If not, w is said to avoid P. A pattern is *avoidable* if there are infinitely many words of A^+ avoiding it, which is equivalent (because A is finite) to the existence of an infinite word in A^∞ whose finite factors avoid it. For example, $\alpha_1 \alpha_1$ is avoidable if the alphabet has at least three letters, but is unavoidable on a binary alphabet (see Problem 79).

Zimin patterns Z_n are standard examples of unavoidable patterns. They are defined, for $n > 0$, by

$$Z_0 = \varepsilon \text{ and } Z_n = Z_{n-1} \cdot \alpha_n \cdot Z_{n-1}.$$

In particular, a word contains the Zimin pattern Z_n if it contains a factor whose Zimin type is at least n (see Problem 43). For example, the word aaaaabaabbbaaaabaabb contains Z_3 since its factor aaabaabbbaaaabaa is the image of $Z_3 = \alpha_1 \alpha_2 \alpha_1 \alpha_3 \alpha_1 \alpha_2 \alpha_1$ by the morphism ψ defined by

$$\begin{cases} \psi(\alpha_1) = \text{aa} \\ \psi(\alpha_2) = \text{ab} \\ \psi(\alpha_3) = \text{bba} \end{cases}$$

Question. Show that Zimin patterns Z_n, $n > 0$, are unavoidable.

Solution

Let k be the size of the alphabet A. Define the sequence of lengths, for $n > 1$, by

$$\ell_1 = 1 \text{ and } \ell_n = (\ell_{n-1} + 1) \cdot k^{\ell_{n-1}} + \ell_{n-1} - 1,$$

and consider the following observation before answering the question.

Observation. Any word of length ℓ_n, $n > 1$, in A^* has a factor of the form uvu, where $|u| = \ell_{n-1}$ and $|v| > 0$.

Proof Any word w of length ℓ_n contains $(\ell_{n-1} + 2) \cdot k^{\ell_{n-1}}$ factors of length ℓ_{n-1}. Since the number of distinct factors of length ℓ_{n-1} is at most $k^{\ell_{n-1}}$ there is a word u of length ℓ_{n-1} having at least $\ell_{n-1} + 2$ occurrences in w. Consequently there are two occurrences at distance at least $\ell_{n-1} + 1$ and there should be a non-empty word v between these occurrences. The word uvu is a factor of the required form. ∎

To answer the question, it is enough to show that each word of length ℓ_n, $n > 0$, contains the Zimin pattern Z_n.

The proof is by induction on n. Obviously each non-empty word contains the pattern Z_1. Assuming that each word of length ℓ_{n-1} contains Z_{n-1} we are to show that any word w of length ℓ_n contains Z_n. Due to the above observation w contains a factor of the form uvu, where $|u| = \ell_{n-1}$ and $|v| > 0$.

By the inductive hypothesis u contains Z_{n-1}, hence $u = u_1 u_2 u_3$, where $u_2 = \psi(Z_{n-1})$ for a morphism $\psi : \{\alpha_1, \alpha_2, \ldots, \alpha_{n-1}\}^+ \to \text{A}^+$. Then w contains the factor $u_2 \cdot z \cdot u_2$, where $z = u_3 v u_1$. Extending ψ by setting $\psi(\alpha_n) = z$, w contains a morphic image of Z_n. This completes the proof.

Notes

Denote by $f(n)$ the length of a longest binary word not containing Z_n. Due to the unavoidability result $f(n)$ is finite. However, finiteness here almost meets infinity, since for instance $f(8) \geq 2^{(2^{16})} = 2^{65536}$ (see [48]). Even for short patterns values of $f(n)$ may be large; for example, there are binary words of length 10482 avoiding Z_4.

Pattern unavoidability is decidable as proved by Zimin (see [176, chapter 3]). An algorithm can be based on Zimin words, since it is known that a pattern P containing n variables is unavoidable if and only if it is contained in Z_n. In other words, Zimin words are unavoidable patterns and they contain all unavoidable patterns.

However, the existence of a deterministic polynomial-time algorithm for the pattern avoidability problem is still an open question. It is only known that the problem is in the NP class of complexity.

94 BW Transform of Thue–Morse Words

The goal of the problem is to show the inductive structure of the Burrows–Wheeler transform of Thue–Morse words. The words are produced by the Thue–Morse morphism μ from $\{a,b\}^*$ to itself defined by $\mu(a) = ab$ and $\mu(b) = ba$. Iterating μ from letter a gives the nth Thue–Morse word $\tau_n = \mu^n(a)$ of length 2^n.

The Burrows–Wheeler transform $BW(w)$ of w is the word composed of the last letters of the sorted conjugates (rotations) of w. The list of Thue–Morse words starts with $\tau_0 = a$, $\tau_1 = ab$, $\tau_2 = abba$ and $\tau_3 = abbabaab$ and the transforms of the last two are $BW(\tau_2) = baba$ and $BW(\tau_3) = bbababaa$.

Below the bar, morphism from $\{a,b\}^*$ to itself is defined by $\overline{a} = b$ and $\overline{b} = a$.

> **Question.** Show the Burrows–Wheeler transform $BW(\tau_{n+1})$, $n > 0$, is the word $b^k \cdot \overline{BW(\tau_n)} \cdot a^k$, where $k = 2^{n-1}$.

Solution
The solution comes from a careful inspection of the array of sorted conjugates producing the transform.

Let S_{n+1} be the $2^{n+1} \times 2^{n+1}$ array whose rows are the sorted rotations of τ_{n+1}. By definition $BW(\tau_{n+1})$ is the rightmost column of S_{n+1}. The array splits into three arrays, with T_{n+1} its top 2^{n-1} rows, M_{n+1} its middle 2^n rows and B_{n+1} its bottom 2^{n-1} rows.

Example. Below are the rotations of $\tau_2 = abba$ (R_2 on the left) and its sorted rotations (S_2 on the right). Thus $BW(\tau_2) = baba$.

$$
R_2 = \begin{matrix} a & b & b & a \\ b & b & a & a \\ b & a & a & b \\ a & a & b & b \end{matrix}
\qquad
S_2 = \begin{matrix} a & a & b & b \\ a & b & b & a \\ b & a & a & b \\ b & b & a & a \end{matrix}
$$

The array S_3 gives $BW(\tau_3) = BW(abbabaab) = bbababaa$.

$$
S_3 = \begin{matrix}
a & a & b & a & b & b & a & b \\
a & b & a & a & b & a & b & b \\
a & b & a & b & b & a & b & a \\
a & b & b & a & b & a & a & b \\
b & a & a & b & a & b & b & a \\
b & a & b & a & a & b & a & b \\
b & a & b & b & a & b & a & a \\
b & b & a & b & a & a & b & a
\end{matrix}
$$

The decomposition of S_3 into T_3, M_3 and B_3 shows that $\mathrm{BW}(\tau_3)$ is $\mathrm{b}^2 \cdot \mathrm{abab} \cdot \mathrm{a}^2 = \mathrm{b}^2 \cdot \overline{\mathrm{BW}(\tau_2)} \cdot \mathrm{a}^2$.

$$
T_3 = \begin{array}{|cccccccc|}
a & a & b & a & b & b & a & b \\
a & b & a & a & b & a & b & b \\
\end{array}
$$

$$
M_3 = \begin{array}{|cccccccc|}
a & b & a & b & b & a & b & a \\
a & b & b & a & b & a & a & b \\
b & a & a & b & a & b & b & a \\
b & a & b & a & a & b & a & b \\
\end{array}
$$

$$
B_3 = \begin{array}{|cccccccc|}
b & a & b & b & a & b & a & a \\
b & b & a & b & a & a & b & a \\
\end{array}
$$

Since rows of S_n are sorted, a simple verification shows they remain sorted when μ is applied to them. The last column of $\mu(S_n)$ is then $\overline{\mathrm{BW}(\tau_n)}$ by the definition of μ.

It remains to find rotations of τ_{n+1} that are in T_{n+1} and in B_{n+1}, which eventually proves $M_{n+1} = \mu(S_n)$.

Observation. The number of occurrences of a's and those of b's in τ_n are both equal to 2^{n-1}.

In the word $\tau_{n+1} = \mu(\tau_n)$ let us consider the occurrences of ba that are images of an occurrence of b in τ_n. By the observation, there are 2^{n-1} such occurrences of ba. Equivalently, they start at an even position on τ_{n+1} (there are other occurrences of ba when n is large enough).

Rows of T_{n+1} are composed of rotations obtained by splitting τ_{n+1} in the middle of these factors ba. All rows of T_{n+1} start with a and end with b.

Since there is no occurrence of bbb in τ_n, the (alphabetically) greatest row of T_{n+1} cannot start with ababa and in fact starts with abaa. Thus this row is smaller than the top row of $\mu(S_n)$ that is prefixed by abab, since it is the image of a rotation of τ_n prefixed by aa.

Symmetrically, B_{n+1} is composed of rotations obtained by splitting occurrences of ab starting at an even position on τ_{n+1}. Proving they are all larger than the last row of $\mu(S_n)$ is proved similarly as above.

To conclude, since T_{n+1} and B_{n+1} each have $k = 2^{n-1}$ rows, $M_{n+1} = \mu(S_n)$. Rows of T_{n+1} end with b and provide the prefix b^k of $\mathrm{BW}(\tau_{n+1})$. Rows of B_{n+1} end with a and provide the suffix a^k of $\mathrm{BW}(\tau_{n+1})$.

95   BW Transform of Balanced Words

The Burrows–Wheeler operation maps a word w to the word $\mathrm{BW}(w)$ composed of the last letters of the sorted conjugates of w. The goal of the problem is to characterise primitive words $w \in \{a,b\}^{+}$ for which $\mathrm{BW}(w) \in b^{+}a^{+}$. Such a word w can then be compressed to a word of length $\log|w|$ by representing the exponents of a and of b.

The characterisation is based on the notion of balanced words. The density (or weight) of a word $u \in \{a,b\}^{+}$ is the number of occurrences of letter a in it, that is, $|u|_a$. A word w is said to be balanced if any two factors of w, u and v of the same length have almost the same density. More formally, factors satisfy

$$|u| = |v| \implies -1 \le |u|_a - |v|_a \le 1.$$

We also say the word w is circularly balanced if w^2 is balanced.

> **Question.** For a primitive word $w \in \{a,b\}^{+}$, show that w is circularly balanced if and only if $\mathrm{BW}(w) \in b^{+}a^{+}$.

Fibonacci words are typical examples of circularly balanced words. Below is a graph showing the cycle to recover a conjugate of fib_4 (length $F_6 = 8$ and density $F_5 = 5$), from b^3a^5. Following the cycle from the top left letter, letters of aabaabab are those met successively on the bottom line. Starting from another letter gives another conjugate of $fib_4 = $ abaababa, which itself is obtained by starting from the first occurrence of a on the top line. In fact, any word of length $|fib_n|$ and density $|fib_{n-1}|$ is circularly balanced if and only if it is a conjugate of fib_n.

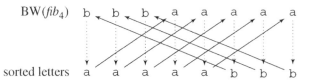

> **Question.** Show that $\mathrm{BW}(fib_n) \in b^{+}a^{+}$ for $n > 0$.

For example, $\mathrm{BW}(fib_1) = \mathrm{BW}(\mathrm{ab}) = \mathrm{ba}$, $\mathrm{BW}(fib_2) = \mathrm{BW}(\mathrm{aba}) = \mathrm{baa}$ and $\mathrm{BW}(fib_3) = \mathrm{BW}(\mathrm{abaab}) = \mathrm{bbaaa}$.

Solution
Transformation of a circularly balanced word. We start with a proof of the direct implication in the first question. First note that $\mathrm{BW}(w)$, composed of letters ending lexicographically sorted factors of length $|w|$ in w^2, is

equivalently composed of the letters preceding occurrences of these sorted factors starting at positions 1 to $|w|$ on w^2. The solution comes readily from the next lemma.

Lemma 7 *For a circularly balanced primitive word w, let $\mathrm{b}u$ and $\mathrm{a}v$ be two factors of w^2 with $|u| = |v| = |w|$. Then $u < v$.*

Proof Let z be the longest common prefix of u and v. Since u and v are conjugates of w and w is primitive, $u \neq v$. Thus either both $z\mathrm{a}$ is a prefix of u and $z\mathrm{b}$ is a prefix of v (like in the above picture) or both $z\mathrm{b}$ is a prefix of u and $z\mathrm{a}$ a prefix of v. But the second case is impossible because $|\mathrm{b}z\mathrm{b}| = |\mathrm{a}z\mathrm{a}|$ and $|\mathrm{b}z\mathrm{b}|_{\mathrm{a}} - |\mathrm{a}z\mathrm{a}|_{\mathrm{a}} = -2$, contradicting the balanced condition. The first case shows that $u < v$. ∎

A direct consequence of the lemma is that any conjugate of w whose occurrence is preceded by b in w^2 is smaller than any conjugate preceded by a. Thus $\mathrm{BW}(w) \in \mathrm{b}^+\mathrm{a}^+$.

Converse implication. To prove the converse implication we show that $\mathrm{BW}(w) \notin \mathrm{b}^+\mathrm{a}^+$ if w is not circularly balanced, which is a direct consequence of the next lemma.

Lemma 8 *If the primitive word $y \in \{\mathrm{a},\mathrm{b}\}^+$ is not balanced then it contains two factors of the form $\mathrm{a}z\mathrm{a}$ and $\mathrm{b}z\mathrm{b}$, for a word z.*

Proof Let u and v be factors of y of minimal length $m = |u| = |v|$ with $||u|_{\mathrm{a}} - |v|_{\mathrm{a}}| > 1$. Due to the minimality of m, u and v start with different letters, say a and b respectively. Let z be the longest common prefix of $\mathrm{a}^{-1}u$ and $\mathrm{b}^{-1}v$. The inequality $||u|_{\mathrm{a}} - |v|_{\mathrm{a}}| > 1$ implies $|z| < m - 2$. Then $u = \mathrm{a}zc\bar{u}$ and $v = \mathrm{b}zd\bar{v}$ for words $\bar{u}$ and $\bar{v}$ and for letters c and d, $c \neq d$. Due to the minimality of m again, we cannot have both $c = \mathrm{b}$ and $d = \mathrm{a}$. Then $c = \mathrm{a}$ and $d = \mathrm{b}$ (see the above picture), which shows that words $\mathrm{a}z\mathrm{a}$ and $\mathrm{b}z\mathrm{b}$ are factors of y, as expected. ∎

To conclude, when w is not circularly balanced, w^2 is not balanced and by the above lemma contains two factors of the forms aza and bzb. Therefore, the conjugate of w prefixed with za and preceded by a is smaller than the conjugate prefixed with zb, and preceded by b. Therefore ab is a subsequence of BW(w), which implies BW(w) $\notin$ b$^+$a$^+$.

Case of Fibonacci words. To prove the statement of the second question, we show that Fibonacci words are circularly balanced. Since their squares are prefixes of the infinite Fibonacci word **f**, it is enough to show that the latter does not contain two factors of the forms aza and bzb for any word z. This yields the result using the conclusion of the first question.

Recall that **f** is generated by iteration of the morphism ϕ from $\{a,b\}^*$ to itself defined by $\phi(a) = $ ab and $\phi(b) = $ a: $\mathbf{f} = \phi^\infty(a)$. The word is also a fixed point of ϕ: $\phi(\mathbf{f}) = \mathbf{f}$.

Related to the question, note that, for example, aa is a factor of **f** but bb is not, and similarly that bab is a factor of **f** but aaa is not. That is, **f** avoids bb and aaa among many other (binary) words.

Lemma 9 *The infinite Fibonacci word* **f** *does not contain two factors* aza *and* bzb *for any word* z.

Proof The proof is by contradiction, assuming **f** contains two factors of the stated forms. Let z be the shortest possible word for which both aza and bzb occur in **f**.

Considering words avoided by **f** like a^3 and b^2, it follows that z should start with ab and end with a. A simple verification shows that the length of z should be at least 4, then $z = $ ab$u$a with $u \neq \varepsilon$ (see picture). Indeed, the two occurrences of a cannot coincide because **f** avoids a^3. Then u cannot be empty because ababab does not occur in **f**, as it would be the image by ϕ of aaa that is avoided by **f**.

The words aab$u$a, a prefix of aza, and abab$u$ab uniquely factorise on $\{a, ab\}$, which is a suffix code. Thus, $\phi^{-1}(\text{aab}u\text{a}) = \text{ba}\phi^{-1}(u)\text{b}$ and $\phi^{-1}(\text{abab}u\text{ab}) = \text{aa}\phi^{-1}(u)\text{a}$ occur in **f**. But this contradicts the minimality of z's length because a$\phi^{-1}(u)$ is shorter than z. Therefore, **f** does not contain two factors of the forms aza and bzb, which achieves the proof. ∎

Notes

The result of the problem was first shown by Mantaci et al. and appeared in a different form in [185]. Part of the present proof uses Proposition 2.1.3 in [176, chapter 2], which states additionally that the word z in the lemma of the above converse implication is a palindrome.

The question is related to Christoffel words that are balanced Lyndon words, as proved by Berstel and de Luca [33] (see also [35, 176]). The result is stated by Reutenauer in [208] as follows: let w be a Lyndon word for which $p = |w|_a$ and $q = |w|_b$ are relatively prime. Then w is a Christoffel word if and only if $BW(w) = b^q a^p$.

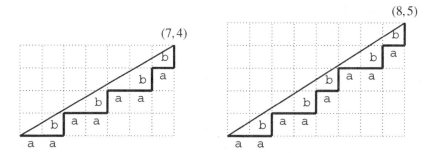

Lower Christoffel words approximate from below segments of the plane starting from the origin. The pictures show the Christoffel word aabaabaabab (left) representing the path on grid lines closely below the segment from $(0,0)$ to $(7,4)$. The Lyndon word conjugate of Fibonacci word $\mathit{fib}_5 =$ abaababaabaab (right) of length $F_7 = 13$ and density $F_6 = 8$ approximates the segment from $(0,0)$ to $(F_6, F_5) = (8,5)$.

96 In-place BW Transform

The Burrows–Wheeler transform (BW) of a word can be computed in linear time, over a linear-sortable alphabet, using linear space. This is achieved via a method to sort the suffixes or conjugates of the word, which requires linear extra space in addition to the input.

The problem shows how the input word is changed to its transform with constant additional memory space but with a slower computation.

Let x be a fixed word of length n whose last letter is the end-marker #, smaller than all other letters. Sorting the conjugates of x to get $BW(x)$ then amounts to sorting its suffixes. The transform is composed of letters preceding suffixes (circularly for the end-marker). For the example of $x = $ banana# we get $BW(x) = $ annb#aa:

BW(x)

a	#						
n	a	#					
n	a	n	a	#			
b	a	n	a	n	a	#	
#	b	a	n	a	n	a	#
a	n	a	#				
a	n	a	n	a	#		

> **Question.** Design an in-place algorithm to compute the Burrows–Wheeler transform of an end-marked word of length n in time $O(n^2)$ using only constant extra space.

Solution

Let initially $z = x$. The goal is to transform (the array) z in-place into $BW(x)$. The computation is performed by scanning z right to left.

Let x_i denote the suffix $x[i \mathrel{..} n - 1]$ of x, $0 \le i < n$. During iteration i, the word $z = x[0 \mathrel{..} i] \cdot BW(x[i + 1 \mathrel{..} n - 1])$ is transformed into the word $x[0 \mathrel{..} i - 1] \cdot BW(x[i \mathrel{..} n - 1])$. To do it, letter $c = x[i]$ is processed to find the rank of x_i among the suffixes $x_i, x_{i+1}, \ldots, x_{n-1}$.

If p is the position of # on z, $p - i$ is the rank of x_{i+1} among the suffixes $x_{i+1}, x_{i+2}, \ldots, x_{n-1}$. Then $z[p]$ should be c at the end of iteration i, since it precedes the suffix x_{i+1}.

To complete the iteration it remains to locate the new position of #. Since it precedes x_i itself we have to find the rank of x_i among the suffixes $x_i, x_{i+1}, \ldots, x_{n-1}$. This can easily be done by counting the number q of letters smaller than c in $z[i + 1 \mathrel{..} n - 1]$ and the number t of letters equal to c in $z[i + 1 \mathrel{..} p - 1]$.

Then $r = q + t$ is the sought rank of x_i. Eventually the computation consists in shifting $z[i + 1 .. i + r]$ one position to the left in z and by setting $z[i + r]$ to #.

Example. For $x =$ banana# the picture below simulates the whole computation. At the beginning of iteration $i = 2$ (middle row), we have $z =$ ban·an#a and we process the underline letter $c =$ n. In an#a there are three letters smaller than c and, before #, one letter equal to it. Then $r = 4$. After substituting c for #, the factor $z[3 .. 3 + 4 - 1]$ is shifted and the end marker inserted after it. This gives $z =$ ba · anna#.

i				x				r
	b	a	n	a	n	a	#	
4	b	a	n	a	<u>n</u>	a	#	$2 = 2 + 0$
3	b	a	n	<u>a</u>	a	n	#	$2 = 1 + 1$
2	b	a	<u>n</u>	a	n	#	a	$4 = 3 + 1$
1	b	<u>a</u>	a	n	n	a	#	$3 = 1 + 2$
0	<u>b</u>	a	n	n	#	a	a	$4 = 4 + 0$
	a	n	n	b	#	a	a	

$$\mathrm{BW}(x)$$

Algorithm INPLACEBW implements the above strategy. It begins with iteration $i = n - 3$, since $x[n - 2 .. n - 1]$ is its own transform.

INPLACEBW(x end-marked word of length n)
```
 1  for i ← n − 3 downto 0 do
 2      p ← position of # in x[i + 1 .. n − 1]
 3      c ← x[i]
 4      r ← 0
 5      for j ← i + 1 to n − 1 do
 6          if x[j] < c then
 7              r ← r + 1
 8      for j ← i + 1 to p − 1 do
 9          if x[j] = c then
10              r ← r + 1
11      x[p] ← c
12      x[i .. i + r − 1] ← x[i + 1 .. i + r]
13      x[i + r] ← #
14  return x
```

As for the running time, instructions at lines 2, 5–7, 8–10 and 12 all run in time $O(n - i)$. Then the overall running time is $O(n^2)$ in the comparison model.

Notes
The material of the problem is from [73]. The authors also show how to invert in-place BW to recover the initial word with the same complexities on a constant-size alphabet. More on the Burrows–Wheeler transform is in the book on the subject by Adjeroh et al. [2].

97   Lempel–Ziv Factorisation

The problem deals with a Lempel–Ziv factorisation of words. The factorisation considered here is the decomposition of a word w into the product $w_0 w_1 \ldots w_k$ where each w_i is the longest prefix of $w_i w_{i+1} \ldots w_k$ that occurs in w before the present position $|w_0 w_1 \ldots w_{i-1}|$. If there is no previous occurrence, w_i is the first letter of $w_i w_{i+1} \ldots w_k$.

The factorisation is stored in the array LZ: $LZ[0] = 0$ and, for $1 \le i \le k$, $LZ[i] = |w_0 w_1 \ldots w_{i-1}|$. For example, the factorisation of abaababbabbbabbb is a · b · a · aba · bab · babb · b, which gives the array $LZ = [0, 1, 2, 3, 6, 9, 13, 14]$.

> **Question.** Show how to compute the array LZ of a word in linear time assuming a fixed-size alphabet.

The same running time can be achieved when the alphabet is linearly sortable, which is a weaker condition than the above one. This is done from the longest previous array (LPF) array of the word that computes in linear time under this condition (see Problem 53).

The LPF array of a word w is defined, for each position i on w, by: $LPF[i]$ is the length of the longest factor of w that starts both at position i and at a smaller position. Below is the LPF array of abaababbabbbabbb.

i	0	1	2	3	4	5	6	7	8	9	10	11	12	13
$w[i]$	a	b	a	a	b	a	b	a	b	b	a	b	b	b
LPF$[i]$	0	0	1	3	2	4	3	2	1	4	3	2	2	1

> **Question.** Design an algorithm that computes in linear time the Lempel–Ziv factorisation of a word given its LPF array.

Solution

Direct computation of LZ. A solution to the first question utilises the Suffix tree $T = \mathcal{ST}(w)$ of w. Its terminal nodes (or leaves if w has an end-marker) are identified with the suffixes of w and can be assumed to be labelled by their starting positions. Additionally, for each node v of T, *first*(v) is the smallest label of a leaf in the subtree rooted at v, which can be computed via a mere bottom-up traversal of the tree.

Assume LZ$[0 \mathinner{.\,.} i - 1]$ is computed and LZ$[i - 1] = j$, for $1 \le i \le k$. To get LZ$[i]$ the tree is traversed from *root*(T) along the path spelling a prefix of $w[j \mathinner{.\,.} n - 1]$ letter by letter. The descent stops if either it cannot continue or the scanned word does not occur before position j. The latter condition is checked in the following way: in a given step the current node of the tree is an explicit node v or possibly an implicit inner node, in which case we look down for the first explicit node v. Checking if a previous occurrence exists amounts to checking if *first*$(v) < j$.

Building the Suffix tree takes linear time on a linearly sortable alphabet (see Problem 47) and traversing it takes linear time on a fixed-size alphabet. It is $O(|w| \log alph(w))$ on a general alphabet.

LZ from LPF. The following algorithm solves the second question.

LZ-FACTORISATION(LPF table of a word of length n)

```
1   (LZ[0], i) ← (0, 0)
2   while LZ[i] < n do
3       LZ[i + 1] ← LZ[i] + max{1, LPF[LZ[i]]}
4       i ← i + 1
5   return LZ
```

It is clear that LZ$[0]$ is correctly set. Let us assume that, at iteration i of the while loop, values LZ$[j]$ are correct for $0 \le j \le i$. In particular, LZ$[i] = |w_0 w_1 \ldots w_{i-1}|$.

Let w_i be the next factor of the factorisation. If w_i is not empty then its length (greater than 1) is LPF$[|w_0 w_1 \ldots w_{i-1}|]$; thus LZ$[i + 1]$ = LZ$[i]$ + LPF[LZ$[i]$]. If w_i is empty then LZ$[i + 1]$ = LZ$[i]$ + 1. In both cases, the instruction at line 3 correctly computes LZ$[i + 1]$.

The algorithm stops when LZ$[i] \geq n$; thus it computes all the values LZ$[i]$ for $0 \leq i \leq k$.

All the instructions of the algorithm run in constant time except the while loop that is iterated $k + 1$ times; thus the algorithm runs in $O(k)$ time.

Notes

An alternative algorithm can be designed with the Suffix automaton (or DAWG) of the word. See [76] for the algorithm of the second question and for applications of the LPF array.

There is a large number of possible variations on the definition of the factorisation. The above version is inspired by the LZ77 compression method designed by Ziv and Lempel [243] (see [37]). Its study has been stimulated by its high performance in real applications.

The factorisation is also useful to produce efficient algorithms for locating repetitions in words (see [67, 167]), outperformed by the computation of runs in [26] (see Problem 87). The factorisation can also deal with repetitions in other applications, such as finding approximate repetitions in words [168] or aligning genomic sequences [88], for example.

98   Lempel–Ziv–Welch Decoding

The Lempel–Ziv–Welch compression method is based on a type of Lempel–Ziv factorisation. It consists in encoding repeating factors of the input text by their code in a dictionary D of words. The dictionary, initialised with all the letters of the alphabet A, is prefix-closed: every prefix of a word in the dictionary is in it.

Here is the encoding algorithm in which $code_D(w)$ is the index of the factor w in the dictionary D.

LZW-ENCODER(*input* non-empty word)

```
 1    D ← A
 2    w ← first letter of input
 3    while not end of input do
 4         a ← next letter of input
 5         if wa ∈ D then
 6              w ← wa
 7         else WRITE(code_D(w))
 8              D ← D ∪ {wa}
 9              w ← a
10    WRITE(code_D(w))
```

The decompression algorithm reads the sequence of codes produced by the encoder and updates the dictionary similarly to the way the encoder does.

LZW-DECODER(*input* non-empty word)

```
 1    D ← A
 2    while not end of input do
 3         i ← next code of input
 4         w ← factor of code i in D
 5         WRITE(w)
 6         a ← first letter of next decoded factor
 7         D ← D ∪ {wa}
```

Question. Show that during the decoding step Algorithm LZW-DECODER can read a code i that does not belong yet to the dictionary D if and only if index i corresponds to the code of aua, where au is the previous decoded factor, $a \in A$ and $u \in A^*$.

The question highlights the only critical situation encountered by the decoder. The property provides the element to ensure it can correctly decode its input.

Solution

We first prove that if just after it writes a code in the output the encoder reads $v = auaua$, with $a \in A$, $u \in A^*$, $au \in D$ and $aua \notin D$, then the decoder will read a code that does not belong to the dictionary.

The encoder starts reading $au \in D$. Then when reading the following a in v the encoder writes the code of au and adds aua to the dictionary. Going on, it reads the second occurrence of ua and writes the code of aua (since the dictionary is prefix-closed aua cannot be extended).

During the decoding step when the decoder reads the code of au, it next reads the code of aua before it is in the dictionary.

We now prove that if the decoder reads a code i that does not belong yet to the dictionary then it corresponds to the factor aua to where au is the factor corresponding to the code read just before i.

Let w be the factor corresponding to the code read just before i. The only code that has not been inserted in the dictionary before reading i corresponds to the factor wc, where c is the first letter of the factor having code i. Thus $c = w[0]$. If $w = au$ then code i corresponds to factor aua.

Example. Let the input be the word ACAGAATAGAGA over the 8-bit ASCII alphabet.

The dictionary initially contains the ASCII symbols and their indices are their ASCII codewords. It also contains an artificial end-of-word symbol of index 256.

Coding

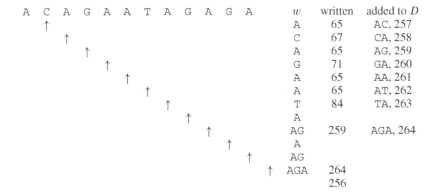

A C A G A A T A G A G A	w	written	added to D
	A	65	AC, 257
	C	67	CA, 258
	A	65	AG, 259
	G	71	GA, 260
	A	65	AA, 261
	A	65	AT, 262
	T	84	TA, 263
	A		
	AG	259	AGA, 264
	A		
	AG		
	AGA	264	
		256	

Decoding

The input sequence is 65, 67, 65, 71, 65, 65, 84, 259, 264, 256.

read	written	added
65	A	
67	C	AC, 257
65	A	CA, 258
71	G	AG, 259
65	A	GA, 260
65	A	AA, 261
84	T	AT, 262
259	AG	TA, 263
264	AGA	AGA, 264
256		

The critical situation occurs when reading the index 264 because, at that moment, no word of the dictionary has this index. But since the previous decoded factor is AG, index 264 can only correspond to AGA.

Notes

The Lempel–Ziv–Welch method has been designed by Welch [239]. It improves on the initial method developed by Ziv and Lempel [243].

---

99   Cost of a Huffman Code

Huffman compression method applied to a text $x \in A^*$ assigns a binary codeword to each letter of x in order to produce a shortest encoded text. Its principle is that the most frequent letters are given the shortest codewords while the least frequent symbols correspond to the longest codewords.

Codewords form a prefix code (prefix-free set) naturally associated with a binary tree in which the links from a node to its left and right children are labelled by 0 and 1 respectively. Leaves correspond to original letters and labels of branches are their codewords. In the present method codes are complete: internal nodes of the tree all have exactly two children.

The cost of a Huffman code is the sum $\sum_{a \in A} freq(a) \times |code(a)|$, where $code(a)$ is the binary codeword of letter a. It is the smallest length of a binary text compressed by the method from a word x in which $freq(a) = |x|_a$ for each letter $a \in alph(x)$. Let us consider the following algorithm applied to frequencies (weights).

HUFFMANCOST(S list of positive weights)
1   *result* ← 0
2   **while** $|S| > 1$ **do**
3   p ← MINDELETE(S)
4   q ← MINDELETE(S)
5   add $p + q$ to S
6   *result* ← *result* $+ p + q$
7   **return** *result*

Question. Prove that Algorithm HUFFMANCOST(S) computes the smallest cost of a Huffman code from a list S of item weights.

[**Hint:** Consider the Huffman tree associated with the code.]

Example. Let $S = \{7, 1, 3, 1\}$. Initially *result* $= 0$.
Step 1: $p = 1, q = 1, p + q = 2, S = \{7, 3, 2\}$, *result* $= 2$.
Step 2: $p = 2, q = 3, p + q = 5, S = \{7, 5\}$, *result* $= 7$.
Step 3: $p = 5, q = 7, p + q = 12, S = \{12\}$, *result* $= 19$.

The Huffman forest underlying the algorithm, which ends up with a Huffman tree, is shown in the picture. Nodes are labelled with weights.

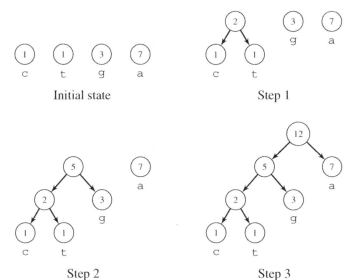

Initial state   Step 1

Step 2   Step 3

The final tree provides codewords associated with letters, summarised in the table.

	a	c	g	t
freq	7	1	3	1
code	1	000	01	001
|*code*|	1	3	2	3

The cost of the tree is $7 \times 1 + 1 \times 3 + 3 \times 2 + 1 \times 3 = 19$. It is the length of the compressed word 000 1 01 1 001 1 1 01 1 01 1 1 corresponding to cagataagagaa, whose letter frequencies fit with those of the example. Encoded with 8-bit codewords, the length of the latter word is 96.

Question. Show how to implement algorithm HUFFMANCOST(S) so that it runs in linear time when the list S is in increasing order.

[**Hint:** Use a queue for inserting the new values (corresponding to internal nodes of the tree).]

Solution
Correctness of HUFFMANCOST. Let S_i denote the value of S at step i of the while loop of the algorithm, $0 \le i \le |S| - 1$.

The loop invariant of the algorithm is: *result* is the sum of total cost of Huffman codewords representing the weights stored in S_i.

Before the first iteration, S_0 is a forest composed of node trees each of depth 0, which corresponds to the initialisation *result* = 0.

During iteration i, the algorithm selects and deletes the least two weights p and q from S_{i-1} and adds $p + q$ to S_{i-1} to produce S_i. This mimics the creation of a new tree whose root has weight $p + q$, thus creating two new edges. Then one more bit is needed to account for all the codewords of letters associated with the leaves of the new tree. Altogether this occurs $p + q$ times and implies that *result* should be incremented by $p + q$ as done at line 6. As a consequence, at the end of iteration i, *result* is the sum of the total cost of Huffman codewords representing the weights stored in S_i.

At the end of the $(|S| - 1)$th iteration only one weight is left in S and *result* is the total cost of the corresponding Huffman code.

It is clear that, at any iteration of the while loop, choosing other values than the two minimal values in S would produce a larger cost than *result*.

Implementation in linear time. To have HUFFMANCOST(S) running in linear time it is enough to insert newly created weights in a queue Q. Since new weights come in increasing order, Q is also sorted and each step runs in constant time, giving the following solution.

HUFFMANCOSTLINEAR(*S* increasing list of positive weights)

```
1   result ← 0
2   Q ← ∅
3   while |S| + |Q| > 1 do
4       (p, q) ← extract the 2 smallest values among
                the first 2 values of S and the first 2 values of Q
5       ENQUEUE(Q, p + q)
6       result ← result + p + q
7   return result
```

Example. Let $S = (1, 1, 3, 7)$. Initially *result* $= 0$ and $Q = ∅$
Step 1: $p = 1, q = 1, p + q = 2, S = (3, 7), Q = (2),$ *result* $= 2$
Step 2: $p = 2, q = 3, p + q = 5, S = (7), Q = (5),$ *result* $= 7$
Step 3: $p = 5, q = 7, p + q = 12, S = ∅, Q = (12),$ *result* $= 19.$

Notes

Huffman trees were introduced by Huffman [144]. The linear-time construction method, once the initial frequencies are already sorted, is due to Van
Leeuwen [235].

100   Length-Limited Huffman Coding

Given the frequencies of alphabet letters, the Huffman algorithm builds an optimal prefix code to encode the letters in such a way that encodings are as short as possible. In the general case there is no constraint on the length of the codewords. But sometimes one may want to bound the codeword length. Building a code satisfying such a constraint is the subject of this problem.

The coin collector's problem is an example of where the constraint is used. Collectors have coins with two independent properties: denominations (currency values) and numismatic values (collector values). Their goal is to collect a sum N while minimising the total numismatic value.

Let denominations be integer powers of 2: 2^{-i} with $1 \leq i \leq L$. Coins are organised as follows: there is a list for each denomination in which coins are sorted in increasing order of their numismatic values.

The method consists in grouping adjacent coins two by two in the list of smaller denominations, dropping the last coin if their number is odd. The numismatic value of a package is the sum of numismatic values of the two coins. Newly formed packages are associated with the coins of the next smallest denomination (sorted in increasing numismatic value). The process is repeated until the list of coins of denomination 2^{-1} is processed.

Question. Design an algorithm that computes for a list of n frequencies an optimal length-limited Huffman code in which no codeword is longer than L and that runs in time $O(nL)$.

[**Hint:** Reduce the problem to the binary coin collector's problem.]

Example. A coin collector has:

- 4 €1/2 coins of numismatic values 4, 8, 13 and 15 respectively,
- 3 €1/4 coins of numismatic values 3, 5 and 6 respectively,
- 5 €1/8 coins of numismatic values 2, 2, 4, 6 and 11 respectively,

and wants to collect 2 euros.

First, €1/8 coins are grouped two by two to form two packages of €1/4 with respective numismatic values 4 and 10, dropping the coin of numismatic value 11.

Then, these two packages are merged with the €1/4 coins and sorted. Coins and packages of €1/4 are grouped, which produces 2 €1/2 packages of respective numismatic values 7 and 11, disregarding the package of numismatic value 10.

Going on, these two packages are merged with the €1/2 coins and sorted. Finally, coins and packages of €1/2 are processed, which gives three packages of respective numismatic values 11, 19 and 28. The picture illustrates the whole process.

The first two packages give the solution: 2 euros composed of 2 €1/8 coins of numismatic values 2 each; 3 €1/4 coins of numismatic values 3, 5 and 6; and 2 €1/2 coins of numismatic values 4 and 8 for a total numismatic value of 30.

Algorithm PACKAGEMERGE(S, L) implements the strategy for a set S of coins with denominations between 2^{-L} and 2^{-1}. PACKAGE(S) groups two by two consecutive items of S and MERGE(S, P) merges two sorted lists.

Eventually, the first N items of the list PACKAGEMERGE(S, L) have the lowest numismatic values and are selected to form the solution.

PACKAGEMERGE(S set of coins, L)

```
1   for d ← 1 to L do
2       S_d ← list of coins of S with denomination 2^{-d}
            sorted by increasing numismatic value
3   for d ← L downto 1 do
4       P ← PACKAGE(S_d)
5       S_{d-1} ← MERGE(S_{d-1}, P)
6   return S_0
```

Both PACKAGE(S') and MERGE(S', P') run in linear time according to $n = |S|$. Thus, provided that the lists of coins are already sorted, the algorithm PACKAGEMERGE(S, L) runs in time and space $O(nL)$.

Solution

Given n letter frequencies w_i for $1 \le i \le n$, the previous algorithm can be applied to collect a sum equal to $n - 1$ by creating, for each $1 \le i \le n$, L coins of numismatic value w_i and of denomination 2^{-j} for each $1 \le j \le L$ to find an Huffman optimal code, where no codeword is longer than L.

Example. Given the following six frequencies sorted in increasing order $w = (1, 2, 4, 6, 8, 20)$ and $L = 4$, the PACKAGEMERGE algorithm operates as illustrated.

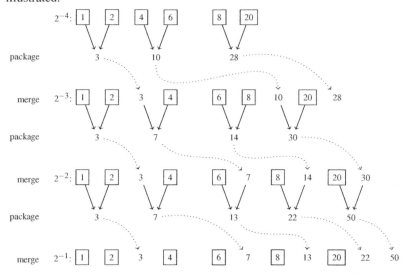

Lengths of codewords corresponding to each frequency are computed by scanning in increasing order the first $2n - 2 = 10$ items of the last level. This is summarised in the table, where, for instance, the 6th item has weight 7 and corresponds to frequencies 1, 2 and 4. The tree corresponds to these codeword lengths.

Item	weight	1	2	4	6	8	20
1	1	1	0	0	0	0	0
2	2	1	1	0	0	0	0
3	3	2	2	0	0	0	0
4	4	2	2	1	0	0	0
5	6	2	2	1	1	0	0
6	7	3	3	2	1	0	0
7	8	3	3	2	1	1	0
8	13	4	4	3	2	1	0
9	20	4	4	3	2	1	1
10	22	4	4	3	3	3	1

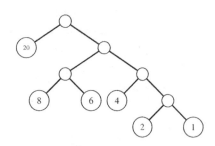

More precisely, L lists of coins are considered, one for each denomination. These lists are sorted in increasing order of numismatic values. Actually, since in this case $L = O(\log n)$, sorting can be done within the given complexity and a solution can be produced in $O(nL)$ time and space complexities.

At the end, the first $2n - 2$ items of the list corresponding to 2^{-1} are processed. In these items, each occurrence of an original frequency accounts for one unit to the length of the associated codeword.

Let $(i, \ell) \in [1, n] \times [1, L]$ be a node of weight w_i and width $2^{-\ell}$. The weight (resp. width) of a set of nodes is the sum of the weights (resp. widths) of its nodes. We define $nodeset(T)$ for a binary tree T with n leaves as follows: $nodeset(T) = \{(i, \ell) : 1 \leq i \leq n, 1 \leq \ell \leq \ell_i\}$ where ℓ_i is the depth of the ith leaf of T.

Thus the weight of $nodeset(T)$ is $weight(T) = \sum_{i=1}^{n} w_i \ell_i$ and its width is $width(T) = n - 1$ (proof by induction).

Lemma 10 *The first $2n - 2$ items of the last list computed by Algorithm* PACKAGEMERGE *applied to L list of n coins sorted in increasing numismatic values w_i, $1 \leq i \leq n$ correspond to a minimum weight nodeset of width $n - 1$.*

Proof Let $C = (k_1, k_2, \ldots, k_n)$ be the codeword lengths produced by Algorithm PACKAGEMERGE. Let $K = \sum_{i=1}^{n} 2^{-k_i}$. Initially $C = (0, 0, \ldots, 0)$ and $K = n$. It can be easily checked that every item among the first $2n - 2$ items produced by the algorithm decreases K by 2^{-1}. Thus the produced nodeset has width $n - 1$. It can also easily be checked that the algorithm at each step greedily chooses the minimal weight so that the produced nodeset is of total minimum weight.   ∎

A nodeset Z is monotone if the following two conditions hold:

- $(i, \ell) \in Z \Longrightarrow (i + 1, \ell) \in Z$, for $1 \leq i < n$,
- $(i, \ell) \in Z \Longrightarrow (i, \ell - 1) \in Z$, for $\ell > 1$.

The following lemmas can be easily proved.

Lemma 11 *For an integer $X < n$, the minimum weight nodeset of width X is monotone.*

Lemma 12 *If $(\ell_1, \ell_2, \ldots, \ell_n)$ is a list of integers for which $1 \leq \ell_i \leq L$ and Z is the nodeset $\{(i, \ell) : 1 \leq i \leq n, 1 \leq \ell \leq \ell_i\}$ then $width(Z) = n - \sum_{i=1}^{n} 2^{-\ell_i}$.*

Lemma 13 *If $y = (\ell_1, \ell_2, \ldots, \ell_n)$ is a monotone increasing list of non-negative integers whose width is equal to 1 then y is the list of depth of leaves of a binary tree.*

We can now state the main theorem.

Theorem 14 *If a nodeset Z has minimum weight among all nodesets of width $n-1$ then Z is the nodeset of a tree T that is an optimal solution to the length-limited Huffman coding problem.*

Proof Let Z be the minimum weight nodeset of width $n-1$. Let ℓ_i be the largest level such that $(i, \ell_i) \in A$ for each $1 \le i \le n$. By Lemma 11, Z is monotone. Thus $\ell_i \le \ell_{i+1}$ for $1 \le i < n$. Since Z is monotone and has width $n-1$, Lemma 12 implies that $\sum_{i=1}^{n} 2^{-\ell_i} = 1$. Then by Lemma 13, $(\ell_1, \ell_2, \ldots, \ell_n)$ is the list of leaf depths of a binary tree T, and hence $Z = nodeset(T)$.

Since Z has minimum weight among all nodesets of width $n-1$ it implies that T is optimal. ∎

Notes
The coin collector's problem and the PACKAGEMERGE algorithm have been introduced by Larmore and Hirschberg in [172]. They also show that finding an optimal length-limited Huffman code can be reduced to the coin collector's problem and solved it in $O(nL)$ time and space. They further show how the space complexity can be lowered to $O(n)$. Other improvements can be found in [156] and in [220].

101   Online Huffman Coding

The two main drawbacks of the static Huffman compression method are that first, if the frequencies of letters in the source text are not known a priori, the source text has to be scanned twice and second, the Huffman coding tree must be included in the compressed file. The problem shows a solution that avoids these drawbacks.

The solution is based on a dynamic method in which the coding tree is updated each time a symbol is read from the source text. The current Huffman tree relates to the part of the text that has already been processed and evolves exactly in the same way during the decoding process.

> **Question.** Design a Huffman compression method that reads only once the source text and does not need to store the coding tree in the compressed text.

[**Hint:** Huffman trees are characterised by the *siblings property*.]

Siblings property. Let T be a Huffman tree with n leaves (a complete binary weighted tree in which all leaves have positive weights). Nodes of T can be arranged in a list $(t_0, t_1, \ldots, t_{2n-2})$ that satisfies

- Nodes are in decreasing order of their weights:
  $weight(t_0) \geq weight(t_1) \geq \cdots \geq weight(t_{2n-2})$.
- For any i, $0 \leq i \leq n - 2$, the consecutive nodes t_{2i} and t_{2i+1} are siblings (they have the same parent).

Solution

The encoding and decoding processes initialise the dynamic Huffman tree as a tree consisting of one node associated with an artificial symbol ART and whose weight is 1.

Encoding phase. During the encoding process, each time a symbol a is read from the source text, its codeword from the tree is appended to the output. However, this happens only if a appeared previously. Otherwise the code of ART followed by the original codeword of a is appended to the output. Afterwards, the tree is modified in the following way: first, if a is a not leaf of the tree a new node is inserted as the parent of leaf ART with a new leaf child labelled by a; second, the tree is updated (see below) to get a Huffman tree for the new prefix of the text.

Decoding phase. At decoding time the compressed text is parsed with the coding tree. The current node is initialised with the root corresponding to ART as in the encoding algorithm, and then the tree evolves symmetrically. Each time a 0 is read from the compressed file the walk down the tree follows the left link, and it follows the right link if a 1 is read. When the current node is a leaf, its associated symbol is appended to the output and the tree is updated exactly as is done during the encoding phase.

Update. During the encoding (resp. decoding) phase, when a symbol (resp. the code of) a is read, the current tree has to be updated to take into account the correct frequency of symbols. When the next symbol of the input is considered the weight of its associated leaf is incremented by 1, and the weights of ancestors have to be modified correspondingly.

First, the weight of the leaf t_q corresponding to a is incremented by 1. Then, if the first point of the siblings property is no longer satisfied, node t_q is exchanged with the closest node t_p ($p < q$) in the list for which $weight(t_p) < weight(t_q)$. This consists in exchanging the subtrees rooted at nodes t_p and t_q. Doing so, the nodes remain in decreasing order according to their weights. Afterwards, the same operation is repeated on the parent of t_p until the root of the tree is reached.

The following algorithm implements this strategy.

UPDATE(a)

```
1   t_q ← leaf(a)
2   while t_q ≠ root do
3        weight(t_q) ← weight(t_q) + 1
4        p ← q
5        while weight(t_{p-1}) < weight(t_q) do
6             p ← p - 1
7        swap nodes t_p and t_q
8        t_q ← parent(t_p)
9   weight(root) ← weight(root) + 1
```

Sketch of the proof. Assume that the siblings property holds for a Huffman tree with a list $(t_0, t_1, \ldots, t_q, \ldots, t_{2n-2})$ of nodes in decreasing order of their weights and assume that the weight of leaf t_q is incremented by 1. Then both inequalities $weight(t_p) \geq weight(t_q)$ and $weight(t_p) < weight(t_q) + 1$ imply $weight(t_p) = weight(t_q)$. Node t_p has the same weight as node t_q and thus cannot be a parent or an ancestor of t_q, since the weight of a parent is the sum of the weights of its two children and that leaves have positive weights. Then swapping t_q with the smallest node t_p such that $weight(t_p) = weight(t_q)$, incrementing *weight*($t_q$) by 1 and applying the same process to the parent of t_p up to the root restore the siblings property for the whole tree, which ensures that the tree is a Huffman tree.

The picture illustrates how the tree is updated during the first five steps of processing the input text cagataagagaa.

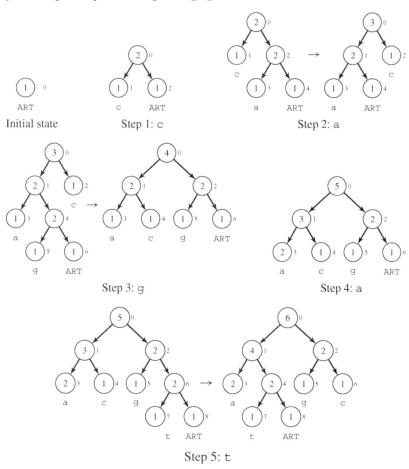

Step 1: c

Step 2: a

Step 3: g

Step 4: a

Step 5: t

Notes

The dynamic version of the Huffman compression method presented here was discovered independently by Faller [108] and by Gallager [125]. Practical versions were given by Cormack and Horspool [62] and by Knuth [161]. A precise analysis leading to an improvement on the length of the encoding was presented by Vitter [236].

There exist myriad variants of Huffman coding; see, for example, [121].

102   Run-Length Encoding

The binary representation (expansion) of a positive integer x is denoted by
$r(x) \in \{0,1\}^*$. The run-length encoding of a word $w \in 1\{0,1\}^*$ is of the
form $1^{p_0} 0^{p_1} \cdots 1^{p_{s-2}} 0^{p_{s-1}}$, where $s - 2 \geq 0$, p_is are positive integers for
$i = 0, \ldots, s - 2$ and $p_{s-1} \geq 0$. Value s is called the run length of w.

In the problem we examine the run length of the binary representation of
the sum, the difference and the product of two integers.

Question. Let x and y be two integers, $x \geq y > 0$, and let n be the total run
length of $r(x)$ and $r(y)$. Show that the run lengths of $r(x + y), r(x - y)$ and
$r(x \times y)$ are polynomial with respect to n.

Solution
Let $r(x) = 1^{p_0} 0^{p_1} \cdots 1^{p_{s-2}} 0^{p_{s-1}}$ and $r(y) = 1^{q_0} 0^{q_1} \cdots 1^{q_{t-2}} 0^{q_{t-1}}$.

Run length of $r(x + y)$. Let us prove by induction on n that the run length of
$r(x + y)$ is polynomial w.r.t. n.

It is straightforward the induction hypothesis holds when $n = 2$, when $s = 1$
or when $t = 1$. Assume it holds when the total run length of $r(x)$ and $r(y)$ is
$k < n$. Now consider the induction case when the total run length of $r(x)$ and
$r(y)$ is n.

- Case $p_{s-1} \neq 0$ and $q_{t-1} \neq 0$.
  Assume w.l.o.g. that $p_{s-1} \geq q_{t-1}$. Then
  $$r(x + y) = (1^{p_0} 0^{p_1} \cdots 1^{p_{s-2}} 0^{p_{s-1}-q_{t-1}} + 1^{q_0} 0^{q_1} \cdots 1^{q_{t-2}}) \cdot 0^{q_{t-1}}.$$

  Since $1^{p_0} 0^{p_1} \cdots 1^{p_{s-2}} 0^{p_{s-1}-q_{t-1}}$ and $1^{q_0} 0^{q_1} \cdots 1^{q_{t-2}}$ have total run
  length no more than $n - 1$ by hypothesis, their sum has a run length
  polynomial w.r.t. n.

  Example. $r(x) = 1^3 0^2 1^2 0^3$ and $r(y) = 1^1 0^3 1^3 0^2$. Then
  $r(x + y) = (1^3 0^2 1^2 0^1 + 1^1 0^3 1^3) \cdot 0^2 = 1^1 0^2 1^1 0^1 1^2 0^1 1^1 0^2$.

	1 1 1 0 0 1 1 0 0 0			1 1 1 0 0 1 1 0
+	1 0 0 0 1 1 1 0 0	=	+	1 0 0 0 1 1 1
	1 0 0 1 0 1 1 0 1 0 0			1 0 0 1 0 1 1 0 1 · 0 0

- Case $p_{s-1} = 0$ and $q_{t-1} \neq 0$.
  If $p_{s-2} \geq q_{t-1}$ then
  $$r(x + y) = (1^{p_0} 0^{p_1} \cdots 1^{p_{s-2}-q_{t-1}} + 1^{q_0} 0^{q_1} \cdots 1^{q_{t-2}}) \cdot 1^{q_{t-1}}.$$

Since $1^{p_0}0^{p_1}\cdots1^{p_{s-2}-q_{t-1}}$ and $1^{q_0}0^{q_1}\cdots1^{q_{t-2}}$ have total run length no more than $n-1$ by hypothesis, their sum has run length polynomial w.r.t. n.

Example. $r(x) = 1^30^21^50^0$ and $r(y) = 1^10^31^30^2$. Then
$r(x+y) = (1^30^21^3 + 1^10^31^3)\cdot1^2 = 1^10^21^10^11^30^11^2$.

	1	1	1	0	0	1	1	1	1	1				1	1	1	0	0	1	1	1
+		1	0	0	0	1	1	1	0	0	=		+		1	0	0	0	1	1	1
1	0	0	1	0	1	1	1	0	1	1			1	0	0	1	0	1	1	1	0	· 1	1

If $p_{s-2} < q_{t-1}$ then
$$r(x+y) = (1^{p_0}0^{p_1}\cdots0^{p_{s-3}} + 1^{q_0}0^{q_1}\cdots1^{q_{t-2}}0^{q_{t-1}-p_{s-2}})\cdot1^{p_{s-2}}.$$

Since $1^{p_0}0^{p_1}\cdots0^{p_{s-3}}$ and $1^{q_0}0^{q_1}\cdots1^{q_{t-2}}0^{q_{t-1}-p_{s-2}}$ have total run length no more than $n-1$ by hypothesis, their sum has run length polynomial w.r.t. n.

Example. $r(x) = 1^30^21^30^11^10^0$ and $r(y) = 1^10^31^30^2$. Then
$r(x+y) = (1^30^21^30^1 + 1^10^31^30^1)\cdot1^1 = 1^10^21^10^11^30^21^1$.

	1	1	1	0	0	1	1	1	0	1			1	1	1	0	0	1	1	1	0
+		1	0	0	0	1	1	1	0	0	=	+		1	0	0	0	1	1	1	0
1	0	0	1	0	1	1	1	0	0	1		1	0	0	1	0	1	1	1	0	0 · 1

- The case where $p_{s-1} \neq 0$ and $q_{t-1} = 0$ can be dealt with similarly.
- Case $p_{s-1} = 0$ and $q_{t-1} = 0$.

Then assume w.l.o.g. that $p_{s-2} \geq q_{t-2}$. Then
$$r(x+y) = (1^{p_0}0^{p_1}\cdots1^{p_{s-2}-q_{t-2}} + 1^{q_0}0^{q_1}\cdots0^{q_{t-3}} + 1)\cdot1^{q_{t-2}-1}0.$$

Since $1^{p_0}0^{p_1}\cdots1^{p_{s-2}-q_{t-2}}$ and $1^{q_0}0^{q_1}\cdots0^{q_{t-3}}$ have total run length no more than $n-1$ by hypothesis, their sum has run length polynomial w.r.t. n.

Example. $r(x) = 1^30^21^50^0$ and $r(y) = 1^10^51^30^0$. Then
$r(x+y) = (1^30^21^2 + 1^10^5 + 1)\cdot1^20^1 = 1^10^21^10^11^10^21^20^1$.

	1	1	1	0	0	1	1	1	1	1				1	1	1	0	0	1	1
+		1	0	0	0	0	0	1	1	1		+			1	0	0	0	0	0
											=	+								1
1	0	0	1	0	1	0	0	1	1	0		1	0	0	1	0	1	0	0 · 1	1	0

The conclusion of all cases answers the question for $r(x+y)$.

Run length of $r(x-y)$. We prove by induction on n that the run length $r(x-y)$ is polynomial w.r.t. n.

The induction hypothesis obviously holds when $n = 2$. Assume it holds when the total run length of $r(x)$ and $r(y)$ is equal to $k < n$. Consider x and y whose total run length of $r(x)$ and $r(y)$ is n.

- Case $p_{s-1} \neq 0$ and $q_{t-1} \neq 0$.

  Assume w.l.o.g. that $p_{s-1} \geq q_{t-1}$. Then
  $$r(x - y) = (1^{p_0} 0^{p_1} \cdots 1^{p_{s-2}} 0^{p_{s-1}-q_{t-1}} + 1^{q_0} 0^{q_1} \cdots 1^{q_{t-2}}) \cdot 0^{q_{t-1}}.$$

  Since $1^{p_0} 0^{p_1} \cdots 1^{p_{s-2}} 0^{p_{s-1}-q_{t-1}}$ and $1^{q_0} 0^{q_1} \cdots 1^{q_{t-2}}$ have total run length no more than $n - 1$ by hypothesis, their difference has run length polynomial w.r.t. n.

  Example. $r(x) = 1^3 0^2 1^2 0^3$ and $r(y) = 1^1 0^3 1^3 0^2$. Then
  $r(x - y) = (1^3 0^2 1^2 0^1 - 1^1 0^3 1^3) \cdot 0^2 = 1^1 0^2 1^5 0^2$.

```
    1 1 1 0 0 1 1 0 0 0              1 1 1 0 0 1 1 0
  -   1 0 0 0 1 1 1 0 0          -     1 0 0 0 1 1 1
  _____      =     _____
    1 0 0 1 1 1 1 1 0 0            1 0 0 1 1 1 1 1 · 0 0
```

- Case $p_{s-1} = 0$ and $q_{t-1} \neq 0$.

  If $p_{s-2} \geq q_{t-1}$ then
  $$r(x - y) = (1^{p_0} 0^{p_1} \cdots 1^{p_{s-2}-q_{t-1}} + 1^{q_0} 0^{q_1} \cdots 1^{q_{t-2}}) \cdot 1^{q_{t-1}}.$$

  Since $1^{p_0} 0^{p_1} \cdots 1^{p_{s-2}-q_{t-1}}$ and $1^{q_0} 0^{q_1} \cdots 1^{q_{t-2}}$ have total run length no more than $n - 1$ by hypothesis, their difference has run length polynomial w.r.t. n.

  Example. $r(x) = 1^3 0^2 1^5 0^0$ and $r(y) = 1^1 0^3 1^3 0^2$. Then
  $r(x - y) = (1^3 0^2 1^3 - 1^1 0^3 1^3) \cdot 1^2 = 1^1 0^1 1^1 0^5 1^2$.

```
    1 1 1 0 0 1 1 1 1 1            1 1 1 0 0 1 1 1
  -   1 0 0 0 1 1 1 0 0          -   1 0 0 0 1 1 1
  _____      =     _____
    1 0 1 0 0 0 0 0 1 1            1 0 1 0 0 0 0 0 · 1 1
```

  If $p_{s-2} < q_{t-1}$ then
  $$r(x - y) = (1^{p_0} 0^{p_1} \cdots 0^{p_{s-3}} - 1^{q_0} 0^{q_1} \cdots 1^{q_{t-2}} 0^{q_{t-1}-p_{s-2}}) \cdot 1^{q_{t-1}}.$$

  Since $1^{p_0} 0^{p_1} \cdots 0^{p_{t-3}}$ and $1^{q_0} 0^{q_1} \cdots 1^{q_{t-2}} 0^{q_{t-1}-p_{d-2}}$ have total run length no more than $n - 1$ by hypothesis, their difference has run length polynomial w.r.t. n.

  Example. $r(x) = 1^3 0^2 1^2 0^1 1^2 0^0$ and $r(y) = 1^1 0^3 1^2 0^3$. Then
  $r(x - y) = (1^3 0^2 1^2 0^1 - 1^1 0^3 1^2 0^1) \cdot 1^2 = 1^1 0^1 1^1 0^5 1^2$.

```
    1 1 1 0 0 1 1 0 1 1            1 1 1 0 0 1 1 0
  -   1 0 0 0 1 1 0 0 0          -   1 0 0 0 1 1 0
  _____      =     _____
    1 0 1 0 0 0 0 0 1 1            1 0 1 0 0 0 0 0 · 1 1
```

- The case where $p_{s-1} \neq 0$ and $q_{t-1} = 0$ can be dealt with similarly.
- Case $p_{s-1} = 0$ and $q_{t-1} = 0$.

If $p_{s-2} \geq q_{t-2}$. Then
$$r(x - y) = (1^{p_0} 0^{p_1} \cdots 1^{p_{s-2}-q_{t-2}} - 1^{q_0} 0^{q_1} \cdots 0^{q_{t-3}}) \cdot 0^{q_{t-2}}.$$

Since $1^{p_0} 0^{p_1} \cdots 1^{p_{s-2}-q_{t-2}}$ and $1^{q_0} 0^{q_1} \cdots 0^{q_{t-3}}$ have total run length no more than $n - 1$ by hypothesis, their difference has run length polynomial w.r.t. n.

Example. $r(x) = 1^3 0^2 1^5 0^0$ and $r(y) = 1^1 0^3 1^2 0^1 1^2 0^0$. Then $r(x - y) = (1^3 0^2 1^3 - 1^1 0^3 1^2 0^1) \cdot 0^2 = 1^1 0^1 1^1 0^5 1^2$.

```
  1 1 1 0 0 1 1 1 1 1              1 1 1 0 0 1 1 1
-   1 0 0 0 1 1 0 1 1         =  -   1 0 0 0 1 1 0
  ─────────────────              ───────────────
  1 0 1 0 0 0 0 1 0 0            1 0 1 0 0 0 0 1 · 0 0
```

If $p_{s-2} < q_{t-2}$. Then
$$r(x - y) = (1^{p_0} 0^{p_1} \cdots 0^{p_{s-3}} - 1^{q_0} 0^{q_1} \cdots 1^{q_{t-2}-p_{s-2}}) \cdot 0^{q_{t-2}}.$$

Since $r(x - y) = (1^{p_0} 0^{p_1} \cdots 0^{p_{s-3}}$ and $1^{q_0} 0^{q_1} \cdots 1^{q_{t-2}-p_{s-2}}$ have total run length no more than $n - 1$ by hypothesis, their difference has run length polynomial w.r.t. n.

Example. $r(x) = 1^3 0^2 1^1 0^1 1^3 0^0$ and $r(y) = 1^1 0^3 1^5 0^0$. Then $r(x - y) = (1^3 0^2 1^1 0^1 - 1^1 0^3 1^2) \cdot 0^3 = 1^1 0^2 1^4 0^3$.

```
  1 1 1 0 0 1 0 1 1 1              1 1 1 0 0 1 0 1
-   1 0 0 0 1 1 1 1 1         =  -   1 0 0 0 1 1 1
  ─────────────────              ───────────────
  1 0 0 1 1 1 1 0 0 0            1 0 0 1 1 1 1 0 · 0 0
```

The conclusion of all cases answers the question for $r(x - y)$.

Run length of $r(x \times y)$. Let us prove by induction on n that the run length of $r(x \times y)$ is polynomial w.r.t. n.

The conclusion readily comes when $n = 2$. Let us assume that the induction hypothesis holds when $r(x)$ and $r(y)$ have total run length $k < n$. Consider $r(x)$ and $r(y)$ whose total run length is n.

• Case $p_{s-1} \neq 0$. Then
$$r(x \times y) = (1^{p_0} 0^{p_1} \cdots 1^{p_{s-2}} \times 1^{q_0} 0^{q_1} \cdots 1^{q_{t-2}} 0^{q_{t-1}}) \cdot 0^{p_{s-1}}.$$

Since $1^{p_0} 0^{p_1} \cdots 1^{p_{s-2}}$ and $1^{q_0} 0^{q_1} \cdots 1^{q_{t-2}} 0^{q_{t-1}}$ have total run length no more than $n - 1$ by hypothesis, their product has run length polynomial w.r.t. n.

Example. $r(x) = 1^3 0^2 1^2 0^3$ and $r(y) = 1^1 0^3 1^5 0^0$. Then $r(x \times y) = (1^3 0^2 1^2 \times 1^1 0^3 1^5) \cdot 0^3$.

```
  1 1 1 0 0 1 1 0 0 0                        1 1 1 0 0 1 1
×   1 0 0 0 1 1 1 1 1        =        × 1 0 0 0 1 1 1 1 1
─────────────────────                ───────────────────
                                                  · 0 0 0
```

- The case when $q_{t-1} \neq 0$ can be dealt with similarly.
- Case $p_{s-1} = 0$ and $q_{t-1} = 0$. Then $r(x \times y)$ is
  $(1^{p_0} 0^{p_1} \cdots 1^{p_{s-2}} \times 1^{q_0} 0^{q_1} \cdots 0^{q_{t-3}+q_{t-2}}) + (1^{p_0} 0^{p_1} \cdots 1^{p_{s-2}} \times 1^{q_{t-2}})$.

  Since $1^{p_0} 0^{p_1} \cdots 1^{p_{s-2}}$ and $1^{q_0} 0^{q_1} \cdots 0^{q_{t-3}+q_{t-2}}$ have total run length no more than $n - 1$ by hypothesis, their product has run length polynomial w.r.t. n. And since $1^{p_0} 0^{p_1} \cdots 1^{p_{s-2}}$ and $1^{q_{t-2}}$ have total run length less than n by hypothesis, their product has run length polynomial w.r.t. n.

Example. $r(x) = 1^3 0^2 1^2 0^0$ and $r(y) = 1^1 0^2 1^3 0^0$. Then
$r(x \times y) = (1^3 0^2 1^2 \times 1^1 0^5) + (1^3 0^2 1^2 \times 1^3)$.

```
  1 1 1 0 0 1 1              1 1 1 0 0 1 1            1 1 1 0 0 1 1
×   1 0 0 1 1 1      =     ×   1 0 0 0 0 0      +   ×         1 1 1
```

The conclusion of all cases answers the question for $r(x \times y)$.

Notes

We can also consider arithmetic operations on succinct representations on numbers in the decimal numeration system. For example,

$$1^{5n} / 41 = 271 \, (00271)^{n-1}.$$

However, it is not a run-length encoding but rather its extension.

103   A Compact Factor Automaton

A Factor automaton is a minimal (deterministic) automaton accepting all the factors of a word. It is also called a directed acyclic word graph (DAWG). All its states are terminal and its edges are labelled by single letters. For certain well-structured words the automaton can be highly compressed by removing nodes having exactly one parent and one child and labelling edges by factors of the word accordingly. The resulting DAWG is called a compact DAWG (CDAWG) or compact Suffix automaton (CSA) if nodes corresponding to suffixes are marked as terminal.

The problem considers words whose CDAWGs are extremely small, namely Fibonacci words fib_n and their shortened version g_n. The word g_n is fib_n with the last two letters deleted, that is, $g_n = fib_n\{a,b\}^{-2}$.

> **Question.** Describe the structure of CDAWGs of Fibonacci words fib_n and of their trimmed versions g_n. Using this structure compute the number of distinct factors occurring in the words.

Solution
The solution is based on the lazy Fibonacci numeration system that uses the fact that each integer $x \in [1 .. F_n - 2]$, $n \geq 4$, is uniquely represented as $x = F_{i_0} + F_{i_1} + \cdots + F_{i_k}$, where $(F_{i_t} : 2 \leq i_t \leq n - 2)$ is an increasing sequence of Fibonacci numbers satisfying

$$(*) \quad i_0 \in \{0,1\} \text{ and } i_t \in \{i_{t-1} + 1, i_{t-1} + 2\} \text{ for } t > 0.$$

For the example of $n = 8$ the sequence of indices $(3,4,6)$ corresponds to 13 because $F_3 + F_4 + F_6 = 2 + 3 + 8 = 13$.

The set of sequences $(F_{i_t} : 2 \leq i_t \leq n - 2)$ satisfying $(*)$ is accepted by a simple deterministic acyclic automaton whose edge labels are Fibonacci numbers and all states are terminal. The picture displays the case $n = 10$ for integers in $[1 .. 53]$.

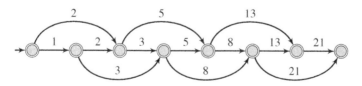

CDAWG of trimmed Fibonacci words. The previous automaton can be easily transformed into the CDAWG of g_n using the following property (introduced in Problem 56). Let R_i denote the reverse of fib_i and let $suf(k,n)$ be the kth suffix $g_n[k .. |g_n| - 1]$ of g_n.

Property. For $n > 2$, $suf(k,n)$ uniquely factorises as $R_{i_0} R_{i_1} \cdots R_{i_m}$, where $i_0 \in \{0, 1\}$ and $i_t \in \{i_{t-1} + 1, i_{t-1} + 2\}$ for $t > 0$.

With the help of the property the previous automaton is changed into CDAWG(g_n) by substituting R_i for each Fibonacci number F_i. The next picture shows CDAWG(g_{10}) after the above picture.

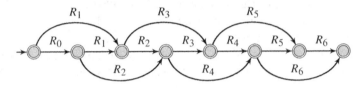

Counting factors in trimmed Fibonacci words. A CDAWG is useful to compute the number of (distinct) non-empty factors occurring in the corresponding word. Indeed, it is the sum of edge lengths multiplied by the number of paths that contain these edges. The number is in fact of $F_{n-1} F_{n-2} - 1$ factors in g_n, that we get using the formula, for $n > 2$: $F_2^2 + F_3^2 + \cdots + F_{n-2}^2 = F_{n-1} F_{n-2} - 1$.

For the example of CDAWG(g_{10}) in the above picture we obtain $1^2 + 2^2 + 3^2 + 5^2 + 8^2 + 13^2 + 21^2 = 21 \times 34 - 1 = 713$ non-empty factors.

CDAWG of Fibonacci words. The compacted DAWG of Fibonacci word fib_n differs only slightly from that of the trimmed Fibonacci word g_n. We just need to append the last two trimmed letters, which lead to a simple modification of CDAWG(g_n), as done in the next picture to get CDAWG(fib_{10}). The compacted structure represents all the 781 factors of fib_{10}.

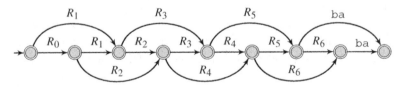

The number of factors in the Fibonacci word fib_n is slightly larger than their number in g_n since we have to consider two additional letters on the two edges reaching the last node. For $n > 2$, fib_n contains $F_{n-1} F_{n-2} + 2F_{n-1} - 1$ non-empty factors.

In the example $n = 10$, the additional word is ba. It is on 34 paths ending in the last node, so we have to add $2 \cdot 34 = 68$ factors. Hence fib_{10} contains $713 + 68 = 781$ non-empty factors.

Notes

The structure of CDAWGs of Fibonacci words is described in [213]. Other very compressed and useful DAWGs appear in the more general context of Sturmian words; see [27]. The number of nodes in the structures reflects the amount of memory space to store them because labels can be represented by pairs of indices on the underlying word.

The Suffix or Factor automaton of a word of length ℓ has at least $\ell+1$ states. In fact on the binary alphabet the lower bound is achieved only when the word is a prefix of a Sturmian word, which a Fibonacci word is [221].

As mentioned at the beginning the simplest strategy to compact a DAWG is to delete nodes with unique predecessor and successor (see [38, 101, 150]). The above method for Fibonacci factors not only gives a smaller CDAWG but also provides a more useful structure.

Below are the Suffix automaton of g_7 of length 11 with 12 states, its ordinary compact version with 7 nodes and the compact version from the above technique with only 5 nodes.

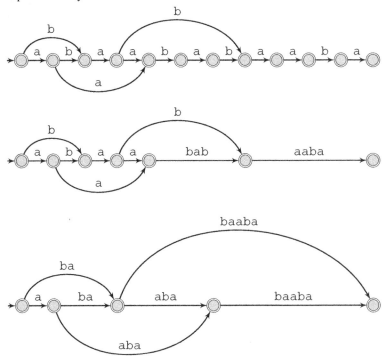

Finite Thue–Morse words have similarly a very short description, see [204], from which one can easily derive that the number of factors in the Thue–Morse word of length $n \geq 16$ is $\frac{73}{192}n^2 + \frac{8}{3}$.

104   Compressed Matching in a Fibonacci Word

Compressed matching refers to the following problem: given compact representations of a pattern and of a text, locate the pattern in the text in a fast manner according to their compressed representations. The representation sizes can be logarithmic with respect to the real input sizes, as it takes place in this problem example.

The input depends on the type of compressed representation. Here we consider a very simple case where the pattern is specified as a concatenation of Fibonacci words and its representation is the sequence of their indices. The searched text is the infinite Fibonacci word $\mathbf{f} = \phi^\infty(\mathrm{a})$, where ϕ is the morphism defined by $\phi(\mathrm{a}) = \mathrm{ab}$ and $\phi(\mathrm{b}) = \mathrm{a}$.

The word b is added with index -1 to the list of Fibonacci words: $fib_{-1} = \mathrm{b}, fib_0 = \mathrm{a}, fib_1 = \mathrm{ab}, fib_2 = \mathrm{aba}, fib_3 = \mathrm{abaab}, \ldots$

Question. Given a sequence of integers $k_1, k_2, \ldots, k_n$ ($k_i \geq -1$) show how to check in time $O(n + k_1 + k_2 + \cdots + k_n)$ if $fib_{k_1} fib_{k_2} \cdots fib_{k_n}$ occurs in the infinite Fibonacci word $\mathbf{f}$.

Solution

The algorithm input is the sequence $w = (k_1, k_2, \ldots, k_n)$ of indices of Fibonacci words. Let $first(w)$ and $last(w)$ denote the first and last elements of w respectively.

COMPRESSEDMATCH(w sequence of indices ≥ -1)

1   **while** $|w| > 1$ **do**
2   **if** w contains a factor $(i, -1), i \notin \{0, 2\}$ **then**
3   **return** FALSE
4   **if** $first(w) = -1$ **then**
5            $first(w) \leftarrow 1$
6   **if** $last(w) = 2$ **then**
7            $last(w) \leftarrow 1$
8   **if** $last(w) = 0$ **then**
9   remove the last element
10   change all factors $(0, -1)$ of w to 1
11   change all factors $(2, -1)$ of w to $(1, 1)$
12   decrease all elements of w by 1
13   **return** TRUE

Example. With the input sequence $w = (0, 1, 3, 0, 1, 4)$ the algorithm makes five iterations and returns TRUE:
$$(0, 1, 3, 0, 1, 4) \to (-1, 0, 2, -1, 0, 3) \to (0, -1, 0, 0, -1, 2)$$
$$\to (0, -1, 0, 0) \to (0, -1) \to (0).$$

Algorithm COMPRESSEDMATCH simply implements the following observations on the sequence $w = (k_1, k_2, \dots, k_n)$.

Case (i): $fib_i fib_{-1}$ is a factor of **f** if and only if $i = 0$ or $i = 2$. Indeed, if $i = 0$, $fib_i fib_{-1} = $ ab, if $i = 2$, $fib_i fib_{-1} = $ abab, and both words appear in **f**. Otherwise $fib_i fib_{-1}$ has a suffix bb or ababab $= \phi(\text{aaa})$ that does not appear in **f**.

Case (ii): If $k_1 = -1$ it can be changed to 1 because the first letter b should be preceded by a in **f** and $fib_1 = $ ab.

Case (iii): Similarly, if $k_n = 2$ it can be changed to 1 because in **f** each occurrence of b is also followed by a, so the suffix aba can be reduced to ab without changing the final output.

Case (iv): Factor $(0, -1)$ can be replaced by 1 since $fib_0 fib_{-1} = $ ab $= fib_1$ and factor $(2, -1)$ by $(1, 1)$ since $fib_2 fib_{-1} = $ abab $= fib_1 fib_1$.

Case (v): The only problematic case is when $k_n = 0$. This corresponds to a match with an occurrence of a in **f**. The correctness proof of this case follows again from the fact that the letter a occurs after each occurrence of b in **f**. There are two subcases depending on the last letter of the penultimate Fibonacci factor.

Case $fib_{k_{n-1}}$ ends with b: Then $fib_{k_1} fib_{k_2} \cdots fib_{k_n}$ occurs in **f** if and only if $fib_{k_1} fib_{k_2} \cdots fib_{k_{n-1}}$ does occur in **f**, since each occurrence of b is followed by a. Hence the last a is redundant and can be removed.

Case $fib_{k_{n-1}}$ ends with a: After 0 is removed and line 12 is executed the algorithm checks if $fib_{k_1 - 1} fib_{k_2 - 1} \cdots fib_{k_{n-1} - 1}$ occurs in **f**. However, $fib_{k_{n-1} - 1}$ now ends with b and $fib_{k_1 - 1} fib_{k_2 - 1} \cdots fib_{k_{n-1} - 1}$ occurs in **f** if and only if $v = fib_{k_1 - 1} fib_{k_2 - 1} \cdots fib_{k_{n-1} - 1}$a does. Hence if v occurs in **f** the word $fib_{k_1} fib_{k_2} \cdots fib_{k_n}$ occurs in $\phi(v)$. This shows that the last element $k_n = 0$ can be removed without spoiling the correctness.

Note that when the algorithm executes the instruction at line 12 all indices of w are non-negative. Thus the argument just considered also applies after execution. This ends the proof of correctness.

As for the complexity, observe that each pair of consecutive iterations decreases the sum of indices by at least 1. Consequently the algorithm achieves the required running time of $O(n + k_1 + k_2 + \cdots + k_n)$.

Notes

The present algorithm has been proposed by Rytter as a problem for the Polish Competition in Informatics. An alternative and completely different algorithm can be found in [238]. Yet another algorithm can be obtained using compressed factor graphs of Fibonacci words.

105   Prediction by Partial Matching

Prediction by Partial Matching (PPM) is a lossless compression technique where the encoder maintains a statistical model of the text. The goal is to predict letters following a given factor of the input. In the problem we examine the data structure used to store the model.

Let y be the text to be compressed and assume $y[0 . . i]$ has already been encoded. PPM assigns a probability $p(a)$ to each letter $a \in A$ depending on the number of occurrences of $y[i + 1 - d . . i] \cdot a$ in $y[0 . . i]$, where d is the context length. Then PPM sends $p(y[i + 1])$ to an adaptive arithmetic encoder taking into account letter probabilities. When there is no occurrence of $y[i + 1 - d . . i + 1]$ in $y[0 . . i]$ the encoder decrements the value of d until either an occurrence of $y[i + 1 - d . . i + 1]$ is found or $d = -1$. In the last case, $y[i + 1]$ is a letter not met before. Each time the encoder decrements the value of d it sends a so-called 'escape' probability to the adaptive arithmetic encoder.

PPM* is a variant of PPM which does not consider a maximum context length but stores all contexts. The initial context at each step is the shortest deterministic context, one that corresponds to the shortest repeated suffix that is always followed by the same letter or it is the longest context if such a suffix does not exist.

Question. Design a data structure able to maintain online the number of occurrences of each context and that can be managed in linear time on a constant-size alphabet.

Solution

The solution is based on a Prefix tree. The Prefix tree for $y[0 .. i]$ is constructed from the Prefix tree of $y[0 .. i - 1]$ and essentially consists of the Suffix tree of $y[0 .. i]^R$.

Let T_i denote the Prefix tree of $y[0 .. i]$. Its nodes are factors of $y[0 .. i]$. The initial tree T_{-1} is defined to be a single node. Prefix links are defined for every node of T_i except for its root and its most recent leaf. A prefix link labelled by letter a from node w points to node wa or to node uwa if every occurrences of wa are preceded by u.

Assume that the Prefix tree for $y[0 .. i - 1]$ is build. Let $head(w)$ denote the longest suffix of w that has an internal occurrence in w.

The Prefix tree is updated as follows. The insertion of $y[i]$ starts at the head of $w = y[0 .. i - 1]$ and ends at the head of $w' = y[0 .. i]$. If $y[i]$ already occurred after w then the node w has a prefix link labelled by $y[i]$ that points to the head of w'. If w does not have a prefix link labelled by $y[i]$, the search proceeds with the parent of w until either a prefix link labelled by $y[i]$ is found or the root of the tree is reached. If the reached node p is w' then only a new leaf q is added to the tree. If the reached node p is uw' for some $u \in A^+$ then a new internal node r and a new leaf q are added to the tree.

All the nodes visited during the process now have a prefix link labelled by $y[i]$ pointing to the new leaf q. When a new internal node r is created some prefix links pointing to p may need to be updated to point to r.

Example. The pictures show the transformation of the Prefix tree when processing $y = \texttt{gatata}$.

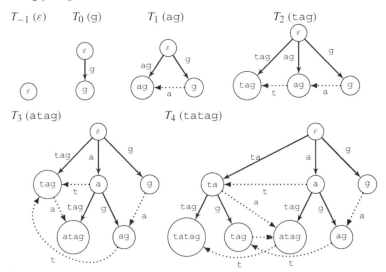

T_5 (atatag)

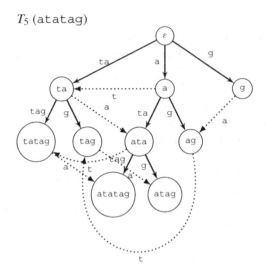

Theorem 15 *The above procedure correctly computes the Prefix tree T_i from the Prefix tree T_{i-1}.*

Proof T_{i-1} contains paths labelled by all the prefixes of $w = y[0..i-1]$ and only these paths. It then only misses a path labelled by $w' = y[0..i]$. Starting from the leaf s corresponding to w in T_{i-1} and going up to find the first node having a prefix link labelled by $a = y[i]$ identifies the node t corresponding to the longest suffix v of w such that va is a factor of w.

- If the prefix link from t labelled by a points to a node p corresponding to va then a new leaf q corresponding to w' must be added to the tree and the branch from p to q is labelled by u, where $w' = uva$. All the nodes scanned from s to t (except t itself) must now have a prefix link labelled by a pointing to q.

- If the prefix link from t labelled by a points to a node p corresponding to $v'va$ then a new internal node r corresponding to va is created having two successors: p and a new leaf q corresponding to w'. The branch from r to p must be labelled by v' and the branch from r to q must be labelled by u, where $w' = uva$. All the nodes scanned from s to t (except t itself) must now have a prefix link labelled by a pointing to q. Then prefix links going from nodes v', v' suffix of v, to p should now point to the new internal node r.

In both cases the tree now contains all the path contained in T_{i-1} and a path corresponding to w'. It is thus T_i. ∎

Theorem 16 *The construction of T_{n-1} can be done in $O(n)$ time.*

Proof   The running time of the construction is dominated by the number of nodes visited during each phase when computing $head(y[0..i])$ for $0 \leq i \leq n-1$. Let k_i denote the number of nodes visited while searching for $head(y[0..i])$. We have $|head(y[0..i])| \leq |head(y[0..i-1])y[i]| - k_i$. Finally $\sum_0^{n-1} k_i = n - |head(y)| \leq n$. Thus at most n nodes are visited during the whole construction of T_{n-1}, which proves the statement.   ∎

Notes

Prediction by Partial Matching was designed by Cleary and Witten [56] (see also [190]). PPM* was first introduced in [55]. The present Prefix tree construction is by Effros [107].

106   Compressing Suffix Arrays

Suffix arrays constitute a simple and space-economical data structure for indexing texts. In addition, there are many compressed versions of suffix arrays. The problem discusses one of them for compressing the array that stores the sorted (partial) list of suffixes (more precisely the partial rank array) of the concerned text. This shows an application of simple number theory.

Number-theoretic tools. A set $D \subseteq [0..t-1]$ is called a *t-difference-cover* if all elements of the interval are differences modulo t of elements in D:

$$[0..t-1] = \{(x-y) \bmod t : x, y \in D\}.$$

For example, the set $D = \{2, 3, 5\}$ is a 6-difference-cover for the interval $[0..6]$ since $1 = 3-2$, $2 = 5-3$, $3 = 5-2$, $4 = 3-5$ (mod 6) and $5 = 2-3$ (mod 6).

It is known that for every positive integer t there is a t-difference-cover of size $O(\sqrt{t})$ and that the set can be constructed in time $O(\sqrt{t})$.

A set $\mathcal{S}(t) \subseteq [1 .. n]$ is called a *t-cover* of the interval $[1 .. n]$ if both $|\mathcal{S}(t)| = O\left(\frac{n}{\sqrt{t}}\right)$ and there is a constant-time computable function

$$h : [1 .. n - t] \times [1 .. n - t] \to [0 .. t]$$

that satisfies

$$0 \leq h(i, j) \leq t \text{ and } i + h(i, j), j + h(i, j) \in \mathcal{S}(t).$$

A *t*-cover can be obtained from a *t*-difference-cover $\mathcal{D}$ (of the interval $[0 .. t - 1]$) by setting $\mathcal{S}(t) = \{i \in [1 .. n] : i \bmod t \in \mathcal{D}\}$. The following fact is known.

Fact. For each $t \leq n$ a *t*-cover $\mathcal{S}(t)$ can be constructed in time $O\left(\frac{n}{\sqrt{t}}\right)$.

Question. Show that the sorted partial list of suffixes of a text of length n can be represented in only $O(n^{3/4})$ amount of memory space and can still allow comparison of any two suffixes in $O(\sqrt{n})$ time.

[**Hint:** Use the notion of *t*-covers on intervals of integers.]

Solution

The answer to the question relies on *t*-covers. Instead of the array SA that stores the sorted list of suffixes of the text w, we use equivalently the array Rank, inverse of SA, that gives the ranks of suffixes indexed by their starting positions. With the whole array, comparing two suffixes starting at positions i and j amounts to comparing their ranks and takes constant time. However, the goal here is to retain only a small part of the table Rank.

Let $\mathcal{S}$ denote a fixed $\sqrt{n}$-cover $\{i_1, i_2, \ldots, i_k\}$ of $[1 .. n]$, where integers are sorted: $i_1 < i_2 < \cdots < i_k$. Its size is then $O(n^{3/4})$. Let $\mathcal{L}$ be the list of pairs

$$((i_1, \mathrm{Rank}[i_1]), (i_2, \mathrm{Rank}[i_2]), \ldots, (i_k, \mathrm{Rank}[i_k])).$$

Since the list is sorted with respect to the first component of pairs, checking if a position i belongs to $\mathcal{S}$ and finding its rank in $\mathcal{L}$ can be done in logarithmic time.

Assume we want to compare lexicographically suffixes starting at positions i and j on w of length n. Let $\Delta = h(i, j)$.

The words $x[i .. i + \Delta - 1]$ and $x[j .. j + \Delta - 1]$ are first compared in a naive way (letter by letter), which takes $O(\Delta)$ time. If they match it remains to compare the suffixes starting at positions $i + \Delta$ and $j + \Delta$. The latter comparison takes logarithmic time because positions $i + \Delta$ and $j + \Delta$ are in $\mathcal{S}$ and we can recover their associated ranks from the list $\mathcal{L}$ in logarithmic time.

Altogether the comparison spends $O(\sqrt{n})$ time since $\Delta = O(\sqrt{n})$.

Example. The set $\mathcal{S}(6) = \{2,3,5,8,9,11,14,15,17,20,21,23\}$ is a 6-cover of $[1 .. 23]$ built from the 6-difference-cover $\mathcal{D} = \{2,3,5\}$. In particular, we have $h(3,10) = 5$, since $3 + 5$, $10 + 5 \in \mathcal{S}(6)$.

If we are to compare suffixes starting at positions 3 and 10 on the word w we have only to compare their prefixes of length 5 and possibly check whether $Rank[3 + 5] < Rank[10 + 5]$ or not.

Notes

By choosing $t = n^{2/3}$ instead of $\sqrt{n}$ in the proof the data structure is reduced to $O(t)$ memory space but then the time to compare two suffixes increases to $O(t)$.

The construction of difference-covers can be found in [178]. It is used to construct t-covers as done, for example, in [47], where the above fact is proved.

A similar method for compressed indexing is the notion of FM-index based on both Burrows–Wheeler transform and Suffix arrays. It has been designed by Ferragina and Manzini (see [112] and references therein). Its applications in Bioinformatics are described in the book by Ohlebusch [196].

107   Compression Ratio of Greedy Superstrings

The problem considers Algorithm GREEDYSCS (presented under different forms in Problem 61) that computes a superstring $Greedy(X)$ for a set X of words of total length n. The superstring can be viewed as a compressed text representing all words in X and from this point of view it is interesting to quantify the gain of representing X by a superstring.

Let $GrCompr(X) = n - |Greedy(X)|$ denote the compression achieved by the greedy algorithm. Similarly define $OptCompr(X) = n - |OPT(X)|$ where OPT is an optimal (unknown) superstring for X.

The fraction $\frac{GrCompr(X)}{OptCompr(X)}$ is called the *compression ratio* of Algorithm GREEDYSCS.

> **Question.** Show the compression ratio of Algorithm GREEDYSCS is at least 1/2.

[**Hint:** Consider the overlap graph of the input set.]

Solution

It is more convenient to deal with the iterative version of Algorithm GREEDYSCS from Problem 61.

ITERATIVEGREEDYSCS(X non-empty set of words)

1   **while** $|X| > 1$ **do**
2   let $x, y \in X, x \neq y$, with $|Overlap(x,y)|$ maximal
3           $X \leftarrow X \setminus \{x,y\} \cup \{x \otimes y\}$
4   **return** $x \in X$

Let us start with an abstract problem for directed graphs. Assume G is a complete directed graph whose edges are weighted by non-negative integers. If $u \to v$ is an edge the operation $contract(u,v)$ identifies u, v and removes the edges out-going from u and in-going to v.

Let $OptHam(G)$ be the maximum weight of a Hamiltonian path in G and $GreedyHam(G)$ be the weight of the Hamiltonian path implicitly produced by the greedy algorithm. In each step the greedy algorithm for graphs chooses an edge $u \to v$ of maximum weight and applies $contract(u,v)$. It stops when G becomes a single node. The chosen edges compose the resulting Hamiltonian path.

Relation between greedy superstring and greedy Hamiltonian path. We introduce the *overlap graph* G of a set X of words. The set of nodes is X and the weight of $x_i \to x_j$ is the maximal overlap between words x_i and x_j. Observe that the statement in line 3 of Algorithm ITERATIVEGREEDYSCS corresponds to the operation $contract(x,y)$. This implies the following fact.

Observation. The greedy Hamiltonian path for the overlap graph of X corresponds to the greedy superstring of X.

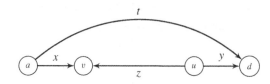

We say that a weighted graph G satisfies condition $(*)$ if in each configuration of the type shown on the above picture we have

$$z \geq x, y \implies z + t \geq x + y.$$

Moreover, we require that it holds for each graph obtained from G by applying any number of contractions.

We leave the following technical but easy proof of the following fact about overlap graphs to the reader (see Notes).

Lemma 17 *The overlap graph satisfies condition $(*)$.*

Lemma 18 *Assume G satisfies condition $(*)$, e is an edge of maximal weight z and G' is obtained from G by applying $contract(e)$. Then $OptHam(G') \geq OptHam(G) - 2z$.*

Proof   Let $e = u \to v$. Let π be an optimal Hamiltonian path in G. Denote by $|\pi|$ the total weight of π. It is enough to show that any Hamiltonian path in G' is of weight at least $|\pi| - 2z$ or (equivalently) to show that any Hamiltonian path π' in G containing the edge $u \to v$ is of total weight at least $|\pi| - z$.

Case v is after u on π. We remove two edges (u, b) and (c, v) of weights at most z and insert edges (u, v) and (c, s) to get a new Hamiltonian path π' (see picture below). Contracting (u, v) decreases the total weight of the path by the sum of weights of (u, b) and (c, v), that is by at most $2z$. We get a Hamiltonian path in G' of total weight at least $|\pi| - 2z$; see the picture below. Consequently $OptHam(G') \geq OptHam(G) - 2z$.

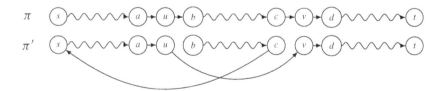

Case v is before u on π. We use condition $(*)$ with $x = weight(a, v)$, $y = weight(u, d)$, $z = weight(u, v)$ and $t = weight(a, d)$. Let $q = weight(v, b)$. Let π' derived from π as in the picture below.

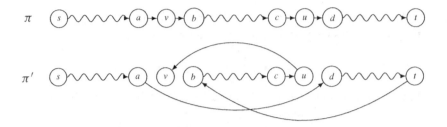

Due to condition (∗) and inequality $q \leq z$ we have

$$|\pi'| \geq |\pi| - x - y + z + t - q \geq |\pi| - z.$$

Consequently $|\pi'| \geq |\pi| - 2z$ and $OptHam(G') \geq OptHam(G) - 2z$. This completes the proof of Lemma 8.   ■

Lemma 19 *If G satisfies condition (∗) then $GreedyHam(G) \geq \frac{1}{2}OptHam(G)$.*

Proof   The proof is by induction on the number of nodes of G. Let z be the maximum weight of an edge in G whose contraction gives G'.

On the one hand, G' is a graph smaller than G, so applying the inductive assumption we have $GreedyHam(G') \geq \frac{1}{2}OptHam(G')$. On the other hand, we have $OptHam(G') \geq OptHam(G') - 2z$ and $GreedyHam(G) = GreedyHam(G') + z$.

Thus: $GreedyHam(G) \geq \frac{1}{2}OptHam(G') + z \geq \frac{1}{2}(OptHam(G) - 2z) + z \geq \frac{1}{2}OptHam(G)$, which proves the statement.   ■

The above observation and Lemmas 17, 18 and 19 imply directly that the greedy algorithm for superstrings achieves a $1/2$ compression ratio.

Notes
The present proof of the problem is a version of the proof given by Tarhio and Ukkonen in [230].

108   Binary Pascal Words

Pascal's triangle displays binomial coefficients following Pascal's rule:

$$\binom{n}{i} = \binom{n-1}{i-1} + \binom{n-1}{i}.$$

The regular structure of the triangle permits fast access to coefficients. In the problem, the nth binary Pascal word P_n is the nth row of Pascal's triangle modulo 2, that is, for $0 \le i \le n$:

$$P_n[i] = \binom{n}{i} \bmod 2.$$

Here are the resulting words P_n for $0 \le n \le 6$:

$$
\begin{array}{lll}
P_0 & = & 1 \\
P_1 & = & 1\ 1 \\
P_2 & = & 1\ 0\ 1 \\
P_3 & = & 1\ 1\ 1\ 1 \\
P_4 & = & 1\ 0\ 0\ 0\ 1 \\
P_5 & = & 1\ 1\ 0\ 0\ 1\ 1 \\
P_6 & = & 1\ 0\ 1\ 0\ 1\ 0\ 1
\end{array}
$$

Question. Given the binary representations $r_k r_{k-1} \cdots r_0$ of n and $c_k c_{k-1} \cdots c_0$ of i, show how to compute in time $O(k)$ the letter $P_n[i]$ and the number of occurrences of 1 in P_n.

[**Hint:** Possibly use Lucas's Theorem.]

Theorem [Lucas, 1852]. If p is a prime number and $r_k r_{k-1} \cdots r_0$, $c_k c_{k-1} \cdots c_0$ are the based p representations of the respective integers r and c with $r \ge c \ge 0$, then

$$\binom{r}{c} \bmod p = \prod_{i=0}^{k} \binom{r_i}{c_i} \bmod p.$$

Solution

The following property leads to a $O(k)$-time algorithm for computing letters in P_n.

Property 1. $P_n[i] = 1 \iff \forall j\ 1 \le j \le k\ (r_j = 0 \Rightarrow c_j = 0)$.

Proof The equivalence is a consequence of Lucas's Theorem. In our situation $p = 2$ and $r_j, c_j \in \{0,1\}$. Then

$$\binom{r_j}{c_j} \bmod 2 = 1 \iff (r_j = 0 \Rightarrow c_j = 0),$$

which directly implies the property.   ∎

Example. $P_6[4] = \binom{6}{4} \bmod 2 = 1$, since the binary representations of 6 and 4 are 110 and 010 respectively.

To answer the second part of the question let $g(n)$ denote the number of occurrences of 1 in the binary representation of the non-negative integer n. The following fact provides a simple algorithm to compute the number of occurrences of 1 in P_n in the required time.

Property 2. The number of ones in P_n is $2^{g(n)}$.

Proof Let $r_k r_{k-1} \cdots r_0$ and $c_k c_{k-1} \cdots c_0$ be the respective binary representations of n and i. Let

$$R = \{j : r_j = 1\} \text{ and } C = \{j : c_j = 1\}.$$

According to property 1 we have

$$\binom{n}{i} \bmod 2 = 1 \iff C \subseteq R.$$

Hence the sought number equals the number of subsets C of R, which is $2^{g(n)}$, due to the definition of $g(n)$. This completes the proof.   ∎

Notes

An easy description of Lucas's theorem is by Fine [114].

Among the many interesting properties of Pascal words let us consider the following. For a word $w = w[0 .. k]$ and a set X of natural numbers, define

$$Filter(w, X) = w[i_1] w[i_2] \cdots w[i_t],$$

where $i_1 < i_2 < \cdots < i_t$ and $\{i_1, i_2, \ldots, i_t\} = X \cap [0 .. k]$. Then, for a positive integer n and the set Y of powers of 2, we get the equality

$$Filter(P_n, Y) = \text{ reverse binary representation of } n.$$

A simple proof follows from the structure of the ith diagonal of Pascal triangle modulo 2, counting diagonals from left to right and starting with 0. The 0th diagonal consists of 1's, the next one consists of a repetition of 10, and so on. Now considering the table whose rows are consecutive numbers, the columns of this table show similar patterns.

109   Self-Reproducing Words

Word morphisms are frequently used to produce finite or infinite words because they are defined by the images of single letters. In the problem we consider another type of function that may be regarded as context dependent and is a kind of sequential transducer.

The working alphabet is $A = \{0, 1, 2\}$. The image by h of a word $w \in A^+$ is the word

$$h(w) = (0 \oplus w[0]) \, (w[0] \oplus w[1]) \, (w[1] \oplus w[2]) \cdots (w[n-1] \oplus 0),$$

where $\oplus$ is the addition modulo 3. Iterating h from an initial word of A^+ produces longer words that have very special properties, as shown with the two examples.

Example 1. When the process is applied to the initial word $x = 1221$, it produces a list of ternary words starting with

$h^0(x)$	=	1	2	2	1							
$h^1(x)$	=	1	0	1	0	1						
$h^2(x)$	=	1	1	1	1	1	1					
$h^3(x)$	=	1	2	2	2	2	2	1				
$h^4(x)$	=	1	0	1	1	1	1	0	1			
$h^5(x)$	=	1	1	1	2	2	2	1	1	1		
$h^6(x)$	=	1	2	2	0	1	1	0	2	2	1	
$h^7(x)$	=	1	0	1	2	1	2	1	2	1	0	1
$h^8(x)$	=	1	1	1	0	0	0	0	0	0	1	1	1
$h^9(x)$	=	1	2	2	1	0	0	0	0	0	1	2	2	1

In particular, $h^9(x) = x \cdot 00000 \cdot x$, which shows that the word x has been reproduced.

Example 2. Applied to $y = 121$, the associated list starts with

$h^0(y)$	=	1	2	1		
$h^1(y)$	=	1	0	0	1	
$h^2(y)$	=	1	1	0	1	1
$h^3(y)$	=	1	2	1	1	2	1

Question. Show that for any word $w \in A^+$ the two properties hold:

(A) There is an integer m for which $h^m(w)$ consists of two copies of w separated by a factor of zeros (i.e., a factor in 0^*).

(B) If $|w|$ is a power of 3 then $h^{|w|}(w) = w\,w$.

Solution

Point (A). Let m be the minimal power of 3 not smaller than the length n of w and denote

$$\alpha(i) = \binom{m}{i} \bmod 3.$$

We use the following fact.

Observation. Let $i \in \{0, 1, \ldots, m\}$. Since m is a power of 3, then we have (obviously) $\alpha(i) = 1$ if $i \in \{0, m\}$; otherwise (slightly less obvious) $\alpha(i) = 0$.

We refer the reader to Problem 108 that shows a relation between the present process and Pascal's triangle.

Starting with the word 1, after m steps, at position i on $h^m(\mathtt{1})$ we have the letter $\alpha(i)$.

Due to the observation after m steps the contribution of a single 1 at position t to the letter at position $t + i$ is $\alpha(i)$. Therefore in the word $h^m(w)$ the prefix w remains as it is, since $\alpha(0) = 1$, and it is copied m positions to the right, since $\alpha(m) = 1$. Letters at other positions in $h^m(w)$ are 0, since $\alpha(i) = 0$ for $i \notin \{0, m\}$. This solves point (A) of the question.

Point (B). Following the above argument, if $|w|$ is a power of 3 the word w is copied m positions to the right, which gives the word ww, since the prefix of size m is unchanged. This solves point (B) of the question.

Notes

When the alphabet is $A_j = \{0, 1, \ldots, j - 1\}$ and j is a prime number we can choose $m = \min\{j^i : j^i \geq n\}$, where n is the length of the initial word w. When j is not prime the situation is more complicated: now we can choose $m = j \cdot n!$, but in this case the word separating the two copies of w can contain non-zero values.

The problem presented here is from [13], where a 2-dimensional (more interesting) version is also presented.

110   Weights of Factors

The *weight* of a word on the alphabet $\{1, 2\}$ is the arithmetic sum of its letters. The problem deals with the weights of all the non-empty factors of a given word of length n. In this limited alphabet, the potentially maximal weight is $2n$ and the maximal number of different weights among factors is $2n - 1$.

For example, the number of weights of factors of the word 2221122 is 10, namely they are $1, 2, \ldots, 8, 10, 12$.

> **Question.** Design a simple linear-time algorithm computing the number of different weights of non-empty factors of a word $x \in \{1, 2\}^+$.

> **Question.** Show that after preprocessing the word x in linear time each query of the type 'is there is a non-empty factor of x of positive weight k?' can be answered in constant time. The memory space after preprocessing should be of constant size.

Solution
Before going to solutions, let us show some properties of weights. For a positive integer k let

$$\text{SameParity}(k) = \{i : 1 \leq i \leq k \text{ and } (k - i) \text{ is even}\}.$$

The size of the set is $|\text{SameParity}(k)| = \lceil \frac{k}{2} \rceil$.

Let $sum(i, j)$ denote the weight of the factor $x[i \mathinner{.\,.} j]$ of x, $i \leq j$. Extremely simple solutions to the questions derive from the following fact.

Fact. If $k > 0$ is the weight of some factor of x then each element of $\text{SameParity}(k)$ is also the weight of a non-empty factor of x.

Proof Let $sum(i, j) = k$ be the weight of $x[i \mathinner{.\,.} j]$, $i \leq j$. If $x[i] = 2$ or $x[j] = 2$ then chopping the first or the last letter of $x[i \mathinner{.\,.} j]$ produces a factor with weight $k - 2$ if it is non-empty. Otherwise $x[i] = x[j] = 1$ and after chopping both end letters we get again a factor with weight $k - 2$ if it is non-empty. Iterating the process proves the fact. ∎

Note that, if $x \in 2^+$, answers to questions are straightforward because x has $|x|$ different weights, $2, 4, \ldots, 2|x|$. In the rest we assume x contains at least one occurrence of letter 1. Let *first* and *last* be respectively the first and the last positions on x of letter 1 and let

$$s = sum(0, n-1) \text{ and } t = \max\{sum(first+1, n-1), sum(0, last-1)\}.$$

In other words, s is the weight of the whole word x and t is the maximum weight of a prefix or a suffix of x that is of different parity than s.

The next observation is a consequence of the above fact.

Observation. The set of weights of all non-empty factors of a word x is the union SameParity$(s) \cup$ SameParity(t).

Number of different weights. Since the number of different weights of non-empty factors of x is

$$|\text{SameParity}(s)| + |\text{SameParity}(t)| = \left\lceil \frac{s}{2} \right\rceil + \left\lceil \frac{t}{2} \right\rceil,$$

its computation amounts to compute s and t, which is done in linear time.

For the word 2221122, we have $s = 12$, $t = \max\{5, 7\} = 7$ and the number of weights of its factors is $\lceil \frac{12}{2} \rceil + \lceil \frac{7}{2} \rceil = 10$ as seen above.

Constant-time query. The preprocessing consists in computing the two values s and t corresponding to the word x, which is done in linear time. After preprocessing, the memory space is used only to store the values s and t.

Then, to answer the query 'is $k > 0$ the weight of a non-empty factor of x?' it suffices to check the condition

$$k \leq t \text{ or } ((s - k) \text{ is non-negative and even}),$$

which is done in constant time.

Notes

What about larger alphabets, for example $\{1, 2, 3, 4, 5\}$? An efficient algorithm is still possible but there is nothing as nice and simple as the above solution.

Let x be a word whose length is a power of 2. An *anchored* interval $[i \mathrel{..} j]$ is a subinterval of $[0 \mathrel{..} |x| - 1]$ with i in the left half and j in the right half of the interval. The associated factor $x[i \mathrel{..} j]$ of x is called an anchored factor. Using fast convolution, all distinct weights of anchored factors of a word x can be computed in time $O(|x| \log |x|)$. We can take characteristic vectors of the sets of weights of suffixes of the left half and of prefixes of the right half of x. Both vectors are of length $O(|x|)$. Then the convolution of these two vectors (sequences) gives all the weights of anchored factors.

Over the alphabet $\{1, 2, 3, 4, 5\}$, using a recursive approach, all distinct weights of factors of a word of length n are computed in time $O(n(\log n)^2)$ because the running time $T(n)$ to do it satisfies the equation $T(n) = 2T(n/2) + O(n \log n)$.

111   Letter-Occurrence Differences

For a non-empty word x, $diff(x)$ denotes the difference between the numbers of occurrences of the most frequent letter and of the least frequent letter in x. (They can be the same letter.)

For example,

$$diff(\texttt{aaa}) = 0 \text{ and } diff(\texttt{cabbcadbeaebaabec}) = 4.$$

In the second word, a and b are the most frequent letters, with five occurrences, and d the least frequent letter, with one occurrence.

> **Question.** Design an $O(n|A|)$ running time algorithm computing the value $\max\{diff(x) : x \text{ factor of } y\}$ for a non-empty word y of length n over the alphabet A.

[**Hint:** First consider $A = \{\texttt{a},\texttt{b}\}$.]

Solution

Assume for a moment that $y \in \{\texttt{a},\texttt{b}\}^+$ and let us search for a factor x of y in which b is the most frequent letter. To do so, y is transformed into Y by substituting -1 for a and 1 for b. The problem then reduces to the computation of a factor with the maximum arithmetic sum and containing at least one occurrence of 1 and of -1.

Before considering a general alphabet, we consider a solution for the binary alphabet $\{\texttt{-1},\texttt{1}\}$ and introduce a few notations.

For a given position i on the word $Y \in \{\texttt{-1},\texttt{1}\}^+$, let sum_i be the sum $Y[0] + Y[1] + \cdots + Y[i]$ and let $pref_i$ be the minimum sum corresponding to a prefix $Y[0..k]$ of Y for which both $k < i$ and $Y[k+1..i]$ contains at least one occurrence of -1. If there is no such k, let $pref_i = \infty$.

The following algorithm delivers the expected value for the word Y.

MAXDIFFERENCE(Y non-empty word on $\{-1,1\}$)

```
1   (maxdiff, prevsum, sum) ← (0, 0, 0)
2   pref ← ∞
3   for i ← 0 to |Y| − 1 do
4       sum ← sum + Y[i]
5       if Y[i] = −1 then
6           pref ← min{pref, prevsum}
7           prevsum ← sum
8       maxdiff ← max{maxdiff, sum − pref}
9   return maxdiff
```

Algorithm MAXDIFFERENCE implements the following observation to compute the maximal difference among the factors of its input.

Observation. Assume $pref \neq \infty$. Then the letter $Y[k]$ is -1 and the difference $diff(Y[k+1 .. i])$ is $sum - pref$. Moreover $Y[k+1 .. i]$ has maximal $diff$ value among the suffixes of $Y[0 .. i]$.

In this way the problem is solved in linear time for a word on a two-letter alphabet.

On a larger alphabet we apply the following trick. For any two distinct letters a and b of the word y, let $y_{a,b}$ be the word obtained by removing all other letters occurring in y. After changing $y_{a,b}$ to $Y_{a,b}$ on the alphabet $\{-1,1\}$, Algorithm MAXDIFFERENCE produces the maximal difference among factors of $Y_{a,b}$, which is the maximal difference among factors of $y_{a,b}$ as well.

The required value is the maximum result among results obtained by running MAXDIFFERENCE on $Y_{a,b}$ for all pairs of letters a and b separately.

Since the sum of lengths of all words $y_{a,b}$ is only $O(n|A|)$, the overall running time of the algorithm is $O(n|A|)$ for a word of length n over the alphabet A.

Notes

This problem appeared in the Polish Olympiad of Informatics for high school students in the year 2010.

---

112   Factoring with Border-Free Prefixes

Searching for a border-free pattern in texts is done very efficiently without any sophisticated solution by BM algorithm (see Problem 33) because two occurrences of the pattern cannot overlap. When a pattern is not border free, its factorisation into border-free words may lead to efficient searching methods.

We say that a non-empty word u is border free if none of its proper non-empty prefix is also a suffix, that is, $Border(u) = \varepsilon$, or equivalently, if its smallest period is its length, that is, $per(u) = |u|$.

The aim of the problem is to show how a word factorises into its border-free prefixes.

Consider for example the word aababaaabaababaa. Its set of border-free prefixes is {a, aab, aabab} and its factorisation on the set is

```
0   1   2   3   4   5   6   7   8   9   10  11  12     134  15
a   a   b   a   b   a   a   a   b   a   a   b   a   b   a   a
        x6              x5      x4              x3           x2  x1
```

> **Question.** Show that a non-empty word x uniquely factorises into $x_k x_{k-1} \cdots x_1$, where each x_i is a border-free prefix of x and x_1 is the shortest border-free prefix of x.

The factorisation of x can be represented by the list of its factor lengths. On the preceding example it is $(5, 1, 3, 5, 1, 1)$ and the list of factors is $x[0 .. 4]$, $x[5 .. 5]$, $x[6 .. 8]$, $x[9 .. 13]$, $x[14 .. 14]$, $x[15 .. 15]$.

> **Question.** Design a linear-time algorithm for computing the border-free prefix factorisation of a word, namely the list of factor lengths.

Solution

Unique factorisation. Let $S(x)$ be the set of border-free prefixes of x. It is a suffix code, that is, if $u, v \in S(x)$ and u and v are distinct words none of them is a suffix of the other. Because on the contrary, if for example u is a proper suffix of v, since u is a non-empty prefix of v, v is not border-free, a contradiction. Then, any product of words in $S(x)$ admits a unique decomposition into such a product. This shows the uniqueness of the factorisation of x into words of $S(x)$, if the factorisation exists.

Let us prove that the factorisation exists. If x is border free, that is $x \in S(x)$, the factorisation contains only one factor, x itself. Otherwise, let u be the shortest non-empty border of x. Then u is border free, that is, $u \in S(x)$. Thus, we can iterate the same reasoning on the word xu^{-1} to get the factorisation. This yields a factorisation in which the last factor is the shortest element of $S(x)$, as required.

Factoring. The factorisation of a non-empty word x can be computed from its border table with the intermediate **shortest-border table** *shtbord*: *shtbord*$[\ell] = 0$ if $x[0 .. \ell - 1]$ is border free and else is the length of its shortest border. The table is computed during a left-to-right traversal of the border table of x.

Here are the tables for the word $x = $ aababaaabaababaa:

i		0	1	2	3	4	5	6	7	8	9	10	11	12	13	14	15
$x[i]$		a	a	b	a	b	a	a	a	b	a	a	b	a	b	a	a
ℓ	0	1	2	3	4	5	6	7	8	9	10	11	12	13	14	15	16
$border[\ell]$	—	0	1	0	1	0	1	2	2	3	4	2	3	4	5	6	7
$shtbord[\ell]$	—	0	1	0	1	0	1	1	1	3	1	1	3	1	5	1	1

The lengths ℓ of the border-free prefixes of x satisfy $border[\ell] = 0$, and are 1, 3 and 5 on the example.

Since the set $S(x)$ is a suffix code it is natural to compute the factorisation by scanning x from right to left. Following the above proof, lengths of factors are picked from the table of shortest non-empty borders until a border-free prefix is found.

FACTORISE(x non-empty word)

```
 1   border ← BORDERS(x)
 2   for ℓ ← 0 to |x| do
 3       if border[ℓ] > 0 and shtbord[border[ℓ]] > 0 then
 4           shtbord[ℓ] ← shtbord[border[ℓ]]
 5       else shtbord[ℓ] ← border[ℓ]
 6   L ← empty list
 7   ℓ ← |x|
 8   while border[ℓ] > 0 do
 9       L ← shtbord[ℓ] · L
10       ℓ ← ℓ − shtbord[ℓ]
11   L ← shtbord[ℓ] · L
12   return L
```

As for the running time of Algorithm FACTORISE, it is clearly linear in addition to the computation of the border table of x, which can also be computed in linear time (see Problem 19). Therefore the overall process runs in linear time.

Notes

It is unclear whether the table of shortest non-empty borders can be computed as efficiently with the technique applied to produce the table of short borders in Problem 21.

113   Primitivity Test for Unary Extensions

A non-empty word x can be decomposed as $x = (uv)^e u$ for two words u and v where v is non-empty, $|uv| = per(x)$ is the (smallest) period of x and e is a positive integer. We set $tail(x) = v$ (not u).

For example, $tail(\text{abcd}) = \text{abcd}$ because the associated words are $u = \varepsilon$ and $v = \text{abcd}$, $tail(\text{abaab}) = \text{a}$ because $\text{abaab} = (\text{aba})^1 \text{ab}$ and $tail(\text{abaababa}) = \text{ab}$ because $\text{abaababa} = (\text{abaab})^1 \text{aba}$. The latter word is the Fibonacci word fib_4 and in general $tail(fib_n) = fib_{n-3}$, for $n \geq 3$.

The goal of the problem is to test whether xa^k is primitive when only little is known about the word x.

Question. Assume the only information on x is

• x is not unary (contains at least two distinct letters)

• $tail(x)$ is not unary or $tail(x) \in b^*$, for a letter b

• $\ell = |tail(x)|$

Show how to answer in constant time if the word xa^k is primitive, for an integer k and a letter a.

[**Hint:** $tail(x)$ is an obvious candidate to extend x to a non-primitive word.]

Solution
The solution relies on the following property, for a non-unary word x:

$$xa^k \text{ is not primitive} \implies tail(x) = a^k.$$

Since the converse obviously holds, the property leads to a constant-time test under the hypotheses in the question because testing the primitivity of xa^k amounts to check if $tail(x) \in b^*$, that is, to check if $a = b$ and $k = \ell$. Although the property is simply stated it needs a tedious proof. We start with an auxiliary fact and go on with the crucial lemma.

Fact. If x is non-unary and $x = (uv)^e u = u'v'u'$, where $|uv| = per(x)$, $e > 0$ and $|u'| < |u|$, then v' is non-unary.

Indeed, if v' is unary, v also is, which implies that u is not (it cannot be unary with a letter different from the letter in v). Since the word u' is both a proper prefix and a suffix of u, we get $u = u'y = zu'$ for two non-empty words y and z that are respectively prefix and suffix of v' with $|y| = |z| = per(u)$. Then both are unary, implying u and x also are, a contradiction.

Unary-Extension Lemma. If x is non-unary, a is a letter, k is a positive integer and $a^k \neq tail(x)$, then xa^k is primitive.

Proof By contradiction, assume xa^k is non-primitive, that is

$$xa^k = z^j, \ j \geq 2, \ |z| = per(xa^k).$$

We deduce $|z| > k$, because otherwise both x would be unary and $|z| \neq per(x)$, since $a^k \neq tail(x)$. Since $|z|$ is a period of x, $|z| > per(x)$. We cannot have $j > 2$ because z^2 would be a prefix of x, which implies $|z| = per(x)$.

Consequently the only remaining case in this situation is when $j = 2$, that is

$$xa^k = z^2 = u'v'u'v', \ x = (uv)^i u = u'v'u', \ v' = a^k,$$

where $v' \neq v = tail(x)$, $|uv| = per(x)$ and $|u'v'| = per(xa^k)$. Let us consider two cases.

Case $|u'| < |u|$: This is impossible due to the above preliminary fact which implies that $v' = a^k$ is non-unary.

Case $|u'| > |u|$: Let us consider only the situation $i = 2$, that is, $x = (uv)^2 u$. The general case $i > 1$ can be treated similarly.

Claim. $|u'| < |uv|$.

Proof (of the claim) By contradiction assume $|u'| \geq |uv|$. Then the word x admits periods $p = |uv|$ and $q = |x| - |u'| = |u'v'|$, where $p + q \leq |x|$. The Periodicity Lemma implies that p (as the smallest period) is a divisor of q. Hence p is also a period of xa^k (which has a period q). Consequently x and xa^k have the same shortest period, which is impossible. ∎

Let w be such that $u'v' = uvw$. Due to the above claim w is a suffix of v' and consequently w is unary. The word u' is a prefix of uvu (as a prefix of x). This implies that $|w|$ is a period of uvu. Since w is unary, uv is also unary and the whole word x is unary, a contradiction.

In both cases we have a contradiction. Therefore the word xa^k is primitive as stated. ∎

Notes

The solution to this problem is by Rytter in [215]. A time–space optimal primitivity test (linear time, constant space) is given in Problem 40 but the present problem provides a much faster solution in the considered particular case.

114   Partially Commutative Alphabets

The study of words over a partially commutative alphabet is motivated by the representation of concurrent processes in which letters are names of processes and commutativity corresponds to the non-concurrency of two processes.

We consider an alphabet A for which some pairs of letters commute. This means that we can transform the word $uabv$ to $ubav$, for any commuting pair (a,b). The corresponding (partial) commutativity relation on A denoted by $\approx$ is assumed to be symmetric.

Two words are equivalent (with respect to the commutativity relation), denoted by $u \equiv v$, if one word can be transformed into the other by a series of exchanges between adjacent commuting letters. Observe that $\equiv$ is an equivalence relation while $\approx$ usually is not.

For example, on the alphabet $A = \{a, b, c, d\}$

$$a \approx b \approx c \approx d \approx a \;\Rightarrow\; abcdabcd \equiv badbdcac$$

due to the following commutations:

```
a  b  c  d  a  b  c  d
b  a  c  d  a  b  c  d
b  a  d  c  a  b  c  d
b  a  d  c  b  a  c  d
b  a  d  b  c  a  c  d
b  a  d  b  c  a  d  c
b  a  d  b  c  d  a  c
b  a  d  b  d  c  a  c
```

> **Question.** Design an equivalence test that checks if $u \equiv v$ for two words u and v of length n in A^* and that runs in time $O(n|A|)$.

[**Hint:** Consider projections of words on pairs of letters.]

Solution
For two letters $a, b \in A$, $\pi_{a,b}(w)$ denotes the projection of w on the pair (a, b), that is, the word resulting from w by erasing all letters except them. Let $|w|_a$ denote the number of times letter a occurs in w. The next property is the basis of our solution.

Property. For two words u and v, $u \equiv v$ if and only if the following two conditions hold:

(i) $|u|_a = |v|_a$ for each letter $a \in A$; and

(ii) $\pi_{a,b}(u) = \pi_{a,b}(v)$ whenever a and b do not commute.

Proof   It is clear that the conditions are satisfied if $u \equiv v$. Conversely, assume conditions (i) and (ii) hold. The proof is by induction on the common length of the two words.

Assume $u = au'$, where $a \in A$. We claim that we can move the first occurrence of letter a in v to the first position using the relation $\approx$. Indeed, if we are not able to do it, there is some non-commuting letter b occurring before a in v. Then $\pi_{a,b}(u) \neq \pi_{a,b}(v)$, a contradiction.

After moving a to the beginning of v we get the word av' with $av' \equiv v$ and the conditions (i) and (ii) hold for u' and v'. By the inductive assumption $u' \equiv v'$, and consequently $u = au' \equiv av' \equiv v$. This completes the proof.   ∎

The equivalence test consists in checking the above two conditions. Checking the first condition is obviously done in time $O(n|A|)$ (or even in time $O(n \log |A|)$ without any assumption of the alphabet).

The second condition it to check if $\pi_{a,b}(u) = \pi_{a,b}(v)$ for all pairs of letters a,b that do not commute. At a first glance this looks to produce a $O(n|A|^2)$ time algorithm. However, the sum of the lengths of all words of the form $\pi_{a,b}(u)$ is only $O(n|A|)$, which is also an upper bound on the running time of the algorithm.

Notes
The material in this problem is based on properties of partial commutations presented by Cori and Perrin in [61].

There is an alternative algorithm for the equivalence problem. We can define a canonical form of a word as its lexicographically smallest equivalent version. Hence given two words one can compute their canonical versions and test their equality. The computation of canonical forms is of independent interest.

115 Greatest Fixed-Density Necklace

A word is called a **necklace** if it is the lexicographically smallest word in its conjugacy class. The **density** of a word on the alphabet $\{0,1\}$ is the number of occurrences of 1's occurring in it. Let $N(n,d)$ be the set of all binary necklaces of length n and density d.

The problem is concerned with the lexicographically greatest necklace in $N(n,d)$ with $0 \le d \le n$. For example, 00100101 is the greatest necklace in $N(8,3)$:

$\{00000111, 00001011, 00001101, 00010011, 00010101, 00011001, 00100101\}.$

And 01011011 is the greatest necklace in $N(8,5)$:

$\{00011111, 00101111, 00110111, 00111011, 00111101, 01010111, 01011011\}.$

The following intuitive property characterises the structure of largest necklaces.

Lemma 20 *Let C be the greatest necklace in $N(n,d)$:*

(i) *If $d \le n/2$ then $C = 0^{c_0}10^{c_1}1 \cdots 0^{c_{d-1}}1$, where both $c_0 > 0$ and, for each $i > 0$, $c_i \in \{c_0, c_0 - 1\}$.*

(ii) *If $d > n/2$ then $C = 01^{c_0}01^{c_1} \cdots 01^{c_{n-d-1}}$, where both $c_0 > 0$ and, for each $i > 0$, $c_i \in \{c_0, c_0 + 1\}$.*

(iii) *In both cases, the binary sequence $w = (0, |c_1 - c_0|, |c_2 - c_0|, \ldots)$ is the largest necklace of its length and density.*

> **Question.** Based on Lemma 20, design a linear-time algorithm for computing the greatest necklace in $N(n,d)$.

Solution
The lemma motivates the following two definitions when the (binary) word w is a necklace of length ℓ:

$$\phi_t(w) = 0^{t-w[0]}10^{t-w[1]}1 \cdots 0^{t-w[\ell-1]}11,$$

$$\psi_t(w) = 01^{t+w[0]}01^{t+w[1]} \cdots 01^{t+w[\ell-1]}.$$

The next two facts are rather direct consequences of the lemma and show that the functions ϕ_t and ψ_t preserve the lexicographic order. They also justify the recursive structure of the algorithm below.

Fact 1. A binary word w of length ℓ is a necklace if and only if $\phi_t(w)$ is a necklace for all $t > 0$.

Fact 2. A binary word w of length ℓ is a necklace if and only if $\psi_t(w)$ is a necklace for all $t \geq 0$.

The following algorithm then solves the problem. Point (iii) of the lemma allows to reduce the problem to a single much smaller problem by a single recursive call.

GREATESTNECKLACE(n,d natural numbers, $d \leq n$)

1   **if** $d = 0$ **then**

2   **return** 0^n

3   **elseif** $d \leq n/2$ **then**

4       $(t,r) \leftarrow (\lfloor n/d \rfloor, n \bmod d)$

5       $w \leftarrow$ GREATESTNECKLACE($d, d - r$)

6   **return** $\phi_t(w)$

7   **elseif** $d < n$ **then**

8       $(t,r) \leftarrow (\lfloor n/(n - d) \rfloor, n \bmod (n - d))$

9       $w \leftarrow$ GREATESTNECKLACE($n - d, r$)

10   **return** $\psi_{t-1}(w)$

11 **else return** 1^n

Example. For $n = 8$ and $d = 3$, we get $t = 2$, $r = 2$ and the recursive call gives GREATESTNECKLACE($3, 1$) $= w = $ 001. Eventually GREATESTNECKLACE($8,3$) $= 0^{2-0}10^{2-0}10^{2-1}1$, which is 00100101, as already seen above.

Example. For $n = 8$ and $d = 5$, we also get $t = 2, r = 2$ (since $n - d = 3$) and the recursive call gives GREATESTNECKLACE($3,2$) $= w = $ 011. This produces GREATESTNECKLACE($8,5$) $=$ 01^{1+0}01^{1+1}01^{1+1}, which is 01011011 as seen above.

The correctness of Algorithm GREATESTNECKLACE essentially comes from the lemma and the two facts.

As for the running time of GREATESTNECKLACE(n,d) note that recursive calls have to deal with words whose length is no more than $n/2$. Therefore the whole runs in linear time to generate the final word.

Notes

The material of the problem is by Sawada and Hartman in [218].

---

116   Period-Equivalent Binary Words

Two words are said to be period equivalent if they have the same set of periods
or equivalently have the same length and the same set of border lengths.
For example, abcdabcda and abaaabaaa are period equivalent since they
share the same set of periods $\{4,8,9\}$ although their letters are not in one-to-one
correspondence.

The goal of the problem is to show that a set of periods of a word can be
realised by a binary word.

Question. Let w be a word over an arbitrarily large alphabet. Show how to
construct in linear time a binary word x period equivalent to w.

[**Hint:** Consider border lengths instead of periods.]

Solution

Dealing with the border lengths of w instead of its periodic structure is more
convenient to solve the question and describe the corresponding algorithm.
The border structure is given by the increasing list $\mathcal{B}(w) = (q_1, q_2, \ldots, q_n)$ of
lengths of non-empty borders of w with the addition of $q_n = |w| = N$. For
example, $(1,5,9)$ is the list associated with abcdabcda.

To answer the question, from the list $\mathcal{B}(w)$ a sequence of words
$(x_1, x_2, \ldots, x_n)$, in which x_i is a binary word associated with the border
list $(q_1, \ldots, q_i)$, is constructed iteratively. The binary word period equivalent
to w is $x = x_n$.

Let x_1 be a border-free word of length q_1. The word x_i of length q_i with
longest border x_{i-1} is either of the form $x_i y_i x_i$ if this fits with its length or
built by overlapping x_{i-1} with itself. Word y_i is unary and its letter is chosen
to avoid creating undesirable borders.

Example. Let $(1,3,8,13) = (q_1,q_2,q_3,q_4) = \mathcal{B}(\text{abacdabacdaba})$. Starting
with the border-free word $x_1 = 0$, x_2 is built by inserting $y_2 = 1$ between
two occurrences of x_1. The word x_3 is built similarly from x_2 with the unary
word $y_3 = 00$, whose letter is different from that of y_2. Eventually, $x_4 =$
0100001000010 is built by overlapping two occurrences of x_3.

In Algorithm ALTERNATING that implements the method, $prefix(z,k)$ denotes the prefix of length k of a word z when $k \leq |z|$.

ALTERNATING(w non-empty word)

```
1   (q₁,q₂,...,qₙ) ← B(w)
2   (x₁,a) ← (01^{q₁-1},0)
3   for i ← 2 to n do
4       gapᵢ ← qᵢ − 2qᵢ₋₁
5       if gapᵢ > 0 then
6           a ← 1 − a
7           xᵢ ← xᵢ₋₁ · a^{gapᵢ} · xᵢ₋₁
8       else xᵢ ← prefix(xᵢ₋₁,qᵢ − qᵢ₋₁) · xᵢ₋₁
9   return xₙ
```

Why does Algorithm ALTERNATING work? The proof relies on the next result that is directly implied by the Unary-Extension Lemma (see Problem 113). When z is written $(uv)^e u$ and $|uv|$ is its (smallest) period, by definition $tail(z) = v$.

Lemma 21 *Let z be a non-unary binary word, k a positive integer and a a letter for which $a^k \neq tail(z)$. Then the word $x = za^k z$ has no period smaller than $|za^k|$, that is, has no border longer than z.*

Proof The proof is by contradiction. Assume $x = za^k z$ has a period $p < |za^k|$ and consider two cases.

Case $p \leq |z|$. The word x has two periods $|za^k|$ and p that satisfy $|za^k| + p \leq |x|$. Applying the Periodicity Lemma to them, we deduce that $\gcd(|za^k|, p)$ is also a period of x. This implies that ua^k is non-primitive, since $\gcd(|za^k|, p) \leq p < |ua^k|$. But this contradicts the Unary-Extension Lemma, whose conclusion is that ua^k is primitive under the hypothesis.

Case $|u| < p < |ua^k|$.

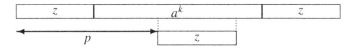

Inequalities of this case imply that there is an internal occurrence of z in $za^k z$, namely at position p. If $p \leq k$, that is, $p + |z| \leq |za^k|$ (see picture) this occurrence is internal to a^k, which contradicts the fact that z is non-unary.

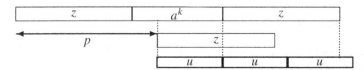

Otherwise $p > k$, that is, $p + |z| > |za^k|$ (see picture). Then the last two occurrences of z overlap, which means that $|za^k| - p$ is a period of z. As a suffix of a^k, the prefix period $u = z[0 .. |za^k| - p - 1]$ of z is unary, which implies that z itself is unary, a contradiction again.

Therefore no period of $za^k z$ is smaller than $|za^k|$.   ∎

To prove the correctness of Algorithm ALTERNATING we have to show that filling the gap between occurrences of x_{i-1} with a unary word at line 7 does not generate a redundant period.

To do so, assume $q_1 > 1$. The case $q_1 = 1$ can be treated similarly starting with the first i for which x_i is non-unary. Algorithm ALTERNATING has the following property: if $gap_i > 0$ then $x_i = x_{i-1} y_i x_{i-1}$ where $y_i = a^{gap_i} \neq tail(x_{i-1})$ and x_{i-1} is not unary. Due to the lemma $x_{i-1} y_i x_{i-1}$ has no border longer than x_{i-1}. Thus no redundant border is created, which shows the correctness of ALTERNATING.

Computing the list of border lengths, for example, with Algorithm BORDERS from Problem 19, and running the algorithm takes linear time $O(N) = O(|w|)$, as expected.

Notes

The presented algorithm as well as more complicated algorithm for binary lexicographically first words are by Rytter [215].

Note that a sorted list $\mathcal{B} = (q_1, q_2, \ldots, q_n)$ corresponds to the list of border lengths of a word if and only if, for $\delta_i = q_i - q_{i-1}$ when $i > 1$,

$$\delta_{i-1} \mid \delta_i \Rightarrow \delta_{i-1} = \delta_i \quad \text{and} \quad q_i + \delta_i \leq n \Rightarrow q_i + \delta_i \in \mathcal{B}.$$

This is a version of Theorem 8.1.11 in [176]. The above technique provides a compressed description of size $O(n)$, which can be of order $\log N$, of the output word of length N.

117   Online Generation of de Bruijn Words

A binary de Bruijn word of order n is a word of length 2^n on the alphabet $\{0,1\}$ in which all binary words of length n occur cyclically exactly once. For example, 00010111 and 01000111 are (non-conjugate) de Bruijn words of order 3.

A de Bruijn word can be generated by starting from a binary word of length n and then repeating the operation $\text{NEXT}(w)$ below. The operation computes the next bit of the sought de Bruijn word and updates the word w. The whole process stops when w returns to its initial word.

DEBRUIJN(n positive integer)

1   $(x, w_0) \leftarrow (\varepsilon, \text{a binary word of length } n)$
2   $w \leftarrow w_0$
3   **do** $w \leftarrow \text{NEXT}(w)$
4       $x \leftarrow x \cdot w[n-1]$
5   **while** $w \neq w_0$
6   **return** x

The operation NEXT needs only to be specified to get an appropriate on-line generation algorithm. Let $\bar{b}$ denote the negation of the bit b.

NEXT(w non-empty word of length n)

1   **if** $w[1 .. n-1] \cdot 1$ smallest in its conjugacy class **then**
2       $b \leftarrow \overline{w[0]}$
3   **else** $b \leftarrow w[0]$
4   **return** $w[1 .. n-1] \cdot b$

Question. Show that the execution of DEBRUIJN(n) generates a binary de Bruijn word of length 2^n.

Example. Let $n = 3$ and $w_0 = 111$. The values of w at line 4 of Algorithm DEBRUIJN are $11\underline{0}, 10\underline{1}, 01\underline{0}, 10\underline{0}, 00\underline{0}, 00\underline{1}, 01\underline{1}, 11\underline{1}$. Underlined bits form the de Bruijn word 01000111.

For $n = 5$ and $w_0 = 11111$ the consecutive values of w are
$1111\underline{0}, 1110\underline{1}, 1101\underline{1}, 1011\underline{1}, 0111\underline{0}, 1110\underline{0}, 1100\underline{1}, 1001\underline{1}, 0011\underline{0},$
$0110\underline{0}, 1100\underline{0}, 1000\underline{1}, 0001\underline{0}, 0010\underline{1}, 0101\underline{1}, 1011\underline{0}, 0110\underline{1}, 1101\underline{0},$

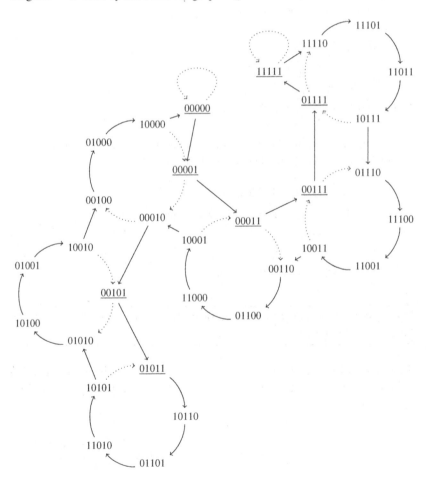

10101, 01010, 10100, 01001, 10010, 00100, 01000, 10000, 00000,
00001, 00011, 00111, 01111, 11111, generating the de Bruijn word

01110011000101101010010000011111.

Solution

The correctness of Algorithm DEBRUIJN can be proved by interpreting its run as a traversal of a tree whose nodes are shift cycles connected by two-way 'bridges'. Vertices of shift cycles are words of length n that are in the same conjugacy class. The representative of a cycle is its lexicographically minimal word (a necklace or Lyndon word if primitive). Edges in cycles stand for shifts, that is, are of the form $au \rightarrow ua$, where a is a single bit, and u is a word of length $n - 1$. Shift cycles form the graph G_n.

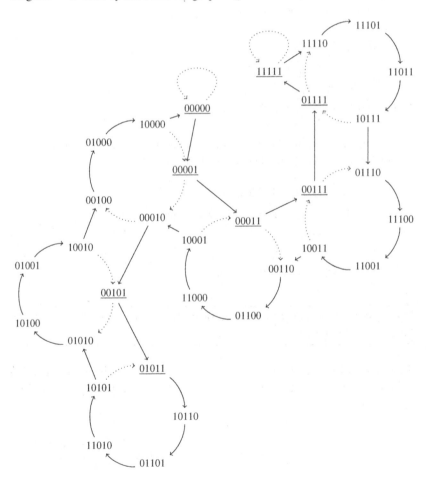

Graph G_n is transformed into the graph G'_n (see picture for G'_5) by adding bridges connecting disjoint cycles and by removing some cycle edges (dotted edges in picture) with the following procedure.

BRIDGES(G graph of cycles)

1   **for** each node u of G **do**
2   **if** $u1$ smallest in its conjugacy class **then**
3   remove edges $1u \to u1$ and $0u \to u0$
4   create edges $1u \to u0$ and $0u \to u1$
5   **return** modified graph

All solid edges in G'_n are associated with the function NEXT and used to traverse the graph. The graph G'_n consists of a single Hamiltonian cycle containing all words of length n. Bridges that connect a cyclic class of a word to another cyclic class of words with more occurrences of 0 form a (not rooted) tree whose nodes are cycles.

Observation. For a word w of length n, $v = $ NEXT(w) if and only if $w \to v$ is an edge of G'_n.

Hence the algorithm implicitly traverses the graph using the Hamiltonian cycle. This completes the proof of correctness.

Notes
The algorithm is by Sawada et al. [219]. The present proof is completely different from their. The for loop of function BRIDGES can be changed to the following:

1   **for** each node u of G **do**
2   **if** $0u$ smallest in its conjugacy class **then**
3   remove edges $0u \to u0$ and $1u \to u1$
4   create edges $0u \to u1$ and $1u \to u0$

Doing so we obtain a different graph of shift cycles connected by a new type of bridges and an alternative version of operation NEXT corresponding to the new Hamiltonian cycle.

118   Recursive Generation of de Bruijn Words

Following Problem 117, the present problem provides another method to generate a de Bruijn word on the alphabet $B = \{0, 1\}$. The method is recursive and its description requires a few preliminary definitions.

Let us first define *Shift*. When a word u occurs circularly exactly once in a word x, $|u| < |x|$, $Shift(x, u)$ denotes the conjugate of x admitting u as a suffix. For example, $Shift(001011101, 0111) = 010010111$ and $Shift(001011101, 1010) = 010111010$.

Let us then define the operation $\oplus$ between two words $x, y \in B^N$, $N = 2^n$, for which the suffix u of length n of x has a unique circular factor occurrence in y: $x \oplus y$ denotes $x \cdot Shift(y, u)$. For example, with $n = 2$, $0010 \oplus 1101 = 0010\,1110$ since $Shift(1101, 10) = 1110$.

Eventually, for a binary word w, let $\Psi(w)$ be the binary word v of length $|w|$ defined, for $0 \le i \le |w| - 1$, by

$$v[i] = (w[0] + w[1] + \cdots + w[i]) \bmod 2.$$

For example, $\Psi(0010111011) = 0011010010$. Also denote by $\overline{x}$ the complement of x, that is, its bitwise negation.

> **Question.** Show that if x is a binary de Bruijn word of length 2^n then $\Psi(x) \oplus \overline{\Psi(x)}$ is a de Bruijn word of length 2^{n+1}.

[**Hint:** Count circular factors of $\Psi(x) \oplus \overline{\Psi(x)}$.]

Example. For the de Bruijn word 0011, we have $\Psi(0011) = 0010$ and $\overline{\Psi(0011)} = 1101$. Then $0010 \oplus 1101 = 0010\,1110$, which is a de Bruijn word of length 8.

Solution

Let $Cfact_k(z)$ denote the set of circular factors of length k of a word z. We start with the following fact.

Observation 1. If two words x and y of length N have a common suffix of length $n < N$, $Cfact_{n+1}(x \cdot y) = Cfact_{n+1}(x) \cup Cfact_{n+1}(y)$.

The second observation is a consequence of the first.

Observation 2. Let x and y be binary words of length $N = 2^n$. When both $Cfact_{n+1}(x) \cup Cfact_{n+1}(y) = B^{n+1}$ and the suffix of length n of x belongs to $Cfact_n(y)$, the word $x \oplus y$ is a de Bruijn word.

Proof   We can assume that x and y have the same suffix of length n because this does not change the result of the operation $\oplus$ and then we have $x \oplus y =$ $x \cdot y$. Observation 1 implies, due to the hypothesis, that $Cfact_{n+1}(x \oplus y) =$ $Cfact_{n+1}(x \cdot y) = Cfact_{n+1}(x) \cup Cfact_{n+1}(y) = B^{n+1}$. Since $x \oplus y$ has length 2^{n+1}, every binary word of length $n + 1$ occurs circularly exactly once in it. This means that $x \oplus y$ is a de Bruijn word as expected.   ∎

To answer the question, let x be a de Bruijn word of length 2^n. The operation Ψ satisfies the following two properties:

(i) $Cfact_{n+1}(\Psi(x)) \cap Cfact_{n+1}(\overline{\Psi(x)}) = \emptyset$;

(ii) $|Cfact_{n+1}(\Psi(x))| = 2^n$ and $|Cfact_{n+1}(\overline{\Psi(x)})| = 2^n$.

Properties (i) and (ii) imply that the words $\Psi(x)$ and $\overline{\Psi(x)}$ satisfy the assumptions of Observation 2. Consequently $\Psi(x) \oplus \overline{\Psi(x)}$ is a de Bruijn binary word of length 2^{n+1}.

Notes

The recursive approach used to build de Bruijn words is from [206]. It is also a syntactic version of Lempel's algorithm that uses a special type of graph homomorphism, see [174].

It is an example of a simple application of algebraic methods in text algorithms. A more advanced application of algebraic methods is the generation of de Bruijn words based on so-called *linear shift registers* and related *primitive polynomials*, see [131].

The algorithm has a surprising graph-theoretic property. Assume we start with $w_2 = 0011$ and define, for $n \geq 3$,

$$w_n = \Psi(w_{n-1}) \oplus \overline{\Psi(w_{n-1})}.$$

Then, in the de Bruijn graph G_{n+1} of order $n + 1$ having 2^n nodes, w_n corresponds to a Hamiltonian cycle C. After removing C and disregarding two single-node loops, the graph G_{n+1} becomes a big single simple cycle of length $2^n - 2$.

119   Word Equations with Given Lengths of Variables

A word equation is an equation between words whose letters are constants
or variables. Constants belong to the alphabet $A = \{a, b, \ldots\}$ and variables
belong to the disjoint alphabet of unknowns $U = \{X, Y, \ldots\}$. An equation is
written $L = R$, where $L, R \in (A \cup U)^*$ and a solution of it is a morphism
$\psi : (A \cup U)^* \to A^*$ leaving constant invariant and for which the equality
$\psi(L) = \psi(R)$ holds.

In the problem we assume that the length $|\psi(X)|$ is given for each variable
X occurring in the equation and is denoted by $|X|$.

For example, $XYbX = aYbXba$ with $|X| = 3$ and $|Y| = 4$ admits a
(unique) solution ψ defined by $\psi(X) = aba$ and $\psi(Y) = baba$:

$$
\begin{array}{ccc}
X & Y & X \\
\overline{a\ b\ a} & \overline{b\ a\ b\ a} & \overline{b\ a\ b\ a} \\
\end{array}
$$

a b a b a b a b a b a
      Y   X

On the contrary, the equation $aXY = YbX$ has no solution, because $a\psi(X)$
and $b\psi(X)$ must be conjugate, which is incompatible with both $|a\psi(X)|_a =
1 + |\psi(X)|_a$ and $|b\psi(X)|_a = |\psi(X)|_a$, while the equation $aXY = YaX =$
has $A^{|X|}$ solutions when $|X| = |Y| - 1$.

> **Question.** Given a word equation with the variable lengths, show how to
> check in linear time with respect to the equation length plus the output length
> if a solution exists.

Solution

Let ψ be a potential solution of the equation $L = R$. If $|\psi(L)| \neq |\psi(R)|$
according to the given variable lengths the equation has obviously no solution.
We then consider that variable lengths are consistent and set $n = |\psi(L)| =
|\psi(R)|$.

Let $G = (V, E)$ be the undirected graph defined by

- $V = \{0, 1, \ldots, n - 1\}$, set of positions on $x = \psi(L) = \psi(R)$.
- E set of edges (i, j) where i and j correspond to the same relative position
  on two occurrences of $\psi(X)$ in $\psi(L)$ or in $\psi(R)$, for some variable X. For
  example, i and j can be first positions of occurrences.

To build the graph, the list of positions on x covered by an occurrence of $\psi(X)$
in $\psi(L)$ or in $\psi(R)$ can be precomputed.

We say that two positions are *conflicting* if they index two distinct constants.

Observation. The equation is solvable if and only if there is no conflicting position in the same connected component of G.

Quadratic-time algorithm. After the graph is computed, its connected components are built and the condition on conflicting positions is checked. Using a standard efficient algorithm for computing the connected components the overall takes $O(n^2)$ time because the size of the graph is $O(n^2)$.

Example. Alignment and graph associated with the above equation $XYbX = aYbXba$ with $|X| = 3$ and $|Y| = 4$. The graph has two connected components $\{0, 2, 4, 6, 8, 10\}$ and $\{1, 3, 5, 7, 9\}$. Positions 0 and 10 correspond to letter a and positions 5, 7 and 9 to letter b in the equation. There is no conflicting position and only one solution, producing the word abababababa.

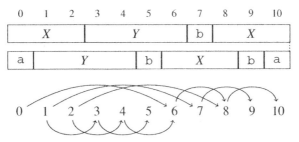

Linear-time algorithm. The algorithm is accelerated by reducing the number of edges of G in a simple way. It is enough to consider edges (i, j), $i < j$, where i and j are positions of consecutive occurrences of $\psi(X)$ in $\psi(L)$ or in $\psi(R)$ (see picture), possibly merging two lists. The connected components of the new graph satisfy the observation and the algorithm now runs in linear time because the size of the graph is linear, with at most two outgoing edges starting from each position.

Notes

When the lengths associated with variables are not given, the problem has been shown to be decidable by Makanin [181]. The problem is known to be NP-hard, but the big open question is its membership to the class of NP problems.

The fastest known algorithms work in exponential time (see [176, chapter 12] and references therein). If we knew that the shortest solution is of (only) single-exponential length then there is a simple NP algorithm to solve the problem. There is no known example of an equation for which a shortest solution is longer than a single exponential, but it is an open problem to prove it is always true.

120   Diverse Factors over a Three-Letter Alphabet

A word w is called diverse if the numbers of occurrences of its letters are pairwise different (some letters may be absent in w). The problem deals with diverse factors occurring in a word $x \in \{a, b, c\}^*$.

Example. The word aab is diverse but aa and the empty word are not. The word abbccc itself is diverse but the word abcabcabc has no diverse factor. The longest diverse factor of cbaabacccbba is cbaabaccc.

Obviously any word of length at most 2 has no diverse factor and a word of length 3 is not diverse if it is a permutation of the three letters. The straightforward observation follows.

Observation 1. The word $x \in \{a, b, c\}^*$, $|x| \geq 3$, has no diverse factor if and only if its prefix of length 3 is not diverse, that is, is a permutation of the 3 letters, and is a word period of x.

Question. Design a linear-time algorithm finding a longest diverse factor of a word x over a three-letter alphabet.

[**Hint:** Consider the Key property proved below.]

Key property. If the word $x[0 .. n - 1] \in \{a, b, c\}^*$ has a diverse factor, it has a longest diverse factor $w = x[i .. j]$ for which either $0 \leq i < 3$ or $n - 3 \leq j < n$, that is,

$$w \in \bigcup_{i=0}^{2} Pref(x[i .. n - 1]) \cup \bigcup_{j=n-3}^{n-1} Suff(x[0 .. j]).$$

Solution

Since testing the condition in Observation 1 takes linear time it remains to consider the case where the word x contains a diverse factor. Before discussing the algorithm, we start with a proof of the Key property.

The proof of the property is by contradiction. Assume x has a longest diverse factor w for which $x = uwv$ with both $|u| \geq 3$ and $|v| \geq 3$. In other words x has a factor of the form $abcwdef$ for letters a, b, c, d, e and f. We consider all cases corresponding to the occurrence numbers of letters in w and in the neighbouring three positions of w, to the left and to the right in x, and assume w.l.o.g. that

$$|w|_a < |w|_b < |w|_c.$$

The following observation limits considerably the number of cases to examine.

Observation 2. If w is a longest diverse factor of $abcwdef$, where a, b, c, d, e and f are single letters and $|w|_a < |w|_b < |w|_c$, then

$$c \notin \{c, d\} \text{ and } |w|_a + 1 = |w|_b = |w|_c - 1.$$

Unfortunately there are still several cases to consider for letters a to f, but all of them lead to a contradiction with the non-extendability of the diverse factor w in the local window $abcwdef$. Eventually the question reduces to six cases whose proofs are left to the reader.

As a consequence of the Key property, the problem amounts to several applications of a simpler version: the diverse prefix and suffix problems, that is, compute a longest diverse prefix and a longest diverse suffix of a word. They are to be computed respectively for the three suffixes $x[i .. n - 1], 0 \le i < 3$, and for the three prefixes $x[0 .. j], n - 3 \le j < n$ of x to get the result.

Linear-time solution for the longest diverse prefix. We describe only the computation of a longest diverse prefix of x, since the other cases are either similar or symmetric.

Example. The longest diverse prefix of $y = $ cbaabacccbba is cbaabaccc as shown on the table at index 8. In fact it can be checked that it is the longest diverse factor of y.

i		0	1	2	3	4	5	6	7	8	9	10	11
$y[i]$		c	b	a	a	b	a	c	c	c	b	b	a
$|y|_a$	0	0	0	1	2	2	3	3	3	**3**	3	3	4
$|y|_b$	0	0	1	1	1	2	2	2	2	**2**	3	4	4
$|y|_c$	0	1	1	1	1	1	1	2	3	**4**	4	4	4

The computation to find a longest diverse prefix of x is done on-line on x. The occurrence numbers of the three letters are computed in consecutive prefixes. The largest index where the vector has pairwise different numbers provides the sought prefix.

Notes

Note that a longest diverse factor can be much shorter than the word, like ccbaaaaaa in aaaabccbaaaaaa, and that the boundary distance 3 in the Key property cannot be reduced to 2: a counterexample is the word abcacbacba whose longest diverse factor is cacbac.

The problem appeared in the 25th Polish Olympiad in Informatics under the name 'Three towers'.

---

121   Longest Increasing Subsequence

In this problem we consider a word x on the alphabet of positive integers. An increasing subsequence of x is a subsequence $x[i_0]x[i_1]\cdots x[i_{\ell-1}]$, where $0 \le i_0 < i_1 < \cdots < i_{\ell-1} < |x|$ and $x[i_0] \le x[i_1] \le \cdots \le x[i_{\ell-1}]$.

Example. Let $x = 3\ 6\ 4\ 10\ 1\ 15\ 13\ 4\ 19\ 16\ 10$. A longest increasing subsequence of x is $y = 3\ 4\ 10\ 13\ 16$ of length 5. Another such subsequence is $z = 3\ 4\ 10\ 13\ 19$. If 21 is appended to x this lengthen y and z to increasing subsequences of length 6. But if 18 is appended to x only $y\ 18$ becomes a longest subsequence, since $z\ 18$ is not increasing.

Question. Show that Algorithm LIS computes in place the maximal length of an increasing subsequence of a word x in time $O(|x| \log |x|)$.

LIS(x non-empty word over positive integers)

```
1   ℓ ← 1
2   for i ← 1 to |x| − 1 do
3       (a, x[i]) ← (x[i], ∞)
4       k ← min{j : 0 ≤ j ≤ ℓ and a < x[j]}
5       x[k] ← a
6       if k = ℓ then
7           ℓ ← ℓ + 1
8   return ℓ
```

Example followed. The tables display x before and after a run of Algorithm LIS.

i	0	1	2	3	4	5	6	7	8	9	10
$x[i]$	3	6	4	10	1	15	13	4	19	16	10

i	0	1	2	3	4	5	6	7	8	9	10
$x[i]$	1	4	4	10	16	∞	∞	∞	∞	∞	∞

Inspecting carefully Algorithm LIS, it should be noticed that the word $x[0..\ell-1]$ computed when the algorithm terminates is increasing but not usually a subsequence of x, as shown by the example, which leads to the next question.

Question. Design an algorithm that computes a longest increasing subsequence of a word x in time $O(|x| \log |x|)$.

Solution

Complexity. Note that values stored in the prefix $x[0 .. \ell - 1]$ of x satisfy $x[0] \leq x[1] \leq \cdots \leq x[\ell - 1]$ and are followed by ∞. (They can be different from the initial values in $x[0 .. \ell - 1]$.) Thus, the instruction at line 4 can be implemented to run in $O(\log |x|)$ time and in fact in $O(\log \ell)$ if ℓ is the length of a longest increasing subsequence of x. This amount to a total of $O(|x| \log |x|)$ or $O(|x| \log \ell)$ running time. It is clear that the required memory space in addition to the input is constant.

Correctness. The correctness of Algorithm LIS relies on this invariant of the for loop: for any $j, 0 \leq j < \ell$, $x[j]$ is the smallest value, called $best[j]$, that can end an increasing subsequence of length j in $x[0 .. i]$.

This obviously holds at start with $j = 0$ and $x[0]$ unchanged. The effect of lines 4-7 is either to decrease $best[k]$ or to enlarge the previously computed longest increasing subsequence.

Longest Increasing Subsequence. Algorithm LIS can be upgraded to compute it. Values stored in $x[0 .. \ell]$ or rather their positions on x can be kept in a separate array with their predecessors inside an increasing subsequence. The main instruction to manage the new array, after initialisation, is to set the predecessor of the current element $x[i]$, when added to the array, to the predecessor of the element it replaces. When the algorithm terminates, a longest increasing subsequence is retrieved by traversing the predecessor links from the largest/rightmost value in the array.

Below is the predecessor array defined on indices for the above example, with which the two longest increasing subsequences are retrieved by tracing them back from indices 9 or 8.

j	0	1	2	3	4	5	6	7	8	9	10
$pred[j]$	–	0	0	2	–	3	3	2	6	6	3

Notes

Observe that the algorithm solves a dual problem, and computes the smallest number of disjoint strictly increasing subsequences into which a given word can be split.

Computing a longest increasing subsequence is a textbook example of dynamic programming (see for example [226]).

When the word is composed of a permutation of the nth smallest positive integers the question is related to the representation of permutations with Young tableaux; see the chapter by Lascoux, Leclerc and Thibon in [176, Chapter 5] for a presentation of Schensted's algorithm in this context. In this case, the running time of the computation can be reduced to $O(n \log \log n)$ (see [241]) and even to $O(n \log \log \ell)$ (see [95] and references therein).

---

122   Unavoidable Sets via Lyndon Words

Lyndon words often surprisingly appear in seemingly unrelated problems. We show that they appear as basic components in certain decompositions, which are the main tool in the problem.

The problem deals with unavoidable sets of words. A set $X \subseteq \{0,1\}^*$ is unavoidable if any infinite binary word has a factor in X.

To start with, let $\mathcal{N}_k$ be the set of necklaces of length k, $k > 0$. A necklace is the lexicographically smallest word in its conjugacy class. Each necklace is a power of a Lyndon word.

Example. The set $\mathcal{N}_3 = \{000, 001, 011, 111\}$ is avoidable, since $(01)^\infty$ has no factor in $\mathcal{N}_3$. But after moving the last 1 to the beginning we get the set $\{000, 100, 101, 111\}$ that is unavoidable.

Observation 1. If $X \subseteq \{0,1\}^k$ is unavoidable then $|X| \geq |\mathcal{N}_k|$.

Indeed, for each $w \in \{0,1\}^k$, length-k factors of w^∞ are all conjugates of w and at least one of them should be in the unavoidable set X. The first question provides a more flexible condition to be unavoidable.

> **Question.** Show that if for each necklace $y \in \{0,1\}^*$, $|y| \geq 2k$, the word y^2 contains a word in $X \subseteq \{0,1\}^k$ then X is unavoidable.

An ingenious construction of an unavoidable set is based on the notion of pre-primes. A pre-prime w is a prefix of a necklace.

Observation 2. A pre-prime is a prefix of a power of a Lyndon word.

The observation justifies the special decomposition of a pre-prime w as $u^e v$, where u is a Lyndon word, $e \geq 1$, $|v| < |u|$ and u is the shortest possible. Head and tail of w are defined by $head(w) = u^e$ and $tail(w) = v$.

Example. $w = 0101110$ factorises as $01^2 \cdot 110$, $01011 \cdot 10$ and $010111 \cdot 0$ over its Lyndon prefixes 01, 01011 and 010111 respectively. Its special decomposition is $01011 \cdot 10$, $head(w) = 01011$ and $tail(w) = 10$.

Note that v is not necessarily a proper prefix of u, that is, $|u|$ is not usually the period of w. It is clear that such factorisation of a pre-prime always exists. The factorisation is the key-concept in this problem.

Question. Show that there is an unavoidable set $X_k \subseteq \{0, 1\}^k$ of size $|\mathcal{N}_k|$. Consequently, $|\mathcal{N}_k|$ is the smallest size of such a set.

[**Hint:** Consider words of the form $tail(w) \cdot head(w)$.]

Solution

We first prove the statement in the first question, which provides a restricted condition for a subset of $\{0, 1\}^k$ to be unavoidable, getting rid of infinity.

By contradiction, assume there is an infinite word x having no factor in $X \subseteq \{0, 1\}^k$. Consider a word u with two non-overlapping occurrences in x, so that uvu is a factor of x and $|u|, |v| \geq k$. Let y be the necklace conjugate of uv. The hypothesis implies that there is a word $w \in X$ factor of y^2; however, due to the inequalities $|u|, |v| \geq k$ this word also occurs in uvu and thus in x. This contradicts the assumption that x does not contain any word from X and completes the proof.

A smallest unavoidable set. The sought unavoidable set is

$$X_k = \{tail(w) \cdot head(w) : w \in \mathcal{N}_k\}.$$

For example $X_4 = \{0000, 0001, 1001, 0101, 1011, 1111\}$ and X_7 contains the 20 words (tails are underlined):

0000000, 0000001, <u>1</u>000001, <u>01</u>00001, <u>11</u>00001, <u>00</u>10001, <u>01</u>10001,
<u>10</u>10001, <u>111</u>0001, <u>1</u>001001, <u>01</u>00101, <u>11</u>00101, <u>011</u>0011, <u>101</u>0011,
<u>111</u>0011, <u>1</u>010101, <u>11</u>01011, <u>1</u>011011, <u>111</u>0111, 1111111.

Before proving X_k is an answer to the second question, we state a useful property of necklaces and special decompositions; its technical proof is left to the reader (see Notes).

Observation 2. Let $w \in \{0,1\}^k$ be a pre-prime prefix of a necklace y of length at least $2k$ and with decomposition $u^e \cdot v$. Let z be the suffix of y of length $|v|$. Then $u^e \cdot z$ is a necklace with decomposition $u^e \cdot z$.

Theorem. The set X_k is unavoidable.

Proof   Due to the first question it is enough to show that for each necklace y of size at least $2k$ the word y^2 has a factor in X_k. Let us fix any such y and let $u^e \cdot v$ be the decomposition of the pre-prime, prefix of length k of y. The goal is to find a factor of y^2 that belongs to X_k.

Let z be the suffix of length $|v|$ of y. According to Observation 2 the word $w = u^e z$ is a necklace and $u^e \cdot z$ is its decomposition. Hence $z \cdot u^e \in X_k$. Since z is a suffix of y and u^e is a prefix of y, zu^e is a factor of y^2 (see picture). This completes the proof.   ■

Notes

The solution of the problem is by Champarnaud et al. [53]. Testing if a word is a pre-prime is addressed in Problem 42.

123   Synchronising Words

The problem deals with the synchronisation of the composition of functions from $I_n = \{0, 1, \ldots, n - 1\}$ to itself for a positive integer n. For two such functions f_a and f_b, a word $w \in \{a,b\}^+$ encodes their composition $f_w = h_0 \circ h_1 \circ \cdots \circ h_{|w|-1}$ when $h_i = f_a$ if $w[i] = a$ and $h_i = f_b$ if $w[i] = b$. (Note functions h_i are applied to elements of I_n in decreasing order of i as usual, i.e., from right to left according to w.) The word w is said to be *synchronising* if the set $f_w(I_n)$ contains a single element.

A useful notion is that of a pair synchroniser: a word $u \in \{a,b\}^*$ is a synchroniser of the pair (i, j), $i, j \in I_n$, if $f_u(i) = f_u(j)$.

Example. Consider the two functions: $g_a(i) = (i + 1) \bmod n$, $g_b(i) = \min\{i, g_a(i)\}$. For $n = 3$ they are illustrated by the automaton. As shown on the table below the word $w = \text{baab}$ is synchronising since the image of the set $\{0, 1, 2\}$ by g_w is the singleton $\{0\}$. The word obviously synchronises every pair but the table shows additional synchonisers like b for the pair $(0, 2)$, baa for the pair $(0, 1)$ and ba for the pair $(1, 2)$.

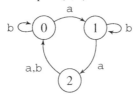

w		b		a		a		b	
$g_w(0)$	=	0	←	2	←	1	←	0	←	0
$g_w(1)$	=	0	←	0	←	2	←	1	←	1
$g_w(2)$	=	0	←	2	←	1	←	0	←	2

For any positive integer n the word $w = b(a^{n-1}b)^{n-2}$ is a synchronising word of the functions g_a and g_b. It is more difficult to see that it is a shortest such word in this particular case. This yields a quadratic lower bound on the length of a synchronising words.

Question. Show that a pair of functions admits a synchronising word if and only if there exists a synchroniser for each pair (i, j) of elements of I_n.

[**Hint:** Compute a synchronising word from synchronisers.]

Question. Show how to check in quadratic time if a pair of functions admits a synchronising word.

[**Hint:** Check pair synchronisers.]

Solution

The 'only if' part of the statement in the first question is obvious because a synchronising word is a synchroniser of every pair of elements of I_n. Then we just have to prove the 'if' part, that is, show that a synchronising word exists when there is a synchroniser for each pair (i, j) of elements $i, j \in I_n$. Algorithm SYNCWORD constructs a global synchronising word.

SYNCWORD(f_a, f_b functions from I_n to itself)

1   $J \leftarrow I_n$
2   $w \leftarrow \varepsilon$
3   **while** $|J| > 1$ **do**
4       $i, j \leftarrow$ any two distinct elements from J
5       $u \leftarrow$ a synchroniser of (i, j)
6       $J \leftarrow f_u(J)$
7       $w \leftarrow u \cdot w$
8   **return** w

Existence of pair synchronisers. To answer the second question, we need to check whether each pair of elements has a synchroniser or not.

To do so, let G be the directed graph whose nodes are pairs (i, j), $i, j \in I_n$, and whose edges of the form $(i, j) \to (p, q)$ are such that $p = f_a(i)$ and $q = f_a(j)$, for a letter $a \in \{a, b\}$.

Then the pair (i, j) has a synchroniser if and only if there is a path from (i, j) to a node of the form (p, p). Checking the property is done by a standard algorithm for traversing the graph.

If some pair has no synchroniser, the functions have no synchronising word by the first statement. Otherwise there is a synchronising word.

The running time for processing the graph is $O(n^2)$, as required. But running Algorithm SYNCWORD to get a synchronising word takes cubic time provided operations on words are done in constant time.

Notes

When the two functions are letters acting on the set of states of a finite automaton, a synchronising word is also called a reset word; see, for example, [29].

Although the above method works in quadratic time (it is enough to test the existence of local synchronisers) the actual generation of a synchronising word could take cubic time. This is due to the fact that the length of the generated word can be cubic. The so-called Cerny's conjecture states that the upper bound on a synchronising word is only quadratic, but the best known upper bound is only $\frac{114}{685}n^3 + O(n^2)$ (improving on the best previous bound of $\frac{114}{684}n^3 + O(n^2)$); see [229] and references therein.

124   Safe-Opening Words

The problem addresses a special non-deterministic version of synchronising words. We are given a graph G with edges labelled by symbols and with a unique sink node s on which all edges loop. We are to find a synchronising word S for which each non-deterministically chosen path labelled by S goes to s independently of the starting node.

The problem is generally difficult but we consider a very special case called *safe-opening words*. It shows some surprising operations on words over the alphabet $B_n = \{0, 1\}^n$.

Narrative description of the problem. The door of a *rotating safe* has a circular lock, which has n indistinguishable buttons on its circumference with equal spacing. Each button is linked to a switch on the other side of the door, invisible from outside. A switch is in state 0 (off) or 1 (on). In each move, you are allowed to press several buttons simultaneously. If all switches are turned on as a result, the safe door opens and remains open. Immediately before each move the circular lock rotates to a random position, without changing the on/off status of each individual switch. The initial configuration is unknown.

The goal is to find a sequence called a *safe-opening word*

$$S(n) = A_1 \cdot A_2 \cdots A_{2^n - 1}$$

of moves $A_i \in B_n$ having a prefix that opens the safe.

Assuming button positions are numbered 1 to n from the top position clockwise, a move is described by an n-bit word $b_1 b_2 \cdots b_n$ with the meaning that button at position i is pressed if and only if $b_i = 1$. Positions are fixed though buttons can move, that is, change positions.

Example. It can be checked that the unique shortest safe-opening word for 2 buttons is $S(2) = 11 \cdot 01 \cdot 11$.

> **Question.** Let n be a power of two. Construct a safe-opening word $S(n)$ of length $2^n - 1$ over the alphabet B_n.

Abstract description of the problem. Each move A_i is treated as a binary word of length n. Let $\equiv$ be the conjugacy (cyclic shift) equivalence. Let $G_n = (V, E)$ be the directed graph in which V is the set of binary words of length n, configurations of the circular lock, and edges are of the form, for $A \in B_n$:

$$u \xrightarrow{A} (v \text{ xor } A)$$

for each $v \equiv u$ if $u \neq 1^n$, and $1^n \xrightarrow{A} 1^n$ otherwise.

Example. For $u = 0111$ and $A = 1010$ there are four nodes v conjugate of u, $0111, 1110, 1101, 1011$, and consequently edges:

$$u \xrightarrow{A} 1101, u \xrightarrow{A} 0100, u \xrightarrow{A} 0111, u \xrightarrow{A} 0001.$$

The aim is to find a word $S = A_1 \cdot A_2 \cdots A_{2^n-1}$ in B_n^* for which each non-deterministically chosen path in G_n labelled by S leads to the sink 1^n independently of the starting node.

Solution

Two operations on words $X, Y \in B_n^*$ are defined to state recurrence relations:

$$X \odot Y = X \cdot Y[0] \cdot X \cdot Y[1] \cdot X \cdots X \cdot Y[N-1] \cdot X$$

is a word in B_n^* and, when $|X| = |Y| = N$, $X \otimes Y \in \Sigma_{2n}^*$:

$$X \otimes Y = X[0]Y[0] \cdot X[1]Y[1] \cdots X[N-1]Y[N-1].$$

For example, $(01 \cdot 11 \cdot 10) \otimes (10 \cdot 11 \cdot 00) = 0110 \cdot 1111 \cdot 1000$.

Recurrence relations. Let $Z(n) = (0^n)^{2^n-1}$, word of length $2^n - 1$ over B_n. Let $S(n)$ be a safe-opening word for $n \geq 2$. Then $S(2n)$ can be computed as follows:

(i) $\mathcal{B}(n) = S(n) \otimes S(n)$, $C(n) = Z(n) \otimes S(n)$.

(ii) $S(2n) = \mathcal{B}(n) \odot C(n)$.

Example. Knowing that $S(2) = 11 \cdot 01 \cdot 11$, we get

$\mathcal{B}(2) = 1111 \cdot 0101 \cdot 1111$,
$C(2) = 0011 \cdot 0001 \cdot 0011$ and
$S(4) = 1111 \cdot 0101 \cdot 1111 \cdot \mathbf{0011} \cdot 1111 \cdot 0101 \cdot 1111 \cdot \mathbf{0001} \cdot 1111 \cdot 0101 \cdot 1111$

$\cdot \mathbf{0011} \cdot 1111 \cdot 0101 \cdot 1111$.

Claim. If n is a power of 2 the recurrence from Equation (ii) correctly generates safe-opening words.

Proof The word $\mathcal{B}(n)$ treats exactly in the same way buttons whose positions are opposite on the cycle. In other words, buttons at positions i and $i + n/2$ are both pressed or both non-pressed at the same time. Hence at some moment the word $\mathcal{B}(n)$ achieves the required configuration, if it starts from the configuration in which for each pair $(i, i + n/2)$ the corresponding buttons are synchronised, that is, in the same state.

This is precisely the role of the word $C(n)$. After executing its prefix $C_1 \cdot C_2 \cdots C_i$, for some i, all pairs of opposite buttons are synchronised.

Then the forthcoming application of the whole word $\mathcal{B}(n)$ opens the safe, as required. ∎

Illustration on the compacted graph. The alphabet B_n has exponential size but in the solution only its small part, denoted by B'_n, is used. Instead of G_n let us consider its compacted version G'_n in which nodes are (smallest) representatives of conjugacy classes and edges have labels from B'_n only. The figure shows G'_4, in which letters 0001, 0011, 0101, 1111 of B'_4 are abbreviated as $1, 3, 5, 15$, and nodes $0000, 0001, 0011, 0101, 0111, 1111$, necklaces representing conjugacy classes, are abbreviated as A, B, C, D, E, F respectively.

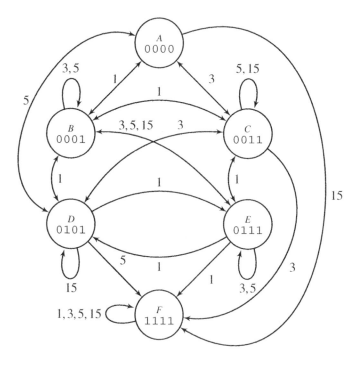

Observe that, independently of the starting node in G'_4, every path labelled with $15, 5, 15, 3, 15, 5, 15, 1, 15, 5, 15, 3, 15, 5, 15$ leads to 1111.

The correctness of this sequence can be shown by starting from the whole set of nodes and applying consecutive transitions. At the end we should get the set $\{F\}$. Indeed we have

$$\{A,B,C,D,E,F\} \xrightarrow{15} \{B,C,D,E,F\} \xrightarrow{5} \{A,B,C,E,F\} \xrightarrow{15}$$
$$\{B,C,E,F\} \xrightarrow{3} \{A,B,E,D,F\} \xrightarrow{15} \{B,E,D,F\} \xrightarrow{5} \{A,B,E,F\}$$
$$\xrightarrow{15} \{B,E,F\} \xrightarrow{1} \{A,D,C,F\} \xrightarrow{15} \{D,C,F\} \xrightarrow{5} \{A,C,F\}$$
$$\xrightarrow{15} \{C,F\} \xrightarrow{3} \{A,D,F\} \xrightarrow{15} \{D,F\} \xrightarrow{5} \{A,F\} \xrightarrow{15} \{F\}.$$

Notes

The content of the problem is adapted from its original version by Guo at https://www.austms.org.au/Publ/Gazette/2013/Mar13/ Puzzle.pdf. The length of safe-opening words is not addressed but it is shown that there is no such word if n is not a power of 2.

There is an alternative description of the safe-opening sequence. Assume binary words are represented as non-negative integers in a standard way. Then $S(2) = 3 \cdot 1 \cdot 3$ and

$$S(4) = 15 \cdot 5 \cdot 15 \cdot 3 \cdot 15 \cdot 5 \cdot 15 \cdot 1 \cdot 15 \cdot 5 \cdot 15 \cdot 3 \cdot 15 \cdot 5 \cdot 15.$$

The recurrence equations (i) and (ii) now look much shorter:

$$S(2n) = (2^n \times S(n) + S(n)) \odot S(n),$$

where the operations $+, \times$ are here component-wise arithmetic operations on sequences of integers.

---

125   Superwords of Shortened Permutations

On the alphabet of natural numbers, a word is an n-permutation if every number from $\{1, 2, \ldots, n\}$ appears exactly once in it (see Problems 14 and 15). A word is a shortened n-permutation (n-shortperm, in short) if it is an n-permutation with its last element removed. The bijection between standard permutations and shortened ones for a given n implies there are $n!$ shortened n-permutations.

The subject of the problem is the construction of a shortest superword for all n-shortperms. They are of length $n! + n - 2$, which meets the obvious lower bound. For example, 3213123 is a shortest superword for 3-shortperms since it contains all shortened 3-permutations

32, 21, 13, 31, 12 and 23.

Question. Show how to construct a superword of length $n! + n - 2$ for shortened n-permutations in linear time w.r.t. the output length.

[**Hint:** Consider an Eulerian cycle in an appropriate graph.]

Solution

The problem reduces to finding an Eulerian cycle in a directed graph $\mathcal{J}_n$ (Jackson graph) that is very similar to a de Bruijn graph. The set V_n of nodes of $\mathcal{J}_n$ consists of all words that are $(n - 2)$-combinations of elements in $\{1, 2, \ldots, n\}$. For each $w = a_1 a_2 \ldots a_{n-2} \in V_n$ there are two outgoing edges:

$$a_1 a_2 \cdots a_{n-2} \xrightarrow{b} a_2 \cdots a_{n-2} b,$$

where $b \in \{1, 2, \ldots, n\} - \{a_1, a_2, \ldots, a_{n-2}\}$. Each such edge labelled by b corresponds to the shortened permutation $a_1 a_2 \cdots a_{n-2} b$. The graph $\mathcal{J}_4$ is displayed in the picture below, where labels of edges are implicit.

Observation. If $b_1 b_2 \cdots b_m$ is the label of an Eulerian cycle starting from $a_1 a_2 \cdots a_{n-2}$, $a_1 a_2 \cdots a_{n-2} b_1 b_2 \ldots b_m$ is a shortest superword for n-shortperms.

Example. In $\mathcal{J}_4$, the Eulerian cycle $12 \rightarrow 23 \rightarrow 34 \rightarrow 41 \rightarrow 12 \rightarrow 24 \rightarrow 43 \rightarrow 32 \rightarrow 21 \rightarrow 14 \rightarrow 43 \rightarrow 31 \rightarrow 14 \rightarrow 42 \rightarrow 21 \rightarrow 13 \rightarrow 32 \rightarrow 24 \rightarrow 41 \rightarrow 13 \rightarrow 34 \rightarrow 42 \rightarrow 23 \rightarrow 31 \rightarrow 12$ produces the superword of length $26 = 4! + 4 - 2$ prefixed by 12:

$$12\ 34124321431421324134 2312.$$

To answer the question it is sufficient to show that the graph $\mathcal{J}_n$ is an Eulerian graph.

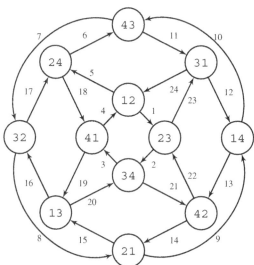

Lemma 22 *For two n-shortperms with the same set of elements one is reachable from the other in the Jackson graph $\mathcal{J}_n$.*

Proof It is enough to show that for each shortperm $a_1 a_2 \cdots a_{n-2}$ there is a path in $\mathcal{J}_n$ to its cyclic shift $a_2 \cdots a_{n-2} a_1$ and to $a_2 a_1 a_3 \cdots a_{n-2}$ (transposition of the first two elements) because any permutation can be decomposed into a series of such permutations.

We sketch it for a shortperm of the form $123 \cdots n-2$ using the representative example of 12345 for $n = 7$. Let $a = 6$ and $b = 7$. In $\mathcal{J}_7$ we have the path

$$12345 \to 2345a \to 345ab \to 45ab2 \to 5ab23 \to ab234$$
$$\to b2345 \to 23451,$$

which shows that there is a path $12345 \xrightarrow{*} 23451$ from 12345 to its shift 23451. There is also a path $12345 \xrightarrow{*} 345ab$. Then using them both we get the path

$$12345 \xrightarrow{*} 345ab \xrightarrow{*} ab345 \longrightarrow b3452 \longrightarrow 34521 \xrightarrow{*} 21345,$$

which corresponds to the transposition of the first two elements. This completes the sketch of the proof. ∎

The lemma induces that the Jackson graph is strongly connected. It is also regular, that is, the in-degree and out-degree of each node equal 2. It is known that these conditions imply that it is an Eulerian graph. Following the observation we can extract a required superword from an Eulerian cycle.

Notes
The problem of constructing a shortest superword for all shortened n-permutations has been completely solved by Jackson [151, 211].

The problem is equivalent to finding a Hamiltonian cycle in the *line graph* $\mathcal{H}_n$ of $\mathcal{J}_n$. The nodes of $\mathcal{H}_n$, identified with shortened permutations, correspond to edges of $\mathcal{J}_n$: there is an edge (e, e') in $\mathcal{H}_n$ if and only if the starting node of the edge e' in $\mathcal{J}_n$ is the end node of e.

Edges of $\mathcal{H}_n$ can be labelled as follows. For each node $a_1 a_2 \cdots a_{n-1}$ of $\mathcal{H}_n$ the graph has two labelled edges

$$a_1 a_2 \cdots a_{n-1} \xrightarrow{1} a_2 \cdots a_{n-1} a_1 \text{ and } a_1 a_2 \cdots a_{n-1} \xrightarrow{0} a_2 \cdots a_{n-1} a_1 a_n,$$

where $a_n \notin \{a_1, a_2, \ldots a_{n-1}\}$. The Eulerian tour in $\mathcal{J}_n$ corresponds now to a Hamiltonian cycle in $\mathcal{H}_n$. For example, the Eulerian cycle in $\mathcal{J}_4$ from the previous example is associated with the Hamiltonian cycle in $\mathcal{H}_4$, after adding one edge at the end:

$$123 \xrightarrow{0} 234 \xrightarrow{0} 341 \xrightarrow{0} 412 \xrightarrow{1} 124 \xrightarrow{0} 243 \xrightarrow{1} 432 \xrightarrow{0}$$
$$321 \xrightarrow{0} 214 \xrightarrow{0} 143 \xrightarrow{1} 431 \xrightarrow{1} 314 \xrightarrow{0} 142 \xrightarrow{1} 421 \xrightarrow{0}$$
$$213 \xrightarrow{1} 132 \xrightarrow{0} 324 \xrightarrow{0} 241 \xrightarrow{0} 413 \xrightarrow{1} 134 \xrightarrow{0} 342 \xrightarrow{1}$$
$$423 \xrightarrow{0} 231 \xrightarrow{1} 312 \xrightarrow{1} 123.$$

The Hamiltonian cycle starting at 123 is identified by the word of labels $x = 000101000110101000101011$.

Interestingly there is a family of words x_n describing a Hamiltonian cycle in the graph $\mathcal{H}_n$ and having a very compact description. We use the interesting operation $\odot$ on words defined as follows. For two binary words u and $v = v[0 . . k-1]$, let

$$u \odot v = u\, v[0]\, u\, v[1]\, u\, v[2] \cdots u\, v[k-1].$$

Let $\bar{u}$ denote the operation of negating all symbols in u. Then for $n \geq 2$ let

$$x_2 = 00 \text{ and } x_{n+1} = 001^{n-2} \odot \overline{x_n}'.$$

For example, $x_3 = 00 \odot 11 = 001001$ and $x_4 = 001 \odot 110110 = (0011\,0011\,0010)^2$. It is shown in [211] that for $n \geq 2$ the word x_n describes a Hamiltonian cycle starting from $123 \cdots n - 1$ in $\mathcal{H}_n$.

The connection between words and Hamiltonian cycles happening here is similar to the relation between de Bruijn words and Hamiltonian cycles in de Bruijn graphs.

Bibliography

[1] Z. Adamczyk and W. Rytter. A note on a simple computation of the maximal suffix of a string. *J. Discrete Algorithms*, 20:61–64, 2013.

[2] D. Adjeroh, T. Bell and A. Mukherjee. *The Burrows-Wheeler Transform*. Springer, 2008.

[3] A. V. Aho and M. J. Corasick. Efficient string matching: An aid to bibliographic search. *Commun. ACM*, 18(6):333–340, 1975.

[4] A. V. Aho, J. E. Hopcroft and J. D. Ullman. *The Design and Analysis of Computer Algorithms*. Addison-Wesley, 1974.

[5] C. Allauzen, M. Crochemore and M. Raffinot. Factor oracle: A new structure for pattern matching. In J. Pavelka, G. Tel and M. Bartosek, eds., *SOFSEM '99, Theory and Practice of Informatics, 26th Conference on Current Trends in Theory and Practice of Informatics*, Milovy, Czech Republic, 27 November–4 December 1999, Lecture Notes in Computer Science, vol. 1725, pp. 295–310. Springer, 1999.

[6] J. Allouche and J. O. Shallit. The ubiquitous Prouhet-Thue-Morse sequence. In C. Ding, T. Helleseth and H. Niederreiter, eds., *Sequences and Their Applications, proceedings SETA 98*, pp. 1–16. Springer-Verlag, 1999.

[7] J. Allouche and J. O. Shallit. *Automatic Sequences: Theory, Applications, Generalizations*. Cambridge University Press, 2003.

[8] J. Almeida, A. Costa, R. Kyriakoglou and D. Perrin. Profinite semigroups and symbolic dynamics, volume 2274 of Lecture Notes in Mathematics, Springer, 2020.

[9] M. Alzamel, M. Crochemore, C. S. Iliopoulos, et al. How much different are two words with different shortest periods? In L. S. Iliadis, I. Maglogiannis and V. P. Plagianakos, eds., *Artificial Intelligence Applications and Innovations AIAI 2018 IFIP WG 12.5 International Workshops, SEDSEAL, 5G-PINE, MHDW, and HEALTHIOT*, Rhodes, Greece, 25–27 May 2018, IFIP Advances in Information and Communication Technology, vol. 520, pp. 168–178. Springer, 2018.

[10] A. Amir and M. Farach. Efficient matching of nonrectangular shapes. *Ann. Math. Artif. Intell.*, 4:211–224, 1991.

[11] A. Amir, M. Farach and S. Muthukrishnan. Alphabet dependence in parameterized matching. *Inf. Process. Lett.*, 49(3):111–115, 1994.

[12] A. Amir, C. S. Iliopoulos and J. Radoszewski. Two strings at Hamming distance 1 cannot be both quasiperiodic. *Inf. Process. Lett.*, 128:54–57, 2017.

[13] S. Amoroso and G. Cooper. Tessellation structures for reproduction of arbitrary patterns. *J. Comput. Syst. Sci.*, 5(5):455–464, 1971.

[14] A. Apostolico and M. Crochemore. Optimal canonization of all substrings of a string. *Inf. Comput.*, 95(1):76–95, 1991.

[15] A. Apostolico and R. Giancarlo. Pattern matching machine implementation of a fast test for unique decipherability. *Inf. Process. Lett.*, 18(3):155–158, 1984.

[16] A. Apostolico and R. Giancarlo. The Boyer-Moore-Galil string searching strategies revisited. *SIAM J. Comput.*, 15(1):98–105, 1986.

[17] G. Assayag and S. Dubnov. Using factor oracles for machine improvisation. *Soft Comput.*, 8(9):604–610, 2004.

[18] G. Badkobeh. Infinite words containing the minimal number of repetitions. *J. Discrete Algorithms*, 20:38–42, 2013.

[19] G. Badkobeh and M. Crochemore. Fewest repetitions in infinite binary words. *RAIRO Theor. Inf. Applic.*, 46(1):17–31, 2012.

[20] G. Badkobeh, G. Fici and S. J. Puglisi. Algorithms for anti-powers in strings. *Inf. Process. Lett.*, 137:57–60, 2018.

[21] R. A. Baeza-Yates. Searching subsequences. *Theor. Comput. Sci.*, 78(2):363–376, 1991.

[22] H. Bai, A. Deza and F. Franek. On a lemma of Crochemore and Rytter. *J. Discrete Algorithms*, 34:18–22, 2015.

[23] B. S. Baker. A theory of parameterized pattern matching: Algorithms and applications. In S. R. Kosaraju, D. S. Johnson and A. Aggarwal, eds., *Proceedings of the Twenty-Fifth Annual ACM Symposium on Theory of Computing*, 16-18 May 1993, San Diego, CA, pp. 71–80. ACM, 1993.

[24] B. S. Baker. Parameterized pattern matching: Algorithms and applications. *J. Comput. Syst. Sci.*, 52(1):28–42, 1996.

[25] H. Bannai, M. Giraud, K. Kusano, W. Matsubara, A. Shinohara and J. Simpson. The number of runs in a ternary word. In J. Holub and J. Zdárek, eds., *Proceedings of the Prague Stringology Conference 2010*, Prague, Czech Republic, 30 August–1 September 2010, pp. 178–181. Prague Stringology Club, Department of Theoretical Computer Science, Faculty of Information Technology, Czech Technical University in Prague, 2010.

[26] H. Bannai, I. Tomohiro, S. Inenaga, Y. Nakashima, M. Takeda and K. Tsuruta. The "runs" theorem. *SIAM J. Comput.*, 46(5):1501–1514, 2017.

[27] P. Baturo, M. Piatkowski and W. Rytter. Usefulness of directed acyclic subword graphs in problems related to standard sturmian words. *Int. J. Found. Comput. Sci.*, 20(6):1005–1023, 2009.

[28] M. Béal, F. Mignosi and A. Restivo. Minimal forbidden words and symbolic dynamics. In C. Puech and R. Reischuk, eds., *STACS 96, 13th Annual Symposium on Theoretical Aspects of Computer Science*, Grenoble, France, 22-24 February 1996, Lecture Notes in Computer Science, vol. 1046, pp. 555–566. Springer, 1996.

[29] M. Béal and D. Perrin. Synchronised automata. In V. Berthé and M. Rigo, eds., *Combinatorics, Words and Symbolic Dynamics. Encyclopedia of Mathematics and Its Applications*, pp. 213–240. Cambridge University Press, 2016.

[30] M.-P. Béal, M. Crochemore, F. Mignosi, A. Restivo and M. Sciortino. Forbidden words of regular languages. *Fundam. Inform.*, 56(1,2):121–135, 2003.

[31] J. L. Bentley and R. Sedgewick. Fast algorithms for sorting and searching strings. In M. E. Saks, ed., *Proceedings of the Eighth Annual ACM-SIAM Symposium on Discrete Algorithms*, LA, 5–7 January 1997, New Orleans, pp. 360–369. ACM/SIAM, 1997.

[32] J. Berstel. Langford strings are square free. *Bull. EATCS*, 37:127–128, 1989.

[33] J. Berstel and A. de Luca. Sturmian words, Lyndon words and trees. *Theor. Comput. Sci.*, 178(1–2):171–203, 1997.

[34] J. Berstel and J. Karhumäki. Combinatorics on words: A tutorial. *EATCS*, 79:178, 2003.

[35] J. Berstel, A. Lauve, C. Reutenauer and F. Saliola. *Combinatorics on Words*, CRM Monograph Series, vol. 27. Université de Montréal et American Mathematical Society, 2008.

[36] J. Berstel and D. Perrin. *Theory of Codes*. Academic Press, 1985.

[37] J. Berstel and A. Savelli. Crochemore factorization of sturmian and other infinite words. In *Mathematical Foundations of Computer Science 2006, 31st International Symposium, MFCS 2006*, Stará Lesná, Slovakia, 28 August–1 September 2006, Lecture Notes in Computer Science, vol. 4162, pp. 157–166. Springer, 2006.

[38] A. Blumer, J. Blumer, D. Haussler, A. Ehrenfeucht, M. T. Chen and J. I. Seiferas. The smallest automaton recognizing the subwords of a text. *Theor. Comput. Sci.*, 40:31–55, 1985.

[39] K. S. Booth. Lexicographically least circular substrings. *Inf. Process. Lett.*, 10(4/5):240–242, 1980.

[40] J. Bourdon and I. Rusu. Statistical properties of factor oracles. *J. Discrete Algorithms*, 9(1):57–66, 2011.

[41] R. S. Boyer and J. S. Moore. A fast string searching algorithm. *Commun. ACM*, 20(10):762–772, 1977.

[42] F. Brandenburg. Uniformly growing k-th power-free homomorphisms. *Theor. Comput. Sci.*, 23:69–82, 1983.

[43] D. Breslauer. An on-line string superprimitivity test. *Inf. Process. Lett.*, 44(6):345–347, 1992.

[44] D. Breslauer, L. Colussi and L. Toniolo. Tight comparison bounds for the string prefix-matching problem. *Inf. Process. Lett.*, 47(1):51–57, 1993.

[45] D. Breslauer, R. Grossi and F. Mignosi. Simple real-time constant-space string matching. *Theor. Comput. Sci.*, 483:2–9, 2013.

[46] S. Brlek, D. Jamet and G. Paquin. Smooth words on 2-letter alphabets having same parity. *Theor. Comput. Sci.*, 393(1–3):166–181, 2008.

[47] S. Burkhardt and J. Kärkkäinen. Fast lightweight suffix array construction and checking. In R. A. Baeza-Yates, E. Chávez and M. Crochemore, eds., *Combinatorial Pattern Matching, CPM 2003*, Lecture Notes in Computer Science, vol. 2676, pp. 55–69. Springer, 2003.

[48] A. Carayol and S. Göller. On long words avoiding Zimin patterns. In H. Vollmer and B. Vallée, eds., *34th Symposium on Theoretical Aspects of Computer Science, STACS 2017*, 8–11 March, 2017, Hannover, Germany, vol. 66 of LIPIcs, pp. 19:1–19:13. Schloss Dagstuhl – Leibniz-Zentrum fuer Informatik, 2017.

[49] Y. Césari and M. Vincent. Une caractérisation des mots périodiques. *C. R. Acad. Sci.*, 286:1175, 1978.

[50] S. Chairungsee and M. Crochemore. Efficient computing of longest previous reverse factors. In Y. Shoukourian, ed., *Seventh International Conference on Computer Science and Information Technologies*, CSIT 2009, pp. 27–30. The National Academy of Sciences of Armenia Publishers, Yerevan, Armenia, 2009.

[51] S. Chairungsee and M. Crochemore. Using minimal absent words to build phylogeny. *Theor. Comput. Sci.*, 450(1):109–116, 2012.

[52] S. Chairungsee and M. Crochemore. Longest previous non-overlapping factors table computation. In X. Gao, H. D. and M. Han, eds., *Combinatorial Optimization and Applications - 11th International Conference, COCOA 2017*, Shanghai, China, 10-18 December, 2017, Proceedings, Part II, vol. 10628 *Lecture Notes in Computer Science*, pp. 483–491. Springer, 2017.

[53] J. Champarnaud, G. Hansel and D. Perrin. Unavoidable sets of constant length. *IJAC*, 14(2):241–251, 2004.

[54] S. Cho, J. C. Na, K. Park and J. S. Sim. A fast algorithm for order-preserving pattern matching. *Inf. Process. Lett.*, 115(2):397–402, 2015.

[55] J. G. Cleary, W. J. Teahan and I. H. Witten. Unbounded length contexts for PPM. In J. A. Storer and M. Cohn, eds., *Proceedings of the IEEE Data Compression Conference, DCC 1995*, Snowbird, UT, 28–30 March, 1995, pp. 52–61. IEEE Computer Society, 1995.

[56] J. G. Cleary and I. H. Witten. A comparison of enumerative and adaptive codes. *IEEE Trans. Inf. Theory*, 30(2):306–315, 1984.

[57] J. Clément, P. Flajolet and B. Vallée. The analysis of hybrid trie structures. In H. J. Karloff, ed., *Proceedings of the Ninth Annual ACM-SIAM Symposium on Discrete Algorithms*, 25-27 January 1998, San Francisco, 25–27 January 1998, pp. 531–539. ACM/SIAM, 1998.

[58] P. Clifford and R. Clifford. Simple deterministic wildcard matching. *Inf. Process. Lett.*, 101(2):53–54, 2007.

[59] R. Cole. Tight bounds on the complexity of the Boyer-Moore string matching algorithm. *SIAM J. Comput.*, 23(5):1075–1091, 1994.

[60] R. Cole and R. Hariharan. Tighter upper bounds on the exact complexity of string matching. *SIAM J. Comput.*, 26(3):803–856, 1997.

[61] R. Cori and D. Perrin. Automates et commutations partielles. *ITA*, 19(1):21–32, 1985.

[62] G. V. Cormack and R. N. Horspool. Algorithms for adaptive Huffman codes. *Inf. Process. Lett.*, 18(3):159–165, 1984.

[63] T. H. Cormen, C. E. Leiserson, R. L. Rivest and C. Stein. *Introduction to Algorithms*, 3rd Edition. MIT Press, 2009.

[64] M. Crochemore. An optimal algorithm for computing the repetitions in a word. *Inf. Process. Lett.*, 12(5):244–250, 1981.

[65] M. Crochemore. Sharp characterization of square-free morphisms. *Theor. Comput. Sci.*, 18(2):221–226, 1982.

[66] M. Crochemore. *Régularités évitables*. Thèse d'état, Université de Haute-Normandie, 1983.

[67] M. Crochemore. Transducers and repetitions. *Theor. Comput. Sci.*, 45(1):63–86, 1986.

[68] M. Crochemore. Longest common factor of two words. In H. Ehrig, R. A. Kowalski, G. Levi and U. Montanari, eds., *TAPSOFT'87: Proceedings of the International Joint Conference on Theory and Practice of Software Development*, Pisa, Italy, 23-27 March, 1987, Volume 1: Advanced Seminar on Foundations of Innovative Software Development I and Colloquium on Trees in Algebra and Programming (CAAP'87), vol. 249, Lecture Notes in Computer Science, pp. 26–36. Springer, 1987.

[69] M. Crochemore. String-matching on ordered alphabets. *Theor. Comput. Sci.*, 92(1):33–47, 1992.

[70] M. Crochemore, A. Czumaj, L. Gasieniec, S. Jarominek, T. Lecroq, W. Plandowski and W. Rytter. Speeding up two string-matching algorithms. *Algorithmica*, 12(4/5):247–267, 1994.

[71] M. Crochemore, C. Epifanio, R. Grossi and F. Mignosi. Linear-size suffix tries. *Theor. Comput. Sci.*, 638:171–178, 2016.

[72] M. Crochemore, S. Z. Fazekas, C. S. Iliopoulos and I. Jayasekera. Number of occurrences of powers in strings. *Int. J. Found. Comput. Sci.*, 21(4):535–547, 2010.

[73] M. Crochemore, R. Grossi, J. Kärkkäinen and G. M. Landau. Computing the Burrows-Wheeler transform in place and in small space. *J. Discrete Algorithms*, 32:44–52, 2015.

[74] M. Crochemore, C. Hancart and T. Lecroq. *Algorithms on Strings*. Cambridge University Press, 2007.

[75] M. Crochemore, A. Héliou, G. Kucherov, L. Mouchard, S. P. Pissis and Y. Ramusat. Absent words in a sliding window with applications. *Inf. Comput.*, 270, 2020.

[76] M. Crochemore and L. Ilie. Computing longest previous factors in linear time and applications. *Inf. Process. Lett.*, 106(2):75–80, 2008.

[77] M. Crochemore and L. Ilie. Maximal repetitions in strings. *J. Comput. Syst. Sci.*, 74(5):796–807, 2008.

[78] M. Crochemore, L. Ilie, C. S. Iliopoulos, M. Kubica, W. Rytter and T. Waleń. Computing the longest previous factor. *Eur. J. Comb.*, 34(1):15–26, 2013.

[79] M. Crochemore, L. Ilie and E. Seid-Hilmi. The structure of factor oracles. *Int. J. Found. Comput. Sci.*, 18(4):781–797, 2007.

[80] M. Crochemore, L. Ilie and L. Tinta. The "runs" conjecture. *Theor. Comput. Sci.*, 412(27):2931–2941, 2011.

[81] M. Crochemore, C. S. Iliopoulos, T. Kociumaka et al. Order-preserving indexing. *Theor. Comput. Sci.*, 638:122–135, 2016.

[82] M. Crochemore, C. S. Iliopoulos, T. Kociumaka, et al. The maximum number of squares in a tree. In J. Kärkkäinen and J. Stoye, eds., *Combinatorial Pattern Matching: 23rd Annual Symposium, CPM 2012*, Helsinki, Finland, 3–5 July,

2012. Proceedings, Lecture Notes in Computer Science, vol. 7354, pp. 27–40. Springer, 2012.

[83] M. Crochemore, C. S. Iliopoulos, T. Kociumaka, et al. Near-optimal computation of runs over general alphabet via non-crossing LCE queries. In S. Inenaga, K. Sadakane and T. Sakai, eds., *String Processing and Information Retrieval - 23rd International Symposium, SPIRE 2016*, Beppu, Japan, 18–20 October, 2016, Proceedings, vol. 9954, *Lecture Notes in Computer Science*, pp. 22–34, 2016.

[84] M. Crochemore, C. S. Iliopoulos, M. Kubica, J. Radoszewski, W. Rytter, K. Stencel and T. Walen. New simple efficient algorithms computing powers and runs in strings. *Discrete Appl. Math.*, 163:258–267, 2014.

[85] M. Crochemore, C. S. Iliopoulos, M. Kubica, J. Radoszewski, W. Rytter and T. Walen. On the maximal number of cubic runs in a string. In A. Dediu, H. Fernau, and C. Martín-Vide, eds., *Language and Automata Theory and Applications, 4th International Conference, LATA 2010*, Trier, Germany, 24–28 May, 2010. Proceedings, vol. 6031, *Lecture Notes in Computer Science*, pp. 227–238. Springer, 2010.

[86] M. Crochemore, C. S. Iliopoulos, M. Kubica, J. Radoszewski, W. Rytter and T. Walen. The maximal number of cubic runs in a word. *J. Comput. Syst. Sci.*, 78(6):1828–1836, 2012.

[87] M. Crochemore, C. S. Iliopoulos, M. Kubica, W. Rytter and T. Waleń. Efficient algorithms for three variants of the LPF table. *J. Discrete Algorithms*, 11:51–61, 2012.

[88] M. Crochemore, G. M. Landau and M. Ziv-Ukelson. A subquadratic sequence alignment algorithm for unrestricted scoring matrices. *SIAM J. Comput.*, 32(6):1654–1673, 2003.

[89] M. Crochemore and T. Lecroq. Tight bounds on the complexity of the Apostolico-Giancarlo algorithm. *Inf. Process. Lett.*, 63(4):195–203, 1997.

[90] M. Crochemore, M. Lerest and P. Wender. An optimal test on finite unavoidable sets of words. *Inf. Process. Lett.*, 16(4):179–180, 1983.

[91] M. Crochemore and R. Mercas. On the density of Lyndon roots in factors. *Theor. Comput. Sci.*, 656:234–240, 2016.

[92] M. Crochemore, F. Mignosi and A. Restivo. Automata and forbidden words. *Inf. Process. Lett.*, 67(3):111–117, 1998.

[93] M. Crochemore, F. Mignosi, A. Restivo and S. Salemi. Text compression using antidictonaries. In J. Wiedermann, P. van Emde Boas, and M. Nielsen, eds., *International Conference on Automata, Languages an Programming* (Prague, 1999), Lecture Notes in Computer Science, pp. 261–270. Springer-Verlag, 1999. Rapport I.G.M. 98-10, Université de Marne-la-Vallée.

[94] M. Crochemore and D. Perrin. Two-way string-matching. *J. ACM*, 38(3):651–675, 1991.

[95] M. Crochemore and E. Porat. Fast computation of a longest increasing subsequence and application. *Inf. Comput.*, 208(9):1054–1059, 2010.

[96] M. Crochemore and W. Rytter. *Text Algorithms*. Oxford University Press, 1994.

[97] M. Crochemore and W. Rytter. Squares, cubes, and time-space efficient string searching. *Algorithmica*, 13(5):405–425, 1995.

[98] M. Crochemore and W. Rytter. *Jewels of Stringology*. World Scientific Publishing, Hong-Kong, 2002.

[99] M. Crochemore and G. Tischler. Computing longest previous non-overlapping factors. *Inf. Process. Lett.*, 111(6):291–295, 2011.

[100] M. Crochemore and Z. Troníček. On the size of DASG for multiple texts. In A. H. F. Laender and A. L. Oliveira, eds., *String Processing and Information Retrieval, 9th International Symposium, SPIRE 2002*, Lisbon, Portugal, 11–13 September, 2002, Proceedings, vol. 2476, *Lecture Notes in Computer Science*, pp. 58–64. Springer, 2002.

[101] M. Crochemore and R. Vérin. On compact directed acyclic word graphs. In J. Mycielski, G. Rozenberg, and A. Salomaa, eds., *Structures in Logic and Computer Science, A Selection of Essays in Honor of Andrzej Ehrenfeucht*, vol. 1261 *Lecture Notes in Computer Science*, pp. 192–211. Springer, 1997.

[102] A. Deza and F. Franek. A d-step approach to the maximum number of distinct squares and runs in strings. *Discrete Appl.Math.*, 163(3):268–274, 2014.

[103] A. Deza, F. Franek and A. Thierry. How many double squares can a string contain? *Discrete Appl. Math.*, 180:52–69, 2015.

[104] F. Durand and J. Leroy. The constant of recognizability is computable for primitive morphisms. *CoRR*, abs/1610.05577, 2016.

[105] J. Duval. Factorizing words over an ordered alphabet. *J. Algorithms*, 4(4):363–381, 1983.

[106] J. Duval, R. Kolpakov, G. Kucherov, T. Lecroq and A. Lefebvre. Linear-time computation of local periods. *Theor. Comput. Sci.*, 326(1-3):229–240, 2004.

[107] M. Effros. PPM performance with BWT complexity: A new method for lossless data compression. In *Data Compression Conference, DCC 2000*, Snowbird, UT, 28–30 March, 2000, pp. 203–212. IEEE Computer Society, 2000.

[108] N. Faller. An adaptive system for data compression. In *Record of the 7th Asilomar Conference on Circuits, Systems, and Computers*, pp. 593–597, 1973.

[109] H. Fan, N. Yao and H. Ma. Fast variants of the Backward-Oracle-Marching algorithm. In *ICICSE '09, Fourth International Conference on Internet Computing for Science and Engineering*, pp. 56–59. IEEE Computer Society, 2009.

[110] M. Farach. Optimal suffix tree construction with large alphabets. In *38th Annual Symposium on Foundations of Computer Science, FOCS '97, Miami Beach*, FL, 19–22 October, 1997, pp. 137–143. IEEE Computer Society, 1997.

[111] S. Faro and T. Lecroq. Efficient variants of the Backward-Oracle-Matching algorithm. *Int. J. Found. Comput. Sci.*, 20(6):967–984, 2009.

[112] P. Ferragina and G. Manzini. Indexing compressed text. *J. ACM*, 52(4):552–581, 2005.

[113] G. Fici, A. Restivo, M. Silva and L. Q. Zamboni. Anti-powers in infinite words. *J. Comb. Theory, Ser. A*, 157:109–119, 2018.

[114] N. J. Fine. Binomial coefficients modulo a prime. *Am. Math. Mon.*, 54(10, Part 1):589–592, December 1947.

[115] J. Fischer and V. Heun. Theoretical and practical improvements on the RMQ-problem, with applications to LCA and LCE. In M. Lewenstein and G. Valiente, eds., *Combinatorial Pattern Matching, 17th Annual Symposium, CPM 2006*,

Barcelona, Spain, 5–7 July, 2006, Proceedings, vol. 4009 *Lecture Notes in Computer Science*, pp. 36–48. Springer, 2006.

[116] J. Fischer, Š. Holub, T. I and M. Lewenstein. Beyond the runs theorem. In *22nd SPIRE*, Lecture Notes in Computer Science, vol. 9309, pp. 272–281, 2015.

[117] A. S. Fraenkel and J. Simpson. How many squares must a binary sequence contain? *Electr. J. Comb.*, 2, 1995.

[118] A. S. Fraenkel and J. Simpson. How many squares can a string contain? *J. Comb. Theory, Ser. A*, 82(1):112–120, 1998.

[119] F. Franek, A. S. M. S. Islam, M. S. Rahman and W. F. Smyth. Algorithms to compute the Lyndon array. *CoRR*, abs/1605.08935, 2016.

[120] H. Fredricksen and J. Maiorana. Necklaces of beads in k colors and k-ary de bruijn sequences. *Discrete Math.*, 23(3):207–210, 1978.

[121] A. Fruchtman, Y. Gross, S. T. Klein and D. Shapira. Weighted adaptive Huffman coding. In A. Bilgin, M. W. Marcellin, J. Serra-Sagrista and J. A. Storer, eds., Data Compression Conference, DCC 2020, Snowbird, UT, 24–27 March 2020, pp. 368–385. IEEE, 2020. http://arxiv.org/abs/2005.08232vl.

[122] Z. Galil. On improving the worse case running time of the Boyer-Moore string matching algorithm. *Commun. ACM*, 22(9):505–508, 1979.

[123] Z. Galil and R. Giancarlo. On the exact complexity of string matching: Upper bounds. *SIAM J. Comput.*, 21(3):407–437, 1992.

[124] Z. Galil and J. I. Seiferas. Time-space-optimal string matching. *J. Comput. Syst. Sci.*, 26(3):280–294, 1983.

[125] R. G. Gallager. Variations on a theme by Huffman. *IEEE Trans. Inf. Theory*, 24(6):668–674, 1978.

[126] J. Gallant, D. Maier and J. A. Storer. On finding minimal length superstrings. *J. Comput. Syst. Sci.*, 20(1):50–58, 1980.

[127] P. Gawrychowski, T. Kociumaka, J. Radoszewski, W. Rytter and T. Walen. Universal reconstruction of a string. In F. Dehne, J. Sack and U. Stege, eds, *Algorithms and Data Structures: 14th International Symposium, WADS 2015*, Victoria, BC, Canada, 5–7 August, 2015. Proceedings, vol. 9214, *Lecture Notes in Computer Science*, pp. 386–397. Springer, 2015.

[128] P. Gawrychowski, T. Kociumaka, W. Rytter and T. Walen. Faster longest common extension queries in strings over general alphabets. In R. Grossi and M. Lewenstein, eds., *27th Annual Symposium on Combinatorial Pattern Matching, CPM 2016*, 27–29 June, 2016, Tel Aviv, Israel, vol. 54, LIPIcs, pp. 5:1–5:13. Schloss Dagstuhl – Leibniz-Zentrum fuer Informatik, 2016.

[129] P. Gawrychowski and P. Uznanski. Order-preserving pattern matching with k mismatches. In A. S. Kulikov, S. O. Kuznetsov and P. A. Pevzner, eds., *Combinatorial Pattern Matching: 25th Annual Symposium, CPM 2014*, Moscow, Russia, 16–18 June , 2014. Proceedings, vol. 8486, *Lecture Notes in Computer Science*, pp. 130–139. Springer, 2014.

[130] A. Glen, J. Justin, S. Widmer and L. Q. Zamboni. Palindromic richness. *Eur. J. Comb.*, 30(2):510–531, 2009.

[131] S. W. Golomb. *Shift Register Sequences* 3rd rev. ed. World Scientific, 2017.

[132] J. Grytczuk, K. Kosinski and M. Zmarz. How to play Thue games. *Theor. Comput. Sci.*, 582:83–88, 2015.

[133] C. Guo, J. Shallit and A. M. Shur. On the combinatorics of palindromes and antipalindromes. *CoRR*, abs/1503.09112, 2015.

[134] D. Gusfield. *Algorithms on Strings, Trees and Sequences: Computer Science and Computational Biology*. Cambridge University Press, 1997.

[135] D. Gusfield and J. Stoye. Linear time algorithms for finding and representing all the tandem repeats in a string. *J. Comput. Syst. Sci.*, 69(4):525–546, 2004.

[136] C. Hancart. On Simon's string searching algorithm. *Inf. Process. Lett.*, 47(2):95–99, 1993.

[137] T. Harju and T. Kärki. On the number of frames in binary words. *Theor. Comput. Sci.*, 412(39):5276–5284, 2011.

[138] A. Hartman and M. Rodeh. Optimal parsing of strings. In A. Apostolico and Z. Galil, eds., *Combinatorial Algorithms on Words*, vol. 12, NATO ASI Series F: Computer and System Sciences, pp. 155–167, Springer, 1985.

[139] M. M. Hasan, A. S. M. S. Islam, M. S. Rahman and M. S. Rahman. Order preserving pattern matching revisited. *Pattern Recogn. Lett.*, 55:15–21, 2015.

[140] D. Hendrian, T. Takagi and S. Inenaga. Online algorithms for constructing linear-size suffix trie. *CoRR*, abs/1901.10045, 2019.

[141] D. Hickerson. There are at most $2n$ distinct twins in any finite string of length n. Personal communication by D. Gusfield, 2003.

[142] C. Hohlweg and C. Reutenauer. Lyndon words, permutations and trees. *Theor. Comput. Sci.*, 307(1):173–178, 2003.

[143] R. Houston. Tackling the minimal superpermutation problem. *CoRR*, abs/1408.5108, 2014.

[144] D. A. Huffman. A method for the construction of minimum redundancy codes. *Proc. I.R.E.*, 40:1098–1101, 1951.

[145] R. M. Idury and A. A. Schäffer. Multiple matching of parameterized patterns. *Theor. Comput. Sci.*, 154(2):203–224, 1996.

[146] L. Ilie. A simple proof that a word of length n has at most $2n$ distinct squares. *J. Comb. Theory, Ser. A*, 112(1):163–164, 2005.

[147] L. Ilie. A note on the number of squares in a word. *Theor. Comput. Sci.*, 380(3):373–376, 2007.

[148] L. Ilie and W. F. Smyth. Minimum unique substrings and maximum repeats. *Fundam. Inform.*, 110(1-4):183–195, 2011.

[149] C. S. Iliopoulos, D. Moore and W. F. Smyth. A characterization of the squares in a Fibonacci string. *Theor. Comput. Sci.*, 172(1–2):281–291, 1997.

[150] S. Inenaga, H. Hoshino, A. Shinohara, M. Takeda, S. Arikawa, G. Mauri and G. Pavesi. On-line construction of compact directed acyclic word graphs. In A. Amir and G. M. Landau, eds., *Combinatorial Pattern Matching, 12th Annual Symposium, CPM 2001*, Jerusalem, Israel, 1-4 July 2001, Proceedings, vol. 2089, *Lecture Notes in Computer Science*, pp. 169–180. Springer, 2001.

[151] B. W. Jackson. Universal cycles of k-subsets and k-permutations. *Discrete Math.*, 117(1-3):141–150, 1993.

[152] N. Johnston. All minimal superpermutations on five symbols have been found. www.njohnston.ca/2014/08/all-minimal-superpermutations-on-five-symbols-have-been-found/, 2014.

[153] J. Kärkkäinen and P. Sanders. Simple linear work suffix array construction. In J. C. M. Baeten, J. K. Lenstra, J. Parrow and G. J. Woeginger, eds., *Automata, Languages and Programming, 30th International Colloquium, ICALP 2003*, Eindhoven, The Netherlands, 30–4 June, 2003. Proceedings, vol. 2719, *Lecture Notes in Computer Science*, pp. 943–955. Springer, 2003.

[154] J. Kärkkäinen P. Sanders and S. Burkhardt. Linear work suffix array construction. *J. ACM*, 53(6):918–936, 2006.

[155] T. Kasai, G. Lee, H. Arimura, S. Arikawa and K. Park. Linear-time longest-common-prefix computation in suffix arrays and its applications. In A. Amir and G. M. Landau, eds., *Combinatorial Pattern Matching, 12th Annual Symposium, CPM 2001*, Jerusalem, Israel, 1–4 July 2001, Proceedings vol. 2089, *Lecture Notes in Computer Science*, pp. 181–192. Springer, 2001.

[156] J. Katajainen, A. Moffat and A. Turpin. A fast and space-economical algorithm for length-limited coding. In J. Staples, P. Eades, N. Katoh and A. Moffat, eds., *Algorithms and Computation, 6th International Symposium, ISAAC '95*, Cairns, Australia, 4–6 December 1995, Proceedings vol. 1004, *Lecture Notes in Computer Science*, pp. 12–21. Springer, 1995.

[157] D. Kempa, A. Policriti, N. Prezza and E. Rotenberg. String attractors: Verification and optimization. *CoRR*, abs/1803.01695, 2018.

[158] A. J. Kfoury. A linear-time algorithm to decide whether A binary word contains an overlap. *ITA*, 22(2):135–145, 1988.

[159] D. K. Kim, J. S. Sim, H. Park and K. Park. Constructing suffix arrays in linear time. *J. Discrete Algorithms*, 3(2-4):126–142, 2005.

[160] J. Kim, P. Eades, R. Fleischer, S. Hong, C. S. Iliopoulos, K. Park, S. J. Puglisi and T. Tokuyama. Order-preserving matching. *Theor. Comput. Sci.*, 525:68–79, 2014.

[161] D. E. Knuth. Dynamic Huffman coding. *J. Algorithms*, 6(2):163–180, 1985.

[162] D. E. Knuth, J. H. Morris Jr. and V. R. Pratt. Fast pattern matching in strings. *SIAM J. Comput.*, 6(2):323–350, 1977.

[163] P. Ko and S. Aluru. Space efficient linear time construction of suffix arrays. *J. Discrete Algorithms*, 3(2-4):143–156, 2005.

[164] T. Kociumaka, J. Pachocki, J. Radoszewski, W. Rytter and T. Walen. Efficient counting of square substrings in a tree. *Theor. Comput. Sci.*, 544:60–73, 2014.

[165] T. Kociumaka, J. Radoszewski, W. Rytter, J. Straszynski, T. Walen and W. Zuba. Efficient representation and counting of antipower factors in words. In C. Martín-Vide, A. Okhotin and D. Shapira, eds., *Language and Automata Theory and Applications: 13th International Conference, LATA 2019*, St. Petersburg, Russia, 26–29 March, 2019, Proceedings, vol. 11417, *Lecture Notes in Computer Science*, pp. 421–433. Springer, 2019.

[166] W. Kolakoski. Problem 5304. *Am. Math. Mon.*, 72(674), 1965.

[167] R. M. Kolpakov and G. Kucherov. Finding maximal repetitions in a word in linear time. In *40th Annual Symposium on Foundations of Computer Science, FOCS '99*, 17–18 October 1999, New York, pp. 596–604. IEEE Computer Society, 1999.

[168] R. M. Kolpakov and G. Kucherov. Finding approximate repetitions under Hamming distance. In F. Meyer auf der Heide, ed., *Algorithms - ESA 2001*,

9th Annual European Symposium, Aarhus, Denmark, 28–31 August 2001, Proceedings, vol. 2161, Lecture Notes in Computer Science, pp. 170–181. Springer, 2001.

[169]   K. Kosinski, R. Mercas and D. Nowotka. Corrigendum to 'a note on Thue games' [Inf. Process. Lett. 118 (2017) 75-77]. Inf. Process. Lett., 130:63–65, 2018.

[170]   M. Kubica, T. Kulczynski, J. Radoszewski, W. Rytter and T. Walen. A linear time algorithm for consecutive permutation pattern matching. Inf. Process. Lett., 113(12):430–433, 2013.

[171]   P. Kurka. Topological and Symbolic Dynamics. Société Mathématique de France, 2003.

[172]   L. L. Larmore and D. S. Hirschberg. A fast algorithm for optimal length-limited Huffman codes. J. ACM, 37(3):464–473, 1990.

[173]   A. Lefebvre and T. Lecroq. Compror: On-line lossless data compression with a factor oracle. Inf. Process. Lett., 83(1):1–6, 2002.

[174]   A. Lempel. On a homomorphism of the de Bruijn graph and its applications to the design of feedback shift registers. IEEE Trans. Comput., 19(12):1204–1209, 1970.

[175]   M. Lothaire. Combinatorics on Words. Addison-Wesley, 1983. Reprinted in 1997.

[176]   M. Lothaire. Algebraic Combinatorics on Words. Encyclopedia of Mathematics and Its Applications. Cambridge University Press, 2002.

[177]   M. Lothaire. Applied Combinatorics on Words. Cambridge University Press, 2005.

[178]   M. Maekawa. A $\sqrt{N}$ algorithm for mutual exclusion in decentralized systems. ACM Trans. Comput. Syst., 3(2):145–159, 1985.

[179]   M. G. Main and R. J. Lorentz. An $O(n \log n)$ algorithm for recognizing repetition. Report CS-79-056, Washington State University, Pullman, 1979.

[180]   M. G. Main and R. J. Lorentz. Linear time recognition of square-free strings. In A. Apostolico and Z. Galil, eds., Combinatorial Algorithms on Words, vol. 12, Series F: Computer and System Sciences, pp. 271–278. Springer, 1985.

[181]   G. S. Makanin. The problem of solvability of equations in a free semi-group. Math. Sb., 103(2):147–236, 1977. In Russian. English translation in: Math. USSR-Sb, 32, 129-198, 1977.

[182]   A. Mancheron and C. Moan. Combinatorial characterization of the language recognized by factor and suffix oracles. Int. J. Found. Comput. Sci., 16(6):1179–1191, 2005.

[183]   S. Mantaci, A. Restivo, G. Romana G. Rosone and M. Sciortino. String attractors and combinatorics on words. CoRR, abs/1907.04660, 2019.

[184]   S. Mantaci, A. Restivo, G. Rosone and M. Sciortino. Suffix array and Lyndon factorization of a text. J. Discrete Algorithms, 28:2–8, 2014.

[185]   S. Mantaci, A. Restivo and M. Sciortino. Burrows-Wheeler transform and Sturmian words. Inf. Process. Lett., 86(5):241–246, 2003.

[186]   W. J. Masek and M. Paterson. A faster algorithm computing string edit distances. J. Comput. Syst. Sci., 20(1):18–31, 1980.

[187]   E. M. McCreight. A space-economical suffix tree construction algorithm. J. ACM, 23(2):262–272, 1976.

[188] J. Mendivelso and Y. Pinzón. Parameterized matching: Solutions and extensions. In J. Holub and J. Žďárek, eds., *Proceedings of the Prague Stringology Conference 2015*, pp. 118–131, Czech Technical University in Prague, Czech Republic, 2015.

[189] T. Mieno, Y. Kuhara, T. Akagi, et al. Minimal unique substrings and minimal absent words in a sliding window, *International Conference on Current Trends in Theory and Practice of Informatics*, pp. 148–160, Springer, 2019.

[190] A. Moffat. Implementing the PPM data compression scheme. *IEEE Trans. Commun.*, 38(11):1917–1921, 1990.

[191] S. P. Mohanty. Shortest string containing all permutations. *Discrete Math.*, 31:91–95, 1980.

[192] E. Moreno and D. Perrin. Corrigendum to 'on the theorem of Fredricksen and Maiorana about de Bruijn sequences'. *Adv. Appl. Math.*, 33(2):413–415, 2004.

[193] G. Navarro and N. Prezza. Universal compressed text indexing. *Theor. Comput. Sci.*, 762:41–50, 2019.

[194] G. Navarro and M. Raffinot. *Flexible Pattern Matching in Strings: Practical On-line Search Algorithms for Texts and Biological Sequences*. Cambridge University Press, 2002.

[195] J. Nilsson. Letter frequencies in the Kolakoski sequence. *Acta Phys. Pol. A*, 126(2):549–552, 2014.

[196] E. Ohlebusch. *Bioinformatics Algorithms*. Oldenbusch Verlag, 2013.

[197] R. Oldenburger. Exponent trajectories in symbolic dynamics. *Trans. AMS*, 46:453–466, 1939.

[198] T. Ota, H. Fukae and H. Morita. Dynamic construction of an antidictionary with linear complexity. *Theor. Comput. Sci.*, 526:108–119, 2014.

[199] T. Ota and H. Morita. On a universal antidictionary coding for stationary ergodic sources with finite alphabet. In *International Symposium on Information Theory and Its Applications, ISITA 2014*, Melbourne, Australia, 26–29 October 2014, pp. 294–298. IEEE, 2014.

[200] T. Ota and H. Morita. A compact tree representation of an antidictionary. *IEICE Trans.*, 100-A(9):1973–1984, 2017.

[201] J. Pansiot. Decidability of periodicity for infinite words. *ITA*, 20(1):43–46, 1986.

[202] N. Prezza. String attractors. *CoRR*, abs/1709.05314, 2017.

[203] S. J. Puglisi, J. Simpson and W. F. Smyth. How many runs can a string contain? *Theor. Comput. Sci.*, 401(1-3):165–171, 2008.

[204] J. Radoszewski and W. Rytter. On the structure of compacted subword graphs of Thue-Morse words and their applications. *J. Discrete Algorithms*, 11:15–24, 2012.

[205] N. Rampersad, J. Shallit and M. Wang. Avoiding large squares in infinite binary words. *Theor. Comput. Sci.*, 339(1):19–34, 2005.

[206] D. Repke and W. Rytter. On semi-perfect de Bruijn words. *Theor. Comput. Sci.*, 720:55–63, 2018.

[207] A. Restivo and S. Salemi. Overlap-free words on two symbols. In M. Nivat and D. Perrin, eds., *Automata on Infinite Words*, Ecole de Printemps d'Informatique Théorique, Le Mont Dore, 14–18 May, 1984, vol. 192, *Lecture Notes in Computer Science*, pp. 198–206. Springer, 1985.

[208] C. Reutenauer. *From Christoffel Words to Markov Numbers.* Oxford University Press, 2018.

[209] G. Rozenberg and A. Salomaa. *The Mathematical Theory of L Systems.* Academic Press, 1980.

[210] M. Rubinchik and A. M. Shur. *Eertree: An efficient data structure for processing palindromes in strings.* CoRR, abs/1506.04862, 2015.

[211] F. Ruskey and A. Williams. An explicit universal cycle for the (n-1)-permutations of an n-set. *ACM Trans. Algorithms*, 6(3):45:1–45:12, 2010.

[212] W. Rytter. A correct preprocessing algorithm for Boyer-Moore string-searching. *SIAM J. Comput.*, 9(3):509–512, 1980.

[213] W. Rytter. The structure of subword graphs and suffix trees of Fibonacci words. *Theor. Comput. Sci.*, 363(2):211–223, 2006.

[214] W. Rytter. The number of runs in a string. *Informat. Comput.*, 205(9):1459–1469, 2007.

[215] W. Rytter. Two fast constructions of compact representations of binary words with given set of periods. *Theor. Comput. Sci.*, 656:180–187, 2016.

[216] W. Rytter. Computing the k-th letter of Fibonacci word. Personal communication, 2017.

[217] A. A. Sardinas and G. W. Patterson. A necessary and sufficient condition for the unique decomposition of coded messages. Research Division Report 50-27, Moore School of Electrical Engineering, University of Pennsylvania, 1950.

[218] J. Sawada and P. Hartman. Finding the largest fixed-density necklace and Lyndon word. *Inf. Process. Lett.*, 125:15–19, 2017.

[219] J. Sawada, A. Williams and D. Wong. A surprisingly simple de Bruijn sequence construction. *Discrete Math.*, 339(1):127–131, 2016.

[220] B. Schieber. Computing a minimum weight-link path in graphs with the concave Monge property. *J. Algorithms*, 29(2):204–222, 1998.

[221] M. Sciortino and L. Q. Zamboni. Suffix automata and standard Sturmian words. In T. Harju, J. Karhumäki and A. Lepistö, eds., *Developments in Language Theory, 11th International Conference, DLT 2007*, Turku, Finland, 3–6 July, 2007, Proceedings, vol. 4588, *Lecture Notes in Computer Science*, pp. 382–398. Springer, 2007.

[222] J. Shallit. On the maximum number of distinct factors of a binary string. *Graphs Combinat.*, 9(2–4):197–200, 1993.

[223] Y. Shiloach. A fast equivalence-checking algorithm for circular lists. *Inf. Process. Lett.*, 8(5):236–238, 1979.

[224] R. M. Silva, D. Pratas, L. Castro, A. J. Pinho and P. J. S. G. Ferreira. Three minimal sequences found in ebola virus genomes and absent from human DNA. *Bioinformatics*, 31(15):2421–2425, 2015.

[225] I. Simon. String matching algorithms and automata. In R. Baeza-Yates and N. Ziviani, eds., *Proceedings of the 1st South American Workshop on String Processing*, pp. 151–157, Belo Horizonte, Brasil, 1993. Universidade Federal de Minas Gerais.

[226] S. S. Skiena. *The Algorithm Design Manual.* 2nd ed., Springer, 2008.

[227] T. Skolem. On certain distributions of integers in pairs with given differences. *Math. Scand.*, 5:57–68, 1957.

[228] B. Smyth. *Computing Patterns in Strings*. Pearson Education Limited, 2003.

[229] M. Szykula. Improving the upper bound on the length of the shortest reset word. In R. Niedermeier and B. Vallée, eds., *35th Symposium on Theoretical Aspects of Computer Science, STACS 2018*, 28 February – 3 March 2018, Caen, France, vol. 96, LIPIcs, pp. 56:1–56:13. Schloss Dagstuhl - Leibniz-Zentrum fuer Informatik, 2018.

[230] J. Tarhio and E. Ukkonen. A greedy approximation algorithm for constructing shortest common superstrings. *Theor. Comput. Sci.*, 57:131–145, 1988.

[231] Z. Tronícek and B. Melichar. Directed acyclic subsequence graph. In J. Holub and M. Simánek, eds., *Proceedings of the Prague Stringology Club Workshop 1998*, Prague, Czech Republic, 3–4 September, 1998, pp. 107–118. Department of Computer Science and Engineering, Faculty of Electrical Engineering, Czech Technical University, 1998.

[232] Z. Tronícek and A. Shinohara. The size of subsequence automaton. *Theor. Comput. Sci.*, 341(1–3):379–384, 2005.

[233] K. Tsuruta, S. Inenaga, H. Bannai and M. Takeda. Shortest unique substrings queries in optimal time. In V. Geffert, B. Preneel, B. Rovan, J. Stuller and A. M. Tjoa, eds., *SOFSEM 2014: Theory and Practice of Computer Science: 40th International Conference on Current Trends in Theory and Practice of Computer Science*, Nový Smokovec, Slovakia, 26–29 January 2014, Proceedings, vol. 8327, Lecture Notes in Computer Science, pp. 503–513. Springer, 2014.

[234] E. Ukkonen. On-line construction of suffix trees. *Algorithmica*, 14(3):249–260, 1995.

[235] J. van Leeuwen. On the construction of Huffman trees. In *ICALP*, pp. 382–410, 1976.

[236] J. S. Vitter. Design and analysis of dynamic Huffman codes. *J. ACM*, 34(4):825–845, 1987.

[237] N. Vörös. On the complexity measures of symbol-sequences. In A. Iványi, ed., *Conference of Young Programmers and Mathematicians*, pp. 43–50, Budapest, 1984. Faculty of Sciences, Eötvös Loránd University.

[238] B. Walczak. A simple representation of subwords of the Fibonacci word. *Inf. Process. Lett.*, 110(21):956–960, 2010.

[239] T. A. Welch. A technique for high-performance data compression. *IEEE Computer*, 17(6):8–19, 1984.

[240] W. A. Wythoff. A modification of the game of Nim. *Nieuw Arch. Wisk.*, 8:199–202, 1907/1909.

[241] I.-H. Yang, C.-P. Huang and K.-M. Chao. A fast algorithm for computing a longest increasing subsequence. *Inf. Process. Lett.*, 93(5):249–253, 2005.

[242] E. Zalinescu. Shorter strings containing all k-element permutations. *Inf. Process. Lett.*, 111(12):605–608, 2011.

[243] J. Ziv and A. Lempel. A universal algorithm for sequential data compression. *IEEE Trans. Inf. Theory*, 23(3):337–343, 1977.

Index

332